Song of the Vineyard

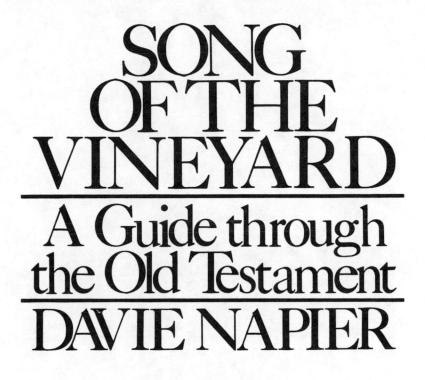

SONG
OF THE
VINEYARD

A Guide through the Old Testament

DAVIE NAPIER

Revised Edition

FORTRESS PRESS   PHILADELPHIA

First Fortress Press Edition 1981

Library of Congress Cataloging in Publication Data

Napier, Bunyan Davie.
  Song of the vineyard.

  Bibliography: p.
  Includes indexes.
    1. Bible. O.T.—Introductions. 2. Bible. O.T.—
Theology. I. Title.
BS1140.2.N36 1981   221.6   78-14672
ISBN 0-8006-1352-X

7407D80   Printed in the United States of America   1-1352

TO JOY
JOHN AND ANNE

CONTENTS

III. Positive Judgment: Classical Prophetism

IV. Existence: The Meaning of Yahwism

Faith and the World's Wisdom: Proverbs,
Ecclesiastes, Song of Solomon
Judaism and the World: Daniel, Esther, Jonah

Preface to the Revised Edition

The preface to the original *Song of the Vineyard* is left unchanged, of course, although if it, too, were revised, some
changes there would surely be (for example, the phrase in the last
paragraph, "men [sic] in the biblical field")! But what was chiefly
emphasized then is, in intention, reiterated now; and the revision
holds even more assiduously to the purpose of encouraging the
reader of *Song* to be, first and always, a careful reader of the Old
Testament.

I have not appreciably lengthened the book. I see it as a "text"
(an ill-fitting term in biblical courses where the true text is the Bible) for introductory one-semester or one-term courses aimed
precisely and only at "introducing" the Old Testament. More
voluminous and technical introductions have their place as texts,
to be sure; but in shorter courses they are more likely to be pursued *in lieu of* reading the Bible.

To this end, also, I have simplified footnotes; and on the
assumption that not many readers will know German and
Hebrew, I have reduced the transliteration of Hebrew (and where
retained, spelled it as pronounced and not with the scholars' ap-
paratus); and, except in a few instances where outstanding works
have not been translated into English, I have excised from the first
edition all references to books in German. Happily for us all,
some of these have since appeared in English, and these do appear
throughout *Song*.

What is different for me, and what is reflected throughout this
revision, is the living and thinking and reading of the days and
years of the sixties and seventies. The ancient texts do not change;
but it is the wonder of the Bible that it is able always to speak to us
in terms appropriate to the turbulently changing world which is
our home. One of those changes has to do with the increased sensitivity of many of us to the long-held habits of male-dominated
language. Although I have not always felt justified in modifying

the RSV text in this regard, my own language in this revision is (I hope) consistently inclusive.

It is important that I acknowledge my indebtedness, often unconscious, to students and colleagues at Stanford University (1966–1972) and Pacific School of Religion (1972–1980). And I am deeply grateful to my former student, Dr. John M. Bullard, Albert C. Outler Professor of Religion at Wofford College, for his assistance and sensitive contribution to this revised edition.

DAVIE NAPIER

Eugene, Oregon

Preface to the First Edition

In the common but not the technical sense of the word, this is an introduction to the Old Testament. I have tried to restrain my professional instincts by constant address to the question, "What is *essential* to a genuine understanding of the Old Testament?" This is a short introduction; and, since every "problem" of Old Testament study is faced only in the context of the Old Testament itself, the method is always inductive. Since this is a short, inductive introduction, the emphasis is on *meaning* and especially on the meaning of the ancient text in the life and faith of that ancient people, Israel.

I hope I have made some suggestions which will be profitable or stimulating to my colleagues in the biblical field. But in writing this book I have had in mind primarily the formal student, both the college and the seminary student. I have also found myself looking into the faces of that diversified company of informal students embracing, for example, my colleagues teaching in other fields, as well as those other friends from all walks with whom I spend sustaining nonworking hours and who, ever and again even in the midst of play, put me back to work with "simple" innocent questions about the Bible. I have also remembered former students at Judson College, Alfred University, the University of Georgia, Wesleyan University in Middletown (in a gratifying interim), the hundreds of men in Yale College who elected Religion 21a in the decade of the fifties[1] and the more than a thousand men and women at Yale Divinity School who have had no choice. I remember gratefully all of these who "saw the movie" and who may have some interest now in "reading the book."

I have thought of still others in writing this: Sunday school teachers, that brave breed, who give so much and are so often given too little; and those wonderful, ubiquitous "people in the street" who want questions answered without theological indoctrination and in such fashion as to be spared professional initia-

---

[1]This was B. C. Yale College, i.e., before coeducation, which began in 1969.

tion. And always I have found myself in conversation with working clergy whose hard and rewarding role I have known in my own parishes and to whom biblical meaning is of the essence.

Whoever reads this must know that it is not and cannot be a substitute for the Old Testament. The reader's time and my own effort are wasted if this is attempted. The book is conceived and written as a "companion" (that abused word), a knowledgeable companion whose sole reason for existence is to aid in understanding the text of the Old Testament. In the life of learning, nothing is so injurious as the usurpation of the role of the *subject* of instruction by the *medium* of instruction, whether the medium be the lecturer on the subject or the book about the subject. Here is another reason why this is, as such books go, a short introduction. Many students in many courses have been discouraged from reading adequately in primary sources by the sheer bulk of the secondary material pushed in their direction. Courses in Bible are, alas, all too often courses about the Bible. Let Old Testament study be the study of the Old Testament.

The reviewer of a previous book of mine very kindly complimented my total appearance in the book but regretted that my "Christian slip was showing." I suspect this condition persists—which is only to say, or which is at least to say, that I affirm the essential continuity of Old and New Testaments. I also insist that the Christian is fundamentally ignorant of the New Testament who does not know and understand the Old. On the other hand, and most emphatically, I have tried here not to reduce the Old Testament—as it never should be—simply to an introduction to the New Testament. For the most part, I have left the reader to draw his own conclusions on the relationship *in meaning* of the Old to the New. The story of ancient Israel is a story worth knowing in and for itself, and the most ardent Christian interpreter does himself and his own faith a disservice if he fails to see and acknowledge this.

My debts are so extensive as to defy specific acknowledgment, but the range is from my own instructors here, my family, my present colleagues, this university, and its students to men in the biblical field in scores of cities in this country, this hemisphere, and around the world.

B. DAVIE NAPIER

Yale University
New Haven, Connecticut
Christmas, 1961

THE SONG OF THE VINEYARD

Let me sing for my beloved
  a love song concerning his vineyard:
My beloved had a vineyard
  on a very fertile hill.
He digged it and cleared it of stones,
  and planted it with choice vines;
he built a watchtower in the midst of it,
  and hewed out a wine vat in it;
and he looked for it to yield grapes,
  but it yielded wild grapes.

And now, O inhabitants of Jerusalem
  and men of Judah,
judge, I pray you, between me
  and my vineyard.
What more was there to do for my vineyard,
  that I had not done in it?
When I looked for it to yield grapes,
  why did it yield wild grapes?

And now I will tell you
  what I will do to my vineyard.
I will remove its hedge,
  and it shall be devoured;
I will break down its wall,
  and it shall be trampled down.
I will make it a waste;
  it shall not be pruned or hoed,
  and briers and thorns shall grow up;
I will command the clouds
  that they rain no rain upon it.
For the vineyard of the Lord of hosts
  is the house of Israel,
and the men of Judah
  are his pleasant planting;

and he looked for justice,
but behold bloodshed;
for righteousness,
but behold, a cry!

ISA. 5:1–7

In that day:
"A pleasant vineyard, sing of it!
I, the Lord, am its keeper;
every moment I water it.
Lest anyone harm it,
I guard it night and day;
I have no wrath.
Would that I had thorns and briers to battle!
I would set out against them,
I would burn them up together.
. . . .

In days to come Jacob shall take root,
Israel shall blossom and put forth shoots,
and fill the whole world with fruit.

ISA. 27:1–5,7

Introduction

Thus says Yahweh.

The Old Testament is a story. It is an expression of the full range of human emotions from exalted or passionate love to bitterest hate. The story has been narrated and written in prose and poetry, song and hymn, liturgy and prayer; it uses allegory, humor, irony, hyperbole, and all other literary devices to convey its meaning.

It is the story of a people—ancient Israel's history over a period of some fifteen hundred years. But it is not merely a record of the past, for as the people of Israel told and wrote the story it was continuously re-created as a commentary on the meaning of Israel and the life of its people. Although the events related took place in the centuries long before our era, the meaning Israel found in its own history has had persistent relevance to all subsequent human existence, not only to Judaism but to Islam and Christianity.

It has been common to label the Old Testament as literature, history, or theology, but it is all three and cannot be categorized so simply as to its purpose and form. It offers examples of consummate literary skill; parts can be ranked with the best of the contemporary ancient histories; and nowhere else in all the world's literature and history is God so consistently and passionately the center of action and contemplation.

But to label the Old Testament as simply *literature* may be to obscure its relationship to the life and faith of a people. The term literature sometimes conveys the impression of a single individual independently creating in his or her own art form. The Old Testament is the product of many individuals using many forms, and the content must be identified not merely with individuals but with an entire people and their faith, for the Old Testament developed out of a spoken "literature," much of it anonymously, corporately, and even spontaneously formed.

To call the Old Testament *history* distorts its true character, if we think of history as simply a record of the past. Thomas Mann

1

said of myth that "It is, it always is, however much we may say, it was." And history, too, is recounted and compiled not simply for its "wasness" but for its 'isness." A record of the past for its own sake, a past that is not continuous with the present or that has no meaning for the present, is a denial of the true character of history. The Old Testament was created to give expression to a people's self-understanding, to convey the meaning of their existence. The event of the past evokes little interest in itself, but is recorded as a clue to the meaning of the present.

Old Testament history is even further removed from the rubric of history by the emphasis on the event as a witness in Israel to the One in whom all life has meaning, to whom belong the earth and its fullness, the world, and those who inhabit it. Ancient Israel takes for granted in its story that the determinative factor in all human events and in all creation is outside and above event and time. There is no history merely of people and events, since these are determined by the impingement of God's life and will on the plane of human history. Thus, the Old Testament remains essentially existential and suprahistorical.

Then why not give the Old Testament the primary designation of *theology*? Even here the emphasis may be misleading. The term suggests a self-conscious preoccupation with the discipline of one "science" or with one organization of reality as opposed to others. In the Old Testament there is no "other." Our distinctions, with their common connotations, of mind and soul, secular and religious, would be incomprehensible in ancient Israel with its prevailing emphasis on the oneness of personality and experience. Women and men are God's creatures, inhabiting God's world, subject to God's laws. When the totality of experience is theological, the use of the term becomes misleading.

Thus, the Old Testament is literature, history, and theology, and more. Based on faith in the knowledge of God, it is the story of ancient Israel's life as given form, coherence, and meaning by the life and purpose and power of God—by what the story characteristically calls the Word of God.

The Framework of the Story

The varied events and numerous components of the story of the people and the Word, which spans two thousand years, tend to group around four central events, each one radically affecting

Israel, and, at least implicitly, the world as well. Each of these four events is seen as a disclosure of the nature and purpose of God acting through the instrument of the Word. Three events are concrete; they occur and are treated in the story in detail, from anticipation to realization to reflection.

The first event is the Exodus from Egypt. The nucleus of this event is the actual escape of a group of slaves from Egypt in the thirteenth century B.C.E. But the total event also included the expansive prelude (composed in its final form in full knowledge of the event) and the more expansive sequel, the consequences of the Exodus leading finally to the settlement and domination of a new land.

The Exodus found a brief "confessional" formulation very early in Israel's life as a people. "Confessional" is used here in an affirmative sense, as a declaration of faith and recitation of firm belief:

"We were Pharaoh's slaves in Egypt; and the Lord brought us out of Egypt with a mighty hand; and the Lord showed signs and wonders, great and grievous, against Egypt and against Pharaoh and all his household, before our eyes; and he brought us out from there, that he might bring us in and give us the land which he swore to give to our fathers."

(Deut. 6:21–23)

A similar credo appears in Deut. 26:5–9, with only one significant difference. The second credo begins, rather than ends, with reference to the ancestors of Israel, and therefore more closely retains the present form contained in the first six books of the Old Testament, from Genesis to Joshua.

"A wandering Aramean was my father; and he went down into Egypt and sojourned there, few in number; and there he became a nation, great, mighty and populous. And the Egyptians treated us harshly, and afflicted us, and laid upon us hard bondage. Then we cried to the Lord the God of our fathers, and the Lord heard our voice and saw our affliction, our toil, and our oppression; and the Lord brought us out of Egypt with a mighty hand and an outstretched arm, with great terror, with signs and wonders; and he brought us into this place and gave us this land, a land flowing with milk and honey."

These are two forms of Israel's earliest credo. Both forms had wide and continued use at Israel's sanctuaries as a confession of faith defining Israel's existence as the purposive creation of God and its present relatively secure environment as his gift. (A third, longer variation of the same essential confession of God's crucial relationship to this event appears in Joshua 24.) The credo constitutes a Hexateuch in miniature (Genesis to Joshua), and provided the original nucleus and outline for the centuries-long process of the production and completion of the Hexateuch.[1]

The second central event of the Old Testament story is the establishment of the monarchy under David in Jerusalem. If, for the sake of creating convenient chronological pegs, we center the total Exodus event in the date 1200 B.C.E., we can date the David-Jerusalem (or David-Zion) event about 1000 B.C.E. Saul, from one of the northern tribes in the confederation of Israelite tribes, formed an uneasy and incomplete monarchy in Palestine in the eleventh century B.C.E. with the help of the prophet-priest Samuel. But it was David, of the southern tribe of Judah, who completed the consolidation and organization of the tribes and took the last hostile Canaanite fortress city, Jerusalem, with its hill of Zion. The actions of David's son and successor Solomon led to the tragic division of the monarchy with the original tribes seceding from the union with Judah and the Davidic monarchy. The kingdom of Judah no doubt continued to acknowledge the event of the Exodus, but the David-Zion event was celebrated more prominently, and sometimes exclusively, as the primary, creative event by which God indicated his purposive choice and election of his people and established an indestructible covenant.

The David-Zion event was also given expression in the cultus, that is, in the liturgies of the Jerusalem temple which Solomon built upon the hill of Zion. Yahweh:

> . . . rejected the tent of Joseph,
>   he did not choose the tribe of Ephraim;[2]
> but he chose the tribe of Judah,
>   Mount Zion, which he loves.
> He built his sanctuary like the high heavens,
>   like the earth, which he has founded for ever.
> He chose David his servant,
>   and took him from the sheepfolds;

---

[1]This view of the relationship between credo and Hexateuch originated with G. von Rad in his *Problem of the Hexateuch and Other Essays,* New York, 1966. Also see von Rad's *Genesis,* trans. J. Marks, rev. ed., 1972, pp. 10 ff., and M. Noth, *A History of Pentateuchal Traditions,* trans. B. W. Anderson, Englewood Cliffs, N.J., 1972. Since the death of von Rad on Oct. 31, 1971, his view of the three credos as a kind of "Hexateuch in miniature" has been occasionally challenged, in my view unsuccessfully.

[2]Joseph and Ephraim represent the tribes of the seceding North.

from tending the ewes that had young he brought him
to be the shepherd of Jacob his people,
of Israel his inheritance.

(Ps. 78:67–71)

The psalm does not question the relationship of David and Mount Zion to all Israel.[3] In its moods of deepest despair, the Old Testament story finds hope for the future of all Israel in the certainty that God would realize his purpose in the David-Zion covenant with the reestablishment of that rule in some form.

I will establish his line for ever
and his throne as the days of the heavens.
. . . . . .
I will not violate my covenant,
or alter the word that went forth from my lips.
. . . . . .
His line shall endure for ever,
his throne as long as the sun before me.

(Ps. 89:29 ff.)

The third dominating event represents the Word of God effecting harsh judgment in the apparent demise of all Israel. The northern segment of the severed monarchy suffers political execution at the hands of Assyria in the last quarter of the eighth century B.C.E., and Judah at the hands of resurgent Babylon in the first quarter of the sixth century. In prophetic utterance of that time and in later cultic liturgy, the catastrophe was deemed to be (no less than Exodus or Zion) the disclosure and effects of God's will and power.

Therefore thus says the Holy One of Israel,
"Because you despise this word,
and trust in oppression and perverseness,
and rely on them;
therefore this iniquity shall be to you
like a break in a high wall, bulging out, and about to collapse,
whose crash comes suddenly, in an instant;
and its breaking is like that of a potter's vessel
which is smashed so ruthlessly
that among its fragments not a sherd is found
with which to take fire from the hearth,
or to dip up water out of the cistern."

(Isa. 30:12–14)

[3]Cf. Psalm 132 and Ezek. 34:23 f.

In cultic language, the event is recalled in abject misery in the same psalm which extols the grace of God in the David-Zion covenant:

> Thou hast renounced the covenant with thy servant;
>   thou hast defiled his crown in the dust.
> Thou has breached all his walls;
>   thou hast laid his stronghold in ruins.
> All that pass by despoil him;
>   he has become the scorn of his neighbors.
> Thou hast exalted the right hand of his foes;
>   thou hast made all his enemies rejoice.
>   . . . . . .
> How long, O Lord? Wilt thou hide thyself for ever?
> How long wilt thy wrath burn like fire?
>   (Ps. 89:39 ff.)

The fourth event is and is not a concrete event. It is elusive. When the story appears ready to identify and affirm this fourth event, it dissipates as event and any affirmative word in the story is projected into the future. The fourth event is concerned with fulfillment, completion, consummation. If God acted and covenanted with Israel with grace and steadfast love in the events of Exodus and Zion; if, in order to purify rather than to punish Israel, he put Israel through the furnace[4] what and when is the end of all this? If this is the story of Israel and the Word, what has this to do with the world? What of the promise, even expectation, of Israel's blessing to the world? What of the covenant with Israel and the world that cannot really be broken? What of healing, God's healing—the healing of hate, bitterness, animosity, alienation, hostility, fear, terror, anguish, poverty, oppression? Can this be the end—a broken Israel in a broken world, with a broken God?

The fourth event never quite comes. Israel's existence as a political, though not autonomous, entity is reestablished in the closing decades of the sixth century, and for a brief moment the event of reconstitution is hailed with eloquent rapture as the fulfilling event (Isa. 40 ff.). And yet at the same time this particular identification of the event is rejected.

Still, this undefined consummation remains. It is affirmed in

[4]Cf. Isa. 1:25.

prophetic faith-knowledge even before the third event—the purification. The Word of fulfillment has been spoken:

> "For as the rain and the snow come down from heaven,
>   and return not thither but water the earth,
> making it bring forth and sprout,
>   giving seed to the sower and bread to the eater,
> so shall my word be that goes forth from my mouth;
>   it shall not return to me empty,
> but it shall accomplish that which I purpose,
>   and prosper in the thing for which I sent it."
>
> (Isa. 55:10–11)

And what is the nature of the event? The blessing of the families of the earth (Gen. 12:3). Someone "upon the throne of David, and over his kingdom, to establish it, and to uphold it with justice and with righteousness from this time forth and for evermore" (Isa. 9:7). The healing of the world's internal estrangements (Isa. 11:6–9). The bridging of the chasm between God and people in a redefined and recreated covenant (Jer. 31:31 ff.). The restoration of God's creation of humankind symbolized and allegorized in the words:

In that day Israel will be the third with Egypt and Assyria, a blessing in the midst of the earth, whom the Lord of hosts has blessed, saying, "Blessed be Egypt my people, and Assyria the work of my hands, and Israel my heritage."

(Isa. 19:24–25)

And, equally incredibly, the cessation of all fear, all war, and all violent, arbitrary death:

> For out of Zion shall go forth the law,
>   and the word of the Lord from Jerusalem.
>   . . . . . .
> nation shall not lift up sword against nation,
>   neither shall they learn war any more;
> but they shall sit every [one] under [one's own] vine and
>   under [one's own] fig tree,
>   and none shall make them afraid;
>   for the mouth of the Lord of hosts has spoken.
>
> (Mic. 4:2 ff.)[5]

Will this fourth event occur? Can it have tangible existence in

[5]Cf. Isa. 2:2–4

any meaningful form? Is there a real sense in which the fourth event was and is accessible? Has the fourth event an "isness" as well as a "to-be-ness"? The Old Testament answers with a powerful affirmative. If the fourth event is only the stuff of dreams, the three preceding events around which the whole story revolves are meaningless, and the God who speaks and in speaking acts in these events is not only dead—that God never was.

1

CREATION:
ORDER OUT OF CHAOS

1

Yahweh and People

Israel in Egypt:
Exodus 1–2

> Jacob and his children went down to Egypt.
> *Josh. 24:4*

The story of Israel as a people begins here. Everything of enduring significance that ancient Israel became, believed, and proclaimed is ultimately influenced not only by what actually occurred in the time of the Exodus, but by the *story* of the Exodus —the story as it was first remembered and repeated; the story as it assumed relatively fixed classical forms in different areas, in the North or South; the story as its multiple versions, written and oral, were compared, mutually "corrected," and finally composed into the single, unified narrative that is before us now. It is not alone the *event* of the creation of order and meaning out of chaos that conditions the mind and faith of Israel, but also Israel's own sustained, fluid reading and interpretation of the event.

It is important to add that in the tradition of biblical faith, historical revelation, which is the self-disclosure of God in history, is never deemed to inhere simply in the event as event, but also in the interpretation of the event. The motion picture industry fails utterly and with almost unexceptional regularity in its stupendous efforts to reproduce segments of the biblical story because it assumes a self-validating character in the divine disclosure and is apparently unable to deal with the admittedly difficult, illusive, and profound factor of interpretation. The significant biblical event is always the event as faith sees, remembers, tells, and celebrates it. That God is disclosed in the event—if indeed God *is* disclosed in the event—is an affirmation made possible only because God reveals the fact of that self-disclosure in the faith of the human interpreters of the event.

We hold that it was precisely *not* demonstrable that God was in any direct, causative, and purposive way related to the Exodus events. Any impartial observer—for example, an ancient counterpart of a United Nations representative—would surely have been astonished at Israel's subsequent claims about this epoch. We can only assume that the Egyptians, some of whom were participants or even victims, regarded the Egyptian involvement in the Exodus event very differently. Indeed, Egypt thought so lightly of the whole episode that no mention of it was made anywhere in the rather extensive Egyptian historic records thus far discovered.

In the Old Testament the Israelite participants, actual or empathic, impute to the event of the Exodus the actual relationship of deity to human event, the responsibility of God's Word in and through the total event. Recall only that the ancient Israelites were able to say, generation after generation, "*We* were Pharaoh's slaves in Egypt and the Lord brought *us* out. . . ." Were they right or wrong in this *interpretation* of the event? Were they inspired or deluded? Was this affirmation itself revealed or was this fundamentally the prideful projection of a people's self-image? These and other questions can, of course, be answered only according to one's own interpretation of the biblical interpretation of the biblical event, that is, according to one's own position vis-à-vis the life of faith. But all must interpret the interpretation; and all must acknowledge and respond to the role of interpretation in the Bible's claim to be a historical revelation of God. And whatever we may ultimately judge to be the historical nature and structure of the biblical event, we must reckon with Israel's reading of it if we are to understand historical Israel.

1:1–7　　Seventy persons into Egypt—no doubt a round number,[1] but also doubtlessly the accurate recollection of a small group, hardly more than a large Eastern-type family. Twelve names representing twelve tribes—how idealized is this? There is no doubt that David's kingdom embraced twelve dominant tribal groups, nor any doubt that many or all of these tribal entities were earlier involved in one or several confederations of tribes. The question is: were the progenitors of these subsequently confederated tribal groups all present in pre-Exodus Israel? Or does the story spontaneously idealize by reading back into its origins the numbers and

---

[1]It is essential that the Bible be read *in conjunction with* this book, since constant reference is made to specific words and passages.

entities of its subsequently developed components? We pass, and advise you to do the same. Equally competent scholars answer emphatically yes, emphatically no, and emphatically no one can know. But if we are not permitted to pass, then we stress that it appears probable to us that many, or even most, of Israel's components were not biologically represented in Egypt. How much the more remarkable that subsequently all Israel espoused, confessed, and lauded the Exodus event! But then, all who stand in biblical faith in all time have so confessed and appropriated the Exodus event. People in all times find something profound in their own existence given articulation in the words, "We were Pharaoh's slaves and God redeemed us." The image and language of the Exodus faith are timeless.

Five phrases (v. 7) stress the initial benign environment of Egypt. Let the story have its head. The land was full of Egyptians, not Israelites, of course; but how more effectively can the story make its point?

This is Israel's story. Egypt's words are as Israel heard them, thought it heard them, or wanted to hear them. If they do not instruct us in the language of Egypt, they are marvelously penetrating in the language and thought of Israel.

It is the story's way, and a part of its gift, to be imprecise. On the basis of multiple lines of evidence (as convincing as such evidence can be) the "new king over Egypt" refers either to Seti I (c. 1310–1290) or his son Ramses II (c. 1290–1224). These two kings of the Nineteenth Dynasty (c. 1310–1200) were both ambitious builders, and work probably started by Seti, at Pithom (Tell er-Rerabeh) and Ramses (Tanis, in the eastern Delta), was completed by Ramses. Perhaps there was, for varying reasons, a growing antipathy between Israelite and Egyptian (v. 12); but work became for the slaves more intense and bitter because Egypt now embarked on a program of building to the glory of Egypt and the Nineteenth Dynasty and, more pointedly, to the glory of Ramses the Great! Certainly the story is idealized and condensed, but it vividly highlights the essence of the crisis: the life of Israel— of whatever size and constituency—was now made bitter with hard, rigorous service (v. 14).

1:15–22   The term *Hebrew* appears prominently now (1:15,16,19; 2:6,7,11,13) to remind us of the nature of this group in relation to the life of the ancient Near East. Elsewhere—in the archives of the kings of Egypt of the Eighteenth Dynasty of the fourteenth century—we read of *'Apiru,* a term probably related to Hebrew, denoting not a state or political unit, but rather a widespread *type* of communal existence. The term represents the character of the groups who were not permanently identified with the area of their occupation, not indigenous to the territory. They were aliens who nevertheless were able on occasion to move with effective force on their own behalf.[2]

The Old Testament story recalls realistically this quality of Israel's origin, quite without apology. Indeed, the story here stresses with satisfaction the contrast between the physical constitution of the Hebrew and the Egyptian. In this Exodus chapter the total resources of the Hebrew are pitted against the total resources of the Egyptian. It is, of course, the divine resource which is to be the decisive factor; but the form of the story betrays Israel's vast sense of enjoyment of sophisticated Egypt's embarrassment and humiliation through the instrument of the rough Hebrew, the mixed Jacob-Joseph *'Apiru.*

The critical reader will observe here (and over and over again throughout the Old Testament story) a logical contradiction, an item suspicious, if not incredible, if judged from the standpoint of factual probability. Would an absolutely autocratic master administration, involved in gigantic building operations, voluntarily and radically reduce its potential slave labor? From the practical point of view, the answer would, of course, be no. Then what is the relationship of the narrative to the actual historical episode?

Let us acknowledge, not apologetically, but positively, that this is not a pedestrian enumeration of mere factual details. We know that the factual details cannot be reconstructed from the present story. Rather, what appears here is only that which is essential to the theme—the astounding victory of Israel over Pharaoh. Pharaoh had at his disposal all the wealth, power, and resources that human ingenuity, the earth, and the Egyptian gods could create, whereas Israel, a sad segment of *'Apiru,* had only its deity, unknown to humankind, the earth, and the gods.

What precipitated the action that resulted in the creation of the people of Israel from a band of *'Apiru* existing on Egypt's edge around 1300 B.C.E.? The appearance of a death motif in the

[2]Cf. M. Greenberg's thesis, "The Hab/piru," in the *American Oriental Series,* vol. 39, New Haven, 1955; and A. Alt, *Essays on Old Testament History and Religion,* trans. R. A. Wilson, New York (Anchor), 1968, pp. 216 ff.

answer to this question is inevitable. Stated symbolically in terms of killing the firstborn, the fact is that for these people existence was no longer life, but a living death. Human life was reduced to subhuman existence and was deprived of all essentially human expressions—freedom, leisure, exercise of choice and self-determination, opportunity to be creative.[3] In *essence,* if not in *fact,* Egypt decreed death. Thus, the relationship between story and event, narrative and fact, is much closer than the superficially critical eye discerns.

The Figure of Moses

We must remember that we are dealing with a text that assumed its present form over a period of about eight centuries, that is roughly between 1200 and 400 B.C.E. In the course of this development, it has drawn from many sources, both oral and written, which were produced and modified in different times, in different geographical areas, and therefore from different perspectives. The mechanical process by which the present Exodus story developed explains some of the characteristic features of the text.

Beyond a doubt, the image of Moses in these pages of the Bible is much more than a simple "unretouched" photograph. Moses appears in the story as something more than a mere man. But it could not possibly be otherwise in view of the fact that, in the subsequent life, recollection, and meditation of Israel, he *was* more than a man. For the continuing generations of Israel no "photo" could convey the form, stature, achievement, and "immortality" of Moses. In Old Testament Israel, he rightly remains the first person, the unique person, the prophet *par excellence,* the peculiarly Godlike figure playing the role of human creator-sustainer-redeemer in the first epoch of Israel's life. Ordinary facts of birth, life, and death (Deut. 34:6) cannot contain, nor indeed adequately represent, the "truth" of Moses and his enduring meaning to those whose existence he shaped, and to whom in a sense he gave life.[4]

We know, of course, that Moses was a mortal, fallible human

[3]Little wonder that oppressed minorities in this country, especially blacks, and oppressed people around the world (notably in the globe's Southern Hemisphere) see in God's identification with downtrodden ancient Israel in the whole Exodus event a meaningful paradigm of their own existence.

[4]For a description of the continuing modification of the character of Moses in tradition, see G. von Rad, *Old Testament Theology,* trans. D. M. G. Stalker, New York, 1962, vol. 1, pp. 289–96.

being, and in the story he is so represented on occasion (for example, Ps. 106:32–33 in reference to Num. 20:10 ff.; cf. Exod. 17:1–7). But to present him consistently in this manner would inevitably be false to his status and his meaning in the life of Israel. It is no wonder that a corporate, intensely subjective, and adoring memory should produce the image of Moses as it now appears.

2:1–10   The Old Testament story has its inconsistencies and contradictions. These are inevitable in the nature of the story and were certainly evident to those involved in its development. We should not be overly concerned with internal ambiguities, remembering the underlying multiple sources and the relatively fluid status of the developing text, and also that those who developed the story were not primarily concerned with factual details, but rather with the dominant themes and their enduring meaning in the life of the people of Israel.

The initial episode in the life of Moses echoes a familiar theme in the lore and traditions of ancient peoples. Here is a part of a comparable account of the origins of Sargon I, king of Akked about twelve hundred years before the time of Moses.

Sargon, the mighty king, king of Agade, am I.
My mother was a changeling, my father I knew not
. . . .
My changeling mother conceived me, in secret she bore me.
She set in a basket of rushes, with bitumen she sealed my lid.
She cast me into the river which rose not (over) me.
The river bore me up and carried me to Akki, the drawer of water.
Akki, the drawer of water, lifted me out as he dipped his e[w]er.
Akki, the drawer of water, [took me] as his son (and) reared me.[5]

We cite this parallel to show the similar theme; but note also the contrast between the two accounts—the relative tenderness and intimacy of the Moses story, the implicit quality of deep human compassion, the unspoken but acute sensitivity to human relationships. Above all, we see the irony which contributes so forcefully to the central theme of Moses-Hebrew versus Pharaoh-Egypt: the fascinating "accident" by which all of Egypt's richest gifts and

[5]From the translation in James B. Pritchard, ed., *Ancient Near Eastern Texts*, 2nd ed., Princeton, N.J., 1955, p. 119. The brackets indicate the translator's reconstruction of the original text; the parentheses he adds simply for clarity. The translator notes that the meaning of the Akkadian word for changeling is doubtful.

endowments are lavished upon him who is to conduct the campaign that ends in Egypt's abysmal frustration.

We have stressed the close relationship between the Old Testament story and the cultic life of Israel, the institutionalized devotional expression. Remember that relationship especially through the first fifteen chapters of Exodus. Israel's corporate memory of Moses, God, and the Hebrews in Egypt is certainly shaped and accented in devotional use, in the annual celebration and reenactment of the glorious event of divine creation in the triumphal Exodus from Egypt, much in the fashion of the church's annual memorialization of the birth, crucifixion, and resurrection of Christ.[6]

The character of the story is better defined in the word "tradition," than in the word "history." Tradition, though not necessarily divorced from all implements of history, is nevertheless fundamentally determined in Israel by the mind of faith which is theology and by the worship institution which is the cultus. We can see the result in this idealized, simplified story of Moses' birth and rearing. The form is dictated by the primary concern of both faith and cultus to render praise to God. The story is *in intention* a powerful affirmation: in God's grace the very princess of Egypt is brought into the service of Moses and the Hebrews!

The name Moses is Egyptian. It means "son" and is compounded in Egyptian names like Tutmose and Ahmose. But rather characteristically, the story must find a Hebrew etymology; and it comes up with a naming-narrative (v. 10) tying the Egyptian name to a Hebrew word meaning "to draw out." The story gives a passive reading to the name: Moses is the one "drawn out" from the water. But to make this etymology legitimate, the Hebrew form of the name can only be the active participle, a fact certainly not lost in the story's implicit understanding. The name Moses, adapted from the Egyptian into the Hebrew, means the one who executes the "drawing out," and so points to the essence of Moses' life, his role of leadership in the deliverance of Israel.

2:11–25   Moses' identification with his future role of deliverer is made

[6]Cf. J. Pederson, *Israel*, Copenhagen, 1940, vols. 3–4, pp. 728 ff. Pederson sees Exodus 1–15 as "obviously of a cultic character" aiming "at glorifying the god of the people of the paschal (Passover) feast through an exposition of the historical event that created the people" (p. 728).

clear in verses 11-15a. The great act of deliverance is fore-shadowed as he acts decisively and violently in sympathetic iden-tification with the abused, as Hebrew is tormented not only by Egyptian (v. 11), but by fellow Hebrew as well (v. 13). The episode affirms his compassionate character (cf. Num. 12:3).

As a result of the episode, Moses seeks refuge in the land of Mi-dian (vv. 15b-22). Midian is only vaguely defined, partly because the Midianites were a seminomadic people. But the general area is sure—near the northern shores of the Gulf of Aqabah, south of and adjacent to the territory of Edom (cf. 1 Kings 11:14-18). Moses fled east from Egypt, across the Sinaitic peninsula.

An example of the use of realistic detail of symbolic importance is found in the story of Moses by the well. Obviously, this cannot be proved factually, but the story's sense of reality is sound. In the semidesert, in all parched lands, life literally flows to and from the source of water (compare the role of the place of the well of the Jacob story, Genesis 29). What transpires is (as in the Jacob scene) romantic; but the episode again emphasizes Moses' charac-ter as deliverer.

Corporate memory recalls Moses' adopted home in Midian as the home of a priest. Moses is subsequently called upon to be not only premier-commander, but prophet-minister-priest as well, and so here another role is foreshadowed. Indirectly (and directly, see 18:1-27) Moses is indebted to his father-in-law for his ad-ministrative skills, "civic" as well as religious. However, in Mi-dian, Moses is but a "sojourner in a foreign land" (v. 22), and this episode ends with a return to the theme of Egyptian oppres-sion and the task which he cannot, even if he would, avoid (vv. 23-25).

It is the function of the concluding verses of chapter 2 to make clear what has gone before and what is about to take place—the call and commission of Moses. If the story is correct in recording the death of an Egyptian pharaoh during Moses' stay in Midian, we suspect it was Seti I, who died about 1290, although it could be Ramses II, who died about 1224. Evidence of varying sorts points preponderantly to a thirteenth-century date for the Exodus, and perhaps favors a date earlier rather than later in the century. We shall here assume that the "new king over Egypt" of 1:8 was Seti I (c. 1310-1290), under whose administration the lot of all 'Apiru in Egypt grew less tolerable; and that following his death (2:23) and the accession of Ramses II (c. 1290-1224) the condition of slave and semislave laborers degenerated still further, precipitating the Exodus of the group under Moses.

Moses' people are in hard bondage. They now take their place in the vast, timeless company of the exploited and the wretched of the earth. Israel—it is now Israel—has cried out to God. God hears, God sees, God knows, God also "remembers." God remembers the covenant with Abraham and Sarah, Isaac and Rebekah, and Jacob and Leah and Rachel. Now, we do not suppose that in this pre-Exodus time the confessional formula of ancestral covenant was invoked, since the formula itself is dependent upon the Exodus event and the subsequent identification of Israel as a covenant people. The story verbalizes the faith that the Exodus event is *in meaning* consequent to what God had purposed long ago in Abraham and Rebekah, Isaac and Sarah (see Isa. 51:1 f.), and Jacob, Leah, and Rachel. Thus, the story impresses on the hearer or reader the enormous dimensions implicit in what is happening. This is an act of covenant fulfillment; God is remembering and performing the covenant program. And this act has universal implications, for the promise to the company of the ancestors is a promise ultimately to all the families of the earth (see Gen. 12:3). It is a promise to *all* who are "in Egypt," who are in bondage, who are exploited and oppressed, that God hears, sees, knows, and remembers. The story affirms its own universal and timeless significance.

Moses in Midian:
Exodus 3–4

> I sent Moses.
> *Josh. 24:5*

Three words in the first two verses of chapter 3 raise questions about the framework of the story. In these verses, Moses' father-in-law is Jethro, but in 2:18 he is Reuel. The sacred mountain, "the mountain of God," is called Horeb, a name used less than twenty times in the Old Testament, but it is called Sinai—quite apparently the same mountain—about forty times. In the first two chapters of Exodus, God is designated only by the Hebrew word *'Elohim,* which also underlies the word "God" in 3:1. But in 3:2 ff. another term appears, "the Lord," in Hebrew originally simply four consonants: YHWH. For centuries Hebrew was written without vowels. The probable pronunciation is Yahweh, although in Israelite-Jewish tradition this specific and particular *name* of God was commonly deemed too sacred to be pronounced. The reader or speaker simply said *'Adonai,* meaning the Lord. The term *Jehovah* is a hybrid, combining the consonants YHWH with the vowels of *'Adonai.*

Jethro-Reuel (and perhaps also called Hobab, see Num. 10:29; Judg. 4:11); Horeb-Sinai; *'Elohim-*Yahweh—these variants point unmistakably to different sources in the oral tradition, the first writing, and later "editorial" stages. Through the nineteenth century of our era and into the twentieth, biblical scholars have worked productively at the analysis of the Old Testament by means of a documentary hypothesis—the theory (supported by many variants such as these) that multiple documents or sources were employed and combined in the present text. We see no reason to abandon this theory if the hypothesis is not rigidly or arrogantly employed; if we remember that often it is impossible to untangle the "sources"; if we recognize that there is artistic, even theological, meaning in the way in which the sources have been combined; and if we recall that what we choose to designate as a single source may itself be the product of multiple lesser sources.

The pioneers of documentary analysis are three nineteenth-century European scholars: Graf, Kuenen, and Wellhausen. Early in the twentieth century S. R. Driver (*Literature of the Old Testament,* 1913) gave a mature and now classic formulation to their essential position; and more recently Robert Pfieffer in this country (*Introduction to the Old Testament,* rev. ed., 1948) and Otto Eissfelt in Germany (*The Old Testament: An Introduction,* 1965) continued to analyze and interpret the Old Testament in the tradition of literary criticism.

Other scholars use more radically modified methods of literary criticism proceeding from the basic assumption of multiple sources; and in Germany in the past few decades interest has shifted to a different approach known as form criticism, which asks different questions of the text. The "literary" critic first attempts to determine the source, its extent, date, and even authorship. The form critics address themselves first to questions of the community which produced a given segment of Old Testament text, the possible role of that segment in the life of the community, and such insights into the faith of ancient Israel as may be derived from the passage. But the form critic utilizes the work of literary critics, for example, in the inspired work of the father of form criticism, Hermann Gunkel, in the early decades of this century, and G. von Rad in the middle decades.[7] Only relatively few, notably among Scandinavian scholars, have completely abandoned the presuppositions of literary criticism.

We will use here the standard symbols, J, E, and P, to designate the three most conspicuous narrative strands interwoven in Exodus (as well as in Genesis, Numbers, and perhaps Joshua). The symbol J represents the source in which Jahweh-Yahweh is the preferred style of this divine name, and which seems to have originated in the south (*J*udah). It is generally taken to be the record of traditions current and fluid down to the tenth century, when the J-work was done, and it appears to be the work of an individual.[8] The symbol E represents not an individual's work of collection and editing, but a varied, unintegrated assortment of stories and traditions circulating in the north (*E*phraim) and preferring the divine name *'Elohim*. Drawn from the traditions current in Israel to perhaps the eighth century, it was combined with the material in J to augment, supplement, or pose a significant variant to the J body of tradition. P (for the characteristic *p*riestly perspective), the latest process of collection to attain a fixed form, also draws from the common mine of tradition until its development was arrested in the fifth century when it was combined with JE, probably by the same continuing community of priests who formed it.

The Call of Moses

3:1–10 Exodus 3 is JE, but E is dominant since the term "God" (*'Elohim*) occurs more frequently than the term "the Lord" (Yahweh). Exodus 4–5 (including 6:1) is also JE, but here J dominates. P, following brief appearances in chapters 1 and 2 (1:1–5,13–14; 2:23–25), first takes over the Exodus story in 6:2–7:13. This description of the text before us now explains some of the superficial phenomena of the story as it stands, but it also

---

[7]Cf. H. Gunkel, *The Legends of Genesis,* trans. W. H. Carruth, Chicago, 1901, available in paperback, with an introduction by W. F. Albright, as a Schocken Book, 1964; *What Remains of the Old Testament,* trans. A. K. Dallas, London, 1928; See also G. von Rad, *Studies in Deuteronomy,* in the series *Studies in Biblical Theology,* London, 1953; and other works of his already cited.

[8]M. Noth argues convincingly for a pre-J collection of traditional materials. See his *A History of Pentateuchal Traditions,* trans. B. W. Anderson, Englewood Cliffs, N.J., 1972. See also Brevard S. Childs, *Introduction to the Old Testament as Scripture,* Philadelphia, 1979, pp. 145–50 for a review of the use and role of sources in Genesis.

speaks of the relationship of the story to the total life of ancient Israel.

The scene is Horeb (E and Deuteronomy) or Sinai (J and P). We are not positive about its location. The traditional site is the mountain Jebel Musa in the southern Sinai peninsula; but if Jethro and the Midianites were here, they had ranged rather far out of their customary orbit east and perhaps north of the Gulf of Aqabah. In part on the strength of the proposition that the description of God's appearance on the sacred mountain in Exodus 19 presupposes volcanic phenomena (a view supported by the guiding cloud and pillar of fire?), some would locate Horeb/Sinai in the territory of Midian proper where alone in the whole area there is evidence of volcanic action. Still others would find the sacred mountain to the north and west of the northern extremities of the Gulf of Aqabah in the area loosely defined as the wilderness of Paran. This location satisfies the inference from a number of passages that Horeb/Sinai was not far removed from Kadesh-barnea ('ain el-Qudeirat?) which, though not positively identified, was surely situated just south of the Negeb (Canaan's southernmost territory) and considerably to the northwest of the tip of Aqabah. We incline to this third alternative.

We may now dispense with the minor problems of internal ambiguity, for we understand the structure of the story. For example, one of the story's components identified the reality behind Moses' vision as Yahweh (v. 4), but another as an angel, the authorized representative of Yahweh (v. 2). There is nevertheless unity in the narrative in its central affirmation—that Moses knew beyond any possible doubt the firm call of Yahweh/God to "bring forth my people, Israel, out of Egypt!" On the strength of what is recorded, we do not presume to reconstruct the "facts" of the event. We take this as testimony of Israel's faith in Yahweh and Moses. We take this for nothing more or less than *the way Israel remembered.*

Israel remembers the texture of this encounter between Yahweh and Moses—the texture rather than the concrete structure. The quality rather than the literal substance of Moses' overwhelming and ultimately indescribable experience of the call is reproduced. Moses' tiny space, the world of a moment, is exploded by the invasion of the Fullness of Time. His word is in conversation with the Word—*Moses, Moses, you may not walk here with shoes, since this, being ground of meeting, is holy ground. Do not walk here with shoes, since in this place of holiness your uncovered feet acknowledge that you, Moses, stand uncovered and naked in the holy place, this island, this enclosure, this tomb of your existence now entered by the Word of Yahweh!*

Israel remembers the essence of the call; the word of Moses is in conversation with the Word; the person of Moses, bared to the soul, is engulfed in glory. And to what end, the call? *That My people, Israel, may be delivered from their oppression in Egypt!*

Moses' Four Protests

3:11–12   *I will send you to bring all of this to pass.* And Moses responds, in effect—By all means, Lord, bring it to pass, but not through me.

1. Moses' first protest is essentially—Who am I to do this? Child of Israel-Egypt; fugitive; priest's son-in-law; and Midianite shepherd. This is my identity. I am obviously not qualified. But he is answered that he must now identify himself in terms of his relationship to God, "I will be with you."

Moses' problem when confronted by the Word is everyone's problem when so confronted. The story of Moses always "is" however much we may be concerned with its "wasness." The coin which reads "Faith" on one side and "Unfaith" on the other is universal. The two faces may not be separated or significantly altered, even by a Moses.

3:13–22   2. Moses is willing, for the sake of argument, to accept this definition of true identity. But to define himself in terms of a relationship to another, he must know the other. He must again protest and ask, in effect—Who are you, Lord? Tell me your *Name,* lest when they ask me, as ask me they will, I will have no name, and having no name, no real knowledge of who or what you are, to say nothing of who and what I am.

Six possible interpretations of the name are given. The J work —as we have suggested, the earliest identifiable collection of Israel's stories and traditions—takes for granted the knowledge of the divine name, Yahweh, from earliest times (Gen. 4:26). In E and P, the personal name, as opposed to the titles by which God was known, was first revealed to Moses. This is the view of verses 3:13–22 (traditionally assigned to E) as well as of 6:2 (P). Now it may well be, as a matter of fact, that God *was* worshiped in the south (J's provenance) by the name Yahweh long before the Moses-Joshua group entered Canaan, bringing with them the sacred name which only then became normative in the north. It may also be, as a number of competent scholars have maintained, that Jethro the Midianite was a Kenite, a clan related to tribes long in residence in south Canaan, and that the form, structure, and even the terminology of Moses' faith was influenced by the relationship. It is certain, as we shall see (chap. 18), that Moses was significantly indebted to Jethro.

However varied the historical details related to this question may be, the story is unequivocal in its most crucial point. Moses has a fresh, immediate, and unprecedented encounter with God, out of which new and deeper insights into the nature of the deity are gained.[9] In response to the question, "Who are you, Lord?" we are given six possible meanings of the name.

I am who I am or *I will be what I will be* (v. 14)
I am or *I cause to be* (all that comes into existence!)
YHWH (v. 15) here related to the verb "to be" but possibly derived
   from a root meaning "to blow" or perhaps "to sustain, to maintain"
God of your fathers
God of Abraham . . . Isaac . . . Jacob
God of the Hebrews (v. 18)

The uncertainty as to the derivation of the name YHWH results in a totally remarkable confession of faith: the God of the Hebrews, these particular *'Apiru* enslaved in Egypt, is the fathers' God and, surely, the mothers' God, the God of Abraham, Isaac, and Jacob, who is and will be, who causes to be, who manifests power (blowing), who sustains all life. This is the God of the fugitive Moses and the Hebrew slave!

4:1–9 3. But there is a third protest—Will he be believed? A note of impatience creeps into the divine response as Yahweh reveals to Moses the power he now possesses to perform the magician's acts. Here again the Old Testament story shapes itself according to the principle of essential meaning, subordinating details of events and the external forms of the past. Was there an actual contest between Moses and Pharaoh's magicians? We cannot say. But in the essential contest between Yahweh-Moses-Israel and Pharaoh-staff-Egypt, Egypt is defeated on its own terms—the magicians' apparent power over objects of the environment—and the story highlights and augments this motif.

4:10–19 4. The story moves to Moses' fourth protest. "I am not eloquent . . . I am slow of speech and tongue."

[9]On the name and nature of Yahweh, see W. F. Albright, *From the Stone Age to Christianity,* New York, 1957, pp. 15 ff.; D. N. Freedman, "The Name of the God of Moses," *Journal of Biblical Literature,* 79, June 1960, pp. 151 ff.

Yahweh's answer is double-pronged. The story presents, in Yahweh's words, a stirring affirmation of the biblical creation faith—God is the creator and sustainer of the life and time and total environment of humankind. This is all implicit in the rebuke, "Who has made man's mouth?" And this sharp response is accompanied by the promise, "I will be with your mouth!"

Now Moses breaks Yahweh's patience. The RSV translates, "Oh, my Lord, send, I pray, some other person" (v. 13). The sense of the Hebrew is much stronger: Send whom you jolly well please. I'm not your man! The story acknowledges Yahweh's surging anger against Moses, but nevertheless represents the long-suffering Yahweh still countering a recalcitrant Moses, this time with the assurance that eloquence can be had in the person and service of Moses' brother Aaron.

Reaction and Response

4:18–23
The significant events between Moses' call and his program of deliverance (chap. 5) are culled from sources both ancient and primitive, and late and sophisticated. There has been a considerable time lapse since Moses came to Midian (v. 19). His recently acquired powers of magicianship will not effect deliverance, and inferentially faith declares that only Yahweh can bring this about (v. 21). Pharaoh is to be informed (vv. 21 ff.) that Israel is Yahweh's firstborn (cf. Hos. 11:1, "my son"); and the demand theme, which is to be the refrain in the following chapters, is sounded—"Let my people go that they may serve me!" If the demand is refused, retaliation will be in kind—"If you refuse to let them go, behold, I will slay *your* firstborn son."

4:24–26
The form of this strange little narrative of Moses' near brush with death probably reaches back to a time not far removed from the Exodus era.[10] It is impossible to say precisely what facts gave rise to the account. Moses must be circumcised. Is his uncircumcision an affront to the deity? Or more positively, is it now essential that Moses seal and affirm by circumcision his own covenant with Yahweh just described in his call (cf. Genesis 17)? The narrative may present something of both. In any case, since Moses, near death, is physically unable to tolerate the rite, it is performed

---

[10]But see the illuminating suggestion of H. Kosmala, "The Bloody Husband," *Vetus Testamentum*, 12, January 1962, pp. 14 ff.

vicariously upon Moses' son, and this act of covenant-making effects the cure of Moses' sickness-unto-death.

4:27–31   Finally the story records Israel's response to Moses of unqualified faith: "And the people believed; . . . they bowed their heads and worshiped."

It is the Word of Yahweh which effects Israel's deliverance from oppression, from chaos, from meaninglessness. But it is also unmistakable in the story that this deliverance followed only upon the response of faith from within the life of oppression, chaos, and meaninglessness!

Israel Out of Egypt: Exodus 5–18

> I brought you out.
> *Josh. 24:5*[11]

We must again repeat that we are here commenting on a story which cannot be taken for objective external history. It is, in a manner of speaking, internal history; it portrays a people's inner life, self-understanding, and faith. The inescapable questions of possible correspondence between the inner and outer history must ultimately be answered by each individual reader and interpreter of the story.

The Preliminary Meetings

5:1–7:13   The issue is joined. Pharaoh is confronted with the Word's demand. His natural response is: Whose word is this? Who is Yahweh? I never heard of him and the answer is no.

Following the story's colorful and imaginative development of the plot (to 5:21), Moses reacts to Egypt's increasingly oppressive measures and the animosity of his own people as he is to react in the face of bitterness again and again. He turns to Yahweh. He appeals to the Word. And on the final outcome, at least, he is reassured (6:1).

It is the P stratum of the story (6:2 ff.) which now reports its own "memory" of Moses' call; or if, in the unified story's intent, this is, at a critical moment, a reiteration of the call experience, it brings to mind the earlier episode of the mountain of God, the burning bush, and the holy ground (JE, 3:1–6). There are dif-

[11]Cf. Psalms 77; 81; 105; 106.

ferences in the two accounts. The scene here is Egypt. There is no attendant vision. The sense of awe and mystery in the earlier encounter gives way here to a relatively developed theology; it is here a highly articulate Word giving eloquent expression to the nature and purpose of Yahweh. And where in JE the sense of covenant is only implied, however emphatically, in P the term "covenant" itself is explicit.

It is nevertheless the same covenant. It is the same Word. It is the revelation of the same divine name YHWH (6:3) for the first time to Moses. It is a brilliant and realistic stroke to repeat Moses' transforming encounter with the Word at Horeb/Sinai at this moment of abysmal discouragement following the first appearance before Pharaoh and the bitter verbal abuse of the Israelite foremen. The story understands and would have us understand that Moses is able to continue only on the strength of a renewal of purpose effected by a vivid reappropriation of the Word which first moved him from Midian to Egypt.

If the P stratum has its dull genealogies (for example, 6:14 ff.), if it embraces large blocks of legal material, if it sometimes exercises an unnecessarily minute interest in the external accountrements of institutionalized religion, it also incorporates some of the Old Testament's most beautiful and eloquent lines. Read aloud the content of the moving Word to Moses in 6:2–8. It ought to be read aloud. Its form strongly suggests that it existed for generations first as a spoken liturgy or confession of faith, habitually recited in the round of formalized worship, that is, in the cultus. Note that the quality of divine compassion, mercy, and grace comes through here as it has not previously in Exodus; that this is a recital of faith in the nature and purpose of God (observe the emphasis even more pronounced in Hebrew, on the divine "I" and compare the same feature in Joshua 24); and that all this is an expansion of the simple, eloquent theme which opens and closes the recital—"I am Yahweh"—conveying in the very name all the essential meaning of the divine life.

The Moses-Word dialogue breaks off at 6:13 to resume at 6:28 through 7:9. The intervening verses (6:14–27) constitute (except vv. 14–15; cf. Gen. 46:9 ff.) Levite genealogy concerning Moses and Aaron but more particularly Aaron, through whom the line of the institutional priesthood is derived (vv. 23, 24).

Now Moses repeats his self-deprecation: his lips are uncircumcised. This time the Word responds (7:1; cf. 4:14–16), "I will make you as God to Pharaoh" (*'Elohim,* not Yahweh), that is,

Moses will possess vis-à-vis Pharaoh certain attributes of deity; "Aaron your brother shall be your prophet," that is, Aaron is to be his spokesman. The story here pays magnificent tribute to Moses.

As evidence of the story's use of variant traditions, Aaron now (7:8–13) wields the rod endowed with magical powers, not Moses (as in 4:2–4). This is P, and priestly tradition understandably magnifies the role of the father of priests. Aaron's act with the rod is promptly duplicated by the whole complement of Egyptian magicians; but it is quickly added, with the humor and zest of a good story, that Aaron's rod-into-serpent swallowed up the Egyptian equipment.

Still Pharaoh's heart was hard (7:13); might remained unmoved, power remained corrupt. Still, as it were, the world turned a deaf ear to the cry of faith. The preliminary meetings were all abortive.

The Plagues

7:14–13:16   Literary critics see the three major source-strata all intermingled here. No single source appears to have embraced all ten plagues. Some plagues may well be duplicates; for example, plagues 3 (gnats, 8:16–19, P?) and 4 (flies, 8:20–32, J?) are both plagues of insects. At the same time, form critics remind us that any interpretation must take into account the confessional form of the story, that is, its present structure, intent, and emphasis as derived from its cultic use, as imparted from its repeated recitation throughout Israel's generations on the occasion of the annual celebration of the great deliverance. The entire unit, Exodus 1–15, is the product of a multiform literary tradition, but a relatively uniform cultic-liturgical tradition—a fact which again leaves quite beyond recovery the external-objective structure of the event.

What is preserved is the fact and the quality of the faith of the participants—the actual or sympathetic participants (probably both, but who can say in what proportions?). It is the central affirmation of the story that calamities falling with such severity upon Egypt were occasioned and controlled by the purposive Word of Yahweh. The event, this sequence of disastrous episodes, is interpreted as revelatory event, disclosing the nature and intent of Yahweh—an event celebrating and underscoring Yahweh's *nature* as Creator, and Yahweh's *intent* to make of Israel a people.

All else is subordinated to this theme. Thus, the present form of the story is obviously unconcerned with consistency. For example, is all of Egypt's water affected (7:19, P?) or only the Nile waters (7:17-18, J?)? Or, in general, who is the immediate agent of the wonders produced, Yahweh (J?), Moses (E?), or Aaron (P?)? As another consequence of the story's preoccupation with the faith-meaning theme, the major roles are unmistakably drawn in idealized and simplified fashion, more according to theological than to historical function. Most conspicuous in this regard is, of course, Pharaoh, representing "unfaith," brought repeatedly to the brink of submission but never persuaded, and therefore ultimately the victim of crushing defeat.

What of Pharaoh's actual role, whether Ramses II, his successor Merneptah, or, a more remote possibility, some predecessor of Ramses? This is simply an impossible question. The overwhelming significance with which the event of the Exodus is charged in the story obviously and appropriately reflects Israel's estimate, not Egypt's. Since the episode is mentioned nowhere in contemporary Egyptian records thus far uncovered, we assume that from Egypt's perspective it was nothing remotely resembling the momentous event it seemed to Israel. But this is Israel's birth as a people, its very creation out of formlessness and void, and therefore the varying strands of tradition must represent this event as of critical consequence to the very person of the Pharaoh of Egypt.

Essential truth and bare fact are not necessarily coincident, coextensive, or identical. It may well be, as some astute Old Testament historians maintain, that 14:5a preserves the historical fact that Israel fled without Pharaoh's knowledge and was pursued only subsequently when he was for the first time informed of their escape. But in the internal sense of faith, the fundamental significance of what is conveyed is profoundly true. To the mind of faith, Pharaoh's role and response in this event are authentic. "Let my people go, that they may serve me!" (7:16; 8:1,20; 9:1,13; 10:3; cf. 3:12; 4:23; 10:7). The answer of Pharaoh is a perennial paradigm of the defiance of the claims of faith by the oppressors of the earth's people: These are not Your people, but mine, and they shall not serve You but me.

11:1-13:16   In the round of the Old Testament cultic year, the most prominent and probably the oldest festival is the Passover. From the time of Moses on, it was celebrated in the spring of the year, commemorating the Exodus and particularly the "passing over"of the Israelite homes (12:23) when death invaded Egypt and claimed its firstborn. But the festival appears to have had a pre-Exodus history among pastoral folk as a spring celebration of the birth of the lambs with attendant rites for the consecration of the flocks and probably a communion meal shared by the shepherd group and the deity. Exodus 5:1 may refer to this parent festival of the Passover.

Together with the tenth and decisive plague, the Exodus story includes the full prescription for the Passover celebration (12:1-13,21-27,43-49). A second closely associated festival, the feast of unleavened bread, is similarly given its first prescription here (12:14-20; 13:3-10). In subsequent centuries when Israel had become a settled people, this agricultural festival also commemorated the Exodus (12:17; 13:8). A third cultic rite is also introduced—the rite of the dedication of the firstborn (13:1-2, 11-16). It is introduced here because of its natural association with the moving "firstborn" theme which dominates these chapters.

The first simple Passover was no doubt in a real sense celebrated in the episode of the last plague, which was considered by the Israelite participants to be decisive to their escape. This seems probable whatever the external structure of that moment of time. But the present story gives us a form of celebration developed over the seven or eight following centuries (12:21-27 appears to derive from the older J stratum; but 12:1-13,43-49 is of the P character). And this is as it should be in the case of all three rites, since the story is concerned primarily with the meaning of the episode in the life of Israel. Only the developed matured rites could effectively convey what Israel understood to be the meaning of its birth-night: that Yahweh, in this event, is made known as Lord of life and creation, of time and history. In converting (certainly long after entrance into Canaan) an agricultural festival of unleavened bread celebrating the fertility of nature and a nature-deity into a rite memorializing the action of Yahweh and the Word-to-Moses in history, Israel underscores its faith in the purposive, effective reign of God in time and history. And in relating the rite of dedication of the firstborn to that same momentous night, Israel declares this meaning in its deliverance from Egypt—that the same Yahweh who brought Israel forth out of Egypt also gives and sustains, and so rightfully owns and possesses, all life.

The Crossing

13:17–14:31   We can be very sure that this little band of escaping *'Apiru* did not go out "equipped for battle" (see RSV, v. 18). We probably ought to read the text here "by fifties" or "in five divisions." It is a point of the story and surely a fact of the real event that the escape was won in spite of the complete vulnerability of the escapers.

In the Hebrew text, there is no reference to the Red Sea but to the Reed Sea, mentioned first in 10:19, again in 13:18, and repeatedly thereafter. The sea in question, then, was never purported to be the present Gulf of Suez. Unhappily, we have as yet no consensus as to where and what it was, other than the remarkably astute observation that it must have been a body of water in which reeds commonly grew. Was it Lake Sirbonis, east of Egypt and adjacent to the Mediterranean? Or is it not more likely that the crossing took place at the northern end of Lake Timsah or the southern tip of Lake Mensaleh, both bodies of water being situated along the course of the present Suez Canal? We cannot be sure, in part because as yet we have been unable to identify Etham (13:20) and Pihahiroth, Migdol (14:2), is probably to be located just beyond Egypt's northeast border, and may therefore indicate that escaping Israel followed initially the main route from the Egyptian delta to Palestine.

We shall not here attempt to reconstruct Egypt's pursuit (14:5–21),[12] save to insist that the whole episode has been dramatically heightened in keeping with Israel's sense of its overwhelming significance. It was, by the story's own admission, "a mixed multitude" (12:38), a conglomerate lot of hangers-on to Egypt's relatively lush land, some of whom must have been to Egypt more liability than asset. That Ramses II or any other pharaoh of the Eighteenth or Seventeenth Dynasty, put himself in person at the head of his entire complement of chariotry (14:7,9) is, to say the least, improbable.

The story nevertheless comprehends and intends to highlight the tensions of faith and unfaith. We were Pharoah's slaves! We lived and we continue to live and relive that experience. We remember the tension because we know the tension now. We recall what we felt, what we always existentially feel—our freedom to serve God is only a dim possibility, the pursuit of

---

[12]Cf. B. D. Napier, *Exodus,* Richmond, 1962.

which means the abandonment of such security as we have. How can we face the quest of freedom in God's service when the quest propels us into an existence that is a vacuum, devoid of all the familiar symbols of security, ground to walk on, means of subsistence, and some reasonable assurance of continuity? Let us go back to Egypt. Let us return to life and meaning tangibly supported by human means and human devices, even Egyptian. In the life of faith this tension always exists.

Source critics long ago divided the scene of the dramatic crossing (14:10–31) into J and P (E figures here insignificantly if at all) accounts:

J	P
21b. And Yahweh drove the sea back by a strong east wind all night, and made the sea dry land.	21a,c. Then Moses stretched out his hand over the seas, and the waters were divided.
24. And in the morning watch Yahweh looked down upon the host of the Egyptians.	22. And the people of Israel went into the midst of the sea on dry ground, the waters being a wall to them on their right hand and on their left.
25. And clogged [or bound, or caused to bog down] their chariot wheels so that they drove heavily; and the Egyptians said, "Let us flee from before Israel; for Yahweh fights for them against the Egyptians."	23. The Egyptians pursued, and went in after them into the midst of the sea, all Pharaoh's horses, his chariots, and his horsemen.
27b. And the sea returned to its wonted flow [the inference is clear: the wind abated and the water returned to its customary level] when the morning appeared and Yahweh routed the Egyptians in the midst of the sea.	26. Then Yahweh said to Moses, "Stretch out your hand over the sea, that the water may come back upon the Egyptians."
	27a. So Moses stretched forth his hand over the sea.
	28a. The waters returned and covered the chariots and the horsemen and all the host of Pharaoh.

In J the event is recorded as crucially conditioned by "natural" phenomena—an abnormally low water level at one end of the lake produced by uncommonly strong winds, the return of the water, the Egyptian chariots rendered inoperable by the now miry shallows, and the necessary abandonment of the chase. While P represents an event more impressed with the quality of the miraculous, it is important to acknowledge the fact that both interpretations affirm with equal insistence the decisive role of Yahweh. Essentially the same two interpretations are to be seen combined in the account of the plagues. Incidentally, we shall encounter this motif of the phenomenally dry crossing again in the story of Israel's entrance into Canaan (Josh. 3:1 ff.; cf. 2 Kings 2:8).

15:1–21   The climax of the crossing is unambiguous in the present text. This bitterly oppressed people, this company of the lost, this weak, diffuse body, suddenly given unity and entity by Yahweh, all break forth into a spontaneous hymn of praise, more shout than song, more chant than anthem, more cry of ecstasy than artistic creation (15:21; cf. 15:1):

> Sing to Yahweh for he has triumphed gloriously;
> The horse and his rider he has thrown into the sea!

The Song of Moses or Miriam (15:1–18) has usually been taken as a later expansion of the original, very ancient two lines (15:21) attributed to Miriam, although some have more conservatively maintained the originality and antiquity of the long poem.[13] In any case, we affirm its relative antiquity, subject of course to modification (for example, to accommodate the reference to the tenth-century temple in Jerusalem, vv. 13b,17), and its immediate relationship from the beginning to the cultus, to the annual celebration and reenactment of the event.

In the Wilderness

5:22–17:16   We cannot trace the route of march, nor can we hope to reconstruct the sequence of events. We are unable to define the geographical limits of the wilderness of Shur (15:22) or the wilderness of Sin (16:1, from the name Sinai?).[14] And as we have seen, the location of the sacred mountain itself, Sinai/Horeb, remains uncertain.

[13]Cf. F. Cross and D. N. Freedman, "Song of Miriam," *Journal of Near Eastern Studies,* 14, no. 4 (October 1955). Cross and Freedman argue that the long poem is in its entirety the "Song of Miriam" and in its original form dates from a time no later than the twelfth century B.C.

[14]The two wildernesses of Sin (17:1 and Num. 33:11–12) and Zin (Num. 13:21; 20:1; 27:14; 33:36; 34:3; Deut. 32:51; Josh. 15:1,3) may in reality be one and the same, located south of Judah and embracing Kadesh. The Septuagint assumes the identity of the two.

The story employs four somewhat random narratives to emphasize the quality of Israel's existence upon first emerging from Egypt. The first days in the wilderness were days of intense anxiety and crisis over survival. In near panic the first cry—always the first cry in parched lands—is, "What shall we drink?" (15:22-27). It must have been raised repeatedly in the wilderness years (17:7; Num. 20:1-2). This band of escapers also faced the problem of hunger, and the second narrative centers on the cry, "What shall we eat?" (16:1-36). The third episode recounted to illustrate the crisis of survival repeats the motif of the people's thirst, but poses a more sweeping question, "Is Yahweh among us or not?" (17:1-7). The fourth in this series concerns another basic threat to existence, attack from hostile forces (17:8-16).

Was Moses in fact knowledgeable in the art of "healing" unpalatable waters? Did Israel on occasion gather quail near the Mediterranean shore, when, as still happens, they had flown south over the sea to fall exhausted on the ground of northern Sinai? Was their "bread" (manna, RSV 16:15, note; and cf. bdellium, Num. 11:4-9) on occasion a sweet substance found adhering to the tamarask tree, a honeylike sap sucked out by insects to form a fragrant edible gum? Did Moses, wise in nature's ways, uncover or make available the waters of a natural rock spring? Did he in fact possess the powers of the primitive medicine man, to gain or seemingly to gain by magic means the victory over Amalek?

We cannot but ask these questions, even though no answer is forthcoming. These four episodes have been employed, apparently deliberately in this sequence, for primarily theological reasons—to illustrate simply and effectively the Yahweh-Moses-Israel conquest of the fundamental threats to Israel's existence in its first breath of independence following the hazardous birth out of Egypt.

18:1-27   Now the story turns, as Israel must have turned, to the crucial matters of consolidation and organization.

Jethro, Moses' father-in-law, was a Midianite, and more specifically, apparently a Kenite (Judg. 1:16). Whether and to what extent the *religion* of Moses was initially borrowed from the Kenite priest Jethro (a theory long maintained under the designation the Kenite hypothesis) remains unresolved. But there can be little doubt, in view of chapter 18, that Jethro gave Moses significant advice in matters of civil administration. The parallel, though differing, account in Numbers 11 places full responsibility for this action on Moses and Yahweh; Jethro is not even mentioned. Now if Jethro, the Midianite-Kenite, never served in such a relationship to Moses, it is difficult to understand how and why tradition (in tendency always disposed to magnify the stature of Moses) would create an account giving so decisive a role not simply to another person, but to a non-Israelite. The fact that Moses followed the advice of Jethro (18:13–27) lends support to the general proposition of Israelite Yahwism's ultimate (if unmeasurable and indefinite) indebtedness to the faith and cultus of Jethro.[15]

Jethro takes his leave of Moses (18:27. The parallel narrative in Num. 10:29–32 records Moses' urging his father-in-law to stay with them—"you will serve as eyes for us" in the wilderness—thus agreeing in the very positive estimate of Jethro and his relationship to Moses and Israel.) The Exodus story now moves on to a block of material centering on events and experiences at the sacred mountain. The act of Israel's creation-deliverance, offering initially a miserable prognosis and fulfilled against seemingly insuperable odds, is rounded out with the establishment of some order and stability. Yahweh and Yahweh's Word through Moses have effected the impossible—deliverance from Egypt; salvation from the threats of extinction by thirst, famine, and sword; and now a workable administrative structure adequate to the needs of a group increasingly involved in the problems of a new people, with a new freedom and a new and uneasy responsibility.

[15]This proposition, the Kenite hypothesis, has had wide acceptance among Old Testament scholars for more than a century. For bibliography and an able defense of the hypothesis, see H. H. Rowley, *From Joseph to Joshua,* London, 1950, pp. 149 ff. For arguments in rejection of the view, see Martin Buber, *Moses,* New York, 1958, pp. 94 ff.

2

Yahweh and World

Creation:
Genesis 1–2

> Let us make 'adam [humankind].
> *Gen. 1:26*[1]

The Context

Anyone acquainted with political life, even merely as observer, knows how viciously a public figure may be maligned from his own words *lifted out of context.* The treacherous device of damning by out-of-context quotation has served in the past and unhappily continues to serve effectively in the disastrous defamation of persons in public life.

One commonly hears it said, with a shrug, "You can prove anything in the Bible." And in a sense this comment is true: interpret the biblical verse or the brief narrative or in a couple of instances even the Old Testament book in isolation and it becomes in meaning something totally different from what was clearly its intent *in context.*

This is pointedly true of the whole Genesis story. Source critics see here the same three primary strata of tradition—J, E, and P— which we have already seen in Exodus; but we will do well to remind ourselves again that these symbols represent by and large the collection and arrangement of smaller units of oral and written material, at least some of which were already long in existence. There can be no doubt that what we identify in the Tetrateuch (Genesis–Numbers) as P employs and incorporates in the fifth

---

[1]Cf. Psalms 8, 104.

century some material as old as or possibly older than J. And J in the tenth century may well have had as a primary source an earlier effort to bring together coherently a wide assortment of stories deemed to have significant bearing on the life of the people Israel.[2] Certainly individual units in the J corpus had been in existence for centuries before they were integrated; and beyond any doubt these units were often strikingly modified in meaning in the *context* of the J work.

We must always interpret the part in the light of the whole. We will read the whole book of Genesis in the context of the faith of the people of Israel—a people who, as we have seen, deem their life to be the gift of Yahweh and their destiny the subject of Yahweh's Word. And the varied components of the present book of Genesis we will read as for the most part purposively and meaningfully related to the whole work.

In briefest outline, Genesis falls into two parts. The pivotal point is chapter 12, the call of Abraham—at once the climax and interpretive key to the first eleven chapters, and the opening, thematic scene of the second division of Genesis, chapters 12–50. The J work no doubt supplied Genesis with its earliest outline and its profound theological bearing. But the *form* of this remarkable introduction to the life of the people of Israel remained fluid from the tenth century to the fifth century and the final Genesis story may with all justification be termed a meditation on history. It is as such both an informed and an informing introduction, which is simply to say that like any good introduction, it is *informed by* that which it introduces and is therefore also *informative to* that which it seeks to present meaningfully.

The first section, 1–11, intends to set the particular story of Israel against the background of all creation and in the midst of universal human existence. It has commonly been termed the "primeval history," but this overemphasizes the quality of "wasness." The faith of Israel, the interpretation of its historical life in Yahwism, inevitably poses the question: If the Word of Yahweh thus creates, shapes, and informs our life, if the life of Yahweh thus impinges effectively upon human history, what is Yahweh's relationship, and ours, to the wide world? In the first

[2]Noth calls the hypothetical, but very plausible, pre-J source G for *Grundlage,* meaning "basic source." See *The Laws in the Pentateuch and Other Studies,* trans. D. R. Ap-Thomas, Philadelphia, 1967.

two chapters of Genesis, Israel affirms in two totally different ways that all order in the universe is both introduced *and maintained* by God, and that the meaning of human existence, and indeed of all lower forms of life, derives solely from Yahweh. Creation is the control of chaos and the gift and the support of meaning. It always is, however much we may say it was.

Chapters 3–11, to which we will return in the next section, demonstrate *in full context* the intention to introduce a central proposition of biblical faith: *all* humankind (not excepting Israel, obviously) contend, in one way or another, that order and meaning are *not* thus created and sustained, but are subject to arbitrary human manipulation. This results in a state of existence intolerable both for humanity and God—a state of existence into which Yahweh introduced the Word through Abraham and Israel for the restoration of creation. "In you all the families of the earth will be blessed" (12:3 RSV margin).

The Creation Stories

Israel's Yahwism was from the beginning in tension or even sometimes in bitter conflict with the widespread indigenous fertility cults of Canaan. Local sanctuaries abounded enshrining the male deity, *Ba'al*, and often his consort, *'Asherah* (later and elsewhere, Astarte, Ishtar, and other names). Fertility rites, practiced in the interests of securing fertility and productivity, both human and natural, involved cultic prostitution—the sex act performed with cult personnel to bring efficacious union with the deity and the consequent guarantee of fertility of field and body.

Against this widely prevailing understanding of the "creation faith," we suspect that in Yahwistic circles the very term "creation" may have been a dirty word and that the development and discussion of Israel's creation faith was suppressed as part of the long, anguished struggle against religious syncretism and the loss of the distinctly moral-ethical-historical character of the Yahweh faith. It is, in any case, a fact that Israel's creation faith—certainly a basic element of the structure of Yahwism from early times—receives scant specific mention (apart from the J story of Gen. 2:4b ff.) until relatively late, and no absolutely unqualified elaboration and application until the latter part of the sixth century (in Isaiah 40–66), when also, at the earliest, the creation story of Genesis 1 became a part of the accepted cultic instructional idiom.

For this is what it is. The style is strongly didactic. A few phrases occur repeatedly: And God said, and God saw, and God called, and God made, and God created, and God blessed. The story is a precisely ordered piece, with each of its six creative acts rounded out with the same refrain: and there was evening, and there was morning, one day, a second day, a third day, and so on. (In ancient Israel as in the practice of Judaism now, the course of a day is marked from evening to evening.) No word is anywhere wasted, no phrase ill-conceived, unpondered. And the climax? It is the verification of the Sabbath institution, the ultimate authorization:

So God blessed the seventh day and hallowed it, because on it God rested from all his work which he had done in creation.[3] (2:3)

Yet this story's *origin* is emphatically *not* full-blown out of the demands of a revitalized cultic-religious program centered on the rebuilt city and temple of Jerusalem in the closing years of the sixth century. The story had its dim beginnings and it betrays its distant involvement in an ancient myth of creation out of the Near and Middle East, which survived in various forms but best and most fully in the Babylonian *Emma Elish* (a title derived from its opening words, "When on high").[4] Here chaos is represented in the goddess Tiamat, a name perhaps echoed in the Hebrew word for "deep" *tehom* (1:2). Creation is effected when the god Marduk-Bel, with the assistance of lesser gods, carves up Tiamat's carcass to form from it the earth and its arching canopy, the firmament. Neither the Hebrew nor the Akkadian (Babylonian) accounts envisage creation out of nothing, since in both creation results from the radical transformation of a prior chaos.

But gone from the Hebrew account is any suggestion of "biological" relationship between chaos and God. Gone is the long gory struggle. Gone is the stupendous effort of Tiamat's defeat. Genesis 1 does preserve the notion of creation by work in the frequent use of the verb "make" and the thrice-repeated verb

[3]Cf. G. von Rad, *Old Testament Theology,* trans. D. M. G. Stalker, New York, 1962, vol. 1, pp. 147 f.; and *Genesis,* trans. J. Marks, Philadelphia, 1961, pp. 59 ff.

[4]For the translated text of the seven tablets, by E. A. Speiser, see James B. Pritchard, ed., *Ancient Near Eastern Tests,* 2nd ed., Princeton, N.J., 1955, pp. 60 ff.

"create" (of "the heavens and the earth," v. 1; of "every living creature that moves," v. 21; and of man, v. 27). But the measure of the story's theological refinement is nowhere more conspicuous than in its confident, if subtle, superimposition of creation by Word—the Word which, effortlessly spoken, effortlessly calls into being that which was not. " 'Let there be light!' And *there was* light."

Not *creatio ex nihilo* but creation conceived in terms analogous to Israel's own creation. Israel *was* prior to the call of Moses, but it was chaos. It was without order, meaningless. Israel was, in the onomatopoetic phrase of verse 2, *tohu vavohu,* "formless and void." God called it into being (not from nonbeing but from "antibeing"[5]) by the Word. So, analogously, Israel understands and articulates its faith in the world's and humanity's creation: all that now exists is brought into being by Yahweh and the Word out of chaos and continues in nonchaotic existence only in and by the creating-sustaining Yahweh. Creation, in Israel and the world, is continuous. In the faith of Israel the story of creation always *is*.

2:4b–24 The origins, background, and history of the second creation story remain obscure. It was apparently available to the J work in the tenth century and was there appropriated to J's uses as the opening chapter of the corpus. It became stabilized, so to speak, very early and therefore displays a spontaneity, charm, and naïveté which contrast sharply with the preceding story. The ordered sequence of Genesis 1, the specific citing of the range and depth of creation, the refined theological concept of creation by Word, and any institutionally motivated purpose (Sabbath)—all this is absent. There *is* concurrence that Yahweh God (2:4b ff.; but "God," *'Elohim* alone, in 1:1 ff.) worked "in the beginning" (1:1), that is, "in the day that Yahweh God made earth and the heavens" (2:4b) from preexistent matter—chaos (an earth formless, void, engulfed in darkness, 1:2) or, and this is part of the concurrence, an earth utterly barren, a sterile world (2:5). Both stories understand creation as essentially transformation. The thought of ancient Israel is always characterized by the nonspeculative. One rarely encounters in the Old Testament any

[5]The term is suggested by N. H. Gottwald. See his discussion of the creation motif in Babylon and Israel in *A Light to the Nations,* New York, 1959, pp. 455–63.

disposition to probe beyond time, concrete existence, matter, and history. There is even syntactical concurrence: the two stories open with sentences similarly structured:

When God began to create [RSV margin] the heavens and the earth, [when] the earth was without form and void, . . . *then God said* . . . .

In the day that Yahweh God made the heavens, when no plant of the field was yet in the earth, . . . *then the Lord God formed man* [Hebrew, *'adam*-humankind] . . . .

But perhaps the most fundamental contrast is also here apparent: the J story proceeds at once to the creation of *'adam* (literally, "formation" for this story does not use the word "create"). The language is raw, earthy, concrete, and pictorially three dimensional. Here it is not the conceptual "created . . . in the image of *'Elohim''* (1:27) but the graphic "formed [molded] of dust from the ground." And this lifeless but shaped mass of clay is now animated by Yahweh's breath, the breath of life, blown without benefit of any intermediate devices into the cold clay nostrils of the sculptor's figure.

Here is a primitive, even crude etiology (a creation myth explaining present, persistent phenomena of existence). This was its intentional meaning in the centuries of its circulation before J employed it. As such, it is interesting as one in the growing collections of ancient mythologies, but it is now irrelevant, if not also aesthetically and theologically unpalatable. But we must ask after the story's J-meaning, its Israel-meaning. What intentional interpretation is imparted to the story *contextually?* How does the J-work understand the story? Why do Israel's traditionists through the centuries retain the story and hold it inseparably joined in the unit Genesis 1-2 and the larger unit Genesis 1-11?

The quality of naïveté is capable of great depth and subtlety. The *present* intention of the story is to give expression to what J and all true Yahwists in Israel deemed to be the essence of the relationship, not as in Genesis 1 between God and all creation, but pointedly and existentially between Yahweh and *human* life. The one essential, universal datum of human life is its immediate, direct, total dependence on Yahweh. Yahweh gives it form out of formless ground. Yahweh imparts life to lifeless form. Yahweh gives the productive environment in which human life is set with only the one condition (symbolized in the story in the forbidden tree) that humankind acknowledge their status as creature by observing this single restriction to their freedom imposed by the Creator. Aside from this, human autonomy is complete and includes full jurisdiction over all lesser creatures, as is testified to in *'adam*'s *naming* these creatures and thereby assuming toward them the superior and controlling relationship of the namer to the named.

And this creation-faith is articulated in Israel always in terms analogous to the Exodus experience of formation out of the lifeless ground of Egyptian oppression, animation by Yahweh's breath and Word in escape, and autonomy, unqualified save by the creator-creature relationship, in Canaan's productive environment.

An etiological story out of the common fund of Middle Eastern mythologies becomes in the context of Israel's life and faith profoundly theological. Thus, not once but twice in the opening lines of Israel's long, intimate story Israel declares its faith that its story, which is to follow, is inseparably related to the world's story; that the world and Israel's own role in it have meaning only in the proposition that the earth and all who dwell in it are Yahweh's; and that the stuff of chaos rendered unchaotic by the creative power of Yahweh alone nevertheless resides in all, restrained only by the living God and God's living Word.

Alienation:
Genesis 3–11

> Where are you?
> *Gen. 3:9*[6]

The Human Condition

Briefly surveyed, this block of chapters is comprised of four major narrative units and two extended genealogies in chapters 5 and 10. The self-contained tales of the Garden (3), the Brothers (4), the Flood (6–9), and the Tower (11) all bear the marks of a pre-J origin and history and, with the exception of the Flood, which is now combined with a strong P strand, appear substantially as selected and employed by J. E has a part in Genesis only

---

[6]Cf. Psalm 29.

beginning, probably, in chapter 15. Genealogies are offered by both J (4:17-25; 5:29; 10:8-19,21,25-30) and P (5:1-28,30-32; 10:1-7,20,22-23,31-32). J's are colorful, anecdotal, and etiological (for example, Jubal "was the father of all those who play the lyre and pipe," 4:21), whereas P's are boringly businesslike with only slight relief from the enumerated weight of human years and procreation. Both J and P thus testify to Israel's historicizing of these timeless tales, originally disjointed, single, homeless, and dateless, but always relevant and deemed in Israel's faith to describe the universal human situation, the perennial condition of human existence.

We may term the block of chapters, then, JP, a designation which serves at least to remind us that the work is composite and that it reflects the meditation and faith of Israel over a good five-hundred-year span, from the Yahwist in the tenth century to the priests of the fifth century. The latter, through whose hands the whole Pentateuch finally passed before it was elevated to the relatively unmodifiable status of holy canon, are responsible for the superficial editorial framework of Genesis. It is P that would divide Genesis into sections by use of the formula "These are the generations of . . . ," or a comparable phrase at 2:4 (perhaps originally standing before 1:1 and introducing "the generations" of heaven and earth?); 5:1, Adam; 6:9, Noah; 10:1, sons of Noah; 11:10, Shem; 11:27, Terah, Abram, Lot; 25:12, Ishmael; 25:19, Isaac, Esau, and Jacob; 36:1, Esau; 37:2, Jacob. But certainly the basic sequence and structure of Genesis—the arrangement of its principal components—still derives from the J work.

As Etiology

It was not many decades ago that serious discussion (and heated debate) still commonly centered on the question of the literal truth of these tales, including, of course, the creation stories. Defenders of the truth of the Bible, who erroneously assumed that the truth of a narrative is found precisely in the measure of its literal accuracy, its concrete facticity, were constrained to interpret so as to substantiate the objective or scientific reliability of the account. For example, to bring Genesis 1 into conformity with relatively modern theories viewing creation as a developmental-evolutionary process over vast eons of time, the word "day" was arbitrarily interpreted to mean just that, eons of time! And this despite the fact that this same word, in Hebrew yōm, is habitually used with great frequency for the span of time from evening of one day to evening of the next.

Happily, this debate has appreciably subsided, although in certain quarters there are still those ready to tilt to the death on behalf of what is, alas, an idol—a deified book representing the reduction of Israel's Yahweh (and in the New Testament Christ's God) to a particular combination of ink letters preserved on lifeless sheets of paper bound together between a pair of cardboard or leather covers and known as the Bible. In Judaism as in Christendom, the area in which this old debate can now be revived is greatly reduced. With characteristic British understatement and with admirable humor (intentional or not), the ghost of the argument for objectivity was firmly laid in the clipped accents of Professor A. S. Peake of the preceding generation of Old Testament scholars, in address to the tale of the flood:

The question of the historical character of the narrative still remains. The terms seem to require a universal deluge, for all the flesh on the earth was destroyed (6:17; 7:4, 21–23), and "all the high mountains that were under the whole heaven were covered" (7:19 f.). But this would involve a depth of water all over the world not far short of 30,000 ft., and that sufficient water was available at the time is most improbable. The ark could not have contained more than a very small proportion of the animal life on the globe, to say nothing of the food needed for them, nor could eight people have attended to their wants, nor apart from a constant miracle could the very different conditions they required in order to live at all have been supplied. Nor, without such a miracle, could they have come from lands so remote. Moreover, the present distribution of animals would on this view be unaccountable. If all the species were present at a single centre at a time so comparatively near as less than five thousand years ago [dating by genealogical tables returns a date for creation around 4000 B.C.E. and Noah and company about a thousand years later], we should have expected far greater uniformity between different parts of the world than now exists. The difficulty of coming applies equally to return. Nor if the human race took a new beginning from three brothers and their three wives (7:13; 9:19) could we account for the origin, within the very brief period which is all that our knowledge of antiquity permits, of so many different races, for the development of languages with a long history behind them, or for the founding of states and the rise of advanced civilizations. And this quite understates the difficulty. . . .[7]

[7]"Genesis," *Peake's Commentary on the Bible,* London, 1937, p. 143. Alas, this vigorous word from Professor Peake did not survive subsequent revisions and does not appear in Black and Rowley's final revision of *Peake's Commentary on the Bible,* New York, 1962.

Of course, the flood story may preserve the memory of not infrequent inundations in the Tigris-Euphrates valleys, as is also no doubt the case in the somewhat parallel Babylonian *Gilgamesh Epic* (whose Noah bears the grand name of Utnapishtim). But the story is taken over into biblical use not from what in any sense we could call "historical" form, but from a prior and predominant etiological function—to give, in charming, interest-holding narration, an "explanation" of such common phenomena as the rainbow (9:13), the cultivation of wine (9:20 f.), "racial" distinctions and divisions (9:24-27), the occurrence of people of abnormally large stature (in the originally separate and probably truncated tale of the sons of God and the daughters of women and men, which now introduces the account, 6:1-4), and many other etiologies more blunted in present form.

The same is true of the three other tales which form the main body of the section Genesis 3-11. We list some of the most conspicuous etiologies: pain of childbirth, 3:16; the relative position of man and woman in society, 3:16; the intractability of earth's natural environment and the consequent necessity of hard labor, 3:17-19; the irrevocable consignment to death, 3:19; the antipathy between the nomad and the agriculturalist and perhaps also the origin of violence in human relationships in the Brothers, 4:1-16; and the frustrating fact in the human situation of fundamental communication thwarted by plurality of speech and wide geographical dispersion, 11:1-9.

The stories do not appear to have been radically altered in the course of their appropriation into the biblical corpus. It has been aptly remarked that, for example, the Yahwist's "editing" is hardly more than the placing of accents of refinement on the story in the use, say, of the name Yahweh where earlier some amorphous term for deity stood in the story.[8] And in the formation of JP it is obvious that editors regard it as essential that the distinctive forms of both existent flood accounts, for example, be retained, a fact accounting for present "discrepancies" in the tale in the form of duplicates and contradictions.[9]

[8]Cf. von Rad, *Genesis*, op. cit., pp. 31 ff.
[9]Cf. B. D. Napier, *From Faith to Faith*, New York, 1955, pp. 48-52. See also D. L. Peterson, "The Yahwist on the Flood," *Vetus Testamentum* 26, 1976, p. 438.

As Theology

What is editorially—and theologically—affirmed first by the Yahwist and tacitly by all subsequent handlers of the tradition (since they do not see fit to make any radical alteration in the Yahwist's outline) comes about not from the heavy-handed use of the red pencil, so to speak, but by the much more subtle editorial-izing achieved by the selection, arrangement, and juxtaposition of stories originally independent of one another. The stories thereby play a different role and say something very different. Israel shares with its neighbors the fascination of etiology and certainly continues to delight in the charm of the stories *at this level.* But clearly in the J work, the P work, and the JP work, emphatically in the context of the history of Israel, *in this subsequent level* of the life and interpretation of these etiological tales, the character and quality of the etiological is transformed to make of the scattered individual etiologies a single, all-embracing explanation — an etiology conceived not in the area of prescientific observation but in profound faith. In Israel and the world Yahweh's good intent in creation is thwarted and the good order of creation is tragically disfigured. In the faith of Israelite Yahwism, this is an empirical fact. If creation has not yet reverted to chaos, divine order and meaning are nevertheless woefully disfigured. The single, characteristic, and comprehensive biblical etiology, the etiology of all etiologies, is concerned with the how and why of distorted, aborted creation. It attempts to answer this one vast theological phenomenon of existence with the explanation, *alienation.* The problem of human life, out of which all of the problems of the human situation issue, is the chasm by which people are separated from God, the creatures from the Creator. It is a condition epitomized in Yahweh's first address to liberated autonomous beings, "Where are you?" (3:9). "Who told you that you were naked" (3:11), that you must run from me and hide from me, that you must separate yourself from me, so that we are alienated and estranged? "Have you eaten of the [forbidden] tree" (3:11), the only symbol limiting your freedom and denoting so long as it is inviolate your acknowledgment of your creatureliness? "What is this that you have done" (3:13) in the role of creature with which I endowed you?

The primitive etiology becomes in the JP-Israel story a profoundly theological etiology. All people willfully violate the favorable and, on the whole, nonrestrictive terms of human existence. When the terms are violated in an *act* of alienation, the conditions of human tenure in creation (the Garden) are so altered that woman and man must be expelled. The good order and clear meaning of creation become obscured, and though existence continues under Yahweh's sustenance, scrutiny, and concern, it is now beset with the bitter fruits of rebellion against Yahweh, against God's creation, and against humankind's status within it.

Of course, we do not suppose that the Yahwist in the tenth century B.C.E. would or could thus have analyzed his purposes in the composition and unification of these tales. But we think this is nevertheless the essence of even the Yahwist's interpretation of Israel and the world. And we are sure that the maturing Yahweh faith in subsequent Israel interpreted the sequence of Creation, Garden, Brothers, Flood, and Tower stories as the only key to understanding Israel's story: God called Abraham out of Haran (11:31) and Israel out of Egypt in order to bless the alienated families of the earth, to end the victimization of the weak by the strong (Cain and Abel), to effect the healing of the estrangement of folk and God, creature and Creator, and to restore and redeem the order and meaning of creation. This is the etiology—the explanation in terms of origins that *are,* not *were,* that extend not vertically but in comprehensive horizontal fashion over all time and history. This is the etiology of the one great phenomenon of existence, the fact of the relationship between Israel, the Word of Yahweh, and the world.

The etiological story can be set, then, without violence to Israel's essential understanding, in our own terms. The four tales of Garden, Brothers, Flood, and Tower are variations on a theme. Humankind is creature. Rebellion occurs (in four different modes) against that status in an act of pride by which the Creator is wittingly defied. The resulting alienation is perforce responded to by Yahweh, since the conditions of creation have in any case already been altered; or perhaps there is a sense in which the ensuing alienation is itself the positive judgment of God.

In the Garden story, sin (which is the expression vis-à-vis God of unwarranted and rebellious pride) takes the form of trust in human understanding in defiance of the Word. The one tree from which the created man and woman may not eat, and by not eating may glorify God, is observed to be good for food, a delight to the eyes, and, much more, is deemed to convey to the eater the gift of wisdom (3:6). Their consequent reasonable (to them) appropriation of *all* creation, their calculated denial of essential status, the implicit arrogation to themselves of the prerogatives of creator bring the Creator's unhappy response of judgment. What existence might be, *it is not.*

In the Brothers, as in all of the tales, the very naïveté is made to serve the profounder uses of theology. All folk are represented in Cain and Abel. All are brothers and sisters responsible to and for one another (4:9 f.). All are Yahweh's, ultimately responsible to God. But one arrogates to oneself prerogatives in the very nature of creation that are Yahweh's. One (person, group, sex, association, race, or nationality) acts against another and in judgment suffers alienation not only from the victim, the lost brother or sister, and from the human community but from Yahweh as well (4:14).

The Flood is a tale different in character from the other three. It is not only longer, but much more complex, diffuse, composite, and in its long history much more heterogeneously motivated. Nevertheless it is made to conform to the same essential theme of sin and judgment—the violation of creation and the necessary response of the Creator. Here human depravity is cited, that human condition in which the thoughts of the heart are only evil (6–5). The cataclysmic judgment this time is destruction. But as Yahweh is concerned for the creature in the Garden and in the Brothers stories, here also the story affirms a positive theology: the divine response in judgment is not without continuing mercy, since the creature is now given a fresh beginning. Alas, how quickly it comes to grief (9:20–27), even in the very person of Noah, "a righteous man, blameless in his generation," who "walked with God" (6:9). At Israel's level of interpretation, the story would remind the listener-reader that the strength of sheer righteousness is inadequate and that human estrangement in creation can be met effectively only with faith—a motif we shall see made central in the cycle of stories about Abraham.

11:1–9 In the last of this sequence of stories, the Tower, all humankind is represented as a single clan or tribe wandering aimlessly over the East—or through history. To manipulate their own security, they will build themselves a tower to reach into heaven and so guarantee control over that sphere; they will build the imperishable city; and they will establish for themselves the indestructible name. "And Yahweh came down" utterly uninvoked, unmentioned, ignored. From Yahweh's point of view, this is willful alienation of the most painful sort. The terms of creation are not defied; they are simply ignored. This is the ultimate act of rebellion and estrangement in which all the controls of creation and existence are unhesitatingly assumed by the creature. This is the final expression of apostasy by which trust in ultimate security is totally transferred from God to man and woman.

If there is a climactic quality in this fourth variation on the theme of sin, the response of judgment is also more enduringly bitter. Only in this one of the four stories is the judgment unmediated by any expression of Yahweh's continuing grace. The human situation is (apparently) irremediably afflicted with the accursed quality of the divisive, both in language and in geographical dispersion.

And yet it is just here that the primeval story is inseparably linked to the story of salvation: Abraham is called out of the multitude of peoples "in order that in him all the families of the earth may be blessed." So it is that the introduction of the story of salvation [in the call of Abraham, Genesis 12] answers the unresolved question of the primeval story—the question of God's relationship to the totality of peoples. This point where the story of salvation is brought in, Gen. 12:1-3, is not only the conclusion of the primeval story—it is the only real key to its interpretation. In thus inseparably uniting primeval story and salvation story the Yahwist expresses the meaning and goal of the function of redemption which Yahweh has charged to Israel. He gives the etiology of all etiologies of the Old Testament . . . on grounds neither rational nor documented by particulars, he proclaims that the ultimate goal of salvation effected by God through Israel's history is the overcoming of the chasm between God and all [folk] everywhere.[10]

The chasm to be overcome is, of course, an interhuman chasm as well, the result of a proliferation of interhuman alienations—sexual, racial, regional; political and economic; between rich and poor, powerful and powerless, exploiter and exploited, East and West, but now, more significantly in our world, North and South. The promise repeated five times (see on) to the ancestors of Israel is that what is begun in them will ultimately effect the blessing of

[10]von Rad, *Genesis,* trans. by the author from the German, p. 23. See the English, op cit., p. 24.

all the families of the earth—and obviously those most in need of blessing. The term conveys, among other qualities, human dignity and fulfillment; the actualization in man and woman of "the image of God"; freedom from oppression, extortion, impotence, hunger, abuse; "growth, success, increase, provision . . . peace . . . prosperity . . . security, and tranquility."[11]

[11]Claus Westermann, *Blessing: In the Bible and the Life of the Church,* trans. Keith Crim, Philadelphia, 1978, pp. 13, 64.

3

Yahweh and Covenant

In the Ancestors:
Genesis 12–50

> All the families of the earth.
> *Gen. 12:3*

These chapters should be read in a single sitting, or in as few sessions as possible. The reader should read uncritically and not be concerned if parts of the whole refuse to fit into *any* scheme of interpretation or any pattern of meaning.

Three fairly well-defined subunits appear, which at one time were probably three separate cycles of stories. The subunits center on (1) Abraham and Sarah and Isaac and Rebekah, 12–26; (2) Jacob (and Esau) and Leah and Rachel, 27–36; and (3) Joseph, 37–50 (except 38, which deals with Judah and Tamar).

Areas of Meaning

The questions we must address to these patriarchal stories fall into three categories. How are these stories to be interpreted (1) historically, (2) etiologically, and (3) theologically?

Historical Interpretation

The "age of the patriarchs" is roughly the first half of the second millennium B.C.E. (2000–1500). Several archaeological finds illuminate this epoch in the life of the Middle East. We know from evidence gathered all over the productive lands around the vast Arabian desert (long ago the historian J. H. Breasted designated this area as the Fertile Crescent) of a widespread eruption of desert peoples, Semitic nomads, into the more sedentary areas. The invaders were called Amorites ("Westerners") and for centuries they dominated the life of the Fertile Crescent, with city-states firmly established at such sites as Haran (from whence came Abraham, 11:31), Ugarit, Mari, and Babylon, which was ruled in the decades around 1700 by the renowned Hammurabi. Ugarit and Mari and Ebla, among other ancient sites, have yielded profuse contemporary information of several kinds. At Nuzi, southeast of Ninevah, clay tablets from the patriarchal age further inform of that epoch's practices and customs. All of these, together with a still-growing body of contemporary information from the exciting fields of archaeology, confirm the credibility of the whole atmosphere of the ancestral stories. If no shred of *specific* evidence substantiating the historicity of the patriarchs has appeared, it is, on the other hand, impossible now to maintain that the stories are of no historical value. Whatever may be the ultimate "historical" decision with respect to the plot and the players themselves, the stage-settings are indisputably authentic.[1]

Etiological Interpretation

The array and variety of etiological stories in Genesis is striking.[2] Three primary types recur again and again.

1. The *ethnological* story explains in terms of the "past" observable phenomena relating to known tribes and ethnic groups. The relatedness of Ammon and Moab, recognized in Israel, is explained in the simple terms of the brothers Abram and Lot (13) and the literal father-sons relationship of Lot to Ammon and Moab (19). Their consignment to territory beyond the Jordan and to the south of Israel is etiologically explained and justified in the story of Lot's voluntary choice of that area (13).

2. The *etymological* legend betrays Israel's (and, in general, the East's) profound interest in names, their meaning, and the relationship between meaning and innate character or performance, or between meaning and situation of origin. The explanation of Isaac's name (from a word meaning "laughter") is thrice repeated (17:17; 18:12; 21:2) as is Ishmael's ("God hears" 16:11; 17:20; 21:17). An alleged peculiarity of Jacob's birth and the subsequent, continuing relationship between the descendants of Jacob and Esau is etymologically explained ("heel-holder"—born holding his twin brother's heel, 25:26); while the same man's

[1]Cf. W. F. Albright, *The Biblical Period,* Pittsburgh, 1950, pp. 1-6; John Bright, *A History of Israel,* 2nd ed., Philadelphia, 1972, pp. 76-95. This conservative judgment is opposed by M. Noth, *The History of Israel,* 2nd ed., rev. trans., London, 1960, pp. 12 ff. and *Vetus Testamentum Supplement* 7, 1959.

[2]Cf. H. Gunkel, *The Legends of Genesis,* trans. W. H. Carruth, Chicago, 1901; and B. D. Napier, *From Faith to Faith,* New York, 1955, pp. 71 ff.

character (and in their own eyes, surely, that of his descendants who bear the name) is etymologically defined in his other name, Israel (perhaps "Striver with God" 32:28).

3. The *cult* etiology explains the existence of a sanctuary or a cultic ritual. Israel's major sanctuaries are thus all domesticized by association with the patriarchs, as, for example, Abraham at Jerusalem (Salem, 14:18) and Jacob at Bethel (28:10 ff.). Cult etiology attributes the origin of the rite of circumcision to Abraham (17, but also to Moses, Exod. 4:24–26; and Josh. 5:2 ff.).

Theological Interpretation

But in the present context, historical and etiological relations are subservient to the broadly theological bearing of the narratives. The "literary" judgment, for what it is worth, sees the whole, 12–50, as a JEP compendium. E is deemed to enter the structure at 15 (a prominent feature of E is the dream motif). P's role is in substance seen to be relatively slight except in 17 (covenant by circumcision, the P parallel to the JE covenant in Yahweh's promise, the response of faith, and Yahweh's irrevocable commitments to promise in chap. 15); in 23 (the charming story of Abraham's negotiation for a burial ground, a narrative we suspect to be of very different stuff indeed from 17); and in 25, 34, and 36. The rest is mainly JE except the very odd chapter 14, which continues to defy both historical and literary analysis. But again, this "documentary" structure serves to remind us of the centuries from J to P, from Israel's days as political state to its reconstitution as theocratic state, during which the fluid collection of traditions, the still pliable story of Israel, continued to serve as a living commentary on this people's existence. In the following sections on the ancestors, it is essentially this meditative, theological perspective that we shall pursue.

Abraham and Isaac

12–26   The theological theme, sometimes subdued and even momentarily lost, is unmistakable. Abraham is a *chosen* person. The chooser is Yahweh. The reasons behind the choice of Abraham (and not some other) are decidedly unclear, but the purpose behind the choosing is most explicitly affirmed. It is to give a land (remember the Garden, 3), peoplehood (recall the Brothers, 4), the blessing (contrast the Flood, 6–9), and a name (see the Tower, 11):

Go . . . to the land that I will show you. And I will make of you a great nation, and I will bless you, and make your name great. . . .

$$(12:1–2)$$

It is, in short, to create a people, a people of Yahweh, a people of God, a covenant people. Yahweh *said* this to Abraham (12:1). This is the Word to and on behalf of a people.

But Abraham's election by Yahweh is not confined to the two-member relationship of Word and people. It is, in its end function, of universal import. It is Word and people—and world:

In you all the families of the earth will be blessed.[3]

(12:3, RSV margin)

One strongly suspects that in ancient Israel the first ancestor was seen in terms analogous to Israel's first historical epoch. One notes an unmistakable correspondence between Abraham and Moses. Both respond to an exceedingly difficult call in an act of profound faith. There is a sense in which neither is fully Hebrew-Israelite. Both come into Egypt and go out again with ringing success. Both are committed to covenant in circumcision (Genesis 17; Exod. 4:24–26). In both the role of intercessor is featured (Gen. 18:22 ff.; Exod. 32:30 ff.). And although both are represented as models of faith, there are notable instances of gross unfaith in each.

If Israel tends to see its own first epoch essentially "anticipated" in the Abraham cycle of stories, there can be no doubt that Israel also sees the many in the one, identifies itself as people with Abraham the patriarch, and gives concrete articulation to its own tensions of faith in his fluctuations from faith to unfaith. In short, Abraham is at once both Abraham and Israel. This identification of one and the many accounts in part for the remarkable realism with which all the other primary ancestral figures are viewed—Sarah as well as Abraham, Isaac and

---

[3]Here as well as in 18:18 and 28:14 the form of the Hebrew verb is *niph'al*, permitting either a passive ("be blessed") or reflexive ("bless themselves") reading. In two other occurrences of the covenant promise of universal blessing, 22:15–18 and 26:2–5, the verb form *hithpa'el* requires the reflexive. From a theological point of view, the distinction is immaterial.

Rebekah, and Jacob and Leah and Rachel. This kind of story shows the *tendency* to idealize; and the tendency to cast Abraham as the epitome of faith is apparent especially in the story of the near-sacrifice of Isaac, the climax of the Abraham cycle of stories (22; but cf. 15). But Israel holds its one and its many to be indivisible. Israel knows its own repeated, irrepressible acts of faith, its own unceasing disposition to deny the response of faith in which it was created, by which it was sustained, and through which alone its existence has order and meaning. What Israel knows to be true of itself, it knows also to be true of its fathers and mothers and heroes; and Israel records their stories in the realistic awareness that faith always exists in tension with unfaith, generosity with meanness, magnanimity with selfishness, and honesty with deceit.

Jacob

27-36   We do not deny that the partriarchs may, as it were, speak their own lines on occasion; and we have already testified to the authenticity of the settings. But Genesis 12–50 is an incomparable and intimately informed *historical* document in its revelation of ancient Israel's inner life. In depth and degree quite without parallel, this is the internal history of a people—self-understanding, self-deprecation, pride, shame, fears, hopes, aspirations. The ideal response of faith so movingly portrayed in Genesis 22 is Israel's deepest confession of its own calling: to be ready to suffer the loss of its own historical life in response to the Word and at the same time maintain its faith in the Word's declared purpose to bless the world through Israel. And at the other extreme of the confessional scale are the stories of Jacob's lies and deceits, his unscrupulous, calculated operations conducted with some considerable finesse for his own self-interest; these reveal as conventional "history" never could Israel's acknowledgment of its own share in the distortion of creation and its own particular form of rejection of status.

For Jacob *is* Israel. Israel is his name (Gen. 32:28, J; and 35:10, P). The identity of the one and the many is unmistakable and unforgettable. The Jacob cycle thus effectively silences those who would persist, innocently or maliciously, in interpreting "the chosen people" as self-righteous, self-inflated, and self-praising. In Yahwistic-prophetic circles, in the core Yahweh-faith of Israel, Israel knew that Jacob was Jacob-Israel, and that Israel was

Israel-Jacob. Israel knew and through its prophets acknowledged that it shared with all folk the faithless, self-worshiping corruption of motive and action by which all creation and all human life within it are defaced and distorted.

Popular Yahwism in ancient Israel (like popular Christianity in our own day) commonly cheapened and reduced the faith. The notion of chosenness for mission and responsibility was popularly perverted to signify exclusivism and superiority. Israel certainly knew arrogant pride. But consistently in the core representation of Yahwism Israel acknowledged this pride and deplored it. The Jacob cycle is a declaration of realistic self-knowledge—in no sense does Jacob-Israel *merit* election and covenant. It is a candid appraisal of the qualities of deceit and viciousness devoid of the morbid: in the tales of Jacob, Israel accepts its own vigorous participation in the alienations of existence with remarkable candor and even with humor.[4]

In the Bethel and Peniel episodes of Jacob-Yahweh "meetings" (28 and 32), the stories also mirror Israel's faith that, like Jacob, it is finally sustained and justified only by Yahweh.

Joseph

37–50

For whatever reasons, Isaac lacks the impression of substance, color, and vitality returned in the Abraham and Jacob narratives. Nothing significant is told of him that is not in essence recounted of his father or son.

Four chapters serve to bridge the Jacob and Joseph stories. The story of the rape of Dinah (34) may have strong tribal implications —Dinah is a weak tribe aggressively assaulted by the tribe of Hamor. Certainly the background of the age is reflected—frictions between tribes; a level of sexual morality upon which for a number of reasons we may not sit in judgment; and a consistent representation of Jacob who rebukes his sons not on moral but on utilitarian-prudential grounds (34:30). Chapter 35 also reiterates themes of the Jacob cycle—the tension between Jacob and Yahweh, sin and grace; the faith that Jacob-Israel is redeemed only by Yahweh; and the repetition of the promise and the blessing. In the Edomite genealogy of chapter 36 and its accompanying notices, Israel affirms its claim to the land on grounds other than

---

[4]See further, Napier, op. cit., pp. 88–92.

Yahweh's gift and at the same time recognizes again its close relationship to some of its historical neighbors.

Chapter 38 interrupts the otherwise closely integrated Joseph story. Why? Is it in contrast with, and favorable commentary on, Joseph's sterling moral deportment in the next chapter? Is it in any pious sense to say that this is what, alas, a son of Jacob *is* (38), but this (39) is what a son of Jacob ought to be? We note in any case, and emphatically, that it is, like so much in these narratives, a very good story indeed, especially in the graphic portrayal of Tamar, in its deft integration of plot, and in its fine suspense.[5]

The Joseph story has been called E's masterpiece. But J is very much in evidence as the confusion and contradictions in chapter 37 indicate (for example, E features Reuben and the Midianites, but J, Judah and the Ishmaelites). But although the story is at such points conspicuously composite, it achieves a tightness of coordination that distinguishes it from the much more loosely integrated cycles centering on Abraham and Jacob. Its settings, as for the most part in the preceding stories, are authentic. But again its function in the present context cannot be primarily historical; or rather, and again, its historical value for us lies primarily in its contribution to our historical knowledge of inner Israel.

The Joseph story also sees the many in the one; and the one this time is a projection of Israel's most inspired hopes for what it may be, for what, according to the Word, it must be: a blessing in the earth. Joseph matures and survives to adult manhood against insuperable odds, and having gained full stature he is given to feed not only a starving "Israel" and a starving Egypt, but a starving world (41:57).

Now this kind of correspondence between patriarch and people, as with Abraham and Jacob, is imprecise. In the Joseph story too the players speak their own lines, lines created long before the historical phases to which they bear correspondence. We do not for a moment

---

[5]For a discussion of a novel approach, see J. A. Emerton, "Examination of a Recent Structuralist Interpretation of Genesis 38," *Vetus Testamentum 26,* 1976, pp. 79 f. On the Joseph story, see further articles by J. L. Crenshaw, *Journal of Biblical Literature,* 83, 1969, pp. 129–42; D. B. Redford, *Vetus Testamentum Supplement 20,* 1970, pp. 100–5; G. W. Coats, *Catholic Biblical Quarterly,* 35, 1973, pp. 285–97.

mean to suggest that Gen. 12–50 was created out of whole cloth as an allegorical, fictional, personalized "history" of Israel. . . . the bulk of the material comes *in fact* out of Israel's ancient past, transmitted first orally and given . . . written formulation (first) by the Yahwist. . . . Nor do we mean to say, then, that the story of Joseph came into being as a messianic message with the intention of treating Joseph as a messianic figure. We do mean to suggest . . . that in the unmistakable implications of messianism in Joseph, the *germ* of the later development of the concept (see, e.g., Isa. 49:6) was something already *given* in Israel's early traditions, precisely as the germinal faith in one God as Creator (Gen. 2), Judge (3–11) and Redeemer (12 ff.) was also given in the same traditions received by the Yahwist.[6]

Genesis begins and ends declaring in faith that Israel's created, called life will find fulfillment only in a role of instrumental service to the world. It cannot be only people and Word. It is people, Word, and world. This is the meaning of covenant with the patriarchs.

In the Sinai Decalogue: Exodus 19–20

> These are the words.
> *Exod. 19:6*

These two chapters introduce a very large block of material— Exod. 19:1 to Num. 10:10—of varied sorts and from a broad span of centuries, a block editorially created and given unity in the place, Sinai. In present form, this whole block purports to have its origin there. It has been set in the midst of a section unified in the place Kadesh. Kadesh appears as the center of operations both before and after this extended Sinai complex.

Now although this block is no doubt in its present arrangement the work of priests, it contains a significant nucleus that is not of the priestly cast. Exodus 19–24 and 32–34 we may term Yahwistic-prophetic (though not necessarily limited to the old J stratum); and within this unit, Exodus 19, 20, and 24 appear to have constituted the basic framework. This prior structure was simple, and theologically eloquent. In chapter 19 the glory of Yahweh is

---

[6]Napier, op. cit., pp. 105 ff.

revealed with uncommonly convincing power (the term often used for this is "theophany"), signifying Yahweh's commitment to the covenant made with Israel. In chapter 20 the instigator of the covenant and the senior party, Yahweh, makes known God's will —the Decalogue, the Ten Commandments (literally, ten words)— for the other party to the covenant, Israel. In chapter 24 Israel's commitment to this covenant is symbolized in a cultic act involving the shedding of blood, and a communion meal signifying the irrevocable quality of the commitment.

Here, again, we are faced with unresolvable historical questions. The Sinai block of material is certainly an insertion, from the literary point of view. The oldest forms of Israel's cultic recitations (Deuteronomy 6, 26, and Joshua 24) do not mention Sinai and the giving of the law, so central in later Judaism. Does the present Old Testament story here combine two originally separate "histories"? Is the Exodus-Kadesh tradition the memory of the Egypt-Moses-Israel group, as cultically created and celebrated in the northern hills of Canaan where this contingent first settled? And is it possible, then, that the Sinai complex is characteristically southern, drawing upon the cultically remembered experiences of a totally different group who were later united in the Israelite monarchy with the descendants of the Exodus group? We simply do not know. What is clear is that the whole entity which we know as Israel and later as Judaism accepted for its own *both* Exodus-Kadish and Sinai-law traditions and, with discerning theological appropriateness, combined them in what we have broadly termed the one great Exodus event.

The Glory of Yahweh

19:1–25
It is important to remember that we are dealing with a part of the Old Testament story which had a long oral history before it assumed written form, and no doubt the oral form was shaped, preserved, and periodically "celebrated" at some particular, ancient cultic center.

Chapter 19 is divided into three scenes: The Initiating Word, 19:1–9a; The People's Preparation, verses 9b–15; and Yahweh's Commitment, verses 16–25.

19:1–9a
Observe the strong emphasis on the spoken word. "Yahweh *called . . . saying,* 'thus shall you *say . . .* and *tell . . .*'" (v. 3). Verses 5–9 contain many further examples:

Obey my *voice*

These are the *words* which you shall *speak*

So Moses *called* . . . and set before them all these *words* which Yahweh had *commanded* him

And all the people *answered* . . . and *said*, All that Yahweh has *spoken* we will do

And Moses *reported* the *words*

And Yahweh *said*

Deuteronomic traditionists (designated by the symbol D) have added to the narrative or modified the language of the story in verses 4–6. Somewhere along the way, these deuteronomic editors have lightly touched the form of the Tetrateuch (Genesis–Numbers) here and there. But the major work of D is Deuteronomy, together with the editing of the block of the Old Testament story from Deuteronomy through Kings. That these verses here show the D mind and vocabulary is apparent in a comparison of verses 4–6 with Deuteronomy 32:11; 7:6; 14:2; and 26:18.

19:9b–15   Ancient cultic practice and belief are still mirrored here. The requirement of ceremonial purification may well reflect old notions of taboo. It is taboo (and risked on pain of death) to be "unclean" in the presence of deity; but if this is a primitive concept, it still appears preferable to us to the all-too-common chumminess of the relationship with God in popular religion of our own time. Better some sense of the old taboo's awe than the reduction of God to the role of buddy, or worse, the intimate partner in a relationship with erotic overtones.

The story means, of course, to laud the stature of Moses. While Israel stands afar off under strict taboo, *Moses* will climb to the summit of the mountain and enter the very cloud of the presence!

19:16–25   The closing verses here, 21–24, are a fine example of the sort of disaster that can befall the biblical text. This is a little collection of debris which cannot be explained and out of which little or no sense can be made. It does serve to remind us, however, that this whole treasure of the Old Testament story is given to us in earthen vessels (cf. 2 Cor. 4:7, in the New Testament), and serves sharply to check anyone who would *equate* the Word and the vessel which contains it.

Verses 16–20 are something else. Is it storm or volcano? Or is it intentionally metaphoric language to convey the overpowering awe, mystery, and power in the manifestation of the glory of God? If this is unclear, the testimony of faith is utterly unambiguous: to every instrument of human perception Yahweh made known the presence and glory of deity. It is not the *self* of Yahweh that is revealed, but the unqualified fact of Yahweh's immediately impinging life and nature and will. The motive? It is the validation of the Word that is given and of the covenant, which here comes into being.

The Decalogue

20:1–17   Other such compact definitions of covenant responsibility appear in the Old Testament. We shall be looking at some of them in Deut. 27:15 ff.; Exod. 21:12,15–17; and Lev. 19:13–18. And the present Decalogue appears a second time in slightly modified form in Deut. 5:6–21.

It would be rash indeed to attempt to toss away the vast weight of a tradition which insists on the role of Moses as law-giver. But we think it would be equally arrogant to attempt to define in any detail the content of actual Mosaic law. One *can* discern non-Mosaic regulations in "words" that speak to Israelite existence in demonstrably post-Mosaic times, such as statutes unquestionably aimed at conditions of monarchic political existence in Canaan, or at the control of problems presupposing a settled agricultural life.

The Decalogue is not, as one might casually infer, an original nucleus around which was formed the ever-expanding Old Testament law—or better, *torah,* which means "instruction." Rather, it is a self-conscious, skillfully conceived and executed effort to *reduce* to its most significant essence a relatively comprehensive body of *torah.* The Decalogue is the *summation* of the will of Yahweh for Israel drawn from an established and relatively extensive legal-instructional corpus.[7]

20:1–12   The first five commandments are concerned with Yahweh's (1) identity, (2) nature, (3) name, (4) day, and (5) claim.

Identity of Yahweh

Most of Protestantism considers verse 3—"no other gods"—as the first commandment and verses 4–6, prohibiting images, as the second. Roman Catholics and Lutherans combine these as the first commandment and count two commandments in verse 17,

[7]See further on the Decalogue: M. Noth, *Exodus (The Old Testament Library)* Philadelphia, 1962, pp. 160–68; Georg Fohrer, *Introduction to the Old Testament,* Nashville, 1968, pp. 68 f.; John H. Hayes, *Old Testament Form Criticism,* San Antonio, 1974, pp. 122-24.

against coveting. Judaism, whose reckoning we shall follow here, counts verse 2—the definition of Yahweh's identity vis-à-vis Israel —as the first commandment and verses 3-6, combining in one commandment the prohibition of other gods and any physical representation of deity, as the second.

I am Yahweh your God, who brought you out of the land of Egypt, out of the house of bondage.

(20:2)

This *is* a commandment. Know and acknowledge Yahweh as the God without whom you, Israel, would not exist; without Yahweh's creative, sustaining, redeeming Word, chaos, formless and void, would still embrace you. Only in Yahweh's *identity* are you an entity. Know and acknowledge Yahweh who brought Israel out of shackles into freedom, from unmeaning to meaning. I am Yahweh *your* God, who wrought this for you. In terms of your very existence and history, this is my *identity!*

Nature of Yahweh

It is Yahweh's *nature* to be God alone. Yahweh is in fact denied by the notion that there are other gods and by their representation, since the essential divine nature is thus denied (see vv. 3-6).

You shall have no other gods before me.
You shall not make yourself a graven image, or any likeness of *anything* . . . .

(vv. 3-4, emphasis added)

Here again in verses 4-6 (as in 19:3-6) we encounter the deuteronomic cadence, characteristic of the style and point of view of Deuteronomy and commonly dated in the late eighth, seventh, and early sixth centuries. We would ourselves nevertheless affirm the relative antiquity of the essential commandment supporting Yahweh's oneness, aloneness, and uniqueness.

What of a "jealous" Yahweh, verse 5? Is this the projection (primitive?) of a small god, vindictive, petulant, easily flattered? Something of this may still adhere to the commandment. But on the other hand, if Yahweh *is* one-alone-unique, Yahweh then must be "jealous"—which is neither more nor less than to maintain consistently this divine nature. To condone an image, that is, not to be jealous, would be to deny the very godness of God. And this deuteronomic expansion on the "word" (of the original "ten words") respecting the nature of Yahweh concludes on the note of Yahweh's devotion to those who live in accord with God's nature.

Name of Yahweh

The *name* of Yahweh may suffer no abuse because it is inseparable from the reality of Yahweh.

You shall not take the name of Yahweh your God in vain; for Yahweh will not hold guiltless the one who takes that name in vain.

(v. 7, adapted)

The name is of the essence of that which it names; and to push the concept back to its more primitive application, to name the name is to seek to appropriate and command the power of the one named. But Israel, clearly debtor to a broad, common background of Near Eastern culture, repeatedly converts and transforms what it borrows. Folk sought to use the divine name—and Israelites repeatedly the name of Yahweh!—to bring under their own control the power of the deity. This is, of course, magic. The ultimate background of magic is perhaps still discernible, but the *intent* of magic is thwarted by the very prohibition. The power of magic is denied. Those who would gain their own ends by name-incantation incur a breach in the very relationship upon which they presume to act.

Day of Yahweh

The fourth word on Yahweh's *day* is added now to the preceding words on the identity, nature, and name of deity (see vv. 8–11).

Remember the sabbath day, to keep it holy.

(v. 8)

Why? On what authority? In verse 11 the Sabbath institution is validated in the very pattern of creation and in language strongly reminiscent of the conclusion of the P account of creation (cf. Gen. 2:2–3). The present form of the commandment in Exodus would appear to be dependent upon Gen. 1:1–2:4a, the priestly narration of creation.

The form of the Decalogue as preserved in Deuteronomy 5

presents at this point its most considerable deviation. Keep the Sabbath

... that your manservant and your maidservant may rest as well as you. You shall remember that you were a servant in the land of Egypt, and Yahweh your God brought you out thence with a mighty hand and an outstretched arm; therefore [Yahweh] your God commanded you to keep the sabbath day.

(Deut. 5:14b–15)

Here Sabbath observance rests not upon a primeval "event" but upon a historical event. Yet it is essentially the same *quality* of faith. The fundamental sanction of Sabbath in both statements of the commandment is creation—in Deuteronomy of a people and in Exodus of the world. To "remember" and "keep" this day is to acknowledge Yahweh as Creator-Sustainer and to affirm that life continues under God's reign and providence. It is an act of trust. All of fretful labor's anxious preoccupation with the maintenance of life is suspended every seventh day precisely as an affirmation of the providence of Yahweh. And in its most intimate understanding, of course, the Sabbath is the perpetual reminder of the covenant not only with Israel, but through Israel, with all the families of the earth.[8]

Claim of Yahweh

The climax of Yahweh's pentalogue is the establishment of Yahweh's *claim* on every life by and through the parental relationship.

Honor your father and mother. . . .
(20:12)

In context, this is in effect Yahweh's saying,

Your life is my gift. I created you in the image of the divine (Gen. 1:27); the essential breath of life which makes you a living being is my animating breath (Gen. 2:7). The gift is given, the image of the god-like is conveyed, the breath of life is transmitted, through your father and your mother. The life your parents bear and give to you is my life. To dishonor them is to dishonor me.[9]

We think it is the sense of the fifth commandment in its present

[8] On the relationship between the Old Testament Sabbath commandment and the Christian observance of Sunday, see B. D. Napier, *Exodus,* in the series *The Layman's Bible Commentary,* Richmond, 1962, p. 82.
[9] Ibid., p. 83.

place and sequence that mother and father are to be honored not for what they are intrinsically or sentimentally or even out of any particular moral, ethical, or sociological considerations, but pointedly in acknowledgment of Yahweh's claim on every life. *Life* is Yahweh's and therefore sacred and holy. The holiness of life can be upheld only in honor of father and mother through whose joined life the divine image and animating breath are given.

The deuteronomic phrase which concludes the first pentalogue is more than an appeal to the motive of reward. If Yahweh's identity, nature, name, day, and claim are acknowledged, it cannot be otherwise than that your days will be "long," that your life will be fulfilled in order and meaning. Such is the faith always undergirding the Old Testament story.

20:13–17 The second pentalogue is concerned with the integrity of Israel. The first five words define the God-people relationship. The second five are prohibitions of that which is destructive in the relationship of person to person. However, that relationship is in no sense a "secular" relationship, but rather always seen in the scheme of the God-people relationship.

It is the function of the second pentalogue to defend in human community the inviolable mutual respect for (6) life, (7) person, (8) property, (9) reputation, and (10) status.

Life

You shall not kill (v. 13). Everyone's life is God's life. This is the reason, powerfully implicit in context, why no one may violate the life of another (recall the Brothers story, Gen. 4:2–14). This prohibition seeks to maintain the integrity of every individual life as basic to the life of the community, both the community of person-person and the community of God-people.[10]

Person

You shall not commit adultery (v. 14). If community is to be community, neither life nor *person* may be violated. What is in-

[10]On the sense of the verb "to kill" Martin Noth comments: "The prohibition against killing (Ex. 20–13) uses one of the two words current in Hebrew for 'doing to death.' These verbs apparently express no distinction between premeditated murder and unpremeditated killing, but both evidently include the concept of the arbitrary. It was customary in Hebrew for other expressions to be used for the execution of the death penalty imposed by legitimate trial and for the killing of an enemy in war." *Exodus,* in the series *The Old Testament Library,* Philadelphia, 1962, p. 165.

volved in the sex distinction is purposively and functionally *given* by Yahweh (so in both stories of creation). The abuse of that purpose and function violates the giver, Yahweh, as well as both persons involved; or, where the marriage covenant is also violated, three or even four persons may be involved and violated. The David-Bathsheba episode provides historical commentary on the Old Testament understanding of adultery as disruptive of community between God and people (2 Sam. 12:13; and see also Joseph's classic statement, Gen. 39:9) as well as between person and person (2 Samuel 11).

Property

You shall not steal (v. 15). This is in defense of a personal *property*, but in a sense more dire and stringent than we, economically cushioned, so to speak, would casually suppose. The loss of a garment, put aside during the warmer day, could in parts of the East result not only in the owner's bitter suffering from cold through the night, but in physiological complications leading even to death. Or, in a simple pastoral economy where life is tenuously sustained in a literal hand-to-mouth fashion, the loss of a simple shepherd's meager flock could easily be a life-or-death concern to him and his family. In a society where property and life are directly connected, the prohibition against theft is of a piece with the two preceding prohibitions in defense of life and person. To steal in a society where the vast bulk of property is in an immediate sense the means of subsistence is potentially as great a violation of community as murder or adultery. It is as powerful an assault on human integrity and the God-people relationship as either of these.[11]

Reputation

You shall not bear false witness against your neighbor (v. 16). *Reputation* may not be violated. The language here suggests juridical practice. To bear false witness is to give false testimony in court. Formal "witness" then, in this sense, must be accurate.

At the same time, this commandment, as one of a series of sum-

---

[11]Noth, ibid., pp. 165 f., may be correct in suggesting that the commandment against stealing had *originally* in mind a human object and "the loss of freedom, particularly of free Israelites; it is forbidden to enslave free Israelites." But we think it is probable that in Israel the prohibition came more and more to be applied to property, as the practice of Israelite slavery in Israel disappeared.

mary statements expressing the larger *torah* of Israel, must convey a broader meaning. This, too, reflects the relationship of person to person, but theologically conceived. As in the case of life, person, and property, reputation may not be falsely violated without also violating Yahweh and the aggressor's own relationship to Yahweh. In intention, whatever the juridical overtones, the prohibition means to suppress any and all "witness" that constitutes false testimony against the neighbor and the depreciation, even destruction, of the neighbor's reputation.

Status

You shall not covet your neighbor's house . . . or anything that is your neighbor's (v. 17). This final prohibition is consistent in intent with the four preceding prohibitions. The full *status* of a person—all that is implicit in that inclusive word "house"—must be inviolable not only from physical or material damage, overt abuse, or appropriation, but also (and this is a remarkable concept) from another's *wish,* thought, or dream of appropriation—in short, another's covetousness.

This injunctive word against illicit traffic through the mind is at once sum and climax of the pentalogue in protection of Israel's integrity. All true community finally hangs on how the neighbor's "house" is contemplated. If contemplation is covetous, community is already violated and all possibility of mutuality is crushed.

Ten commandments-prohibitions: a pentalogue whose purpose is to maintain the integrity of Yahweh, author of the covenant with Israel; and another pentalogue concerned with the community *thus created* and with that community's integrity *thus defined.* This is conceived to convey out of Israel's full *torah* the very essence of Yahweh's total will with respect to the Yahweh-people relationship, but at once also to that of person-person covenant.

The place of the Decalogue in the life of ancient Israel can hardly be overemphasized. Once formulated (in its original form, subsequently expanded, not later than the early monarchy) it was understood and celebrated in Israel as a major "event" on a par with and inseparably linked to the event of Israel's deliverance from Egypt. And in that same way it was deemed to be a salvation event, disclosing the fact, meaning, and purposiveness of Yahweh's Word in Israel and the world.

In the Covenant Code:
Exodus 21–24

> These are the ordinances.
> *Exod. 21:1*

The first and oldest considerable code of instruction in the Old Testament is the Covenant Code, Exodus 21–23. The introduction to it, Exod. 20:18–21:1, resumes the Yahweh-manifestation interrupted by the Decalogue; and again the story magnifies the role and stature of Moses. "*You* speak to us," the people cry, "but let not God speak to us lest we die" (20:19). And Moses, reassuring his people, ascends the mountain, disappears in the cloud of the presence, and receives the Word which tradition represents to be the Covenant Code (21:1). One must not overlook the prescription for the simple, unpretentious altar which has been, a trifle irrelevantly, inserted here in 20:24–26. This is an early and discerning protest against the perennial tendency in every cult, ancient and modern, to elaborate the "equipment" of worship so as to make of the material representation of worship an end in itself. This prohibition of the ostentatious altar was, of course, violated in Israel. One can cite examples of rationalization on behalf of pretension: the fault in the elevated altar is not in the altar but in the priest's short skirts; we will robe the officiating priests so that their "nakedness" will not be exposed (Exod. 28:40–43). Elsewhere one encounters open testimony to the disposition to elaborate the structure of the altar (Exod. 27:1–8; 1 Kings 1:50–51; Ezek. 43:13–17). But the demand for the simple altar was not forgotten (Josh. 8:30–31; 1 Kings 18:31).

From 21:2 to 22:17 the Covenant Code presents laws for the most part apparently borrowed from Canaanite practice in the course of the two centuries preceding the establishment of monarchy. On the other hand, in 22:18 to 23:19 cultic regulations predominate which tend much more to express the original character and mind of Israel. The conclusion of the code, 23:20–33, is a Yahweh speech summarizing and reaffirming covenant:

You shall serve Yahweh your God, and I will bless your bread and your water . . . I will fulfil the number of your days . . . .

(23:25 f.)

In its *present form* the code is, of course, no older than this latest concluding section (perhaps the middle of the eighth century). But the full code embraces a span of many centuries and draws both from preoccupation Canaan and pre-Mosaic Yahwism. It is, all in all, a stupendous achievement.

On Servitude and Freedom

21:2-11   On what other theme than slavery could this code so appropriately open? "We were Pharaoh's slaves in Egypt, and Yahweh brought us out!" (Deut. 6:21).

Verses 2-6 regulate the conditions of freedom for the Israelite slave and ought to be compared with the same law in the Deuteronomic Code (Deuteronomy 12-26) which, as a later formulation, represents on the whole considerable refinement of feeling. In Deuteronomy (15:14) the slave is freed not only together with all his family, but with liberal provision from the resources of his master. Still later, in a third major Old Testament collection of *torah* known as the Holiness Code, Leviticus 17-26, the very institution of the slavery of an Israelite to an Israelite is abolished (Lev. 25:39-42), although the practice must have been popularly condemned throughout the period of the kingdoms.

The grounds for the firm protection of the rights of Israelite slaves (Covenant Code), for their generous consideration upon going free (Deuteronomic Code), and for their ultimate removal from the possibility of enslavement (Holiness Code) are emphatically theological. It is implicit in CC; but explicit and emphatic in DC and HC:

> You shall remember that you were a slave in the land of Egypt, and Yahweh your God redeemed you; *therefore* I [thus] command you!
> (Deut. 15:15)

> . . . for they are *my* servants, whom I brought forth out of the land of Egypt; [for this reason] they shall not be sold as slaves!
> (Lev. 25:42)

It is consistently and pointedly Yahweh's historically known grace and redemption in Israel which is responsible for the Old Testament's remarkable regulation of slavery (see further Exod. 12:43 f.; 21:20 f.; Deut. 12:17 f.; 16:10 f.; 23:15 f.; Lev. 25:10).

On Control of Violence

21:12-35   We have what appears to be the mutilated torso of an ancient unit—perhaps an original Decalogue, "ten words"—in four surviving "words" in 21:12,15–17. Here the death penalty is decreed for murder (cf. Gen. 9:6; Lev. 24:17; Num. 35:30 f.), for physical violence against parents, for person-stealing, and for verbal abuse (cursing) of parents. The first has been humanely elaborated (vv. 13–14) to distinguish between voluntary and involuntary homicide. The third has been expanded with the phrase "whether he sells him or is found in possession of him." In common with ancient Hittite and Babylonian codes of law, the Covenant Code compensates the injured (vv. 18–19).

There is apparent tension between the proposition that the slave is property on the one hand and a human being on the other. If verse 21 represents the former principle, verses 26–27 (perhaps originally connected to 21) clearly represent the second, always dominant in the Old Testament: if the slave's owner inflicts the loss of an eye or even a tooth upon the slave, the slave must be given his freedom in compensation!

The *lex talionis*, the law of retaliation (vv. 22–25; cf. Lev. 24:18–21 and Deut. 19:15–21), is a widely held legal principle in antiquity. Looked at positively, this "life for life, eye for eye" sentiment no doubt marked an advance in juridical concept and practice at some time in the distant past, in the sense that it *limited* damages. In the Old Testament as a whole, of course, this principle of exact retaliation is not normative. Israel took it over from Canaan for a period and retained it only for certain particular cases as a standard of judgment in specific instances of injury. In the instance before us, *lex talionis* remained applicable; and this is true also of the two other instances of its use, Lev. 24:18 ff., and Deut. 19:15 ff. But, in general, the Yahweh-covenant quality is dominant, and Israelite law, covenant law, is characterized by relative gentleness and mercy.

The theme of violence continues in verses 28–36, but the focus shifts to the beast, the ox, and the problems created by violence done both by him and to him.

On General Conduct and Responsibility

21:1–23:33 We mark three sections here. The first section, 22:1–17, differs from the second, 22:18–23:19, in form as well as in content. The first is characterized by the structure, "If so and so . . . the offender shall do thus and so . . ." Such *casuistic* formulation derives from the Canaanites and concerns itself with what *we* should call secular, as opposed to religious, law.

The second section occasionally incorporates the casuistic "if" form (22:25, 23:4), but with the second person "you" not the third "he"; but generally it is not casuistic in expression but *apodictic*, stating the noncasuistic, nontheoretical, direct, unqualified commandment or prohibition. Apodictic law explicitly deals with cultic or theological concerns (for example, 22:20); it is implicitly more closely related to the particular life of covenant Israel and the Yahweh faith. Apodictic law is characteristically Israelite in origin and perspective.[12]

The third section, 23:20–33, is the subsequently composed postlude in the form of a hortatory speech of Yahweh.

22:1–17   These verses are casuistic laws of Canaanite origin for the most part; and the theme throughout the section is the determination of appropriate restitution. These are lay regulations as opposed to cultic or religious stipulations. Parallels appear in profusion over the ancient East and in specifically expanded form in, for example, the Code of Hammurabi of Babylon (eighteenth century B.C.E.). Yahweh plays no role (the phrase of verse 11 is intrusive). Deity receives institutional mention under the vague term *'Elohim* (vv. 8 and 9), and theological-ethical content is virtually void.

22:18–23:17   Beginning in 22:18, the characteristic form of expression shifts from the casuistic to the apodictic.

The death sentence is categorically imposed for three offenses —sorcery, sex perversion (with an animal), and idolatrous sacrifice. Hittite (but not Babylonian) law also decrees death for this kind of debased sex act; but in the present context of Israel's *torah*, the law is cast in the same theological perspective as the prohibitions immediately preceding and following. Sorcery (with all divination, witchcraft, and necromancy; cf. 1 Samuel 28; Jer. 7:18 and 44:15; Lev. 20:27; Deut. 18:10; Mal. 3:5) is anathema because it invades the exclusive domain of Yahweh. Non-Yahweh sacrifice, the most vehement of the three prohibitions, denies Israel's very being, since it is Yahweh who "brought us out of Egypt . . . and into this place" (see again Deut. 26:7–9). So, too, by association and context the theological basis of the middle prohibition: to debase and pervert the sex function by which covenant

---

[12]Cf. A. Alt, "The Origins of Israelite Law," in *Essays on Old Testament History and Religion,* trans. R. A. Wilson, Garden City, N.Y., 1967, pp. 79 ff.

life is perpetuated is to deny the covenant, the Yahweh-people relationship, and Yahweh as God.[13]

Verses 21–24 cite three classes of persons repeatedly given special mention in Old Testament *torah:* the sojourner, the widow, and the orphan. The sensitive discernment of relationship between Israel's Egyptian experience and the proper treatment of the sojourner (v. 21) appears again in 23:9. Verses 25–27 (cf. Deut. 23:19 f. and Lev. 25:26–28) regulate aspects of the old institution of credit. Verse 28 is a prohibition in support of authority, divine and human (the Holiness Code, Lev. 24:16, imposes the death sentence for blaspheming "the name of Yahweh").

Cultic requirements constitute verses 29–31. Verse 29b is hardly the survival of an ancient demand in Israel for child sacrifice. The willingness to offer the son and some (here not prescribed) symbolic act to that effect is called for (see 13:2,13,15). In the core Yahweh faith, early and late, literal human sacrifice was consistently repudiated, although apparently sometimes practiced (see, for example, 2 Kings 16:3). An old taboo survives in verse 31, but now with theological justification: it is because you are mine, says Yahweh, that you are not to play the role of scavengers to the beasts of creation.

The Covenant Code's most eloquent lines on the theme of justice appear in 23:1–9. No comment is called for, save to urge the reader not to miss the continued relevance and pertinence (the "isness") of the Egyptian sojourn, or the summary statement in Deut. 16:19–20, perhaps the most moving single plea for justice in the Old Testament:

> You shall not pervert justice; you shall not show partiality; and you shall not take a bribe, for a bribe blinds the eyes of the wise and subverts the cause of the righteous. Justice, and only justice, you shall follow . . . .

Verses 10–19 deal with cultic concerns—the Sabbath year (vv. 10–11), the Sabbath day (vv. 12–13), and the three major annual festivals (vv. 14–19). The feast of unleavened bread (Passover, 34:24) commemorates the Exodus from Egypt. The feast of harvest (feast of weeks, 34:22 and Deut. 16:10, 16) or Pentecost (so named because it came to be celebrated fifty days after the feast of unleavened bread) or the first fruits of wheat harvest (also 34:22) is by whatever name the celebration of the first harvest of

---

[13]It is interesting that in this context there is no prohibition of homosexuality.

the fields, ready in Palestine in April. And a third feast, of in-gathering (so also 34:22; but Deut. 16:13–16, the feast of taber-nacles), celebrates the grape vintage in the fall. These "three times in the year shall all your males appear before Yahweh" (v. 17). Verses 18–19 carry four regulations of the Passover (unleavened bread) festival. Both stipulations in verse 18 warn against carrying the Passover celebration beyond its appointed day. Verse 19a reinterates 16. And verse 19b (also 34:26 and Deut. 14:21), whether originally humanely motivated or not, came to be inter-preted in Judaism as excluding *any* mixture of milk and meat.

23:20–32   From casuistic laws and apodictic *torah,* the Covenant Code turns in its concluding section to what ostensibly lies immediately ahead—the acquisition of Canaan. Deuteronomic editors seem to have had a hand in this (cf. Deut. 7:1–5), but the substantial framework of this Yahweh speech (20–22, 25b–28,31a) is as old as the tenth century. The "predicted" limits of the land to be ac-quired correspond roughly to the peak holding under David and Solomon. The speech is informed of the slow progress of acquisi-tion; and also of some prior attacks upon Canaan unwittingly assisting Israel's task ("hornets" v. 28, cf. Josh. 24:12, Deut. 7:20; and note the fly and the bee of Isa. 7:18). It is in any case a splendid summary section to the Covenant Code, appropriately reaffirming the powers, gifts, and commitment of Yahweh to the covenant with Israel.

The Covenant Sealed

24:1–18   We know that covenants in the ancient east were of several kinds.[14] In the Old Testament story at least two primary types of covenant are emphasized. The earliest understanding of covenant in Israel sees Yahweh as initiator, definer, and sealer of covenant with Israel. It is covenant in which the human role is very nearly passive. Such is the covenant with Abraham in Genesis 15; and such is the *sealing* of the covenant described in Exod. 24:1–2,9–11. Yahweh prepares a communion meal to which Israel's leadership is invited. It is Yahweh who gives the food and in giving it is committed to the covenant.

Ancient covenants sometimes laid greater stress upon the role, obligations, and commitment of the junior or subordinate party

[14]Cf. G. E. Mendenhall, *Law and Covenant in Israel and the Ancient Near East,* Pittsburgh, 1955.

to the covenant. It is covenant in this interpretation which is re-counted in Genesis 17 (P), where Israel's commitment is sealed in the rite of circumcision. And in the passage before us, Exod. 24:3-8, a rite is described by which Israel's acceptance of cove-nant is symbolized—covenant as defined *for Israel*, as its respon-sibility and obligation, in the Decalogue and in the Covenant Code.

In 24:12-18 Moses (and incidentally Joshua) is again set apart, his person and stature lauded. But this closing section of the chapter is also clearly intended to serve as the conclusion of the long section beginning with Exodus 19 and at the same time as ap-propriate introduction to the extended (priestly) section which follows in chapters 25-31, and which has to do exclusively with the institutionalizing of all that has occurred in the making of the covenant. It is the intent of this link not only to laud the role of Moses, but to declare again that the total development of content and form in the practice of Israel's faith presents itself to every succeeding generation with the authority of Yahweh directly mediated through Moses.[15]

Yahweh brings order out of chaos. It is the impingement of Yahweh's life upon history which imparts meaning to the mean-ingless. This is the faith which ancient Israel proclaims in its story. Not alone in Yahweh's creation of a people and a world, but em-phatically also in the creation of covenant, Yahweh's nature and purpose are disclosed. Decalogue and now Covenant Code are deemed to be continually creative, always *now* sustaining order out of the stuff of chaos.

Covenant is the promise of Yahweh, and Yahweh's own ir-revocable act of commitment to that promise, to take Israel for a people, and through Israel to restore to the world the lost blessing of creation, to mend the now fractured meaning of existence, and to heal history's tragically disordered order. But covenant is also deemed to be concretely that by which Israel is to live out all the days of all its years—the ordinances which Moses set before Israel in response to the Word (see 20:1 and 21:1), ordinances in fulfill-ment of which Israel itself alone would be fulfilled. In its covenant-keeping Israel is kept. Sustaining food, sweet water, days without illness, births without accident, parental love

---

[15]Cf. G. von Rad, *Old Testament Theology*, New York, 1962, vol. 1, p. 234.

without frustration, and satisfying length of days (23:25–26)—abundant life in these terms is offered in a covenant relationship in which is created a people to serve Yahweh in faithfulness.

In the Work and Person of Moses: Exodus 32–34

I know you by name.
Exod. 33:17

The conception of the task undertaken in this text rules out any discussion of the two very similar priestly sections of Exodus having to do with the plans of institution (25–31) and the acts of institution (35–40). Both sections are concerned—sometimes in closely corresponding or even identical terms—with the physical means, forms, nature, dimensions, and personnel of the cultic-religious institution, the first section ostensibly as plans and the second as detailing the actual construction, realization, and inauguration of the full-fledged cultic institution.

It is impossible to determine from these sections the actual objects involved in Israel's early cultus. The description of the tabernacle (chaps. 26 and 38), for example, bears no direct relationship to *any* real Israelite sanctuary. Memories of a Mosaic-nomadic tent of meeting *may* be imbedded in the description. It is certain that the form of Solomon's temple (tenth century) influenced the account. But any reconstruction according to these specifications would produce a tabernacle structure which never existed in fact.

The three chapters of Exodus now before us are composite. We have already noted their general Yahwistic-prophetic cast and the nature of the large block of which they are a part (Exod. 19:1–Num. 10:10). What we have termed J and E are both here, with other voices, or other hands. But the finished product is a unified achievement.

Perhaps the reminder is again in order that Israel's interest in the original "event" rests predominantly in its present and continuing *meaning;* that the form of the narrative before us is unquestionably cultically conditioned, that is, shaped by the influences of cultic circles at centers of worship in which the tradition was maintained; and that this cultic tradition returns an image of Moses formed out of long years of meditation on the total significance of his life and time through the succeeding generations of Israel's life.

The Golden Calf: Denial of Covenant

32:1–35   Moses is on Sinai, now himself as mysterious and unapproachable as that presence of Yahweh which he alone may confront and the Word of Yahweh which he alone may hear. The impatient people, to whom the reality of Moses and Yahweh has become only a memory and who know the widespread representation of deity in the form of a calf (probably a young bull, denoting primarily the strength of reproductive power and fertility, natural and human), with Aaron's consent and counsel, make Yahweh (v. 5) in this form, and to Yahweh thus materialized they hold a full-fledged cultic celebration.

Yahweh's immediate repudiation of Israel for this breach of covenant is directly conveyed in the Word to Moses, in form charming and naïve, but in communication of the sense of ruptured relationship, profound and powerful:

Go down, for *your* people, whom *you* brought up out of the land of Egypt, have corrupted themselves.

(v. 7)

Now (such is the sense of the Word) step aside, get out of my way —hold my coat—while I administer—death!

. . . now therefore let me alone, that . . . I may consume them.

Now the thematic note:

. . . of you [Moses] I will make a great nation.
(v. 10)

But Moses will not entertain this complimentary proposal even by mentioning it. Instead he makes successful (v. 14) intercession on Israel's behalf, reminding Yahweh that Israel is Yahweh's people whose destruction would frustrate the glory of the Exodus (vv. 11–12) and constitute a shameful breach of Yahweh's promise to Israel's progenitors (v. 13; the prayer, as other aspects of the narrative, is informed by relatively late traditional stereotypes).

Moses descends the mountain carrying the two stone tablets inscribed with the Decalogue, presumably ("the writing was the writing of God," v. 16); sees what has occurred (Joshua suddenly appears again; cf. 24:13); and in fury breaks the tablets, symbolizing the covenant which Israel has in the same way just shattered.

It all happened "at the foot of the mountain" (v. 19). Tradition recalls that Moses came here first with Jethro's flock and first knew here the piercing of the shell of his existence by the Word of Yahweh out of the undiminished, unconsumed burning bush. To this same mountain Moses brought Israel where it—a people redeemed only yesterday out of slavery—acknowledged Yahweh as the shatterer of its own tight little prison of existence and entered a covenant with this God, accepting Yahweh's commitment to Israel and reciting Israel's own vows of faithfulness. Here at the foot of the mountain, Israel brazenly denied the reality of its encounter, repudiated its emancipator, and shamelessly broke its vows. Here, at the foot of the mountain, Moses cast into the moral rubble the tables of the testimony already in effect reduced to powder and ashes.

When Moses confronts Aaron, the one on whom responsibility clearly falls, he produces a line of evasion, an emphatic disclaimer, which forever ranks with the best, the most ridiculous, and therefore the most humorous of its kind:

I said to them, "Let any who have gold take it off"; so they gave it to me, and I threw it into the fire, and there came out this calf."

(v. 24)

What a remarkable accident! We had absolutely nothing to do with it.

One could wish for restraint in the introduction of the next paragraph (vv. 25–29). We can appreciate the seriousness of the prohibition of images in Israel and (at its highest motivation) the theological maturity which it represents. We are at the same time sure that the human word is given the status of divine Word in the command (v. 27) of indiscriminate slaughter; and we are sure that Moses never regarded such an act as ordination to priesthood (v. 29)!

The narrative concludes on the note of Moses' moving intercession, to be ranked among the greatest prayers ever preserved (vv. 31–32); and with the response of the Word in grace (v. 34a), but with the firm reminder that Yahweh will, when the occasion demands, be known as judge (v. 34b). The final verse (35) is the contribution of a traditionist who obviously feels that Yahweh must be made of sterner stuff, or that Israel must be yet more sternly treated and so produces the disagreeable and anticlimactic notice of the plague.

Among circles of Old Testament students, it has been commonly held, almost taken for granted, that the present narrative was created as a condemnation (with Mosaic-Sinaitic "authority") of the representation of Yahweh in the bull image at the two chief sanctuaries of North Israel, Dan and Bethel, beginning late in the tenth century when the united Israelite kingdom was split (1 Kings 12:28–29). Now, we are sure that tradition reinterpreted and no doubt somewhat modified the story in the light of this heresy; but we are unable to see any reason for denying that the story was already in existence then and that in fact the Yahwistic heresy of image representation began in the beginning of Israel's life as a people, in the first, Mosaic chapter of that life.

Yahweh and Moses: Renewal of Covenant

33:1–34:9   Chapter 33 opens with Yahweh's Word still sounding in bitter tones of reaction to the broken covenant. "You [Moses] and the people whom *you* have brought up out of Egypt" get out of here and move on to the land. But it is the *promised* land; and "I will drive out" those who impede your settlement in the land. And, inconsistently, the negative note resumes in verse 3: Go ahead, but go without Me!

This divine ambivalence plays a role in the plot. Yahweh's Word has been given. That Word cannot be broken. But Israel has behaved in flagrant defiance of all that was implicit in the covenant-Word, so that from any human point of view Yahweh is justified in having no more to do with Israel, indeed in withdrawing for Israel's own protection, since to stay among them in wrath would be to destroy them! The role of this tension and duality is to serve in the delineation of the character of Moses; the person of Moses and his intercession and faith are responsible for the resolution of the divine ambivalence.

In hopes of appeasing the divine anger, the people "stripped themselves of their ornaments, from Mount Horeb [Sinai] onward" (v. 6).

More clearly than in any previous reference, the tent of meeting is the place where Yahweh may be found (v. 7). The use of the two terms "tent of meeting" and "tabernacle" leaves the reader in doubt as to whether they are the same or different structures. Chapters 29 (vv. 4,10,11,31,32,42) and 30 (vv. 16,18,20,36), for example, employ only the first term (cf. also 27:21 and 28:43) and clearly identify tent and tabernacle. In chapter 33 before us it *may* be that the tent of meeting is envisaged as a provisional arrangement, a substitute tabernacle for the duration of Yahweh's withholding the direct divine presence from Israel: Yahweh meets only Moses in the tent of meeting—and that "face to face"! (v. 11; but see the contradiction, v. 20, from another of the sources employed in the shaping of the present account). In subsequent references identity or virtual identity must be assumed (35:21; 38:8,30,32; 39:40 NB; and in 40, repeatedly).

This is all in Moses' praise. Here the uniqueness of Moses is defined in terms of the uniqueness of his relationship to Yahweh. Here the Old Testament story testifies that Israel owes its existence to Yahweh, to be sure, but also to Moses, without whose intercession the Yahweh-Israel enterprise would to all intents and purposes have been dissolved. This is tradition's testimony and tribute to the absolutely incomparable Moses. He goes alone to the tent of meeting for a meeting—*the* Meeting—while all Israel stands in awe and reverence (v. 8). Yahweh follows, and all the people worship from their own doors (vv. 9–10). It is a face-to-face meeting (see above). Moses speaks with such power as to persuade Yahweh of the wisdom of his words and to gain a reversal of the divine decision to withhold the immediate presence of Yahweh from Israel (vv. 12–17). And Yahweh bestows on Moses words of rare occurrence indeed: "I know you by *name* (vv. 12, 17; cf. Matt. 1:21 ff.; 16:13 ff.); "you have found favor in my sight" (vv. 12,17; cf. Mark 1:10; Luke 2:40); "I will give you rest" (v. 14; cf. Matt. 11:28); and "the very thing that you have spoken I will do" (v. 17; cf. Matt. 28:18; 10:32; Luke 12:8; John 16:23).

Finally, in marked contrast to the face-to-face meeting (v. 11; cf. Num. 12:8; Deut. 34:10) Moses' request to behold Yahweh's glory is granted (vv. 18–23; compare and contrast Elijah's great hour on the holy mountain, 1 Kings 19). The quality and meaning of the glory is suggested in the coupling of the proclamation of the name YHWH (33:19; 34:6) with the passing by of the glory, and in the words goodness, graciousness, and mercy (33:19 and 34:6–7). Implicit, of course, is Yahweh's forgiveness of Israel, won through the intercession and devotion of Moses, and assured now in the passing glory of Yahweh's goodness, grace, and mercy. Indeed, the actual description of the passing by of the glory and the rounding out of this intimate Sinai/Horeb scene between Yahweh and Moses (34:6–9) expands on the theme of the graciousness of Yahweh (cf. Joel 2:13; Jon. 4:2), affirms the appropriate humility of Moses before this revelation of the nature of Yahweh, and puts on Moses' lips a prayer which constitutes a fine summary of all that has gone before in chapters 32 and 33. "If *I* [Moses] *have* [in very fact] found favor in thy sight," then (and it is now a moving, timelessly relevant prayer!)

let the Lord . . . go in the midst of us, although it is a stiff-necked people; and pardon our iniquity and our sin, and take us for thy inheritance.

In 34:1–4, the narrative takes up again the subject of stone tables of the law destroyed in Moses' wrath at the sight of the golden calf. Tradition is making a single story of several strands; and since Moses' marvelous vision of Yahweh's glory is also the renewal of covenant with Israel, the broken tablets must be replaced. These verses supply the logically necessary advice that Moses has two new blank tablets at hand and ready.

The Redefined Covenant: The Ritual Decalogue

34:10–28   Accordingly, the covenant between Yahweh "merciful and gracious, slow to anger, and abounding in steadfast love and faithfulness" and a forgiven Israel is instituted afresh. In this completed work of tradition, that is, as the present text of Exodus 34 is handed over to us, the content of the new covenant law differs from the old, the Decalogue of Exodus 20. Following an introductory speech of Yahweh which declares the marvels Yahweh is about to perform and warns against the temptations of Canaan and its religious institutions (vv. 10–13), a decalogue is given which, however, concentrates exclusively on concerns of the cultus, and has therefore come to be known as the Ritual Decalogue, as against what is often called the Ethical Decalogue of Exodus 20 and Deuteronomy 5:

1. (v. 14) You shall worship no other god, for [Yahweh], whose name is Jealous, is a jealous God (cf. 23:13).
2. (v. 17) You shall make for yourself no molten gods (cf. 20:23).
3. (v. 19a) All that opens the womb is mine (cf. 22:29–30).

4. (v. 20b) All the first-born of your sons you shall redeem (cf. 22:29-30).
5. (v. 21) Six days you shall work, but on the seventh day you shall rest; in plowing time and in harvest you shall rest (cf. 23:12).
6. (v. 23) Three times in the year shall all your males appear before the Lord Yahweh, God of Israel (cf. 23:17).
7. (v. 25a) You shall not offer the blood of my sacrifice with leaven (cf. 23:18a).
8. (v. 25b) The sacrifice of the feast of the passover [shall not] be left until the morning (cf. 23:18b).
9. (v. 26a) The first of the first fruits of your ground you shall bring to the house of Yahweh your God (cf. 23:19a).
10. (v. 26b) You shall not boil a kid in its mother's milk (cf. 23:19b).

The parallel references from the Covenant Code (Exod. 20-23; but especially 23:13-19) indicate that this cultic decalogue is unique only in arrangement, and its present form is obviously an expansion of an original "ten words." How old may have been the original Decalogue? Did these cultic prescriptions first appear in the corpus of an extensive code (the Covenant Code of Exodus 20-23), to be distilled into briefer, decalogue form, or was the Ritual Decalogue original and its individual prescriptions subsequently incorporated in the longer code? And how does it happen that tradition comes to record the Ethical Decalogue as the content of the first tables of the law, but the Ritual Decalogue for the second? Questions of this kind remain still without certain answer. It may be that tradition, in combining differing, independent, but parallel accounts of Sinai/Horeb and its covenant, has, without reconciliation, brought together an older version (the nucleus of Exodus, 32-34, J) which "remembers" a Ritual Decalogue, and a somewhat later version (E, having its locus in the North, not the South as J) which associates the Ethical Decalogue with the covenant of the sacred mountain. Or, in that long, unceasingly active process that we call tradition, an original J decalogue, very closely parallel to the E decalogue of Exodus 20, may have been at some point displaced in Exodus 34 by the Ritual Decalogue now before us. This last suggestion has the merit that in an earlier formulation, tradition was not inconsistent but recorded a renewed covenant-decalogue, on new tablets, which was essentially the reproduction of the original tables.[16]

[16]See M. Noth, *Exodus: A Commentary,* Philadelphia, 1962, pp. 265 ff.

Moses: A Terrible Thing

34:29–35 This section on the denial and renewal of covenant (chaps. 32–34) is conceived, of course, in praise of Yahweh. Its theme might be the Yahweh-Word in 34:10, "It is a terrible thing that I will do with you"—terrible in the sense of awe and wonder, not simply dread and horror. But on the terrestrial plane, at the human level, the narrative concentrates on Moses, on his role vis-à-vis Yahweh and Israel, and on his incomparable stature as intermediary between God and people.

Appropriately, then, the section closes (and the J-E or non-priestly stratum of Exodus, since 35–40, like 25–31, is exclusively of priestly quality) with this almost fabulous tribute by tradition —which is, of course, the tribute of all Israel—to Moses. He has prevailed, in a sense, over Yahweh. By a combination of intercession and argument, he has gained for Israel full divine forgiveness. By the strength of his own person and the power of his own commitment to Yahweh, he returns again, descending the sacred mountain with the new tables of the covenant-law in his hands; and he does not know—tradition elsewhere insists that "the man Moses was very meek, more than all that were on the face of the earth" (Num. 12:3)—he does not know that his face is literally aglow, shining with the radiance of the very presence of Yahweh!

This is the ultimate tribute. This is Israel's enduring estimate of Moses. We live because Yahweh gave us life *out* of Egypt for the death that we lived *in* Egypt. By Yahweh's Word (or hand, or presence) Yahweh brought us through the sea, sustained us in the wilderness, made covenant with us at Sinai, forgave us our appalling denial of Word and presence, and renewed in mercy and grace the covenant which we had broken. But by the means of what amazing *human* instrument was all of this the accomplishment of the Word of Yahweh on behalf of Israel?

. . . for the place on which you are standing is holy ground. Moses, Moses! Put off your shoes. I know the affliction of my people. . . . Come, I will send you. . . . I will be with you. . . . I will be with your mouth. . . . and I will bring you into the land . . . .

Come up to me on the mountain and I will give you the tables of stone. . . . Go down; for your people have corrupted themselves. . . . let me alone that my wrath may burn hot against them and I may consume them; but I will make of you a great nation. . . . I will give you rest. . . . you have found favor in my sight. . . . I know you by name. . . . Behold,

I make [again!] a covenant. Before all your people I will do marvels.
. . . it is a terrible thing that I will do with you!

No comment is better able to convey the staggering impression of
such a person upon other folk, not simply in Israel, but in the
world of all time, than this recording of the "memory" of the face
of Moses, so brilliantly shining with the radiance of the very
presence of God that that countenance could be unveiled only in
the presence of the Presence.

This is Moses—by whose offices and through whose leadership
and vision the covenant was first made; against whose devoted
commitment to Israel's life the covenant was shamelessly denied;
and by whose strength of faith and communion with Yahweh
Israel was forgiven and the covenant renewed and reinstituted.

In Priestly Cultus and Ethic:
Leviticus 16, 19, 23–26

> I will make my abode among you.
> *Lev. 26:11*

We turn now to the third book of the Old Testament. In
Hebrew tradition it is customary to call a biblical book by its first
word. Genesis is *Bereshith*, "In the beginning," and Leviticus,
Wayyikra, "And he called." We follow the Septuagint (Greek)
and Vulgate (Latin) translations. This is Leviticus, the Levitical
book—laws, instructions, *torah* collected and arranged (but not
necessarily composed) by the Levitical priests during and after the
period of Babylonian exile, that is, in the sixth and fifth centuries.

Look briefly at the contents of Leviticus:

1–7 Instructions, regulations, relating to sacrifice.
8–10 On the consecration and installation of the priesthood.
11–16 *Torah* relating to ceremonial uncleanness and purification; and
    to the special rites for the Day of Atonement (16).
17–26 The Holiness Code.
27–28 An appendix on offerings and tithes.

This is Lord and covenant, Yahweh and the covenanted people,
as seen from the perspective of priesthood and cultus. In this
perspective Levitical law *is* the covenant, and the keeping of it is
the covenant obligation of the entire community. Leviticus is not
an original unit—the inclusion of the Holiness Code, itself a prior

unit, testifies to this; and in overall editorial design, Leviticus becomes an integral part of the giant Sinai-centered block of material from Exodus 19 to Num. 10:10. The completed canon (the word means "rule" by which the content and limits of holy scripture are determined) affirms that all covenant law, all *torah,* is of Yahweh, and, therefore, essentially of Sinai-Mosaic origin.

What is offered here in very brief commentary presupposes the biblical text. As always, these words of mine are intentionally *dependent.* It is precisely my aim to avoid discussion of the Old Testament which can be appropriated *in lieu of* the biblical text, as a *substitute* for the text.

The Day of Atonement

16:1–34   This day, *Yom Kippur,* has continued in annual celebration in Judaism. It is "a solemn white fast, during which from dusk to dusk the faithful partake of neither food nor drink in token of penitence, but through prayer and confession scrutinize their lives, abjure their evil-doing, and seek regeneration, a returning to God and goodness."[17]

Contrary to the notions of some, belief in the universality and pervasiveness of sin did not originate in the theology of Reinhold Niebuhr, or of Karl Barth, or of Kierkegaard, or of the Protestant reformers, or of St. Augustine, or even of the good Apostle Paul. What is called or miscalled original sin (original in the sense that it is a primary datum of human existence) has its roots in Israel's ancient Yahweh-faith (the Garden, the Brothers, the Flood, and the Tower—these always *are,* in the varied forms of all violations of creation). The priests of Israel and of Judaism (a term appropriate to the Old Testament community after Israel's sixth-century political demise) institutionalized in the Day of Atonement both their conviction of ruptured creation and their faith in the mercy of God.

Indeed, priestly symbolism in the Old Testament underlines a stunning sense of the centrality of sin—and by sin we mean not the mere infraction of rules for the "good" life, but that which *in any respect* violates the biblically defined relationship of God and people. In the priestly-cultic institution the holiest symbol is the mercy-seat, a solid-gold rectangular plate, conforming to the top dimensions of the ark of the covenant (2½ by 1½ cubits; a cubit

---

[17]M. Steinberg, *Basic Judaism,* New York, 1947, pp. 130 f.

was 18 inches?), resting on the ark, supporting the two cherubim above whom resides the invisible Presence. This mercy seat is the footstool of Yahweh, the most sacred symbol within the holy of holies, behind the veil of the tabernacle-temple. At the center of the center, the nucleus of the nucleus, the seat of God's mercy.

Verses 5–10 of Leviticus 16 constitute the earliest stratum of the chapter describing a simple but complete ceremony, subsequently elaborated. The name Azazel (vv. 8,10,26) remains a puzzle. It appears nowhere else in the Old Testament and has been variously interpreted: the chief (or in any case one) of the fallen angels; or as denoting the *place* to which one of the goats was sent (according to Rashi—*Rabbi Sholomon ben Isaac*—the incomparably distinguished medieval commentator); or again, Azazel has been taken as denoting the sins for which the goat atones.

Observe that the priest and the whole house of the priests is not exempt from the necessity of making atonement (v. 6, in the original prescription). A ram (bull) is the specifically priestly sin-offering. Of the two goats, one is sacrificed as a sin offering for the people and its blood, its life-essence, symbolically sprinkled on and before the mercy seat (vv. 15–16). The other goat becomes a scapegoat: the total burden of all Israel's transgressions, all its corporate sins, is symbolically placed upon him and he is driven away "to a solitary land" (vv. 20–22).

In the traditions of the rabbis of Judaism codified in the *Mishnah* about A.D. 200, there is a tractate called "Yoma" which adds details to the development of the celebration of *Yom Kippur*. The priest's moving prayer is recorded, pronounced with his two hands placed upon the goat.

O Lord, thy people the house of Israel have committed iniquity, and transgressed, and sinned before thee. O Lord, pardon now the iniquities, the transgressions, and the sins which thy people, the house of Israel, have inquitously done, transgressed and sinned before thee, as it is written in the law of Moses thy servant, "For on this day shall atonement be made for you, to cleanse you; from all your sins shall you be clean before the Lord" (v. 30).

At various points throughout the ceremony the people respond:

Blessed be the Name of the glory of his Kingdom for ever and ever.

The goat, according to practice detailed in the tractate, is then taken to a place called Zok, about twelve miles from Jerusalem. People follow in sober procession. Arriving there, the goat is pushed backward off the edge of a cliff. Thus profound penitence is confessed; and thus is symbolized God's complete forgiveness and removal of Israel's sins. Thus sang the psalmist (103:12):

> As far as the east is from the west,
> so far does he remove our transgressions from us.

The Holiness Code

19, 23–26   Since A. Klostermann gave the name Holiness Code (*Das Heiligkeitsgesetz*) to this distinctive section (Leviticus 17–26) in 1877, its separate unity within the P corpus has been almost unanimously affirmed. This is chronologically the third major code of *torah* in the Old Testament after the Covenant Code (Exodus 20–23) and the Deuteronomic Code (Deuteronomy 12–26, 28). Its precise date and origin remain uncertain. The code makes use of items of *torah* already long in existence: many of the regulations of the Covenant Code and of Deuteronomy are reproduced. It is not feasible here to detail even the principal supporting arguments. Let it suffice to say that while the three codes, CC, DC, and HC, all incorporate already existent *torah*, they may be deemed to represent in their original codification three successive centuries, the eighth, the seventh, and the sixth, respectively.

The primary quality conveyed in the Hebrew term for holiness is separateness, set-apart-ness (the root of the word, *qdsh*, means to cut, and so, to separate). More particularly in the Old Testament it is a term applied to that which is sacred, that is, set apart for devotional use, for the exercise of the religious function, for purposes pertaining to deity. The root, in varying forms, identifies sacred places and sacred personnel, including both male and female cult prostitutes. In Yahwehism holiness is peculiarly appropriated to Yahweh. Yahweh is holy (Isaiah 6); indeed Yahweh is *the* holy one (Isa. 30:15; Hos. 11:9). Holiness becomes the central attribute of Yahweh, denoting that total aspect of God's being which is disclosed in history. Holiness embraces the full range of God's effective impingement upon human existence. It is that without which Yahweh would not be Yahweh, since without holiness Yahweh would not be known at all. Holiness conveys at once both Yahweh's power and Yahweh's character.[18]

Now the Holiness Code makes the (preposterous?!) affirmation

---

[18]For a fuller and highly perceptive discussion of the term, see von Rad, *Old Testament Theology*, vol. 1, pp. 205–7.

that it shall be, in the Semitic idiom, like Yahweh like people. Israel's full covenant responsibility is to be, like the person of the great Covenanter, holy. "You shall be holy; for I, Yahweh your God am holy" (19:2). "You shall be holy to me; for I Yahweh am holy, and I have *separated* you from the peoples that you should be mine" (20:26; cf. 21:8). This is the intentional force behind the thematic phrase of the code, a phrase repeated almost fifty times: *I am Yahweh*. Thus and so shall you do (the code embraces the full range of *torah*—cultic, ceremonial, civil, sociological, theological), because I am Yahweh, I am holy; and my holiness is fulfilled in you in honoring this *torah;* in obedience to this, you are holy, you appropriate my power, you conform to my character.

And beyond any doubt, the fourth event (see pp. 7 ff.) is implicit in this. The covenant demand of holiness unambiguously conveys the relationship of people and Word to the world: Israel, in its "separation" and appropriation of Yahweh's holiness will convey in the world the power and character of God and his purpose to heal the world's alienation. In doing so, Israel will participate in and bring to realization the fourth event, for which the first three—Exodus, Zion, and Exile—were made.

19:1-37   In this consummately theological conception of the function of Israel's existence and of the force and sanction of its *torah,* it is no wonder that the Holiness Code embraces in Leviticus 19 the Old Testament's supreme articulation of the theological ethic.

The chapter has to do, of course, with the broad concerns of *torah*. Items of the Ethical Decalogue are reiterated—parents and Sabbath (vv. 3,30), other gods (v. 4), stealing (v. 11), Yahweh's name (v. 12). Purely cultic matters are taken up—the eating of the sacrifice (vv. 5–8) and the flesh-blood restriction (v. 26). Husbandry (v. 19) and horticulture (vv. 23–25) are regimented; and the humane law on gleaning again finds eloquent expression (vv. 9–10). All forms of the occult penetration of the unknown are prohibited (vv. 26b,31). Two obviously not uncommon infringements of sexual morality are given attention (vv. 20–22, 29). And the concluding verses of the chapter (33–37) eloquently sound two characteristic thematic notes in the *torah* of prophetic Yahwism: the equality of the foreign-born and the home-born, the stranger (sojourner) and the native (you shall love the stranger *as yourself,* since you know, from Egypt, what it is to be a stranger!); and the need for unqualified integrity in the matter of weights and measures.

The Theo-Ethical Summary

19:11–18 But the heart of the Holiness Code and of Leviticus 19 is verses 13–18. Here is a series of commandments-prohibitions which compares favorably in every significant regard with the Decalogue. Like the Decalogue, the form is prevailingly apodictic —"Thou shalt not" or "Thou shalt." This too represents the effort to give succinct expression to the universal essence of *torah*. And here too the content is theo-ethical; indeed, there is nothing here corresponding to what we have termed Yahweh's pentalogue, but a series in which every member has to do with the relationships of human community.

It is possible to count twelve commandments in the series. Perhaps this, or ten, was the original intent of the unit. It may be that the series was long perpetuated in liturgical use, and that the refrain "I am Yahweh" originally occurred after each one of the commandments. As the text now comes to us, we wonder whether the unit is not best read as an eight-member series; or whether, against prevailing critical opinion, the original unit may not include verses 11–12, and so comprise a decalogue.

Within the covenant community, in the living of your days one with another,

You SHALL NOT

1. (v.11) act corruptly in personal relationships;
2. (v. 12) compound the corruption by a false oath in my name;
     I am Yahweh

3. (v. 13) abuse your neighbor;
4. (v. 13) delay prompt payment of wages and so abuse the worker;
5. (v. 14) abuse the handicapped—specifically the deaf and the blind;
     I am Yahweh

6. (v. 15) commit injustice, either out of sympathy to the poor or out of fear of the mighty: let the consistent principle be *tsda*, righteousness (which is precisely the principle of honor and integrity *as appropriate to* any given relationship);
7. (v. 16) perform (busily, energetically, peripatetically) the function of gossip-slanderer in the community;
8. (v. 16) witness (the primary sense seems to be that of formal witness) so as to put in jeopardy the life of any of your fellows;
     I am Yahweh

9. (v. 17) hate another; but if you do, you shall meet with the one whom you hate and together heal the breach, and so be rid

Yahweh and Covenant / 90

of the sin you bore, which was the hate you knew in the ruptured relationship;

10. (v. 18) avenge or cherish the wrong done you but (and especially in
this situation!) *you shall love your neighbor as yourself.*
I am Yahweh

This is a theological ethic derived from the sense of Yahweh's
holiness and from the conviction that the quality of that holiness
must prevail in all the relationships of the community under covenant with Yahweh. Of course, holiness is translated into elaborate
cultic and ritual rites and regulations and it is with such that the
bulk of the Holiness Code is concerned. But, without apparent
conscious distinction, the HC is also moral-ethical, as the moral
and the ethical are conceived under the primary fact of existence:
"I am Yahweh."

Leviticus 19:11–18 (or 13–18) is a phenomenal series of community controls. A later teacher, nurtured in and informed by this
torah, quoted the concluding line with the observation that
herein, coupled with love of God, is the whole of the law and the
prophets (Matt. 22:34–40).

The Yahweh Speech

26:3–45   We have seen that the Covenant Code concludes with a hortatory speech of Yahweh. The second major collection of *torah*,
the Deuteronomic Code (Deuteronomy 12–26, 28) is similarly
rounded out in Deuteronomy 28; but this we reserve for discussion in a later chapter. As in CC and DC, HC puts in the mouth
of Yahweh the threat of disaster in the event of disobedience and
the promise of unparalleled blessing and fulfillment for the keeping of *torah*.

It is a moving speech, revealing the vitality of the sense of relationship between Yahweh and the covenant people. The lines,
which appear in refrain, are charged with intimate concern: If you
will not hearken to me, if you walk contrary to me, then I shall
perforce walk contrary to you. But to what end? Not simply to
unleash my wrath upon you, but to bring you back, to restore you
in the land, and to renew my covenant.

The present text is obviously informed of the catastrophe of the
early decades of the sixth century. In this crisis, the Holiness
Code, with some of its regulations reaching far back into Israel's
ancient faith and practice, is freshly presented. Here, in this tangible form, is the substance of our life. It has always been the real
substance of our life, and nothing can remove this from us.

An astonishing faith, this covenant faith of ancient Israel, this unquenchable, indestructible Yahwism! In the face of seemingly certain death, annihilation, extinction, this faith in Lord and covenant, in Yahweh and Word, this faith cast in history's fires, this one-track, obstinate Yahwism—*this faith* is articulated in the keynote of the Holiness Code:

... you shall clear out the old to make way for the new . . . I will walk among you, and will be your God, and you shall be my people.

(26:10,12)

Do you fear what has not befallen you? Have you forgotten that

I am Yahweh your God, who brought you forth out of the land of Egypt, that you should not be their slaves; and I have broken the bars of your yoke and made you walk erect.

(26:13)[19]

Walk erect even now—in holiness.

In Narratives of Wilderness and Occupation: Numbers 5–6, 11–17, 20–24; Joshua 1–12, 23–24

> I gave you a land.
> *Josh. 24:13*[20]

The last verse of Leviticus (27:34) reminds us of the structure of the Hexateuch. "These are the commandments which Yahweh commanded Moses for the people of Israel on Mount Sinai." Yahweh to Moses to people, *at Mount Sinai.* This is the platform of Leviticus—in the present *arrangement* of the text. But it is also the foundation of the balance of Exodus from 19:1. And it is the fundamental scheme of the first section of Numbers, to 10:10. At Numbers 10:11 and following "the people of Israel set out by stages from the wilderness of Sinai." The immediate goal, though agonizingly frustrated, is the gaining of Canaan, the acquisition of a land in fulfillment of divine promise.

A glance over the full contents of the book of Numbers returns this outline:

1:1–10:10 varied *torah* as part of the total Yahweh-Moses-Sinai law
10:11–20:13 traditions and *torah* of the wilderness period
20:14–36:13 toward the land: from Kadesh to Moab

[19]See Lev. 19:11–13.
[20]Cf. Psalms 114, 135.

Numbers gets its name from the fact that it opens (1–2) with the numbering of Israel, with complete census lists by tribes.

So the whole number of the people of Israel . . . from twenty years old and upward, every man able to go forth to war in Israel—their whole number was six hundred and three thousand five hundred and fifty.

(1:45 f.)

This would imply a total community of about two million, a preposterous figure which may result from the retrojection of census figures compiled in the days of the monarchy, centuries later, to this early epoch. The figure 603 is hardly the achievement of numerology (it *is* a remarkable coincidence that the Hebrew letters in "children of Israel" total, in the sum of their numerical equivalents, the number 603). This is of course P. In passages commonly assigned to J (Num. 11:21 and Exod. 12:37) the round number 600,000 appears, perhaps, however, as later glosses influenced by P. Is it possible that about six hundred *families* first figured in the tradition? The change from *families* to *thousands* is easy indeed in Hebrew. Again we have to say not only that we do not know but that we shall probably never know. We can only say again that numbers were relatively small, certainly not in excess of a total of ten thousand, and perhaps only about half that number.

5–6   The ordeal of jealousy (5) and the law of the Nazirite (6) represent very ancient belief and practice and ought not to be omitted in reading. Comparable institutions of ordeal in the case of confirmed or suspected unfaithfulness are found all over the ancient world. And the Nazirite (from the Hebrew *nazir*, meaning one who is consecrated—no relation to Nazareth in the New Testament) is later represented in the figures of Samson and Samuel. That widely and justly beloved benediction, the so-called Priestly (or Aaronic) Blessing, is attached to the law of the Nazirite (6:22 ff.). Fortunately, translation only slightly mars its beauty. The Hebrew composition presents three lines of three, five, and seven words each. "In beautiful climax it leads in three members from the petition for material blessing and protection to that of the favour of Yahweh as spiritual blessing, and finally to the petition for the bestowal of the *Shalom*, the peace of welfare in which all the material and spiritual well-being is comprehended."[21]

---

[21] E. Kautzsch, quoted in A. R. S. Kennedy, *Leviticus and Numbers,* in the *Century Bible Series,* Edinburgh, n.d.

The Lord bless you and keep you.
The Lord make his face to shine upon you, and be gracious unto you.
The Lord lift up his countenance upon you, and give you peace.[22]

Between Egypt and Canaan

11:17; 20–21   Not everything in the Old Testament is edifying, or of theological meaning, or even in and of itself worth reading. But everything comes out of Israel's life, and it is part of the genius of the whole Old Testament story that Israel's life is so broadly and deeply represented. Sometimes, then, we are content to read the story simply for what it adds out of the fullness of Israel's experience and memory to our penetration into the entity of that ancient people.

Three narrative units now before us duplicate what we have already encountered in the story as told in Exodus. The cry of hunger (Exodus 16) is here the lament, "O that we had meat to eat!" (11:4). Manna (bdellium, 11:7) is deemed unsatisfactory and "again" (?) quail fall in profusion (11:31 ff.; cf. Exod. 16:13). Chapter 11 begins and ends with a little etymological legend of the sort we have seen before. But the strong feature of this chapter is the delineation of the Yahweh-Moses relationship and the brilliance and vigor of the dialogue. Moses, sick of the fainthearted, self-pitying wails of complaint, turns with impudent irony to Yahweh—"Did I conceive all this people . . ." (see 11:12 ff.); and Yahweh himself carries the day with as fine a speech of sarcasm as is to be found in all antiquity:

Yahweh will give you meat and you shall eat. You shall not eat one day, or two days, or five days, or ten days, or twenty days, but a whole month, until it comes out at your nostrils. . . .

(11:18 ff.)

The cry of thirst (Exodus 17) is also repeated (Numbers 20). This time, Moses responds in such fury (Num. 20:10) that the episode comes to be seen as the explanation for Moses' failure to enter the land of promise (see Ps. 106:33). That the episode is a duplicate of that of Exodus 17 seems likely because of the repetition of the etymological explanation of the name Meribah (Contention).

---

[22]A more sensitive rendering might be: May God bless you and keep you. May the very face of God shine on you and be gracious to you. May God's presence embrace you and give you peace.

The appointment of an administrative staff to ease the fearful load on Moses is also duplicated in Numbers (11:24-29; cf. Exodus 18). But in this account Jethro, Moses' father-in-law, does not figure at all; and in the episode of the somewhat excessive charismatic seizure of the indefatigable Eldad and Medad, Moses is given one of the finest lines ever given a professional to speak of other professionals. When informed by some fortunately nameless busy-body that these two are still inexhaustibly making like prophets, old Moses thunders,

Are you jealous for my sake? Would that all Yahweh's people were prophets . . . !

(11:29)

A notable difference between these three sets of duplicates in Exodus and Numbers is their place in the story: in Exodus these are pre-Sinai episodes; in Numbers, they follow the Sinai sojourn.

In this context where Moses appears with unparalleled vigor, if not violence, it is a remarkable touch that the story incorporates the strange little narrative of Miriam's and Aaron's insubordination (Numbers 12) and the accompanying testimony (unthinkable if untrue) to the essential humility of the man Moses (12:3). Nor is any higher tribute paid Moses than in Yahweh's words of rebuke to Miriam and Aaron (12:6-8).

The area of present occupation is in the vicinity of Kadesh. The Old Testament story now recalls, and surely idealizes, the tentative probe of Canaan (Numbers 13) in hopeful anticipation of occupation, and Caleb's courageous report against all the other cowardly spies who testify that against the stalwart occupants of the land they seemed *in their own eyes* like grasshoppers (v. 33).

It is not at all impossible that Numbers 14 preserves the memory of an abortive attempt to occupy Canaan by approach directly from the south (vv. 39-45). But these narratives of pre-Canaan Israel are not nearly so appropriate to the reconstruction of external as of internal history: it is the grateful impression of a Joshua and a Caleb in the living memory of a people that is best preserved (14:4-10); it is the role of Moses' intercession in their very survival that is celebrated (14:13-20; cf. Exod. 32:30 ff.); it is the enduring shame and remorse of faithlessness, the aggressive rebellion of unfaith that is sounded as a perenially relevant theme in the existence of Israel (14:26-45).

The Rebellion of Korah, Dathan, and Abiram

As it now stands, this narrative confirms the prerogatives enjoyed by the professional hereditary priesthood, the Levites. But here is a fine example of the nature and process of a long-fluid, composite tradition. The present text betrays an original account which was simply a vindication of the position and authority of Moses; a second, variant account combined with the first; and a third account introduced still later (perhaps from a decisive, aggressive editorial hand) providing the final modification. There can be no doubt of the fact of multiple oral and written sources underlying the present Hexateuch, even though our conventional symbols may be inaccurate in certain particulars of representation. Employing these symbols, nevertheless, Numbers 16 presents this interesting history and structure:

1. JE: vv. 1,2a,12–15,25–34 (omitting all references to Korah). Here is a straightforward narrative of a purely secular revolt by the Reubenites Dathan and Abiram against the civil authority claimed by Moses. They are swallowed up.

2. P: Korah, at the head of 250 recognized leaders of Israel, opposes Moses and Aaron in the interests of the entire community, protesting the limitation of priestly rights and privileges to Moses and Aaron and the Levites on the ground that "all the congregation are holy" (v. 3). Korah and company are consumed by fire from Yahweh (v. 35).

3. R (final redactor): Korah, at the head of 250 *Levites*, opposes the exclusive rights of Aaron as against the Levites.

In summary, then: (1) Dathan and Abiram (cf. Ps. 106:16–18, where Korah is not mentioned) protest Moses' civil authority. The motive of the story is, of course, to substantiate the continuing Mosaic authority. (2) Korah and all the congregation challenge the Levites in a variant designed to give ultimate confirmation to the Levitical institution. (3) The third variation centers the controversy within the professional priesthood, and in upholding Aaron against the rebellious Levites, the story serves to give ancient sanction to the relatively late office of high or chief (Aaronic) priest over the Levitical priests.

The Old Testament story, we repeat, tends always toward "isness"; and where questions of external fact are hopelessly obscure (or indeed, as is often the case, irrelevant, the nature of the story being what it is), the subsequent course of Israel's internal history may nevertheless be remarkably illuminated.

Yahweh and Covenant / 96

Approach

An unusual array of fascinating, if problematical, items is presented in this chapter. We can do no more here than call attention to some of them. The broad lines of the story are moving toward the entrance into Canaan. The long period of wilderness occupation is behind. (How, again, are we to assess historically the obviously round number of "forty years," Num. 14:33 f., representing a full generation: was it more or less?) Israel moves now toward Moab, intending to approach Canaan from the southeast.

The place-name Hormah (root, *hrm*, destruction) is etymologically explained as is also, incidentally, the institution of the *herem* (root, *hrm*), in which the enemy is totally destroyed as an act of devotion, a gigantic sacrifice to the deity (vv. 1–4). The bout with fiery serpents (vv. 4–9) is enigmatic: does it preserve the memory of actual casualties inflicted by serpents; is it a cultic etiology to explain the presence of a bronze serpent in the Jerusalem temple in Hezekiah's time (2 Kings 18:4); or is it distantly related to ancient, primitive cultic use of the serpent symbol?

Do not miss the ancient Song of the Well, happily preserved here (vv. 17–18), nor the also very old, if puzzling, song of verses 27 and following. Of serveral possible interpretations of the lines, the most natural and simple is the celebration of a victory of the Amorites (Sihon the king, and Heshbon the capital) over Moab, and incorporated in Israel's story with the sentiment that what Sihon conquered becomes an imputed conquest of those who conquer Sihon, namely, Israel (see vv. 25–31).

If we give literal, historical credence to the narratives of Israel's approach to the land, we can only wonder whether the present sequence is not disordered, with the conquest of Ammon to the *north* of Moab, and still further north, Bashan (vv. 33 ff.), *before* the encounter with Moab represented in Numbers 22 and following.

Balaam, Moab, and Israel

22:1–24:25   Moab hears of what Israel has done to Bashan and Ammon, and a man of vast renown for his powers of efficacious blessing and cursing, Balaam from Aram, is summoned by Moab's king, Balak. Internal conflict in the very charming Balaam story has been conventionally explained as a result of its JE composition: in

J, for example, Balaam sets out without Yahweh's consent; but in E (v. 20) permission has already been given.

The speaking animal is a prevalent theme in antiquity (one remembers the classic example in the Iliad of Achilles' horse Xanthus); but in the Old Testament it occurs only here and in the Garden story (Genesis 3). It is intentionally humorous here. The story says brilliantly that even a man as gifted as Balaam may possess powers of spiritual discernment considerably less than those of an ass. In this connection I recall the finest example I have ever seen of the not uncommon foggy relationship between an undergraduate student and the subject-matter of the course. On an Old Testament quiz, I asked for a one-sentence identification of Balaam and received this answer: Balaam was an ass that went about doing good. Not quite in touch—but almost.

Four remarkable, pro-Israel oracles stand in Numbers 23–24. In the first of these Balaam declares

How can I curse whom God has not cursed?
How can I denounce whom Yahweh has not denounced?

(23:8)

With increasing impatience Balak, king of Moab, tries to secure from Balaam a formal curse against Israel. But twice more (23:18–24 and 24:3–9) the forthcoming oracle takes the form of magnificent, lyrical blessing:

> For there *is* no enchantment against Jacob,
>   no divination against Israel;
> Now it shall be said of Jacob and Israel,
>   "What has God wrought!"

(23:23)

This phrase did not, of course, originate on the wireless, or was it the telegraph?

Humor underlies the whole story. Balak's exasperation is comic when he cries, "Neither curse them at all, nor bless them at all," which, after all, puts the matter very courteously (23:25). Balak's patience nevertheless endures a third oracle; but Balaam's fourth is, from Balak's point of view, utterly gratuitous (24:15–19).

The three short oracles in 24:20–24 are of other and later origin than the four major oracles, which (conventionally seen as E or JE) are certainly not later than the eighth century. They betray characteristics of the tenth-century monarchy, and may rest on still older oracular models. From a purely theological point of view, the second oracle is distinguished for its early and profound definition of the Word, the Yahweh-Word:

> God is not man, that he should lie,
> or a son of man, that he should repent.
> Has he said, and will he not do it?
> Or has he spoken, and will he not fulfil it?
> (23:19)

The sense of the Word as efficacious entity accomplishing itself is further expressed in the next verse:

> Behold, I received a command to bless:
> he *has* blessed, and I cannot revoke it!
> (23:20)

This is the Word that made the covenant that sustained the faith by which Israel survived.

Occupation as Fulfillment of Promise: Joshua 1–12, 23–24

From a *literary* point of view, the first major unit of the Old Testament is not the Pentateuch but the Tetrateuch (Genesis-Numbers). The literary framework is superficial, that is, imposed, and is unmistakably a priestly framework. Upon these four books, the priesthood of exilic and postexilic Judaism has exercised the final, formative influence.

In determining the actual contents and limits of the Old Testament from a *canonical* point of view, the first major unit is, of course, the Pentateuch (Genesis-Deuteronomy). A fifth book is added to the literary unit of the Tetrateuch on the strength of the Mosaic tradition; these five books are "the five books of Moses." In the process of the formation of the Old Testament canon, they fulfill the "rule" of acceptance ("canon"), and so constitute the first unit to achieve canonical status (*c.* 400 B.C.E.?).

But the first *theological* unit is the Hexateuch. Everything in the Pentateuch is in anticipation of the attainment of the land, the fulfillment of divine promise, which is recounted in Joshua. Canonically, Joshua introduces the second major division of the canon (Law, *Prophets*, Writings). Joshua is the first of the Former Prophets: Joshua, Judges, Samuel, Kings (the Latter Prophets are the prophets proper—Isaiah, Jeremiah, Ezekiel, and the twelve, Hosea through Malachi). Judged by the literary norm, Joshua belongs to the Deuteronomic work, Deuteronomy-

Kings—so designated because of its characteristic dominant deuteronomic, editorial framework and cast. As priests have employed older sources, including their own, in the Tetrateuch, so deuteronomists have worked (and apparently more self-assertively than the priests) with the likes of J and E, and their own Deuteronomy, in the Deuteronomic work. Theologically, we repeat, Joshua is the last scene of the first great act of the Old Testament story, the completion of the first great act event, the total event of Egypt-Sinai.

These chapters mark the outline of Joshua. Deuteronomic editors working in the sixth century under the strong influence of the seventh-century Deuteronomic Code (the original Deuteronomy, probably Deut. 4:44–30:20) collected stories of conquest in Joshua 2–11 and added to this collection their own introduction (chap. 1) and conclusion (11:21–12:24). Tribal boundaries and lists of cities dating from the tenth to the seventh centuries comprise, for the most part, Joshua 13–22. The last two chapters of Joshua purport to be the final words of Joshua.

We shall look at some of this in more detail in Part II, to which we are about to turn. It is essential here only to remind ourselves that the shape of the full Hexateuch is theologically and cultically determined, and that a people's memory thus articulated and preserved vastly simplifies and radically idealizes the remembered events. Yahweh's "gift" of the land is theologically dominant in the event and cultically celebrated. Accordingly, the Book of Joshua, while here and there acknowledging a slow, long-sustained process of occupation-acquisition, understandably emphasizes a total and utterly decisive *conquest* of the entire land by force of arms. The question of the relationship of this view to the probable course of events will return. We simply record here our understanding and appreciation of Israel's faith. What is affirmed in Joshua is true of Israel's internal history as it is made articulate in the expanded credo in Joshua 24—the summary, confessional statement of the First Event of Israel's existence. The Old Testament story which we have surveyed thus far is compressed in the credo, with the sharp, tight eloquence of economy, to a half-page recital of Yahweh's creation of Israel.

Let the reading of this recital (24:2–13) round out our review of the Old Testament story's First Event.

II
Rebellion:
Chaos Out of Order

4

Anarchy

Tribal Occupation and Consolidation:
Joshua 1–12; Judges 1–5

> I will not drive them out.
> *Judg. 2:3*[1]

The contents of the Book of Judges may be outlined as follows:

1:1–2:5   Introduction. Efforts at occupation and settlement in Canaan by separate and isolated tribes, with emphasis on the successes of Simeon, Judah, and the house of Joseph.

2:6–16:31   The work of the judges. A collection of narratives originating for the most part independently of one another among tribal groups in Canaan later embraced in Israelite monarchy—a collection wrought and edited by DH (deuteronomic historians responsible for the substantial present form of Deuteronomy-Kings).

17:1–21:25   An appendix of assorted components.

The process by which any record and memory of the past is preserved inevitably involves some screening of the past. This is especially true of history that is predominantly maintained cultically, when past event is the occasion for present praise of God and the celebration of the role of God in the life of a people. The basic cultic formula, *Out of Egypt, into this land,* unquestionably rests upon past events, but it is a past marvelously screened and filtered.

Now it is the genius of ancient Israel that *it knew this.* We have already noted in the stories of Israel's first ancestors and founder (Moses), the irrepressible quality of realism which frustrates all efforts to describe existence—any existence—in ideal terms. In Israel's joyous cultic celebrations it rehearsed the fundamental theological scheme of Yahweh's initiating Word, Israel's response

[1]Cf. Psalm 83.

of faith, and the resultant redemption from slavery into freedom; but at the same time Israel knew (and found itself compelled to record) that the Word is fulfilled always with characteristic imprecision, and in tension and anguish. Israel insists at once on the truth of the theological scheme and on what it also knows to be the realities of existence. Such is the testimony of the Joshua-Judges record.

The Nature of the Story in Joshua

We could call the theological scheme the cult-myth if the term were not so easily misunderstood. The cult-myth is the true theological essence of the celebrated event. It is what faith decrees to be the essential structure and meaning of the event. The myth, then, is historicized, that is, its true essence is clothed with a story which purports to make history of theology. In this case, the account of Canaan's acquisition as told, for the most part, in Joshua represents the historicizing of the cultic confession. Yahweh gave the land. It was the conquest of the people under Joshua, total, complete, easy, and sometimes, as at Jericho (Joshua 6), wrought not at all by force of arms but by potent formula revealed by Yahweh.

So Joshua defeated the whole land, the hill country and the Negeb [the land stretching south of Canaan into the reaches of the desert] and the low-land and the slopes, and all their kings; he left none remaining, but utterly destroyed all that breathed, as Yahweh God of Israel commanded. And Joshua defeated them from Kadesh-barnea to Gaza, and all the country of Goshen [an unidentified but obviously Palestinian, not Egyptian Goshen], as far as Gibeon. And Joshua took all these kings and their land *at one time, because Yahweh God of Israel fought for Israel.*

(Josh. 10:40–42)

In another conspicuous feature, the story confesses its adaptation to the two-member theological scheme *Out of Egypt, into this land.* The two members of the faith-formula take on a striking parallelism: the Joshua-Canaan epoch is seen as a kind of antiphonal response to Moses-Egypt.

Moses-Egypt	*Joshua-Canaan*
1. Spies dispatched: especially to the Hebron area in the south. Num. 13:22 ff.	to the Jericho area. Joshua 2.

Moses-Egypt	*Joshua-Cannan*
2. The dry crossing: "Israel went into the midst of the sea on dry ground." Exod. 14:21 ff.	"All Israel [crossing the Jordan] on dry ground." Josh. 3:14 ff.
3. Circumcision: Exod. 4:24–26; cf. 12:43 ff.	"Circumcise the people of Israel *again the second time.*" Josh. 5:2 ff.
4. Passover: Exodus 12	Josh. 5:10 ff.
5. Commission: "Put off your shoes . . ." Exod. 3:1 ff.	"Put off your shoes . . ." Josh. 5:13 ff.
6. The potent gesture: "Moses held up his hand . . ." against Amelek. Exod. 17:8 ff.	"Stretch out the javelin that is in your hand . . ." against Ai. Josh. 8:18 ff.
7. Law-giving: at Mount Sinai "Moses wrote all the words of Yahweh." Exodus 24	At Mount Ebal (Shechem) Joshua "wrote upon the stones a copy of the law of Moses, which he had written." Josh. 8:30 ff.
8. Cities of refuge: anticipated by Moses. Num. 35:9 ff.	Appointed and named by Joshua. Joshua 20.
9. Covenant-making; at Sinai, "Yahweh our God we will serve, and [Yahweh's] voice we will obey." Exodus 24.	at Shechem, "all that Yahweh has spoken we will do," Joshua 24.

To a considerable extent, the Book of Joshua historicizes the first and fundamental proposition of Israel's faith: Yahweh brought us out of Egypt and gave us this land. It is theology which determines the major theme. But we also observe that etiology has been freely employed, here as in Genesis, to voice and define the theological meaning of names and events which figure prominently in the "history," for example circumcision and Gilgal (5:8 f.), and Achan and the Valley of Achor (chap. 8). In view of all this, it is impossible to reconstruct any firm, full outlines of the concrete structure of events. Nor is archaeology as helpful here as some of the popularizing archaeologists would have us think. The most recent and competent spade work at the site of ancient Jericho returns the verdict that no trace of Israelite violence in the thirteenth century is to be found. Ancient Gilgal may have been located—the identification is not yet certain—but yields nothing significant on the period of Israel's early occupation. Excavations at Ai indicate that the city was already in Joshua's day a long-dead ruin (the attack of the invaders may well have been upon nearby Bethel); Ai, meaning "ruin," may easily have become the object of attack in the story as it circulated in later generations.

Shechem is another matter, of course; but here light is cast chiefly on the times both prior and subsequent to the first entrance of the Joshua group.[2]

The Nature of the Event: Conquest or Occupation?

Of course, it is not *impossible* that an initial, decisive conquest of Canaan under Joshua was effected and the gains largely lost in the generation following his death.[3] But the present book of Joshua warns strongly against its own idealizing tendencies.

But the Jebusites, the inhabitants of Jerusalem, the people of Judah could not drive out [the city finally came into Judah's hands in the time of David, who made it his capital]; so the Jebusites dwell with the people of Judah at Jerusalem to this day.

(Josh. 15:63)

However they did not drive out the Canaanites that dwelt in Gezer; so the Canaanites have dwelt in the midst of Ephraim to this day. . . .

(16:10)

The sons of Manasseh could not take possession of those cities [listed in the preceding verse]; but the Canaanites persisted in dwelling in that land.

(17:12)

A notable instance of accommodation (with the Gibeonites) is recorded in chapter 9. The Book of Judges reflects a process of occupation, settlement, and accommodation stretching over a number of generations, involving numerous mutually independent tribes and resulting ultimately in the amalgamation of Canaanite and "Israelite" into the people of Israel, under covenant to Yahweh. We do not mean to suggest that the process was always without violence: conquest of a sort there surely was, but it was largely localized, involving skirmishes between older and more recent settlers of the land.

The Joshua group (or the Benjamin-Joseph-Ephraimite tribes;[4] and was it also, earlier, the Moses group or have we two originally

---

[2]For bibliography and a summary of the problems and answers of archaeology in this period, see John Bright, *A History of Israel,* 2nd ed., Philadelphia, 1972, pp. 126–30; and G. M. Landes, *Joshua,* in *Interpreter's Dictionary of the Bible,* Supplementary Vol., Nashville, 1976, pp. 472 f.

[3]See G. E. Wright, *Biblical Archaeology,* 2nd ed., Philadelphia, 1960, pp. 79 ff. Cf. B. Anderson, *Understanding the Old Testament,* 3rd ed., Englewood Cliffs, N.J., 1975, pp. 120–25.

[4]M. Noth argues convincingly that the basic account of Joshua 2–9 is the history of the Benjamin tribe, augmented by accounts of the related movements of Joseph and Ephraim. See his *History of Israel,* 2nd ed., rev. trans. S. Goodman, New York, 1960, pp. 74 f., 93.

separate, but now collated, traditions?) occupied a territory in the sparsely settled central hill country of Canaan bounded on the east by the Jordan, on the west by the coastal plains, and on the north and south by strong Canaanite city-states. In the small scattered settlements of this area the inhabitants were distantly or more closely related to the occupying Israelites. They were descendants of Amorite settlers who had moved into Canaan from the fringes of outlying deserts some six to eight centuries earlier; or, indeed, some of these may well have come out of tribes originally closely related to the group which went into Egypt and now, some centuries later, makes its return to the land.

There are some suggestions that perhaps Simeon, along with the Kenites, the Calebites, and the Othnielites (perhaps as a separate but closely related tribe or clan), occupied the southern hill country of Canaan to the south of the powerful Canaanite fortress-city of Jerusalem earlier and independently of the occupation of central Canaan by Yahweh worshipers of the tribe of Judah. In the case of Simeon, Judg. 1:1–3 provides ground for this assumption, although Gen. 34:25 f. sees Simeon and Levi as responsible for the defeat of Shechem in central Canaan. The presence of Kenites is attested to in Judg. 1:16, Calebites in Judg. 1:12 and Josh. 14:13, and the more problematical Othnielites in Judg. 1:13 ff. This thesis is supported by the narrative of Genesis 38 (the story of Judah and Tamar), which strongly suggests Judah's early and permanent occupancy in this area, as well as by the presupposition of some of Israel's earliest beginnings—and even before (Gen. 4:26).

North of the plain of Esdraelon and its defensive chain of strong cities—Megiddo, Taanach, Ibleam, Beth-shan (see Judg. 1:27)—the "conquest" was again an originally separate story involving tribes having no historical association with other tribes ultimately involved in the entity "Israel" until the campaign of Deborah (Judges 4–5). Thus, the entity Israel, formed out of a process of tribal confederation leading to monarchy, has a highly complex, heterogeneous prehistory now understandably simplified and idealized. The ultimate unity of the twelve tribes is imposed upon traditions relating originally to the separate tribes; and most strikingly, the Yahweh-faith which dominates confederation and monarchy appears to have been historically the moving, cohesive force in the long process.

Deuteronomic History and the Judges

"Judge" is a poor term, but since we cannot change it, we must understand that it is not merely an ancient counterpart of our judge. The judge in Israel's tradition is a charismatic (from Greek *charisma* meaning gift, endowment) tribal leader usually responsible for the achievement of at least a temporary respite from harassment or subjugation at the hands of a nearby enemy. In the Old Testament the Hebrew word "to judge" and its derivatives are not exclusively juridical terms, nor do they necessarily connote negative action. Judging is the total task in varied capacities of setting right the wrong and reordering the disordered. As a "history" wrought by the deuteronomic historians, the Book of Judges is obviously and rigidly under theological control. Israel's peaceful, ordered existence in the land promised and given by Yahweh is continually frustrated by Israel's defiance of the giver. The promised life of fulfillment in the land becomes a life of abysmal unfulfillment, an anarchistic existence, because Yahweh is ignored. "You have not given heed to my voice" (Judg. 6:10).

The deuteronomic historians—we will use the symbol DG for them—set all of this in a four-member formula by which the individual stories of the judges are introduced and linked to one another. The formula appears in full for the first time in 3:7 ff. It envisages the long epoch of tribal occupation-settlement-confederation as revolving in the cycle of *apostasy, punishment, penitence,* and finally, through the instrument of the charismatic judge, the restoration of *peace.* Israel forgot Yahweh who in anger "sold" it into subjection to an alien power; Israel came back in penitence to Yahweh, who then effected salvation through the judge. DH has employed tribal stories from all over Canaan without regard for sequence, if, indeed, the sequence was known to DH; and while we do not presume to reconstruct from this a history of Canaan in the twelfth and eleventh centuries, we nevertheless gratefully acknowledge DH's contribution to our understanding of the character of a period which ,*was,* for whatever reasons, predominantly an anarchy. And I, at least, must further acknowledge what appears to me to be beyond dispute; that in an internal sense DH is right; in the Canaanite setting, the Yahweh-worshiping tribe, whether alone or in confederation, achieved order and fulfillment and maintained meaningful entity and self-respect only in the force of its Yahweh-faith.

DH no doubt aimed to include twelve judges, one for (but not from) each of the tribes, although with Deborah and Abimelech (neither is called a judge) there are fourteen. The most important figures are Ehud, Deborah, Gideon, Jephthah, and Samson.

Othniel and Ehud

Judges 3

The Othniel "judgeship" (3:7-11) has often been regarded as spurious. We doubt the historicity of several other judges: Shamgar "who killed six hundred Philistines with an oxgoad" (3:31, and who was created out of whole cloth from the reference in 5:6); Jair who "had thirty sons who rode on thirty asses; and they had thirty cities" (10:4); Ibzan who "has thirty sons; and thirty daughters he gave in marriage outside his clan, and thirty daughters he brought in from outside for his sons" (broad-minded, anyway; 12:8); Abdon who went old Jair one better, gifted in the old game of one-upsmanship: he had "forty sons and thirty grandsons, who rode on seventy asses" (12:14). Is Othniel no more substantial than these, or Tola (10:1), of whom not even an anecdote is told (except perhaps that he is the son of Puah, the son of Dodo), or Elon, who simply judged, died, and was buried (12:11-12)? In Othniel's case, the brief narrative consists almost entirely of the DH formula; and we know nothing else of a Syrian (Aram) king named Cushanrishathaim (the name is etymologically suspect). Othniel is a tribal designation, certainly; but is the episode of Judges 1:11-15, in which Othniel figures ostensibly as an individual, anything other than a tribal encounter, reduced and idealized in terms of personal relationships? Such skepticism may be justified, yet we find ourselves wondering whether DH has not in fact preserved here the very ancient but real encounter of free-ranging Syrian forces with the Yahweh-tribes (notably the Othnielites) inhabiting southern Canaan in the general area south of Hebron.

The story of Ehud's dispatch of Eglon, king of Moab, is one of antiquity's finest examples of graphic, brilliant prose description (3:15-30). Traces of its composite construction still show (vv. 19 and 20, for example, appear to be duplicates) but its impact on the reader is unified and powerful and its disclosure of the life of Canaan in the twelfth century bold, true, and uninhibited.

Deborah

Judges 4-5

The Song of Deborah (Judges 5) is in every respect the finest treasure preserved in the Book of Judges. Without significant dissent, scholars have long regarded it not only as the oldest extant poem of any considerable length in the Old Testament, but also as the work of one who, if not an eyewitness, was nevertheless close to the event and intimately informed about it. It is one of the world's great literary documents, but it is also of incomparable historical value. From no other single narrative of such antiquity do we learn so much of the tribes of Israel in the twelfth century. The song reflects what must have been the first significant effort at a confederation of the tribes of Israel against a Canaanite alliance.

The prose account of the same event (Judges 4) lacks the vigorous authenticity of the poem and is certainly a considerably later creation. We note certain conspicuous differences in the two accounts:

Prose	*Poem*
The oppressor is Jabin, king of Hazor, whose captain is Sisera.	Only Sisera figures.
Deborah's home is situated in the hills between Ramah and Bethel, in Canaan's central region occupied by Benjamin.	Deborah seems to belong to the tribe of Issachar in territory just southwest of what we later know as the Sea of Galilee.
Zebulum and Naphtali alone oppose the enemy; and thus all the principals are in northern Canaan, north of Esdraelon.	The coalition under Deborah embraces tribes in central as well as northern Canaan, that is Manasseh (Machir in Josh. 17:1), Ephraim, and Benjamin, as well as Zebulum, Issachar, and Naphtali.
The battle occurs in the region of Mt. Tabor in the north.	The Canaanite coalition is routed at Taanach along the southern edge of the plain of Esdraelon, near Megiddo.
Jael murders Sisera while he sleeps.	Jael dispatches Sisera in somewhat unorthodox fashion while he stands and consumes "curds in a lordly bowl."

Estimates of the poem's age differ, but we are surely not far wrong if we take the round number of 1100 B.C.E. We note several matters of the utmost significance. If the words *Yahweh* and *Israel* are not later interpolations (that is, insertions by later editors), which seems hardly tenable, then there already existed a conceptual, ideological (if not a formal political) Yahweh-worshiping entity known as Israel. This entity consists *already* not only of the six tribes which "offered themselves willingly" (5:2,9) but also—since their failure to join Deborah is implicitly deemed to be a breach of integrity—four tribes which are specifically rebuked (and in such exquisitely poetic language, vv. 15b–17).[5]

Certainly by the turn of the first full century of occupation by the central tribes of Benjamin, Ephraim, and Joseph/Manasseh (whatever the length of occupation of related or subsequently confederated tribes north and south), a confederation of ten tribes at least is already in existence, embracing roughly the full territory of later monarchic Israel on both sides of the Jordan, but exclusive of the area south of Jerusalem (still a Canaanite stronghold) later identified as the land of Judah. We note further the song's recollection of Yahweh's especially potent self-disclosure in the Kadesh area and of Sinai's location there (vv. 4–5). We commend the poet's consummately sensitive powers of identification with participating leaders and people; with recalcitrant as well as responding tribes; with the whole natural environment of the event, poetically clothed with vital purpose and depicted as a glorious participant (vv. 20–21); in some sense with the enemy, Sisera himself; and of course profoundly, if also with conscious irony, with Sisera's mother.

Most notable is the role of Yahweh in the song. As emphatically as in the story of the Exodus event, or any other comparable Old Testament event, the song is created in praise of Yahweh, as a confessional recitation on the theme of living divine impingement on human history. This is another in Yahweh's series of performances on behalf of a people in quest of a land. It is composed, so it would seem, in the immediate excitement and heat of the encounter between Israelite and Canaanite. In the flush of an astonishing victory the winner exuberantly calls down a fate like Sisera's on all Yahweh's enemies. But it is more than simply a song of victory, for here, as always, it acknowledges the faith that this is Yahweh's world, history, and people, and that victory is meaningful only in terms of Yahweh's purpose.

[5]For a fuller discussion see A. Globe, "The Muster of Tribes in Judges 5:11c–18," *Zeitschrift für die alttestamentliche Wissenschaft*, 87, 1975, pp. 169–83.

So perish all thine enemies, O Lord!
But thy friends be like the sun as he rises
in his might.

(v. 31)

Although from Israel's point of view this was not a time of un-relieved anarchy, it is nevertheless true that during these years of occupation, settlement, skirmish, and consolidation, respite from severe harassment was at best intermittent. In awareness of this and hard-put to rationalize a "gift" of Yahweh so agonizingly achieved, DH finds Israel's prevailing unfaith (not only now but in the subsequent monarchic period as well) the cause of the per-sistence of disorder and chaos in an existence which Yahweh would bless with meaning and fulfillment of life if only Israel would respond appropriately.

The DH formula in Judges repeatedly takes the form of what appears to be an almost crude religious superstition: When Israel did what was evil, Yahweh gave them into the hand of Aram or Moab or Sisera or Midian (Gideon: 6–8) or Ammon (Jephthah: 11–12), or the Philistines (Samson: 13–16). But this is nothing more nor less than the faith of DH that Israel is a covenant people, that to violate the covenant is to make chaos of the life of the people, and that to keep the covenant is to fulfill Israel's crea-tion in order and meaning.

The life of faith in any time and in any variety of acknowledged covenant-existence under God finds itself perennially confronted by the essence of DH's formula. In its unceasing tension with the varied and eminently rational claims of positivism, causality, and aggressive agnosticism, the life of faith must always not merely confront, but confront with decision, the fundamental proposi-tion of the deuteronomic (and so the whole, biblical) faith that human life, the gift of God, is meaningfully fulfilled only in ac-knowledgment of the reign of God in history and in a relationship of response to God's initiation.

Premonarchic Israel:
Ruth; Judges 6–21

You have not given heed to my voice.
Judg. 6:10

Whatever the relationship of the little Book of Ruth to the ac-tual life and history of ancient Israel, it stands as a superb ex-ample of classical Hebrew prose narrative and as an inspired editorial stroke. In the midst of the brutal, violent chaos of premonarchic Canaan, it brings a moment of warm tender, relief.

Ruth is a Moabite woman whose sojourning Israelite husband dies in Moab. She returns with her mother-in-law to Bethlehem in Judah, and there wins love and marriage with Boaz, a kinsman of her deceased husband. With the almost certain exception of 4:18–22 and the possible, even probable, exception of 4:7, the story is a unit, a skillfully and beautifully told tale.

As an artistic creation, Ruth is commonly ranked with the greatest short stories in the literature of the world. Composed around that shamelessly abused theme of they-lived-happily-ever-after, it is the genius of the tale that it successfully avoids what even then must have been the prevailing prostitution of the theme in banal sentimentality. The story of Ruth exploits some of the noblest qualities of human character—tenderness, loyalty, compassion, love—without anywhere sounding noble, without anywhere becoming cloying. And as is true of all classical Hebrew prose, it is a narrative spun with consummately skillful economy and simplicity.

Read *aloud* now the first seventeen verses of the story. This is as it should be rendered, since it was created (whether originally in oral or written form) for the ear rather than the eye, to be heard rather than read. The familiar lines of verses 16–17 are abused in their appropriation to the category of erotic love in popular song or cheap fiction: these are lines all the more magnificent in conveying the love of a younger for an older woman, a Moabite daughter for an Israelite mother!

The Book of Ruth presents two problems. What is the date of its composition and what is its purpose? Not uncommonly a late date, the fifth century, has been argued on the grounds, in part, that in the Hebrew canon, Ruth takes its place in the third and latest collection of writings finally incorporated. The story of the canon cannot be precisely reconstructed, but the three divisions, Law, Prophets, and Writings, did come in that chronological order to the status of canonical, holy scripture between about 400 B.C.E. and the decisive Council of Jamnia, about A.D. 90.[6]

[6]The best brief summary of the origin of the Old Testament canon is in O. Eissfeldt, *The Old Testament: An Introduction,* New York, 1965, pp. 560–71. See also N. H. Gottwald, *A Light to the Nations,* New York, 1959, pp. 29–36; J. Kenneth Kuntz, *The People of Ancient Israel,* New York, 1975, pp. 503–6. For a strongly dissenting judgment, see B. S. Childs, *Introduction to the Old Testament as Scripture,* Philadelphia, 1979, p. 53.

The present Hebrew canon looks like this:

1. Law, *torah:* Genesis-Deuteronomy.
2. Prophets, *nebi'im:*
   A. Former Prophets: Joshua, Judges, 1 and 2 Samuel, 1 and 2 Kings, counted as four books.
   B. Latter Prophets: Isaiah, Jeremiah, Ezekiel, and, reckoned as one book, the Book of the Twelve, Hosea-Malachi in RSV. These four, with the four former prophets, total eight books in the prophetic canon.
3. Writings, *ketubim:* 1 and 2 Chronicles (one book), Ezra-Nehemiah (one book), Esther, Job, Psalms, Proverbs, Ecclesiastes, Song of Solomon, Lamentations, Daniel, and Ruth—a total of eleven books.

Now, it might be assumed that a relatively late date for the Book of Ruth is supported by this division, since, admittedly, the Writings by and large are, in their present form, relatively late. As a matter of fact, however, the *original* Hebrew canon comprised not twenty-four books, as above, but only twenty-two books (this is the count given by the great Jewish historian, Josephus, in the first century A.D.). Ruth was then a part of Judges, and Lamentations was attached to Jeremiah. And we suspect that the argument from canon to date would in any case be indecisive, since there is late and relatively early material in all three divisions.

We doubt, then, that the story is postexilic. A number of distinguished scholars of the Hebrew language have insisted that on the grounds of style, vocabulary, and the form and syntax of the language, it cannot be dated later than the ninth to seventh centuries. In its present form, of course, it can hardly be dated earlier than the tenth century, since it envisages a measure of order in Canaan as well as cordial Moabite-Israelite relationships which were hardly possible before the time of David. And we suspect, too, that it is more in the nature of fiction than history (observe the typological meaning of the names: Mahlon, "sickness"; Chilion, "wasting"; Orpah "stiff-necked"; Naomi, "my sweetness"; and Ruth, a shortened form of a word meaning "companion").

Indeed (to turn to the second question), it has been proposed that the story of Ruth came into existence chiefly as a genealogical narrative—to preserve or comment upon the ancestry of King David: Ruth is David's great-grandmother (4:17; it is the fuller genealogical table of 4:18–22 that appears alien and secondary to the original story). The story then is hardly earlier than the tenth-century age of David and Solomon.

On the question of date, one can say little more than this. The postexilic daters have claimed support in the fact that the ritual of the shoe (4:8) is at odds with the prescription in Deuteronomic law (Deut. 23:3), a fact recognized and commented upon apologetically in the preceding verse 4:7. But that, we suspect, *is* a post-exilic comment added to the story. The custom recounted in the performance of levirate marriage in Ruth 4:8 (by which the brother or the next closest male kin takes the wife of the deceased relative) is, we should judge, considerably earlier than Deuteronomy.

As to the story's purpose, we are confident that it is *not* (as some remarkably allege) a subtle piece of fiction describing the practice of a Bethlehem fertility cult. Ruth *is* a lesson in tolerance, but we doubt that it was first created in response to the crusading spirit of the Israelite Society for Moabite friendship. Nor could it have been produced simply to make concrete some rumor of David's more distant Moabite blood. And we even doubt that the early support and elucidation of levirate marriage was its purpose, although if specific motivation must be assigned, this presents perhaps the strongest claim. We tend to concur in the wise comment that "if the author had an ulterior motive, he concealed it more successfully than is common to story-tellers who write with a purpose"; and, from another source, that the writer "set out to tell an interesting tale of long ago, and he carried out his purpose with notable success."

Gideon, Jotham, and Jephthah

Judges 6–12   Gideon's activities (6–8) center in Ophrah, a site unknown to us, but evidently near Shechem (see 9:1 ff.). His tribe is Manasseh and his problem is that of the age-old incursions into central Canaan of seminomadic Bedouin raiders (6:3, "Midianites and the Amalekites and the people of the East"). The story may well be composite, as witness the two names, Gideon and Jerubaal, and occasional duplicates such as 8:1–3 and 8:4–9. It is nevertheless an exciting and instructive episode in the life of one of the tribes soon to become a part of the nation Israel. Gideon is a charismatic figure, endowed with the spirit of Yahweh. He moves first against the apostate worship of Baal within his own immediate community. By clever stratagem he routs the Midianite enemy with the meager forces of his own clan, Abiezer, and captures and slaughters Midian's two chiefs, Zebah and Zalmunna, in the conventional act of blood-revenge to compensate and set right the loss of life inflicted by them. He takes bitter, but again no doubt conventional, revenge against the towns Succoth and Penuel for the taunting refusal of aid. He makes out of the spoils of battle an ephod, an object in the paraphernalia of a priest (not an image, as a later editor in verse 27 would have it). The ephod was sometimes an apron, but hardly here since it weighs about 65 pounds, and was employed for divining, that is, determining the will of Yahweh. He rejects the popular response that would make of him a monarch in language which no doubt was subsequently put to political use (or perhaps the precise *language* was only then created in the story?) by the Yahweh loyalists and other dissident members of monarchic Israel who deemed the institution of king to be itself an act of apostasy against Yahweh:

I will not rule over you, and my son will not rule over you: Yahweh will rule over you!

(8:23)

Judges 9 Gideon's son, Abimelech, does not share the sentiment attributed to his father and establishes himself for a brief period as king over the city of Shechem. The story of his aggressive rise preserves the exceedingly choice and ancient Fable of the Trees, or Jotham's Fable. The Fable is probably a *contemporary* commentary on one man's consuming ambition played out perhaps sometime around 1100 B.C.E. in the central hill country of ancient Palestine.

Judges 10–12 Although the years prior to Canaan's consolidation in political monarchy cannot be reconstructed in any detail, the stories of Judges do afford a remarkably vivid impression of the tone and character of the age, as well as insight into Israel's later interpretation of the anarchic period. Above all we have the realistic portrayal of a crude and bitter existence, but an existence given persistent light, relief, and meaning by the Yahweh-faith and the (consequent?) redeeming quality of human love. Jephthah is as rough and tough a package of chauvinistic male humanity as one will find anywhere, destined to act out his years in reaction to a human environment with which he always found himself at odds. Yet here he is, remembered and sung for his exploits on behalf of Israel (in Canaan's tribal confederation, however loose, one tribe's victory over a common enemy is other tribes' boon), fighting from the tribe and territory of Gilead east of the Jordan against Ammon. And here the term "shibboleth" (meaning a decisive test or snare) was coined in Jephthah's interconfederation feud with Ephraim (12:1 ff.). The most memorable and poignant feature of the Jephthah story is his tragic vow (but so thoroughly in character) and its genuinely moving sequence (whether interpreted as literal occurrence or as cult-myth). While we spontaneously react in revulsion to the theology of this kind of vow (by no means in principle a thing only of the past), we must understand the character of *that epoch:* this is Jephthah; this is premonarchic Canaan and preprophetic Yahwism; the victory, dear to Jephthah, is only Yahweh's to give, and if he gives it, he must receive in return some commensurate sacrifice. It may seem crude and misconceived by our standards, but our standards may not be imposed on that epoch more than three thousand years ago. All of which may (or may not) justify the comment that, at its highest and purest, the sincere sacrifice was (and is, properly conceived) a rite of communion between person or people and God, and a satisfying means by which created covenant humanity pays its debt of gratitude and love to the Creator.

The Samson Saga

Judges 13–16 The Samson stories probably continue to appeal to readers who read the Bible simply as they read the Iliad and the Odyssey. Samson is not a "judge," since his remarkable exploits are purely personal in character. There *may* have been a real man behind these stories, but what we have is a well-integrated collection of highly exaggerated hero tales. Samson is ancient Israel's Hercules or Paul Bunyan. This is not to say that elements of the Samson saga are not old: the riddles especially convey that age of anarchy, reflecting the ancient delight in the riddle, rough ("out of the strong came something sweet" 14:14) and, shall we say, ready ("If you had not plowed with my heifer you would not have found out my riddle" 14:18).

From Ambrose in the fourth century A.D. to Thomas Hayne and John Milton in the seventeenth century, there have been repeated attempts to maintain a proper "biblicity" for Samson by means of allegorical interpretation. Thus, James Calfhill in 1565 made Samson's victory with the jawbone of an ass an allegorical figure of "how Christ . . . hath overthrown the adversary Power; hath by one death destroyed all the enemies of life." Henoch

Clapham, confusing New Testament Galilean Nazareth with the Hebrew term *nazir* and the dedicated Old Testament order of Nazirite (see p. 93) declared in 1596: "A Nazarite he was, and a figure of our Nazaret anointed." Thomas Hayne saw, among other points, the following allegory early in the seventeenth century:

The Philistines having Sampson in Azza a strong citie, shut the gates upon him thought to hold him fast, and to prevail over him; but hee carried away the gates of the citie, and frustrated their plot.	The Jews and Romans having Christ in his grave a strong prison house, and him shut up with a grave stone sealed and kept with a watch, and thought there to hold him fast; but he conquered death and the grave, and rose again to life, never to die more.

And although Milton drew no overt allegory in his *Samson Agonistes*, 1671, it is probable that he and his readers assumed this kind of allegorical reading and "that this duality was part of —perhaps the center of—the meaning which the poet intended the tragedy to have."[7]

Such allegorizing is, of course, out of the question for us; and beyond this kind of literary-allegorical pursuit of the Samson saga we are able to find nothing. We cannot even appropriate for ourselves the kind of piety that produced this weak effort at salvage: "The important point [in the Samson stories] is Samson's radiant certainty that his tremendous strength, and his successes, were due to Jehovah [Yahweh], who filled him with His (Jehovah's) divine energy."[8]

We reject the sun-myth theory that Samson (Hebrew *shemshon* meaning "little sun") represents the survival of an ancient sun-worshiping cult. Whatever Samson is in the stories, he is because of Yahweh and not the sun; but we find nothing of a "radiant" faith, nor anything else worthy of even the earliest Yahwism in central Canaan. The stories do have some historical importance in that they betray the expanding power of the Philistines in the eleventh century. And this is surely the editorial justification for

[7]See further M. Krouse, *Milton's Samson and the Christian Tradition*, Princeton, N.J., 1949, especially pp. 119 ff.

[8]W. A. L. Elmslie, *How Came Our Faith*, New York, 1948, p. 161. For another interpretation see J. L. Crenshaw, "The Samson Saga: Filial Devotion or Erotic Attachment?" *Zietschrift für die alttestamentliche Wissenschaft*, 86, 1974, pp. 470–504.

Samson's place as the last of the "judges." It was, in the final analysis, the Philistine harassment that forced upon the tribes of Israel and the rest of Canaan a change from loose tribal confederation to monarchy.

"No King in Israel"

Judges 17-21 And since there is no king in Israel, it is a time when everyone does what is right in one's own eyes. This is the theme of these chapters (see 17:6; 18:1; 19:1; and the final verse, 21:25). In a story preserving a sizable nucleus from the purported age (chaps. 17-18), the tribe of Dan migrates from the central coastal area (near the Philistines, who no doubt forced them out) to north Canaan, demonstrating en route the power of any bullies to act as they would (see especially Judg. 18:21-26).

The story of Dan and the story of Gibeah and Benjamin (19-21) remind us of the *kind* of treasure the Old Testament is. It is the story of a people's life and no one denies that any such story, told by any people of themselves, will have its fictional aspects, its idealized accretions, its modifications of episodes and persons in the interests of pride, pretense, and piety. And the self-preserved past will always also undergo an unconscious, psychological screening. It remains nevertheless—and we know that this is repetition—one of the Old Testament's qualities of greatness that the *real* past is withal preserved, albeit not always in detail, not always in sequence, and not always with consistent external precision.

We will probably never be able to vouch for *any* given, specific detail of the marvelous array of stories brought together in the Book of Judges. But in reading them all, we can confidently affirm that we are there, that this is the time, the color, the smell, the feeling of the age. This is Israel and Yahweh when Israel was still becoming Israel and when Yahweh was not yet "the Holy One in your midst" who brought up Israel *and* the Philistines *and* the Syrians (Amos 9:7), who loved and created not only Israel but Egypt and Assyria as well (Isa. 19:25). And this land of Canaan before it was the land of Israel. It is the land of Canaan in anarchy, and in the story of its essential nature there is no mincing of words.

We see certain qualities which have been realistically preserved and recreated—this utterly noneuphemized story of the sojourning Levite and his concubine, the degenerate townsmen, the woman's tragic fate and the unhappy mores which dictated the circumstances (cf. Genesis 19), the Levite's shockingly dramatic response, the attrition of Benjamin, and the episodes of that tribe's very meager reconstitution (was Benjamin in fact depleted by Philistine massacre over the years?).

On this sorry foundation, faith was able to build the emergent prophetic Yahwism of Israel; or better, prophetic Yahwism was able to come intact *through* this hard moral and political debacle with resurgent power beneficial to human existence then and in every subsequent epoch in history.

5

Monarchy

Samuel, Saul, and David:
1 Samuel 1–2 Samuel 8

> See him whom [Yahweh] has chosen.
>
> *1 Sam. 10:24*[1]

Originally one book, and presenting a relatively poorly preserved text, the books of Samuel include:

1 (1–15)   The fortunes of Samuel, Eli, and the ark; and Saul to the point of his rejection by Samuel.

1 (16)–2 (8) Narratives of Saul and David.

2 (9–20)   Events of David's reign (with 1 Kings 1–2).

2 (21–4)   An appendix—a collection of miscellaneous pieces.

We are by now familiar with the "literary" phenomena of a composite text which meet us again here, betraying both the plurality of underlying sources (we shall simply use the symbols A and B for relatively early and late material) and the strong editorial hand of the deuteronomic historian(s), DH, responsible for the unified structure of the block. Deuteronomy-Kings. We are not surprised, then, by duplicate and even triplicate episodes: the fall of Eli's house, 2:31 ff. and 3:11 ff.; Samuel's anointing Saul once privately, 9:26 ff., and twice publicly, 10:17 ff. and 11:15; Saul's double rejection by Samuel in theological but not circumstantial duplicate narratives (1 Sam. 13; 15; and 20:42b); the repeated episode of David's sparing Saul's life (24:3 ff. and 26:5 ff.); the duplicated account of his seeking refuge from Saul with the Philistine Achish, king of Gath (21:10 ff. and 27:1 ff.); the account of Goliath's dispatch by David (1 Samuel 17), and

---

[1]Cf. 1 Chronicles 15; Psalm 132.

again by Elhanan, one of David's distinguished soldiers (2 Sam. 21:19). (The chronicler in 1 Chron. 20:5 seeks to harmonize the contradiction by adding to the account of Elhanan's exploit the words *Lahmi the brother of G*oliath.) And the hand of DH will be recognized: we know something of the character of deuteronomic piety, and we shall see evidence now of the strong DH bias in favor of the southern, Judean half of the short-lived united monarchy.

Prelude to Kingship

1 Samuel 1-8   The story of the making of monarchy is introduced with the somewhat idealized account of the birth and early years of Samuel (Samuel 1-3). This is the most appropriate beginning since it is he who plays the role of kingmaker in Israel. In the utterly tragic figure of old Eli and in the loss of the ark, the symbol of God's presence, from the central sanctuary at Shiloh (probably destroyed by the Philistines in this time), we are further prepared for the establishment of monarchy in Israel: it was Philistine aggression, far too powerful to be checked by the resources of a loose tribal confederation, which precipitated the chain of events leading through Saul and David to a unified and extensive, if short-lived, united Israelite kingdom.

We do not know the ultimate point of origin of the Philistines. They must have settled sometime around 1200 B.C.E. in the coastal plain between the Mediterranean and the Judean hill country. There is some evidence of their earlier, more or less temporary, residence in the Aegean Islands and Asia Minor; and they, or related "maritime people," actually threatened twelfth-century Egypt, as we know from records of Ramses III (*c.* 1175–1144). It is clear in any case that during the twelfth and eleventh centuries they formed a powerful pentapolis made up of the five tightly coordinated city-states of Gaza, Ashkelon, Ashdod, Ekron, and Gath, which ultimately gained control of most of Canaan west of the Jordan. The name Palestine is derived from their name, Philistine.

Do not fail to note the theme of these chapters. Unlike the conditions prevailing earlier, the various tribes of Israel are now reduced by the same enemy; and it is this external threat which ultimately leads to the Israelite monarchy. Philistine control was in some respects minimal and relatively unoppressive, and therefore the threat was not to their existence but to their peace in the full sense of that word—their fulfilled existence. Note also in this prelude to kingship, 1 Samuel 1-8, the following features of the narrative.

"The Song of Hannah" in 2:1-10 is probably later than its context (the institution of monarchy is assumed already in v. 10) and can be removed without injury to itself or the story. In this respect, and others, it compares remarkably to the Magnificat of Mary in Luke 1:46-56. The presence of both of these psalmlike pieces in present context simply testifies again to the faith of the believing community that the life of God impinges on the course of human events with power, purpose, and compassion, and particularly on behalf of the weak, the poor, and the oppressed.

Note the starkly portrayed tragic dimension in old Eli, shamed by his sons, 2:22 ff., in broken relationship to Yahweh, 2:27-36, and dying in the anguished knowledge that his sons have been killed and the ark of Yahweh captured by the Philistines. There is tragedy also in the very words of Philistine to Philistine, 4:9, and in the bitter scene of the birth and naming of the child Ichabod, Eli's grandson, 4:19-22. It is not an unrelieved sense of tragedy: Israel records with humor and glee in 1 Samuel 5-6 the humiliation, in the presence of the ark, of Dagon, god of Philistia, and the humiliation by a plague of the Philistines themselves, regarded as a result of having the ark in their midst. Note also the realistic ancient conviction of taboo reflected in the story of the ark's return to Bethshemesh (6:19 ff.; not to Shiloh because, we suspect, the Philistines had already destroyed it).

Finally, note in these and subsequent chapters the dual, if not conflicting, representations of the person and role of Samuel and of the whole concept of monarchy. Predominantly in chapters 7-8, and also in 10:17-25 and chapter 12, Samuel is a gigantic figure, possessing the greatest attributes of Moses, Joshua, and the most distinguished of the Judges; he is himself adequate for the needs of Israel. This view of Samuel goes naturally hand in hand with a totally negative judgment of the monarchy, which regards it as a grave mistake perversely instituted by sinful Israel against the will of Yahweh and contrary to the judgment of Samuel.

Saul and Samuel

1 Samuel
9–15

According to a second point of view (predominantly, 9–11 and 13–14), Samuel is a seer, a clairvoyant—we might call him a professional occultist. Correspondingly, the monarchy is seen as the will of Yahweh, declared and implemented through Samuel. This representation of the immediate premonarchic time no doubt draws from originally older and more intimately informed narrative strands from what we have called the A stratum. We are nevertheless sure that the present composite narrative constitutes a fuller and even more accurate history. There is every reason to believe that Samuel was in fact a man of many roles: seer but judge; clairvoyant but also prophet; and at the same time kingmaker of ambivalent feeling and motivation.[2] There is every reason to believe that while subsequent disillusionment with kingship in Israel is reflected in B strands of the narrative, an element of sheer realism is also preserved: that is, that there were contemporaneously in Israel Yahweh loyalists, prophets, and others who regarded monarchy as a pagan innovation borrowed from and patterned after the related but generally estranged kingdoms of Moab and Ammon and as such a flagrant rejection not only of the traditional ways of the tribes of Israel, but of course also of Yahweh. And on the essential point of faith, the composite narrative is at one with itself; consenting or disapproving, honored or aggrieved, it is Yahweh and Samuel who are directly responsible for Saul's quasi-kingship and David's ultimate creation of full monarchy. In Israel's ancient faith, Yahweh does not impose divine will arbitrarily upon the covenant people in the midst of their history, but in the course *which they elect,* by one means or another, Yahweh's own historical purposes for them are effected. Yahweh may approve or disapprove of the monarchy which they will have; but that political institution will succeed in serving the ends of Yahweh's covenant purpose: the ultimate, sometime, someway blessing of the families of the earth.

The whole deuteronomic history of Samuel-Kings is a remarkably varied story on a single theme. For Yahweh's own purposes, a people is created as a world was created, out of chaos. The intention of divine purpose and meaning was frustrated by human pride, by the rejection of given order. And the order which Yahweh would create and sustain becomes thus reduced again to the chaos out of which Yahweh will nevertheless still effect the

---

[2]Samuel's ambivalence is discerningly portrayed in D. H. Lawrence's play, *David,* available in *Religious Drama I,* M. Halverson, ed., *Living Age Books,* New York, 1957.

covenant purpose. This is the theological theme repeatedly sounded throughout Samuel-Kings—in the narratives of Israel under the Philistines, of Saul, of David, of Solomon, and of the succession of the kings of Israel, North and South, to the tragic closing of the Israelite monarchy.

See this portrayed vividly and with doubled emphasis in the Samuel-Saul cycle. Saul is surely one of history's greatest and most tragic figures. By his courageous heart, his valiant leadership against Philistia, and his faith that he is Yahweh's choice, he achieves a position of strength and prominence among most of the tribes of Israel, quite exceeding that of any previous "judge" but clearly short of full kingship. In chapters 13 and 15 (theological but not precisely episodical duplicates), he is publicly rejected by Samuel-Yahweh; and with traumatic knowledge that his cause is no longer Yahweh's cause or that Yahweh's cause is no longer his cause, that magnificent man, the courageous heart, the valiant leadership are seen to shrivel, disintegrate, and atrophy. Who can say whether the theological judgment is "right" or "wrong"? We who read of him are nevertheless moved to repeat the lines of David's lament, mourning Saul's (and Johathan's) death: "How are the mighty fallen!" (2 Sam. 1:19,25,27).

David and Saul

1 Samuel 16–31

At Yahweh's behest Samuel annoints David in a strictly private ceremony: this is Samuel's (and therefore Yahweh's) choice for the future (16:1–13, B). Saul, deprived of Samuel's support and no doubt aware of his own inadequacy and Israel's against Philistine aggression, suffers from severe depression and ironically finds the antidote to his illness only in David's musical gifts (16:13–23, A). David comes to Saul with an incomparable recommendation: "skillful in playing, a man of valor, a man of war, prudent in speech, and a man of good presence"; and as if this were not enough, the further word that "Yahweh is with him" (16:18). This is, of course, no incidental comment. This is the point of the narratives: Yahweh is with David. All that is recounted in the progressively deteriorating relationship of David and Saul is intended to illustrate this theme. This is true of the tale of David's conquest of Goliath, chapter 17. In this clearly composite work, David is quite unknown to Saul. The theme that David is peculiarly endowed with the spirit of Yahweh dominates the David-Jonathan relationship and, with greater or less direct control, determines the editor's selection of available narratives that deal with the intricate and tragic Saul-David relationship.

The story is its own best commentary. The greater part of the second half of 1 Samuel is assigned to A, which is simply to say that, by and large, we suspect that these episodes in the lives of Saul and Jonathan and David are accurately informed. They are certainly brilliantly narrated and take the point of view which holds David to be Yahweh's direct choice, in whom the Yahweh-blessing firmly resides. Some modern interpreters feel that every move of this uncommonly gifted man was calculated in terms of its political expediency in achieving his own ambitious ends.[3] Certainly David was ambitious. Undeniably he was a man of almost uncanny political astuteness. Nor do we doubt that some of his acts of magnanimity were *also* calculated to his own advantage. The total political accomplishment of David still stands as a nearly incredible feat, and let no one be so naïve as to suppose that this kind of performance is carried out anywhere, in any time, by unadulterated goodness and nobility of character. These biographical notes on the life of David acknowledge and illustrate David's moral ambivalence and even duplicity, and yet at the same time present us with one who, as mortals go, is superior not only in the qualities of winsomeness and shrewdness, but also in the solid virtues that issue from a dominant integrity.

The Full Accession of David

2 Samuel 1–8

Saul's death (1 Samuel 31) hardly warrants the term suicide unless the narrative deliberately falsifies the facts in order to spare the reputation of Saul—and this is unlikely. He and his sons, including Jonathan, die in a cause they know to be doomed even before that final battle with the Philistines begins; and Saul, this figure of stark tragedy drawn in heroic dimensions, makes his exit from Israel's history with his essential stature of greatness still intact. If the moving lines of the lament (2 Sam. 1:19 ff.) over the death of Saul and Jonathan are in fact David's (as appears to be probable) it becomes more difficult to maintain the interpretation of David as a man of unmitigated, calculating ambition. These

[3]Cf. M. Noth, *History of Israel,* rev. trans. S. Godman, New York, 1960, pp. 179 ff. Noth's position is corroborated by A. D. H. Mayes, "The Rise of the Israelite Monarchy," *Zietschrift für die alttestamentliche Wissenschaft,* 90, 1978, pp. 1–19.

words are more than a lyrical garland tossed toward Saul's adherents in an effort to win them (although we do not suppose for a moment that David was unaware of the positive political implications of his public and phenomenally articulate grief). The lament undeniably expresses genuine sorrow and a profound sense of personal bereavement, and unmistakably attests to David's love and affection for father and son.

We repeat that the narratives here are their own best commentary. This is the unimpeachable stuff of history, history at its best —history articulated and shaped by the very participants in the narrated events and unabashedly interpreted from an internal and involved standpoint, from a position within the history. The participants—David and his contemporaries in Israel—believe that David is Yahweh's own, select person, coming now to the leadership of Yahweh's people, in Yahweh's land, to form Yahweh's kingdom, and (always implicitly at the core of the Yahweh faith) to fulfill Yahweh's purposes in history. Such a record requires no commentary, but only an alert, sympathetic, and sensitive hearer-reader. David, endowed of Yahweh, possesses in these years and through these episodes a kind of Midas-touch. The Philistines, with whom he has earlier been allied, stand confidently by while this old friend is elevated to tribal kingship in Hebron over the small confederation of southern tribes (2:1–4). Internal events in Israel all operate, by accident or manipulation, in David's favor (chaps. 2–4). Now the northern tribes *request* that David assume rule over them; and a narrator gives us his own and what he obviously believes also to be David's interpretation of the whole astonishing sequence of events:

David perceived that Yahweh had established him king over Israel, and that he had exalted his kingdom *for the sake of his people Israel.*

(5:12)

The last major Canaanite (Jebusite) city-fortress, Jerusalem, is taken (5:6–10) and the Philistines, asleep on their feet or successfully lulled by the political charm and machinations of David, suddenly come fully awake (5:17–22). Now the ark is brought to the new capital of Jerusalem (6:1–16: this reminds us of the narrative of the ark's earlier possession of potent taboo during and following its Philistine sojourn) and David secures Saul's daughter Michal, this time surely in an act predominantly politically motivated. The editor adds, from the B complex of narratives, the David-Nathan-Yahweh conversations over the question of a temple in Jerusalem (8:1 ff.; cf. 1 Chron. 28:11–19).

This remarkable section on David's full accession to political kingship over the tribes of Israel and the land of Canaan is summed up and also favorably judged in the words of 2 Sam. 8:15:

So David reigned over all Israel; and David administered justice and equity to all his people.

David, Uriah, and Absalom: 2 Samuel 21–24, 8–20

> Evil out of your own house.
> *2 Sam. 12:11*[4]

The block of chapters 2 Samuel 9–20, with its original conclusion in 1 Kings 1–2, has been justly described as the prose masterpiece of the Hebrew Bible. This is the written work of a highly articulate, gifted, and informed historian who may well have shared as colleague and participant the days of David's mature years. In this remarkable biography, even details appear to be authentic and unimpeachable. And yet, as tends to be true of Old Testament history, this is obviously written not merely for the sake of preserving history of the life of David, the king, but in order to extract from the history its essential meaning in the Yahweh-faith. The historian passionately believes that the sequential events in these years of David's reign are fundamentally shaped by the covenant fact of Yahweh's decisive involvement in the life of Israel and his efficacious impingement upon the life of history. In this sense, therefore, this too is in the nature of prophetic history, that is, history in which the historian, wittingly or involuntarily, acts as representative and interpreter of the Yahweh-faith. Here as in the Saul cycle of stories the *historical* turning point is theologically conceived: both Saul and David are seen to suffer anguished reversal of fortune not in terms of causality, not as the result of mere circumstance, not as blind historical accident, but precisely as the judgment of Yahweh, the

[4]Cf. Psalm 13.

negative response of Yahweh to the misresponse of the king to the covenant God of Israel. Saul is expelled from the kingdom for what is twice represented as an act of unwarranted pride (1 Samuel 13 and 15); the theological "plot" is closely parallel to the story of the Garden in Genesis 3. David's reversal takes the form of alienation within his own communities—family, city, and kingdom—as a result of this violent desecration of community (2 Samuel 11); and here the theological scheme parallels that of the story of the Brothers in Genesis 4. We shall see in the next section that the reign of Solomon is similarly interpreted as turning on an act—apostasy—in violation of the Yahweh-faith (1 Kings 11), in response to which Yahweh brings to violent, tragic rupture the unity of Israel. And this too has its parallel in the Yahwist's prelude to the Old Testament in the story of the Tower, Genesis 11.

And so, for all the intimacy and accuracy of the present record of David, this is not what we would call "objective" history, since the decisive force is without question deemed to be outside and above the plane of history, in the person of Yahweh, who, although effectively involved in history, is nevertheless suprahistorical.

The Situation

2 Samuel
21–24, 8–10

David has attained the pinnacle. His achievement, we think, is the work of a devoted man—devoted certainly to David, but also in uncommon and laudable measure to Israel and to Yahweh. We do not try to maintain that he has reached the summit utterly clean and untarnished. Narratives constituting an appendix to the books of Samuel (2 Samuel 21–24, interrupting the original unit of 2 Samuel 9–20 plus 1 Kings 1–2) remind us of the degree to which David was a product of his own time, and a full-fledged member of the political race. See respectively 2 Sam. 24 and 21:1–14. Both stories are authentic and come from David's earlier years. The former describes how David incurs the active displeasure of Yahweh by taking a census. It is useless to speculate on the "why" of this episode—are population figures deemed to be nobody's business but Yahweh's, or is there implicit condemnation of the possibly sinister *ends* of census-taking, namely, heavy taxation and conscription? In any case, the story reminds us again of the strong sense of group solidarity in the ancient East and specifically in ancient Israel. In the narrative of 2 Sam.

21:1-14, even the most ardent supporter of the winsome David must read with suspicion David's consent to and implementation of the slaughter of the surviving males of the house of Saul (save only one, to whom we will come in a moment). Equally suspect is the rationale for this purge (designed, of course, to put David above political reproach), and David's calculated gesture of rapprochement with the adherents of Saul in the final disposal of all the mortal remains of the male Saulides (2 Sam. 21:12-14).

David's variously motivated ambition is attained. He has trained and fought with a mighty band of warriors, some of whom on occasion have saved his life (21:15-17) or tilted with Philistine giants (21:18-21); and once, in a moving episode of mutual loyalty and admiration, three of their number risked seemingly probable death to answer David's longing for the cool water of Bethlehem's well (23:13-17). Philistia on the coast and Moab across the Jordan are subdued (8:1-2), and more remote potential enemies are unable to offer David any serious threat (8:3-14). The sole male survivor of Saul and Jonathan is, in a gesture at once magnanimous and politically astute, brought into the king's household, to "eat at the king's table," live on the king's bounty—of course under the constant surveillance of the king's staff (chap. 9). With the situation thus in hand both without and within the kingdom the narrative of chapter 10 adds the advice, and brilliantly illustrates it, that in the person of Joab, David has a commander-in-chief not only of fabulous competence, but possessing an admirable quality of Yahweh-faith in the bargain (see 10:12).

Oh what a beautiful morning David has had!

Spring Night in Jerusalem

2 Samuel 11-12

"It happened late one afternoon when David arose from his couch . . ." (11:2). It is spring, "the time when kings go forth to battle." But David has sent Joab against the Ammonites while he, the king, "remained at Jerusalem" (11:1).

There is no combination of situation and season comparable to Jerusalem in the spring. Other cities of renown have laid claim to preeminence in this regard (for example, "Paris in the spring"); and we have met personally the ravishing coincidence of April or May in Athens and Rome, in Washington and New York, in Atlanta and San Francisco, in Cairo and Damascus, in Munich and Berlin, in Nanking and Shanghai and Kobe and Yokohama. Each of these has its peculiar excellence under spring's invasion, but nothing exceeds the intoxication of Jerusalem in early April, a condition lyrically and erotically memorialized by an uncommonly articulate resident of Jerusalem some centuries after David:

> Arise, my love, my fair one,
>   and come away;
> for lo, the winter is past,
>   the rain is over and gone.
> The flowers appear on the earth,
>   the time of singing has come,
> and the voice of the turtledove
>   is heard in our land.
> The fig tree puts forth its figs,
>   and the vines are in blossom;
>   they give forth fragrance.
> Arise, my love, my fair one,
>   and come away.
> (Song of Solomon, 2:10–13)

An idle, aging king in the heady, evening air of a Jerusalem springtime: the beautiful Bathsheba and her incorruptible husband Uriah; the king's prompt, efficient, confident steps to cover the results of his lustful intoxication; Uriah's integrity as soldier and his unwitting and ultimately fatal frustration of David's self-protective scheme merely by the virtue of his extreme loyalty to his compatriots still in the field; David's unhesitating but premeditated resort to murder; the complicity of Joab, always intensely, blindly loyal to David; and continuing this picture of the king's total moral collapse in steps of progressive deterioration, David's calloused words of reassurance to Joab, "Do not let this matter trouble you . . ."; and at last the consummation of the whole sorry episode when Bathsheba is added to David's harem and another son added to his progeny. Here, too, one might murmur, "How are the mighty fallen!"

Such behavior by the king in ancient oriental monarchy was not, we think, as common as is sometimes alleged. On the other hand, it appears certain that the total historical response to this in Israel, and, particularly, within Israelite Yahwism, was unprecedented and unique. It remains one of the distinctive aspects of Israelite monarchy that it was not deemed to be absolute. In Israel the only absolute is Yahweh, and repeatedly Yahweh's "agents" the prophets, assume in Yahweh's name a role of authority above even the king's authority to rebuke, condemn, and declare judgment upon the king.

"The thing that David had done displeased Yahweh" (11:27); and the prophet Nathan is Yahweh's instrument for checking and containing the swollen pride of David (chap. 12). David's response to the prophet's incisive, devastating parable is not the response of a monarch to a brash subject or courtier, but, in this case in full contrition, of a covenant person to the Word: "I have sinned against Yahweh!" The sentence of death, which David himself has meted out, is removed; but the faith which gives form to the biography regards the harassed remainder of David's life as the fulfillment of an irremovable and unalterable judgment. For lust, arrogance, covetousness, adultery, calculated competence in compounding wrong, for deliberate murder, and for highhanded indifference to this wholesale shattering of covenant commandment—for all this, you shall know now the kind of violence you have perpetrated on Uriah, and the same loss of sexual prerogatives which you inflicted upon him. All this evil will come against you *out of your own house!* (see 12:7–12).

The child conceived in that spring night in Jerusalem did not live, and something of the strength of the old David is heard in his courageous response to the death (12:20–23). This sequence, which is the turning point in David's reign, closes with Solomon's birth to David and Bathsheba (12:24), and David's triumphant "conquest" of the Ammonite capital across the Jordan, a farce set up by the loyal Joab (12:26 ff.).

The Grotesque Triangle

2 Samuel 13–14

David is to be succeeded by his (and Bathsheba's) son Solomon, whose despotic, ostentatious reign (contrary to the still glowing Solomonic legends) leads directly to the rupture of the united Israelite kingdom. But, at least in the understanding of David's historian, the real turning point, not merely in the life of David but in the life of the kingdom, is in the center of David's reign. Ultimate responsibility for the collapse of the united monarchy must fall upon David, whose failure is seen as essentially a failure of faith, a moral failure in the broad sense—a failure to act according to covenant faith and in covenant righteousness. And again, the order and meaning which Yahweh would impart to Israel is reduced to chaos by the failure of faith, by the response of unfaith.

The anguish that is now David's—an anguish produced out of his own house—is at least as profound as that of the tragic Saul. There can be no doubt (at least *I* do not doubt) that, in his encounter with the prophet Nathan, David felt the full force of his own despicable role in the David-Bathsheba-Uriah triangle. But if time began to ease his guilt, it was a short-lived reprieve, for in the intimate circle of his own children the primary components of his own heinous behavior are reenacted. Amnon, David's oldest son and heir-apparent, vents a sexual aggression more rampant than his father's not upon another man's wife but upon his own half-sister Tamar, David's daughter and the full-sister of Absalom. Not only does David see his own sexual arrogance manifested in one of his sons, but he must also witness in another son that driving political ambition which he had held in check to some degree, but which in Absalom becomes a ruling and ultimately uncontrollable passion. In a grotesque modification of the triangle in which David played so wretched a role, these traits in his sons lead to the same bleak end—murder. In the Amnon-Tamar-Absalom triangle, David's son Amnon is both the perpetrator of incestuous rape and the victim of homicidal passion—he is, then, David and Uriah. David's daughter Tamar plays the role of violated woman, the victim of her brother. And David's son Absalom reenacts David's role of murderer, unleashing against a brother the same calculated passion of David against Uriah. Amnon blocked Absalom's way to the throne: in both cases, then, the victim threatened the aggressor. Amnon-Tamar-Absalom: "evil out of your own house."[5]

Son with a Chariot

2 Samuel 15–20

The winsomeness of the younger David is incarnate now in Absalom. The deep hurt which Saul knew from his "son" David (see 1 Sam. 24:11,16) David knows in full bitter measure. Absalom is utterly without scruples, a man in whom the vile passions against which David had certainly struggled are in full control.

And he is David's son. Were David and his advisers *at any time* unaware of Absalom's intentions? The structure of David's court

[5]For a fuller commentary on this, and other narratives of the united Israelite kingdom, see B. D. Napier, *From Faith to Faith,* New York, 1955, pp. 108–55. The most distinguished, now classic, study in this area is L. Rost, *Die Ueberlieferung von der Thronnachfolge Davids,* Stuttgart, 1926, a work which unfortunately was never translated into English.

may have been relatively simple (2 Sam. 20:23–26 and 8:16–18), but it was obviously an exceedingly competent organization. If David's normally shrewd and sensitive political faculties were stupefied by his doting love for Absalom, we can hardly expect the same of his advisers, one of whose gifts in counsel is boldly likened to the very oracle of God (2 Sam. 16:23). Under the circumstances, we can only suppose that David's evacuation of the capital, Jerusalem, before Absalom's advance from Hebron in the south (a shrewd choice by Absalom: it was *from Hebron* that David had earlier moved the capital) must have been voluntary and, we suspect, imposed by the king arbitrarily upon a strongly disapproving Joab and army, and indeed the whole of David's staff.

One may repeat here yet again that the text is its own superb commentary. We must not overlook the loyalty of David's mercenary troops (15:19–21); the narrator's conviction of the mature quality of David's faith (15:25 f.; 16:12); the essential gentleness of David in these most wretched hours (16:5–14); the brilliant, carnal symbol of Absalom's irrevocable usurpation (16:20–22) and its portentous recall of the David-Nathan encounter (2 Sam. 12:11–12); the arch Old Testament realist, the remarkable pragmatist Ahithophel (17:1–23); Joab, who always acts like Joab (18:10–15; 19:1–7; 20:4–13); David's pathetic concern, implicit throughout, for the defiant son (18:1–5); the moving grief of a father's utter brokenness at the loss of his son (18:33); the reassertion in this critical time of the old and always fundamental north-south cleavage (19:11,41–43); David's profound and probably chronic annoyance with the crude, brash, "muscular" ways of Joab and his brothers, the sons of Zeruiah (16:10; 19:22; see also 3:34b; 3:38 f.); and finally, in a kind of pausal summary before the last scene of David's reign in 1 Kings 1–2, the statement of David's very modest bureaucracy (20:23–26; cf. the extensive elaboration of this structure under Solomon, 1 Kings 4:1 ff.).

This is the brilliant story of David's mature reign in which order becomes chaos in the form of evil out of David's own house. We, who stand outside the covenant faith of ancient Israel, may want to question or to alter the historian's interpretation of these episodes and events in the king's life, but we must first acknowledge the original interpretation: the king, the kingdom, and the reign—all these that might have been glorious but for the violation of the covenant community, the Yahweh faith, and Yahweh, the Author. What might have been was not, because of the failure of faith, which is the failure of justice and equity and compassion and righteousness in the social fabric of the covenant community.

David, Solomon, and the Kingdom: 2 Samuel 21–24; 1 Kings 1–11

> For David's sake.
> *1 Kings 11:12*

We looked in the preceding section at several of the component pieces in the appendix to the book(s) of Samuel (2 Samuel 21–24). In addition to these (blood revenge upon the house of Saul, 21:1–14; the census, 24; the water of Bethlehem's well, 23:13–17; and the list of warriors, 21:15–22) we find another list of David's "mighty men," the most distinguished of his soldiers (Uriah is one of them, 23:39) in 23:8–39, of which the episode of Bethlehem's well is a part. These two lists, 21:15–22 and 23:8–39, were no doubt originally a unit, broken by the insertion of two psalmlike pieces attributed to David.

The second of these, 23:1–7, appears to be a late composition and purports to be the last words of David. The first, chapter 22, also appears, with a few minor differences, as Psalm 18. That it cannot be *in its present form* a composition of David is on every hand agreed; but whereas most scholars of preceding generations confidently assigned the psalm to a much later age (some as late even as the second century B.C.), there is now strong support for the view that this psalm had its original formulation (subsequently expanded, to be sure) if not from David, then from the time of David or very close to David's time. It takes its place among a considerable number of psalms which may be called Royal Psalms, setting forth (as, for example, Psalm 72) the ideal of righteous kingship under Yahweh which had its origin and, always in tradition, its supreme expression in the Davidic covenant.[6]

---

[6]Cf. A. R. Johnson, *Sacral Kingship in Ancient Israel,* Cardiff, 1955, p. 15; E. Jacob, *Theology of the Old Testament,* New York, 1958, pp. 234–39; Keith R. Crim, *The Royal Psalms,* Richmond, 1962; G. von Rad, *Old Testament Theology,* New York, vol. 1, pp. 318 ff.

The Acts of David's Dotage

1 Kings 1–2 This is the continuation and conclusion of that superb performance of the historian's art, 2 Samuel 9–20. Not in the Old Testament nor anywhere else have we anything comparable to this intimate, eloquent, profoundly moving tragedy of three thousand
years ago.

The opening episode (1 Kings 1:1–4) is emphatically not in
deference to popular taste for smutty or racy details from the life
of a public figure. The narrator brilliantly conveys the senile condition of the king and at the same time introduces the innocent
figure of the warm-bodied, beautiful young woman whose strong
appeal to Adonijah precipitates Adonijah's death and secures his
younger half-brother Solomon's accession to the throne.

As always it is the genius of this narrative that it leaves the
readers quite on their own in the assessment of motives and the interpretation of details. Tradition vastly magnifies Solomon, the
successor to David; and it is easy to assume the illegitimacy and
the "wrongness" of opposing claimants. Adonijah *sounds* and
looks like another Absalom, but with the significant exception
that his father's life is finished and that he has no intention of
usurping his father's place. And he is the next in line (1:6). It is a
point in his favor that he enjoys the support of Joab and Abiathar
the priest: it is difficult if not impossible to think that either of
these would have supported him if David himself were on record
in support of another candidate. We doubt, then, that the
Solomon conspiracy of Nathan, Bathsheba, Zadok, and Benaiah
had David's support as they claimed (1:13). David's senility is successfully put to their uses, and Solomon, son of Bathsheba, is
made king. It may be significant that Nathan, who masterminds
the plot and its execution, is not here represented as acting at the
behest of the Word of Yahweh as twice earlier he is (2 Sam. 7:4 ff.
and 12:1 ff.). If David authorized the bloody purge to remove all
real and potential threats to Solomon's position, it was "authorization" from the surviving body of the already departed David,
from the irresponsible lips of an old man in advanced senility.

One must recall in chapter 2 that verses 3–4, 10–12, and 27 are
editorial additions from the hand of DH (that is, the deuteronomic historians who fashioned the block of Deuteronomy
through 2 Kings from numerous sources). Otherwise, it is a
calculating and merciless Solomon whose "hatchet-man"

Benaiah dispatches in cold blood first Adonijah, then Joab, then Shimei. We are not reading too much into this remarkable narrative of 2 Samuel 9–20; 1 Kings 1–2, when we read the present concluding line, "*So* the kingdom was established in the hand of Solomon."

The Solomon Legend

1 Kings 3–10 Negative evidence against Solomon and his reign is overwhelming. All the more remarkable, then, the persistence and extravagance of what may be called the Solomon legend. The unknown author whose distinguished work of history we have been reading leaves us now. This is material from a variety of other sources. Chapter 3 gives us a highly idealized and stuffily pious account of the wisdom of Solomon. This hard-fisted "fascist" who in the preceding chapter wipes away his potential opposition in a smear of blood appears now a Jekyll to his previous Hyde. To put it mildly, 3:7–9 is out of character: ". . . I am but a little child; I do not know how to go out or come in"(!). Even more out of character are God's words (perhaps significantly not Yahweh's) in verses 11–14: ". . . none like you has been before you and none like you shall arise after you . . . no other king shall compare with you all your days." One could believe that Yahweh might speak so in irony! And one could then also read a meaning certainly not intended by the legend in the following verse: "And Solomon awoke, and behold it was a dream."

But so that we, the readers, will know that this is a dream of substance, the story continues with the famous illustration of the king's wisdom in the disposition of the case of the disputed baby. This legend intends to portray not only the king's wisdom but his accessibility to the meanest of the population—a claim for Solomon, we suspect, even further from the truth. And the essential Solomon legend now moves in a gusty crescendo to its fabulous climax in 4:20–34.

The Solomonic legend continues to be sounded through the more reliable accounts of his prowess as builder and patron of the arts. Solomon was ambitious for the kingdom—of Solomon; and relative to anything ever known in Israel, at least, his public works program was incredibly lavish and, no doubt to the discerning, ostentatious and pretentious. Under Solomon, Israelite art and architectural forms were largely nonindigenous. His alliance with Hiram, king of Tyre (in reality, king of all Phoenicia), provided

Solomon's Israel with the resources of a people singularly advanced both economically and culturally; and Solomon's costly but no doubt magnificent building program, including the temple, employed Hiram's architects, designers, and engineers. Two great pieces of prophetic composition lyrically extol the superior virtues of Tyre, the capital and symbol of Phoenician culture (Isaiah 23 and Ezekiel 27).

The legend of Solomon is not without foundation in fact, as we shall see in a moment; and some of the legend's accretions are superb creations, instructive to the life and faith of Israel and emanating from deep within it. Such is the character of the long speech and prayer put on Solomon's lips on the occasion of the dedication of the temple (1 Kings 8:12-61). This is the work of DH at DH's best, drawn in part from the living liturgy and prayers incorporated in the whole temple institution. If the language of the speech and prayer sometimes appears crassly materialistic by our standards, we must not miss the sensitivity, the depth, and, in the best sense of the word, the sophistication of the theology especially apparent in verses 27-50. Tradition is right in ascribing this to the Solomon of the legend, since indeed such a Solomon might well have prayed for the future of his own people that in every evil contingency Yahweh would hear and would forgive, renew, and restore the life of the people.

Solomon and the Kingdom of David

1 Kings 3-11 David's problems emanated largely from the very considerable community of his own household. David was at his weakest and most inept in these relationships. But the vast structure of the kingdom—indeed, the empire—was securely maintained throughout his reign by his brilliant capacities as political administrator and, of course, by the superior military establishment under Joab. Solomon possessed neither. He conspicuously lacked the political comprehension and sensitivity of David; and while he elaborated the physical facilities of the Israelite military,[7] the fundamental security of the Davidic kingdom was critically undermined, probably early in Solomon's reign, by a resurgent Edom under Hadad

[7]The builder Solomon was at work as far south as the Gulf of Aqabah at the port city of Ezion-geber, as we know from 1 Kings 9:26 and from excavations of his copper mines there. His extensive stables at Megiddo, one of his fortified cities (1 Kings 9:19), have also been uncovered. See further Noth, op. cit., pp. 207 ff.; G. E. Wright, *Biblical Archaeology,* Philadelphia, 1957, pp. 129 ff.

to the south (1 Kings 11:14 ff.), the establishment of incipient Syrian power in Damascus under Rezon to the north (11:23 f.), and, from the very center, the early insurrection of the Ephraimite Jeroboam (11:26–28) who, upon Solomon's death, played a leading role in the North's secession from Israelite union. The kingdom survived Solomon's reign intact and may even have appeared stronger and more extensive than under David's administration. But Solomon permitted the foundations of the kingdom to deteriorate while he built upon them a spectacular superstructure.

David was content with the limits of the old Jebusite city of Jerusalem. Solomon extended the city to the higher hill immediately to the north where he constructed his own extensive royal residence and its probably incorporated royal temple, the renowned temple of Solomon. It was built over or upon a great rock, sacred from time immemorial and held in tradition to be the scene of Abraham's near-sacrifice of Isaac—a rock now enclosed in the magnificent Arab Dome of the Rock in today's old walled city of Jerusalem.[8]

Solomon's ambitious and far-flung building programs were, of course, terribly costly—one might say, fatally costly. The personnel, equipment, and maintenance of the royal establishment became exceedingly heavy and elaborate (see 1 Kings 4:1–28). Legends of Solomon's vast wealth and wisdom are based upon fact. As an avid patron of the arts, Solomon collected in Jerusalem priceless treasures from all over the world (10:14–25), many of them no doubt transported in ships of his own fleet (9:26–28 and 10:11 f.). His "wisdom" consisted, we suspect, in his profligate and ultimately self-flattering sponsorship of native and imported "wisdom" artists—articulate writers and reciters of a kind of prephilosophical moral philosophy current in the Near Eastern world of the tenth century and preserved, in essential character at least, in Proverbs, in many of the psalms, and, in a different vein, in the prologue and epilogue of Job (Job 1–2; 42:7–17).

All of this had to be paid for out of Israelite pockets, with

[8]Any precise reconstruction of the temple is impossible, although Ezekiel 41 may offer tangible assistance where 1 Kings 6 is deficient. See G. E. Wright's attempt at reconstruction and his vivid description in *Biblical Archaeology,* op. cit., pp. 136 ff; and Roland de Vaux, *Ancient Israel: Its Life and Institutions,* trans. John McHugh, New York and London, 1961, pp. 312 ff.

Israelite sweat and blood and tears. The pious statement of 9:22 belies itself—it is the protest which confirms the reality of what is denied:

But of the people of Israel Solomon made no slaves; they were the soldiers, they were his officials, his commanders, his captains, his chariot commanders and his horsemen.

This has always been a great dream—an army made up entirely of officers, a construction gang composed only of overseers, an enterprise employing only executives. But all Israel paid, and paid dearly, to satisfy Solomon's prideful ostentation; and in paying so dearly, the original kingdom of David was destroyed.

The Solomon story is very different in kind from the David story. The sources are more impersonal, further removed, and sometimes ill informed. The embellishment of legend is incomparably greater. The final history is an editorial creation in which a work called "The Book of the Acts of Solomon" (11:41) is no doubt the source of reports of Solomon's varied administrative actions, but which freely incorporates long current lore about that fabulous reign, and here and there the candid editorial judgment of DH. Nevertheless, Yahwism's theological judgment and interpretation of the reign are no less apparent here than in the stories of Saul and David. Unsuppressed by glowing legends of unqualified Solomonic utopia, it is both the explicit and implicit conclusion of the whole Solomon story that Solomon was apostate: by his total performance as king he repudiated the Yahwism of Israel and of his father David. David's kingdom, so runs the perceptible judgment of the Old Testament texts, remained the covenant kingdom of Yahweh. For all his acknowledged weaknesses, David remained to the end a Yahweh loyalist, the Israelite leader of covenanted Israel. But the Solomon story is the Babel story all over again, the story in which Yahweh is repudiated in grossest fashion by being ignored: ". . . let me build *myself* a city and temple, and let me make a name for *myself* . . ." Solomon's sin is apostasy, as the strongly editorial lines of chapter 11 make clear. And consonant with the immutable position of Yahwistic prophetism, whose primary proposition is always the purposeful engagement of divine life in human history, the meaning of Solomon's reign and of events subsequent to it is discerned in the scheme of sin and judgment: like Babel, apostasy results in the rupture of human community. The same Yahweh faith which in Genesis 11 historizes the myth, here clothes history with the myth. Israel's Yahwism understands the failure of the Davidic kingdom to hold together all Israel as a failure of faith.[9] Israel (of course, always in the person of its king in whom all Israel is embodied) must be a Yahweh covenant people or no people; it will be a Yahweh community or a Babel; Israel will be what Yahweh created it to be or chaos.

[9]Cf. D. M. Gunn, "Traditional Composition in the Succession Narrative," *Vetus Testamentum* 26, 1976, p. 214.

6

Rupture

The First Half-Century:
1 Kings 11–16

> I will not take the whole kingdom out of David's hand.
>
> *1 Kings 11:34*

It is time now to look, if briefly, at the form and nature of the books of Kings. Here is a simple, three-part outline of the contents:

1 (1–11)	Solomon.
1 (12)–2 (18:12)	The two kingdoms, North and South, to the North's demise in 722–721.
2 (18:13–25:26)	The South to its own destruction in 587. (The brief narrative of Jehoiachin's release from prison in Babylon some years later. 2 Kings 25:27–30, appears to be in the nature of a postscript to Kings.)

DH and the Sources

Kings is the editorial work of DH, perhaps a school of theologians-historians thoroughly impressed with and largely controlled by the perspectives and even the language and style of Deuteronomy. As we shall see later, the bulk of Deuteronomy appears to date from the seventh century. The total DH work, Deuteronomy through 2 Kings, is probably a sixth-century product as it stands; but Kings may well have been formulated before the fall of the South in 587, since a number of passages suggest the historians' ignorance of that enormous catastrophe. On the other hand, the story carries through the bitter narration of Jerusalem's collapse and destruction, and elsewhere betrays editorial knowledge of this tragic end. We assume, then, the probability of two "editions" of Kings, both deuteronomic, that is, both DH, the work of deuteronomic historians, one edition prior and another subsequent to the final termination of the Israelite monarchy.

The most conspicuous structural feature of Kings is the repeated use of a formula defining and summarizing in brief, rigid categories the reigns of the various kings. It appears first, in an abbreviated form, at the end of 1 Kings 11, to mark the close of the narrative of Solomon's reign. The first *full* use of the formula is in its application to Rehoboam, 1 Kings 14:21–24. The formula appears (with elements here and there omitted, such as the name of the king's mother) in the case of *all* kings, North and South, as an introductory formula, or a concluding formula, or both. It presents two problems in particular. The length of reign of the king in question is characteristically correlated with the reign of the king in the neighboring kingdom, for example, "in the eighteenth year of King Jeroboam [North], Abijam [South] began to reign" (1 Kings 15:1). This exclusively internal synchronism makes absolute dating exceedingly difficult, if not impossible, although our margin of error even at the upper extreme of dates now hardly exceeds more than a few years. The second problem concerns the formula's categorical judgment of each king—a sweeping judgment of the king based, however, on only the single item of the king's relationship to the cultus of the Jerusalem temple. In the sense of the formula, the good king is the faithful king, faithful to the temple institution. Now it follows, of course, that without exception every king of the North is condemned: under the circumstances not one of them could, even if he would, support the South's royal temple. And as a matter of fact, DH's terms being exceedingly demanding, most of the Southern kings are castigated. Hezekiah (2 Kings 18:3–7) and Josiah (2 Kings 22:2) alone are completely exonerated. The praise of four other kings of the South (Asa, 1 Kings 15:11–15; Jehoash, 2 Kings 12:2–3; Azariah, 15:3–4; and Jotham, 15:34–35) is qualified only with the phrase, "but the high places were not taken away."

Inevitably, of course, our own historical sensibilities are sometimes appalled by this parochial and arbitrary basis of judgment. Perhaps the strongest single illustration in Kings is the case of Omri. He inaugurated the North's strongest dynasty. He was able to effect and maintain peace during his reign by various means, including sheer strength of arms. He possessed the wisdom and strategic sense—and the resources—to purchase and begin construction of a capital city on the shrewdly chosen hill of Samaria. A hundred years after his reign an Assyrian historian, an official recorder for the then world-ruling power, termed the whole territory of Palestine "the land of Omri."[1] Yet, aside from the usual formula, which rates him as "more evil than all who were before him" (1 Kings 16:25 ff.), DH includes only one verse (16:24) to inform us of the twelve-year history of his reign.

It is apparent that DH has employed a number of sources in compiling Kings. We have already cited the Book of the Acts of Solomon mentioned in 1 Kings 11:41. DH elsewhere assumes that the readers of Kings have at their disposal the Books of the Chronicles of the Kings of Israel (1 Kings 14:19) and of Judah (1 Kings 14:29). (Incidentally, the *name* Israel is now commonly applied to the North, while the South reverts to the older tribal designation, Judah.) What an incredibly exciting find any one of these ancient works, apparently forever lost, would be! They must have contained detailed and highly diversified material relating to the history of these two kingdoms. For example,

Now the rest of the acts of Jeroboam, *how he warred and how he reigned,* behold, they are written in the Book of the Chronicles of the Kings of Israel.

(1 Kings 14:19)

Now the rest of the acts of Zimri, *and the conspiracy which he made,* are they not written in the Book of the Chronicles of the Kings of Israel?

(1 Kings 16:20)

Now the rest of the acts of Ahab, *and all that he did, and the ivory house which he built, and all the cities that he built,* are they not written in the Book of the Chronicles of the Kings of Israel?

(1 Kings 22:39)

In addition to these three named sources, we suspect the existence of others: perhaps a History of Ahab, comparable to that of Solomon, since we have more material on Ahab than any king since Solomon; almost certainly an Elijah story, since one unique hand appears to be responsible for the bulk of 1 Kings 17-19,21; maybe a collection of stories about Elisha in 2 Kings 1 ff.; and almost certainly the official Temple Records.

[1] In the Annals of Tiglath-pileser III (745-727). See James B. Pritchard, *Ancient Near Eastern Texts,* 2nd ed., Princeton, N.J., 1955, p. 284.

Yahwism, Secession, and Division

1 Kings 11–16 No comment is called for here on the basic conditions of the North's secession. DH provides us with an uncommonly competent narrative in 1 Kings 12. The Northern tribes, now designated Israelite, gather at Shechem, which has served from the beginning as their real, if informal, capital. They gather with the serious intention of making Rehoboam king (12:1)—already established in Jerusalem in the place of his father Solomon. But they are smarting still from Solomon's oppressive measures and when arrogantly assured that these will be in the future only more severe—"My little finger," says Rehoboam, "is thicker than my father's loins" (12:10)—the old cry (cf. 2 Sam. 20:1), "What portion have we in David" (1 Kings 12:16), is heard again, and the one Yahweh-covenant-community becomes two.

Prophetic Yahwism plays again the crucial political role—even if we are unable to assess that role precisely. The function of the prophet Ahijah is primary through the episodes of the catastrophic event of political rupture (Ahijah dominates the narratives of 1 Kings 9:9–39; 12:1–32; and 14:1–18). The mighty protest of the North in which Jeroboam figures centrally is inspired if not led by prophetic Yahwism in the person of Ahijah. Jeroboam is again, like the judges, like Saul and David, a charismatic figure endowed by prophetic declaration and demonstration with the spirit of Yahweh. It is prophetic Yahwism, in the North at least, which perfers the chaos of a broken people to the chaos of a united people under abusive, oppressive, and anti-Yahwistic monarchy.

For roughly the first three-quarters of the tenth century, all the tribes of the unified Israel participate in the reigns of David and Solomon. Now, for a half century—the last quarter of the tenth and the first quarter of the ninth—the larger, stronger North and the smaller but more compactly integrated South know a relationship if not of war, at least of unceasing armed bickering over disputed common boundaries (14:30; 15:7,16). And while they quarrel, the Syrians of Damascus, the Egyptians under Pharaoh Shishak I (1 Kings 14:25–28), and even the old and vastly weakened Philistine enemy make life hazardous for one or the other segment of the broken kingdom. The high hopes of prophetic Yahwism are dashed again. Two prophetic narratives "predict"

Jeroboam's failure. One, 1 Kings 13, is a relatively late legend of a prophet led into disobedience of Yahweh after proclaiming the fall of Jeroboam. It is apparently inserted here to underscore the South's negative view of Jeroboam. In 1 Kings 14, the story of Jeroboam's wife's visit to Ahijah, we have a narrative, late to be sure in its present form, which may well be an expansion of an old narrative better preserved in the Septuagint version. Jeroboam's wife Ano goes to Ahijah *before* Jeroboam is king; Ahijah is not blind, and Ano is not disguised, since she is not yet queen and therefore needs no disguise; Ahijah, giving no reasons, simply foretells the death of the child and the fall of the house of Jeroboam. The point is that both of these prophetic narratives, the one late and Southern, and the other older and out of the North, express prophetic disillusionment with the very course of prophetically inspired events.

This is, of course, the recurring theological tragedy in ancient Israel. Yahweh created Israel (and the world) for purposes totally frustrated. Yahweh brought Israel into a land and an existence free and redeemed from slavery, for purposes which Israel successfully frustrated. Yahweh made a covenant in that land with David on behalf of all Israel, only to have these original covenant intentions frustrated again. Now, Yahweh's intent to salvage order from the chaos of Israel in the person of Jeroboam also comes to the same frustrated end; and prophetism, which had inspired every significant event of Israel's history, once more must declare void the movement in which faith and hope had briefly inhered.

The singular fact is that prophetic faith and hope nevertheless persisted. Prophetic Yahwism—the sustaining force in ancient Israel—*never* abandoned the quest for and expectation of the fulfillment of covenant. Yahweh, *together with Israel in some recognizable form,* will fulfill the purposes of Yahweh's creation and covenant.

We know very, very little of the fifty years from Jeroboam to Omri in the North, from Rehoboam to Jehoshaphat in the South. In Israel—we shall now use that term for the Northern kingdom—it was then, as it was throughout Israel's history, far more turbulent politically than in Judah, where the Davidic line held fast (with the single brief exception of Athaliah). Israel gained previously unprecedented internal security, and Israel and Judah an appreciable measure of concord, with the reign of Omri and the establishment of a short-lived but strong four-member dynasty in the second decade of the ninth century (from *c.* 876–842?).

But the greatness of the Old Testament people in the ninth century B.C. centers not in Omri or any other of Israel's kings, but again in prophetic Yahwism and particularly in the persons of Israel's distinguished prophets.

Emergent Prophetism

> I will put my words in his mouth.
> *Deut. 18:18*

The history of the Old Testament is for the most part transmitted to us through the eye and mind of prophetic Yahwism, a phenomenon to be sharply distinguished from the popular Yahwism of the Old Testament people. Indeed prophetic and popular Yahwism were in unceasing tension, for Israelite prophetism always found its message and action determined by what was deemed to be the prostitution of Yahwism in its popular conception and practice.

In Part III of this book, we shall discuss ancient Israel's most notable development and finest, most widely appropriated legacy to us and the world—classical prophetism. Prophetic Yahwism, certainly already in existence and creatively at work in the whole Exodus event of the thirteenth century, attains its full identity and character in the classical prophets of the eighth to the sixth centuries, most notably in Amos, Hosea, Micah, and Isaiah of the eighth century; in Jeremiah and Ezekiel of the seventh to sixth centuries; and in the so-called Second Isaiah (and probably also Third Isaiah) of the sixth century. But it is important to recognize an essential prophetic Yahwism, a preclassical prophetism, present in Israel from its earliest beginnings and maintained in an unbroken but fluid continuum from Moses to Amos.

The classical prophets from Amos to Second Isaiah strike ancient Israel, and continue to impress all of us, with freshness, vigor, and originality. Indeed, individually and collectively these classical prophets are unique. But in emphasizing a tradition of prophetic Yahwism never significantly broken from Moses in the thirteenth to Malachi in the fifth century, we intend to insist that the classical prophet, albeit proclaiming the *new*, was nevertheless debtor, and consciously debtor, to this core tradition. And we will, of course, understand classical prophetism better in awareness and knowledge of that tradition of prophetic Yahwism.

Prophet and Prophetism

The Hebrew word for prophet is *nabi'* (plural, *nebi'im*). It is a common noun, employed more than three hundred times in the Old Testament to designate a remarkable range of characters from an Aaron (Exod 7:1) to an Elijah, from the "true" to the "false" (1 Kings 22), from the relatively primitive (1 Samuel 10) to the relatively sophisticated (the Isaiahs, for example), from the highly visionary (Ezekiel 1–2) to the concretely ethical (Nathan in 2 Samuel 12 or Elijah in 1 Kings 21), from the seemingly objective perspective (of an Amos) to the intensely participating attitude (of a Jeremiah), from the "maleness" of a Micah to the androgynous Hosea to the female Miriam (Exod. 15:20) or Deborah (Judg. 4:4) or Huldah (2 Kings 22:14).

What does *nabi'* mean? The etymological pursuit is vain: we do not know and cannot now determine the original meaning of the Hebrew root. One strong hypothesis sees it as related to cognate Accadian and Arabic words meaning "to call" or "to announce." In the light of what we know the prophet to be, this commends itself to us. The prophet of the Old Testament *is* "an announcer" or "the one who announces" the force and meaning of the impinging divine Word and life. Or, taking this etymological hypothesis in the passive sense, the prophet is the recipient of the announcement of Yahweh, she or he is "the one who is called."

And how may we define essential prophetism? It may be broadly defined as that understanding of history which accepts meaning only in terms of divine concern, divine purpose, divine participation. Of course, by this definition the bulk of biblical record is emphatically prophetic in its understanding and interpretation of history. In a narrower sense, prophetism refers to the particular succession who are called prophets and who in some real sense fulfill the role of prophet. But in essence, whether referring to person or concept, prophetism presupposes the decisive engagement of Yahweh in human history, and Yahweh's consistent, compassionate demand for justice and righteousness in all interhuman relationships. This constitutes the basic prophetic character. Where this sense of effective partisan (on behalf of the victims of misfortune, injustice, and greed), relationship of Yahweh to history is absent, prophetism is also absent. Where this sense of the interrelatedness of history and deity is present, and where its role is decisive to the utterance or the person, or to the understanding of historical event or human relationship, there is prophetism.

Prophetism *in these terms* was an ingredient of core Yahwism from Israel's earliest days. But the word *nabi'*, "prophet," probably did not come into current use in Israel before the tenth or even the ninth century. First Samuel 9:9 recalls that the one "now called a prophet was formerly called a seer." The role and function and particular identity of the prophet is a development of monarchic times influenced not only by the older institution of "seer" (a professional role illustrated in the Samuel of 1 Samuel 9) but also by the Canaanite phenomenon of organized, contagious prophecy.

In that same, relatively old narrative of 1 Samuel 9:1–10:16, we see that kind of prophetism native to Canaan. This is the first *recorded* instance of its appropriation among the tribes of Israel, by Israelites. We remember this narrative, Saul, with a servant, consults the seer Samuel in his efforts to recover his father's lost asses. Samuel, "seeing" the animals, reassures Saul and then anoints him "to be prince over his people Israel" (10:1, with RSV and the Septuagint). Samuel informs Saul of what is about to take place, and sure enough,

When they came to Gibeah, behold a band of prophets met him; and the spirit of God [the word in Hebrew is not the *name*, Yahweh, but the general term for deity, *'Elohim*] came mightily upon him, and he prophesied among them. And when all who knew him before saw how he prophesied with the prophets, the people said to one another, "What has come over the son of Kish? Is Saul also among the prophets . . ." Therefore it became a proverb, "Is Saul also among the prophets?"
(10:9–12)

First Sam. 19:18–24 repeats the proverb in a more dramatic setting, with even stronger emphasis on the contagious nature of the seizure and with a fuller description of its manifestation. Saul, this time in pursuit of the outlawed David, sends a squadron to take him by force from his position of refuge with Samuel and a band of prophets, who, though perhaps Israelites, exist in the fashion of ecstatic Canaanite bands of prophets. When Saul's company

saw the company of the prophets prophesying, and Samuel standing as head over them, the spirit of God [again *'Elohim*] came upon the messengers of Saul, and they also prophesied.

(19:20)

Two subsequent squads are dispatched by Saul, neither returning since both companies are seized by the same contagion. Now Saul himself comes,

and the spirit of God [*'Elohim*] came upon him also, and as he went he prophesied, until he came to Naioth in Ramah. And he too stripped off his clothes, and he too prophesied before Samuel, and lay naked all that day and all that night. Hence it is said, "Is Saul also among the prophets?"

(19:23 f.)

We cannot be sure of the relationship between these two narratives in 1 Samuel 10 and 19. In literary-critical judgment, it has been common to see the second as a duplicate, and perhaps an historically dubious explanation of the proverb, "Is Saul also among the prophets?" We ourselves see no reason why both passages may not be deemed to portray the phenomenon of Canaanite prophetism as *in that form* it began to be appropriated by Israelites. We shall see how radically the Canaanite institution is transformed in its final adaptation in Israel.

For the sake of comprehending that very transformation, we will do well to understand this form of the Canaanite institution. We note first that the phenomenon of prophecy is *induced*. Samuel says to Saul, "You will meet a band of prophets coming down from the high place with harp, tambourine, flute, and lyre before them, prophesying" (10:5). Second, it produces a *total transformation of personality*. "You shall prophesy with them and be turned into [a different person]" (10:6). It is, further, created and sustained as (3) a *group phenomenon;* and (4) to "prophesy" (from the same root as *nabi'*) primarily denotes *ecstatic behavior*. If this state or action of prophesying is initially induced, it is (5) capable of *spread by contagion*. And it is popularly interpreted as (6) indicative of *seizure* by the deity: the prevailing (but not exclusive—10:6 reads "spirit of Yahweh") term is *'Elohim*.

This kind of prophesying indigenous to Canaan's culture (we will meet it again in the ninth century brilliantly described in the Elijah narratives) is certainly among the antecedents of the classical prophetism which emerges out of prophetic Yahwism. The roots of the great Yahweh prophets are sunk even deeper into the broad culture of the ancient Middle East. Prophetlike persons appear in the Mari texts from the middle Euphrates in the eighteenth century B.C.—a thousand years before Amos. But

. . . even if we assume a historical connection between the messenger of God in the Mari texts and the prophet of the Old Testament, there is a clear difference between the two. This difference lies not in the manner of the appearance, but in the content of that which is announced as the divine message. At Mari the message deals with cult and political matters of very limited and ephemeral importance. Any comparison with the content of the prophetical books is out of the question. The prophetic literature deals with guilt and punishment, reality and unreality, present and future of the Isrealite people as chosen by God for a special and unique service, the declaration of the great and moving contemporary events in the world as part of a process which, together with the future issue of that process, is willed by God.[2]

What Israel freely borrows from all its environment it radically transforms. The distant antecedents at Mari as well as the more immediate antecedents in ecstatic, contagious Canaanite prophetism differ drastically from the prophets of Israel. And the root of the difference is, of course, Yahweh, in whose name Old Testament prophetism always speaks, "who alone disposes of the great powers of world history, and whose will all powers and movement of history serve."[3]

Premonarchic Prophets

Five prominent figures from premonarchic times are awarded the title of prophet by tradition—Abraham (Gen. 20:7); Aaron (Exod. 7:1); Miriam and Deborah (both *nebi'ah*, the feminine form of the noun *nabi'*, Exod. 15:20 and Judg. 4:4); and of course Moses (Deut. 34:10, 18:18; cf. Num. 11:26–29 and 12:5–8). A brief look at why these five were so designated increases our understanding of the place, function, and nature of the prophets in the history of the kingdoms.

[2]M. Noth, "History and the Word of God in the Old Testament." *Bulletin of the John Rylands Library,* 32, no. 2, March 1950, pp. 200 ff.
[3]Ibid.

The patriarchal saga, as we have seen, imputes to Abraham a sense of divinely ordained history which in Israel could only be post-Exodus. As the person of this first patriarch tends in tradition to take typological form, Abraham is able to accept in *faith* (Gen. 15:6) the divine promises of Gen. 12:1–3,7. He is seen in the maturing tradition as being acutely aware of Yahweh's purposive engagement in history. And more than this, he is himself called to play an essential role therein. It is inevitable that in Israel such a figure should be given the ascription "prophet."

The case of Aaron is perhaps less significant, but it instructs us no less in comprehending the *nabi'* of monarchic Israel-Judah.

Yahweh said to Moses, "See I make you as God to Pharaoh; and Aaron your brother shall be your prophet."

(Exod. 7:1, P)

Again, tradition's linking of an early name with a subsequently developed Israelite role presupposes an understanding of prophetism in primary terms of Yahweh's participating, purposive relationship to history. This instance further defines the prophet as one who articulates and proclaims the sense and meaning of the divine impingement, a definition further confirmed in Exod. 4:14 ff. (E) when Yahweh responds to Moses' objection that he is no speaker:

Is there not Aaron. . . . I know that he can speak well. . . . And you shall speak to him and put the words in his mouth.

. . . He shall speak for you to the people; and he shall be a mouth for you, and you shall be to him as God.

Miriam and Deborah (see Exod. 15:21 and Judges 5) come to acquire the designation because both play eloquent and dramatic roles in celebration of what Yahweh is doing in concrete relationship to the historical existence of Israel.

It may be significant that Moses is never called a prophet in the J work, the tenth-century Yahwist's creative, but largely editorial, composition; and on this continuing question of primary "documents," a reiterative, summary word is in order. We have consistently regarded J as a concrete entity, the probably written work of an individual. D (Deuteronomy plus the work of DH) and P are clearly identifiable strata which, unlike J, appear to be more definitely the work of "schools." And E, we submit, continues to require use as a symbol whether or not it ever existed originally as a separate narrative source roughly parallel to J. E is simply that hexateuchal material later than J and earlier than D or P, which reflects the *provenance* of the Northern kingdom.[4]

The term prophet certainly was in use in the Yahwist's day (as witness, again, the authentic, "Saul" proverb, 1 Sam. 10:12 and 19:24), but the *function* and *practice* of prophetism remained still by and large alien, that is, Canaanite. It is, of course, another matter in E, which reflects the period about 850–750, and betrays every evidence of stemming from Israel's early prophetic circles.[5] In the various E material Moses consistently appears not merely in the role of prophet, but prophet *par excellence:*

And there has not arisen a prophet since in Israel like Moses, whom Yahweh knew face to face, none like him for all the signs and wonders which Yahweh sent him to do in the land of Egypt . . . and for all the mighty power and all the great and terrible deeds which Moses wrought in the sight of all Israel.

(Deut. 34:10 ff., E)

Well may one comment:

The prophetism which Moses represents is of a special sort [as understood by E]; he is much more the performing prophet, actively intervening in events. . . . In the last analysis, indeed, Moses towers above all other prophets (Num. 12:7 f.). His *charisma* was so powerful that even a part of it, and that itself further divided among seventy elders, threw the recipients out of their normal senses and transferred them into a state of ecstasy (Num. 11:25 ff.). Even mediation and the intercessory is here (Exod. 18:19; 32:11–13; Num. 12:11); but again we see this quality heightened, augmented in the extreme: in order to save Israel, Moses was prepared to become *anathema* for the people (Exod. 32:32; cf. Rom. 9:3).[6]

In the deuteronomic perspective Moses is the model prophet. Here is Moses reporting what Yahweh has told him:

I will raise up for them a prophet like you from among their brethren; and I will put my words in his mouth, and he shall speak to them all that I command him.

(Deut. 18:18)

[4]Cf. G. von Rad, *Genesis,* trans. J. Marks, Philadelphia, 1961, pp. 23, 27 ff.
[5]Cf. G. von Rad, *Old Testament Theology,* New York, 1962, vol. 1, pp. 292–94.
[6]Ibid. (But this is my own translation from the original German.)

In the century or two separating E and D, a marked change has occurred in the function, and therefore the concept, of the prophet in Israel: by the seventh century, emphasis has passed from the prophet's deed to the prophet's word. The *basic* character of prophetism, however, remains the same—that is, concern with and demonstration of the critical impingement of concerned divine life upon human history. If E and D perpetrate a terminological anachronism in ascribing to Moses the title of prophet, the essential identification is nevertheless sound. Prophetism was—and always *is*—to confront humankind with God-in-history. Timelessly, prophetism is the bringing of Israel up from Egypt into existence under God,[7] the perennial bringing up of the oppressed and victimized, the abused and the exploited into meaningful, fulfilled existence.

The Background of Classical Prophetism:
1 Kings 17–2 Kings 14

> So shall my word be.
>
> Isa. 55:11[8]

Sometime in the second half of the eighth century, but before the destruction of North Israel (722–721), the prophet Isaiah envisaged a catastrophic event to be inflicted upon Judah by the might of Assyria. Contemplating that tragedy (and Judah was in fact severely ravaged by Assyria just before the turn of the century), Isaiah declared to King Ahaz of Judah,

Yahweh will bring upon you and upon your people and upon your father's house such days as have not come since the day that Ephraim departed from Judah!

(Isa. 7:17)

Israel's loss of order and meaning began in the very structure of

---

[7]See E. Voegelin, *Israel and Revelation,* Baton Rouge, 1956, p. 428: "The Moses of the prophets is not a figure of the past through whose mediation Israel was established once and for all as the people under Yahweh the King, but the first of a line of prophets who in the present, under the revelatory word of Yahweh, continued to bring Israel up from Egypt into existence under God." See further B. D. Napier, "Prophet, Prophetism," *The Interpreter's Dictionary of the Bible,* Nashville, 1962; and *Prophets in Perspective,* Nashville, 1963.
[8]Cf. Psalms 2,20,45,72,110.

the David-Zion covenant; took explosive, catastrophic form "the day that Ephraim departed from Judah"; and was climaxed, in seeming hopelessness, first in the North's and subsequently the South's (587–586) destruction.

We have the story only as it was understood and interpreted in core Yahwism, in what we have broadly called prophetism. This is how, in the Yahweh faith, the whole tragic sequence was comprehended. The order which Yahweh would create out of the people Israel is made chaos by Israel's rebelliousness and obstinate refusal to assume, in justice and righteousness, the form and character and identity of the Yahweh covenant. That which Yahweh purposed for Israel from of old was thus frustrated—but not the Yahweh-being, the Yahweh-power, the Yahweh-Word. Israel's unfaith expressed in arrogance, self-aggrandizement, oppression, and injustice brings it back again to the formless and the void, to the meaningless and the chaotic. Israel knows at length a figurative "return to the land of Egypt" (Hos. 11:5). But all of this deterioration of form, this negation and destructive judgment, is seen as the positive work of Yahweh's Word toward that original purpose: the creation in faith and justice and righteousness of a covenant people, and through them the ultimate blessing of all the families of the earth (Gen. 12:1 ff.).

The Yahwist as Prophet

We very briefly surveyed the premonarchic prophets in the preceding section. Among early prophets of the united kingdom, the Yahwist surely has a place. We have already presumed to place the Yahwist within rather narrow limits—somewhere between David's mature years and the death of Solomon. We predicate in the Yahwist a prophetic historian who addressed himself (alas, in that time the possibility that the Yahwist was a woman is remote in the extreme) to the question of the existing form and significance of the entity, Israel. But to comprehend this entity of Israel as it *is,* and to give expression to its meaningful existence, he must articulate all in Israel's past that he deems relevant to the present, and indeed (he does this, of course, in rare, almost involuntary bursts) he must also speak of that to which the present meaning of Israel ultimately points (so, again, Gen. 12:3).

We recall that the creative prophetism of the Yahwist inheres in his still discernible basic organization of the Hexateuch. We assess and affirm his role as prophet not from what is conveyed biographically, since there is not a single word about him, nor from the content of his independent utterances, since no oracles or commentary of his is preserved, but exclusively from his inspired selection, juxtaposition, and broadly conceived arrangement of varied existent materials. By means of this fundamentally editorial process, the Yahwist prophetically proclaimed Yahweh's critical "participation" in history, and brilliantly delineated Israel's form and meaning in terms of its emergence from Egypt into existence under God.[9]

The judgment is surely wrong that "it was Hellenism that created the idea of ecumenical history."[10] The Greek language and hellenistic culture provided the term and a splendid vessel for ecumenical history. But essential ecumenicity inheres, if in quietness and subtlety, in the Decalogue; and it receives its first emphatic description of meaning in the Yahwist's work in the tenth century B.C., a work which proclaims the central thesis of God's particular engagement in the life of ancient Israel, to be sure, but at the same time—such is the historical form of Israel and the meaning of its life—in the world, the whole household of God. The primeval story (see Chap. 2 above) and its structural relationship to the patriarchal stories and all that follows proclaims the Yahwist's sweeping ecumenical perspective.

The Yahwist's place is sure in the story of Old Testament prophetism and the roster of the prophets. Indeed, he renders more credible and comprehensible the roles of Samuel, Nathan, and Elijah, as well as the classical prophets from Amos to Second Isaiah.

Samuel to Elisha: The Tenth and Ninth Centuries

1 Kings 17–
2 Kings 13   Samuel whose career begins in the eleventh century, Nathan and Ahijah in the tenth, and Elijah, Micaiah, and Elisha in the ninth—these six prophets dominate the history of preclassical prophetism. Although they differ radically from one another and appear in widely varied contexts, these early prophets evidence in

---

[9]See above, Chapter 2. See also von Rad, *Genesis* op. cit., pp. 27 ff.; and Voegelin, op. cit., especially chap. 4, "Israel and History."
[10]R. G. Collingwood, *The Idea of History,* Oxford, 1946, p. 32.

two significant ways their place in the movement of prophetism from premonarchic times to the decay and collapse of monarchy and on into the days of Jewish reconstruction. First, they address themselves powerfully and sometimes passionately to the contemporary scene in the characteristic prophetic conviction of Yahweh's concerned involvement in the sociopolitical institution. All six are intimately related to the life of the state and are effectively, if not always decisively, involved in crucial contemporary events; and all six function as prophets to kings, bringing the prophetic perspective to the political institution.

The second characteristic of the pre-Amos prophets, which sets them apart from the prevailing pattern of contagious-ecstatic group prophecy, is their relationship and responsibility to the Word of Yahweh. In all these prophets, the address to history takes its content from the Word, and the concern for and impingement upon history is made articulate and is interpreted by the same Word.

As we have observed, the Word, through Samuel, is responsible for the establishment of monarchy, first tentatively under Saul and then securely and full of promise under David. Through Nathan the Word not only interprets the reign of David but decisively determines the course and nature of that reign. Ahijah and the Word effect the kingdom's tragic rupture. The next fifty years—from about 925 to 875, from Jeroboam and Rehoboam to Omri and Jehoshaphat—were on the whole bleak years in both kingdoms and apparently without prophets of outstanding stature.

Under Omri in Israel and Jehoshaphat in Judah a substantial measure of security was regained in the two kingdoms. Concord was achieved within the family, and relationships with nearby neighbors, except Damascus-Syria, ranged from tolerable to good. Jehoshaphat enjoyed a long reign (873–849, according to the Albright-Bright chronology), and the four-member Omri dynasty survived from 876 until Jehu's bloody revolution in 842.

Elisha the prophet was a younger contemporary of Elijah (1 Kings 19:19–21; 2 Kings 2–13) who died during the reign of Joash, Jehu's grandson (837–800). During the second half of the ninth century, especially under the rule of Jehu, Jehoahaz, and Joash, the Northern kingdom led an increasingly miserable existence brought on by its own internal weakness and the ravaging attacks of Syria (note, for example, 2 Kings 5:7, and the Syrian siege of Samaria, 6:24 ff.). In the closing years of Joash's reign, the North was almost destroyed, but was brilliantly, if briefly and superficially, revived in the long reign of Jeroboam II (786-746), the fourth and strongest member of the Jehu dynasty.

Now, like Samuel and Nathan and Ahijah in the tenth century, Elijah, Micaiah, and Elisha are instrumental in the ninth century in bringing the Word of Yahweh into history in conflict with and in judgment upon the life of king and people, and in effective encounter with the life of Israel.

The Word is at its weakest in Elisha. Indeed, of the six prophets in the preclassical succession, Elisha appears in the least substantial form. This is not to deny his historical reality and his powerful influence on the events of his time. The cycle of stories collected around his name and exploits testifies to his impact on Israel over a long prophetic career; but elements in the cycle partake of the stuff of sheer legend far more than in the shorter Elijah cycle (1 Kings 17-19,21; 2 Kings 2 and even 2 Kings 1 are of different origin). This is true even of one of the theologically more profound stories in the cycle—the story of Naaman's leprosy in 2 Kings 5. The narrative presents insuperable historical problems, but speaks with inspiration to the theme of faith's simplicity and the perennial human problem of the validation of faith. Other stories of the cycle, even less credible historically, are unfortunately at the same time aesthetically or theologically repulsive. One wonders whether the Elisha cycle may not betray efforts to assert the "superiority" of Elisha over Elijah. The only two direct parallels in the two cycles strongly suggest this. The role of the widow, her son, and the prophet is far more realistic in the two episodes of 1 Kings 17 (vv. 8-16; 17-24) than in 2 Kings 4 (vv. 1-7; 18-27). "Sons of the prophets" appear prominently in the Elisha cycle, a circle of prophets over which Elisha presided on occasion. Are these disciples in part responsible for creating out of their prophetic master a figure possessing fantastic magical powers?

The phrase, "the Word of Yahweh" (and the corresponding phrase, "thus says Yahweh") appears in the Elisha cycle. We do not doubt the prophetic authenticity of the historical Elisha, but again, the historical person as well as the prophetic Word are largely obscured in the present cycle of Elisha stories. The most decisive event for which Elisha is responsible is the anointing of

Jehu as king (2 Kings 9). Elisha and his "young man, the prophet" act upon and pronounce what *they* represent to be the Word of Yahweh (9:3,6) with radically effective and appallingly violent results (2 Kings 9:21–10:27). Quite properly, as its seems to us, classical prophetism in the person of Hosea (1:4) subsequently repudiates Jehu and his whole rebellion, and implicitly, therefore, denies that this could be the responsibility of the true Word of Yahweh.

We see the Word of Yahweh imposed upon the king earlier in the eighth century in that brilliant scene of 2 Kings 22 immediately preceding the death of Ahab. The Word through Micaiah works its historical effects, and another preclassical prophet is instrumental in the efficacious juxtaposition of divine life and divine judgment upon human events. Incidentally, the narrative attests the official court adoption in Israel of the originally Canaanite form of group prophecy.[11]

Elijah

1 Kings 17–19, 21[12] Like David (in 2 Samuel 9–20; 1 Kings 1–2), Elijah found a brilliant narrator, whose original brief account of a few episodes from the prophet's life has unfortunately been augmented with some well-intentioned but tedious or offensive details. The narrator wrote with economy of words, as witness the three succinct, eloquent scenes of 1 Kings 17. His use of the Hebrew language was fresh and original: a surprisingly large number of words and forms are unique. His portrayal of character is powerful in its simplicity and subtlety. Nowhere surpassed in the Old Testament are these remarkable delineations of characters: Elijah himself; Ahab, in briefer scenes but especially in chapter 21; even Jezebel, especially in the line omitted in the Hebrew manuscripts but authentically preserved in the Greek translation, the Septuagint, at 19:1—"If you are Elijah, I am Jezebel!" The narrator also wrote with humor, profound sensitivity, and theological insight. His portrayal of the explosively voluble Obadiah (18:7–16) is a masterpiece of humor. The depth of his "psychological" penetration of the prophet himself is astonishing (chap. 19). And only a

[11]The contention that the account of 1 Kings 22 is not authentic and, at best, mistakenly assigned to Ahab's reign is unconvincing. See M. Noth, *History of Israel*, rev. trans. S. Godman, New York, 1960, pp. 243 f.
[12]Cf. 2 Kings 1–2.

man himself nurtured and articulate in the tradition of prophetic Yahwism could record Elijah's racy, earthy verbal devastation of Baal (18:27) and Yahweh's rebuke of Elijah in the climactic Horeb scene (19:9-18), unquestionably simpler, more direct, and even more moving in its original form. And finally, he also intimately comprehended what Elijah comprehended—that the honor of Yahweh in the Yahweh community involves a theological ethic which not even the king may violate (chap. 21).[13] Elijah's brilliant, courageous defense of the brutally, fatally victimized Naboth is consistent with prophetism's thematic insistence on Yahweh's concern for all who are oppressed and dispossessed.

In the prophet Elijah, and certainly also in his narrator, both in the ninth century, the prophetic understanding of the Word of Yahweh has come to full, conscious maturity. Perhaps Elijah and his narrator would not have put it as the Second Isaiah did about three centuries later, but his words express what was essentially their own understanding of the Word-with-power: the entity not merely verbal and descriptive but also instrumental, by its very nature containing the resources for its own accomplishment and fulfillment:

> For as the rain and the snow come down from heaven,
> and return not thither but water the earth,
> making it bring forth and sprout,
> giving seed to the sower and bread to the eater,
> so shall my word be that goes forth from my mouth;
> it shall not return to me empty,
> but it shall accomplish that which I purpose,
> and prosper in the thing for which I sent it.
> (Isa. 55:10-11)

---

[13]If the character of Ahab comes off rather poorly in the Elijah narratives (1 Kings 17-19, 21), 1 Kings 20 and 22 return the impression of an administrator of considerable ability and power and a person of stature. Assyrian records offer one item of significant support. Shalmaneser III (859-824) fought a battle in 853 against a coalition of smaller western states including Israel. Since he does not claim to have destroyed this alliance (see Pritchard, op. cit., pp. 278 f.) historians have assumed that the allies gained at least a draw. Shalmaneser's own records report that Ahab supplied the largest corps of chariots; and it may be that he was the moving force behind the alliance. First Kings 20, probably before this battle of Qarqar, suggests precisely Ahab's long-term strategy aiming at such an alliance with Syria. First Kings 22, which includes the narrative of Ahab's heroic death, makes clear that the alliance did not long survive the battle of Qarqar.

We note in the Elijah narratives the relative frequency of the term, "the Word": 1 Kings 17:2,5,8,16,24; 18:1 (and vv. 31 and 36, which may not be from the original narrator, however); 21:17 (and v. 28, also possibly secondary). Note also that, as in the records of later classical prophetism, the Word here conveys the sense of a formula whose nature and potency are widely known. Note further that the Word is associated not only with the king but with the people as well. It creates and terminates the drought as a judgment upon people and king (chaps. 17, 18). It is surely instrumental in the prophet's indictment of the Carmel assembly (18:20 f.), "How long will you go limping with two different opinions?" It is, of course, the Word which sends the prophet back from Horeb (19:15 ff.) to minister to Israel in the good company of multitudes still faithful to Yahweh.[14] And it is the same Word again confronting and judging the king for murder and theft—thus says Yahweh, "Have you killed, and also taken possession!" (21:19).

Although Elijah belongs to the company of preclassical prophets, more than any other in the company he anticipates in two regards that succession of prophets beginning with Amos. Elijah alone of all prophets properly belongs to both groups. In Elijah the Word has attained substantially full prophetic definition and form. Through him the Word finds its mature expression and application, not merely or even principally to the king, but to the nation, the whole people of the covenant. Yahweh's Word now decisively challenges historical Israel with such force as to involve all history, and the royal house with such intensity as to judge all folk. Jesus, among others, condensed the Old Testament prophetic ethic (quoting from Deuteronomy and Leviticus) when he declared that "all the law and the prophets" depend upon love of God and love of neighbor (Matt. 22:35–40; cf. Mark 12:28–31). But in reality he reached back ultimately to Elijah, in whom these two propositions find impassioned expression, for the first time in biblical record, in a single life. The divine life confronts and decisively qualifies the life of history. To repudiate Yahweh's lordship and his historical engagement ("The people of Israel have forsaken thee"), to delimit it or run in the face of it ("Have

---

[14]This is against the interpretation of some who read in the seven thousand faithful in Israel an early insinuation of the "remnant" idea.

you killed and also taken possession"), to attempt to compromise with it ("How long will you go limping with two different opinions")—all of this is not folly but unqualified disaster. Thus, to deny the Word of Yahweh is to invite loss of meaning and fulfillment and the imposition of chaos and death.

Elijah's address was of course to his own people and his own time; but in his passionate intensity, all humanity, and all history are implicitly embraced. It remains the task and function of classical prophetism to make concrete and specific the decisive involvement of Yahweh in historical existence.[15]

[15]In the foregoing I have borrowed freely from my article "Prophet, Prophetism," op. cit.

III
POSITIVE JUDGMENT: CLASSICAL PROPHETISM

7

Anticipated Judgment: The Eighth Century

Prophetism and the Eighth-Century Indictment: Amos 1–9

> Fallen, no more to rise, is the virgin Israel.
> *Amos 5:2*

The New in Prophetism

There are elements in classical prophetism which are distinctly new. There is the new that is external: a new situation which emerges out of pragmatic history, out of the actual course of real events and which could not have been anticipated. It is a new epoch, which develops out of the wide range of possibilities determined by the past. And in eighth-century Israel it was a new epoch charged with tragedy.

There are, of course, also the new internal elements, but the internal is inseparable from the external. The classical prophets now see Israel's historical existence, first brought into being out of Egypt turning back again into that same essential abyss, chaos, oppression, and unendurable meaninglessness. For the prophets from Moses to Elijah and Elisha, Egypt lay in the past, however wide of Yahweh's mark Israel's performance might be. But now, "Egypt," what Egypt represented, lay in the future as well. Out of the Egyptian existence, formless and void in its misery, Yahweh had created for Israel a life relatively formed, ordered, and fulfilled; certainly in the popular mind this definition of existence continued to be valid and to provide meaning enough for historical consciousness, however strong the opposing judgment from core Yahwism, from prophetic Yahwism.

Here, of course, in Israel's core of Yahweh loyalists, the meaning of the present was not so superficially determined. The present was appraised and its meaning apprehended in terms of Yahweh's participation in Israel's past and his ultimate purpose in the future. But until the eighth century the future *could* be seen in continuum with the present, holding in prospect essentially more of the same, or even, in the prophetic view, the restoration of Yahweh's lost order. Now prophetism envisages discontinuity between the present and the future, the catastrophic imposition from without of disorder and chaos, the abrupt and violent termination of Israel past and present.

The Historical Context

The new aspects of external history and the related internal prophetic mind were initially produced in the middle of the eighth century simply by the aggressive ambition of Assyria backed, for the first time in several centuries, with the leadership and power to implement ambition. Tiglath-pileser III assumed the throne of Assyria in 745 B.C., "the first of an uninterrupted series of great soldiers on the throne of Assyria, who quickly brought the Neo-Assyrian Empire to the zenith of its power and created an empire in the ancient Orient which for the first time united almost the whole of the ancient Orient under Assyrian rule."[1] Indeed, within a single decade of the accession of Tiglath-pileser all of the oriental world that he wanted was clearly either in fact or potentially his. By 721, when the Northern kingdom of Israel fell to Assyria, any hopes of political existence independent of Assyria entertained by smaller neighboring states were simply fatuous. From Tiglath-pileser's days (745–727), through the successive reigns of Shalmaneser V (727–722), Sargon II (to 705), Sennacherib (to 681), and Esarhaddon (to 669), Assyria's position of world domination was beyond serious challenge.

The succeeding reign of Asshurbanipal (669–632), who unlike his predecessors was a patron of the arts rather than of war, was the beginning of the undoing of Assyrian world rule. Assyria slowly succumbed to the vicious powers of the Chaldeans of Babylon, the Medes of the mountains of Iran, and the bands of Umman-manda (apparently Scythians) from the steppes of Russia; and the long death-agony of Assyria was finally ended in decisive battles of 612 and 610 B.C. But unhappily, Assyria's collapse provided only a brief respite for the barely surviving Israelite kingdom of Judah. For now Assyria's position in the world was

[1]M. Noth, *History of Israel,* rev. trans. S. Godman, New York, 1960, p. 253.

appropriated by neo-Babylonian power. The political center of the ancient Middle East was moved from Nineveh to Babylon. The sentence of political death was imposed on Judah in the first quarter of the sixth century. The cycle was complete. Israel became once more void and without form. It was once more swallowed up in the chaos of captivity. From uncreation to creation, Israel was now relegated again to the uncreated. The symbolic word enunciated in Hosea (11:5) was fulfilled: "They shall return to the land of Egypt!"

Classical prophetism rises, then, first in the consciousness that Israel now stands, so to speak, between Egypts, that what it was it will be again. Heretofore in Israelite Yahwism the meaning of the present was taken primarily from the understanding and interpretation of the past (see Deut. 6:20 ff.; cf. 26:5-9). So it is in the old cultic credos:

We were Pharaoh's slaves in Egypt; and Yahweh brought us out of Egypt with a mighty hand . . . that he might bring us in and give us the land which he swore to give to our fathers.

This confession of faith addresses the future, if at all, only implicitly, for the future is of a piece with the present. "Now" embraces tomorrow and tomorrow. The appropriate response to the confessional knowledge of meaning in history is, of course, faithful participation in the Yahweh cultus. Such is the sense of Deut. 6:24 (cf. 26:10, the similar conclusion of a variant of the same basic cultic confession):

And Yahweh commanded us to do all these statutes, to fear Yahweh our God, for our good always, that he might preserve us alive, as at this day.

Yahwism before the eighth century understood the past and the present chiefly in terms of Yahweh's *positive* action on behalf of Israel. If the future is addressed, it is in the confident expectation that it will be in predictable conformity with the past. One sees this in the preclassical prophets. Elijah, for example, believes this, even though he knows full well that Israel's unfaith has already reduced to disorder the order which Yahweh purposed in Israel. But the classical prophets, from Amos on, are forced to reinterpret the meaning of the present not only in terms of a heightened sense of Israel's failure to maintain Yahweh's just order in the present, but also in overwhelming awareness of an immediate future charged with tragedy. This imminent tragedy is deemed to be no less Yahweh's doing than the great formative event of redemption from Egypt, or political self-fulfillment under the David-Zion covenant. For the classical prophet, the old two-part scheme, "out of Egypt, into this land," has become a three-part scheme: "out of Egypt, into this land, back to Egypt again."

Yahweh, who redeemed the nation for special purposes, now finds those purposes thwarted by the unfaith and unrighteousness of Israel. Therefore Israel's God will now commit the nation to its preredeemed status of chaos for the same essential purposes. Why? What lies beyond the second Egypt? Is there, in other words, a fourth member to be added to the three-part scheme. Above all, how does all this qualify the nature of existence under Yahweh in the present time?

These questions and their answers are of the essence of classical prophetism. They are the context of Israelite prophetism in the eighth to the sixth centuries.[2]

Amos: Book and Prophet[3]

The literary-critical problems are few and small. The book is substantially a unit. Some of the woes pronounced upon small neighboring states in chapters 1–2 have commonly been regarded as secondary, particularly the condemnation of Judah (2:4–5). The superbly articulated doxologies of 4:13; 5:8–10; and 9:5–6 *may* be later editorial insertions. The ending of Amos, from 9:8b, has often been regarded as an appendix on the grounds that it represents too radical a change of mood to be a part of the original unit. Now these may be good guesses, but it is important to recognize that this remains a guessing game. We do not even know how the writing first came into existence—whether by the prophet's own hand (unlikely), or at his dictation (possible), or (more likely) from a circle of prophets-disciples among whom the words of Amos were first "recorded" in memory.

The contents of Amos may be surveyed in this fashion:

1–2 A series of oracular indictments (of Damascus, Gaza, Tyre, Edom, Ammon, Moab, Judah, and Israel) climaxed in the final oracle against Israel.

[2]On the foregoing discussion, see G. von Rad, *Old Testament Theology,* New York, 1962, vol. 1, pp. 64–68.
[3]Anyone especially interested in Amos would be well-advised to read Hans Walter Wolff, *Joel and Amos,* in the *Hermeneia* series, Philadelphia, 1977, pp. 89–113.

3-6 The condition of Israel's present unsatisfying, rebellious existence.

7 The three visions of locusts, fire, and plumbline.

8-9 The vision of summer fruit; the pronouncement of Israel's final and irremediable doom; and (whether secondary or not) the proclamation of hope in Israel's future beyond the catastrophe of historical judgment.

One may interpret the astonishing phenomenon of classical Israelite prophetism in two ways. It emerges among the ancient Israelites, one may insist, as a kind of mechanical achievement wrought by the accidents of history. It is, as such, a product of interaction between history and human genius; and it is a perennial problem in the life of faith that this remains a possible and even credible explanation.

The prophets themselves would, of course, resoundingly repudiate this interpretation of prophetism. They would insist, as the Bible insists, as the life of faith continues to insist, that this epoch in Israelite history witnessed an intense series of divine-human encounters, initiated by God and effected by the Word. *In this view* the phrase, the Word of Yahweh, represents no courteous condescension to religion or piety, no innocent lie thoroughly conventionalized to mean in fact the human word. It *means* the Word of God, initiated by God, irresistibly breaking into human life and work from Moses' time on and with peculiar, sustained potency in the classical prophets. In all of these we cannot fail to note—whatever else the work of the Word is—the sharp, specific references to the throbbing life of contemporary human history.

If King Ahab, more than a century earlier, had characterized Elijah in the phrase, "You troubler of Israel!" (1 Kings 18:17), how much more fervently might Jeroboam II have thrown that epithet at Amos. Amos not only condemned the prostitution of Yahwism in Israel and unethical behavior in the king. He heartily damned the whole fabric of society; he repudiated with violence and contempt all of Israel's life and thought and practice, including even its worship of Yahweh (5:21-23). He did so precisely because he saw the will of Yahweh for Israel's life repudiated in the widespread abuse of the weak by the powerful minority, the rife, shameless practice of interhuman injustice (see *now* especially Amos 5:21-24).

Although a native of the Southern kingdom from the little

village of Tekoa, about seven miles southeast of Bethlehem, his one recorded public appearance was at Bethel, the official southern sanctuary of the Northern kingdom. In appreciation of his efforts here, the local authorities cordially expelled him, with the firm invitation for the future to do his preaching at home—or anywhere but Bethel. "It is," said Amaziah, the presiding priest of Bethel, "the king's sanctuary, and it is a temple of the kingdom" (7:13). Amos's only trouble—it is always the prophets' trouble—was his insistence that sanctuary, temple, realm, and people all are Yahweh's!

It would appear from this same exchange between Amaziah and Amos that the term prophet still commonly denoted a certain official status, or some professional affiliation with organized prophetism. We observe that thus far in Old Testament history, professional prophetism has been both of Yahweh and Baal. The professional prophetism of Yahweh appears neutral in quality as associated with Saul, "good" as associated with Obadiah (1 Kings 18:13; cf. 19:14) and Elisha, and on the whole "bad" as associated with Ahab's court as we see the court prophets contrasted with one of their number, Micaiah (1 Kings 22).

Amos denies unequivocally any professional status (7:14): "I am not a prophet, and I am not a son of a prophet" (that is, I belong to no guild, no band, no association of prophets). It is, of course, possible to translate "was" rather than "am." The verb "to be" is commonly supplied in translation, since it does not appear in Hebrew. Grammatically, the imperfect may even be "equally possible" as some have insisted.[4] But in context it does not appear to be natural. Amos is denying, not necessarily in heat and certainly not necessarily in repudiation of the institution of prophetism, that he does not himself represent what Amaziah has just imputed to him. He has had no contact with the professional, associated prophets: "Yahweh took me from following the flock, and Yahweh said to me, 'Go, prophesy to my people Israel!'" (7:15). His action here at Bethel is inspired by this personal confrontation with Yahweh, not by any group apprehension. This is not to say that institutional prophetism may not and does not have this valid, authentic apprehension, or that Amos is unwilling

---

[4]See H. H. Rowley, *The Servant of the Lord and Other Essays on the Old Testament,* London, 1952, p. 114, n. 2.

to be cast in a prophetic role (3:3-8 indicates the contrary!), but simply and exclusively that neither the group phenomenon nor any other official connection happens to be his origin, as charged by Amaziah. Something new comes into the term prophet with Amos. Even Elijah is recognized from the beginning as fulfilling the role of prophet. Amos is freshly created and validated a prophet only and directly by the Word.

He speaks in passionate and apparently unrelieved condemnation. He excoriates the social structure and practice of the nation; in which increasingly during the reign of Jeroboam II wealth was extorted from the poor; in which deceit and dishonesty were the rule; in which great masses of the poor, the dispossessed, the powerless were crushed under the weight of an easy discrimination, a rank, complacent, and brutal injustice.

He damns the religious structure in which the fervent hymns of praise and the devout symbols of dedication were matched by a fervent immorality and a devout pursuit of vanity; in which Yahwism was enthusiastically endorsed at the sanctuaries but—as Amos saw the Yahweh faith—blatantly violated in business, domestic, and personal relationships. Yahweh was acknowledged with the lips, but denied in the preponderant performance of Israel's life.

We first learn from Amos of the popularly expected day of Yahweh. Nothing more brilliantly illustrates the polar disparity between prophetic and popular expectations for the future. Amos declares Israel's certain doom. The jig is up. Time and Yahweh's patience have run out. What Israel calls and anticipates as the day of Yahweh is imminent, but let no one be so foolish as to long for the day's coming. It will be darkness and not light. It will be gloom, with no brightness at all (5:18-20).

Israel has brought upon itself the sentence of death, which Amos proclaims with bitter fury and passion. He is at pains to let Israel know the magnitude of its rejection of the role of Yahweh's people. We read, then, with wonder and appreciation. Here is an incomparably intimate, partisan interpretation of the life of a little Near Eastern state in the second quarter of the eighth century,

the words of Amos, who was among the shepherds of Tekoa, which he saw concerning Israel in the days of Uzziah king of Judah and in the days of Jeroboam the son of Joash, king of Israel. . . .

(1:1)

Contingency and Compassion:
Amos and Hosea 1–14

> How can I give you up, O Ephraim!
> *Hos. 11:8*

The Positive in Amos

It would be woefully wrong to interpret Amos as an exponent of moral law. Israel's doom is for Amos no mechanical, impersonal, and automatically invoked judgment. For Amos, as for all prophetism, justice and righteousness (5:24) are not abstractions or in any sense absolutes. They have no independent meaning. These are terms which have meaning only in specific, familiar relationships, and the particular meaning is determined by the particular relationship. When Amos cries, "Let justice roll along [RSV, roll down] like waters, and righteousness like an everflowing stream!" (5:24), he means specifically justice and righteousness in the Yahweh-Israel relationship, the justice and righteousness in human relationships which honor Yahweh, by which the life of Yahweh's people is fulfilled, and in adherence to which Yahweh's purposes in Israel may be consummated. Morality and ethics subsist only in theology. Justice and righteousness in prophetism are derivatives of faith. Israel's violation is not of principles but of persons, and ultimately the person of Yahweh. The judgment is not a result of the automatic action of some mechanism built into the moral structure of things, but comes directly and personally from Yahweh, whose life and power are thus apprehended primarily *in history*.

Now, if this is true, it is also wrong to read Amos as a prophet of unqualified, unrelieved negation. Contingency and hope are here. The fierce indictment and the proclamation of cataclysmic judgment are predicated on Israel's persistent repudiation of Yahweh, and are implicitly *contingent* upon its refusal to turn back again. But Amos knows Yahweh's love and patience (see 4:6–11, with the essentially tender refrain, "Yet you did not return to me"; but especially 7:2,5); and when he speaks the apparently immutable sentence of death upon Israel (4:12; 7:9; 9:1–8a) it is surely motivated (as the articulation of despair is of necessity always motivated) by hope, indomitable hope, that the pronouncement of judgment will effect decisive change in the conditions which invoked the judgment.

The quality of contingency in prophetism is more marked in

other prophets, but it is implicit in Amos; and no prophet, not even Amos, can be interpreted as holding Yahweh's judgment upon Israel as the last word. The ending of the Book of Amos may be secondary (although this proposition is by no means unassailable), but it remains in a profound sense authentic. The person of the prophet Amos could not have spoken with such passion on behalf of Yahweh except in the faith that the very historical judgment he proclaimed was itself ultimately positive and redemptive in divine purpose. If Amos had deemed Israel's sentence of execution to be the end, he would never have spoken at all!

Hosea: The Time and the Book

Hosea's role of prophet is played out some ten to twenty-five years after Amos. From a number of allusions in the text of Hosea, it appears rather certain that the prophet's career began after the reign of Jeroboam II (786–746) and probably after 740 (despite the reference to Jeroboam in 1:1). Since there is no mention of the fall of Damascus to Assyria in 732, it is possible that his active career ended prior to that date. It is certain that it did not extend beyond the fall of Samaria in 721.

The last generation of the Northern kingdom, to which Hosea belonged, was a period of hectic and brutal confusion. Jeroboam II's reign may have been superficially brilliant but it apparently lacked any fundamental, enduring strength. His son, Zechariah, after a very brief reign (746–745), was assassinated by Shallum, who was himself rather promptly dispatched by Menahem. Menahem (745–738) bought an uneasy security from Assyria in the last year of his reign with the payment of a handsome tribute to Tiglath-pileser, whose annals declare:

As for Menahem I overwhelmed him like a snowstorm and he . . . fled like a bird, alone, and bowed to my feet [?]. I returned him to his place and imposed tribute upon him, to wit: gold, silver, linen garments with multicolored trimmings, . . . great . . . I received from him. Israel [the text reads literally, "Omri-Land," testifying to the power of that reign a century and a half earlier] . . . all its inhabitants and their possessions I led to Assyria. They overthrew their king Pekah and I placed Hoshea as king over them.[5]

[5]As the damaged Assyrian text is reconstructed and translated in James B. Pritchard, *Ancient Near Eastern Texts,* 2nd ed., Princeton, N.J., 1955.

Menahem's son, Pekahiah, reigned for a couple of years (738–737), before he met a violent end at the hands of another assassin, Pekah, who led an anti-Assyrian party in Israel. Pekah (737–732) was rejected by his own people following a pathetic attempt to stop a westward Assyrian advance, and was murdered by Hoshea (2 Kings 15:30), who reigned as a vassal of Assyria. Hoshea (732–724) subsequently revolted and was executed by the Assyrian monarch, Shalmaneser V (727–722). Samaria was besieged for three years, and fell to Shalmaneser's successor, Sargon II, in 721.

The Hebrew text of Hosea is as difficult and confused as the epoch in which it originated. One hesitates to propose anything as definite as an "outline." The present structure does appear to fall into the two divisions:

1–3 The theme, throughout apparent, is Hosea's anguished relationship to Gomer and the tightly analogous relationship of Yahweh and Israel.

4–14 There is nothing here to give form or provide unity. The character of the section is, however, typically prophetic: the broad range of the types of prophetic utterance is embraced, from indictment and judgment to some of the most tender expressions of the compassion which Yahweh holds for Israel.

The more severe textual critics have reduced Hosea largely to a name under which a broad assortment of prophetic oracles from widely varied sources and times has been collected. Preponderant critical opinion has been more conservative and withholds from Hosea (or the immediate Hosea-circle of prophetism) chiefly two kinds of material (and not all examples of these two kinds): (1) the utterance which favorably contrasts Judah with condemned Israel (such as 1:7), and (2) the prediction of an unqualified bright future, usually falling at the end of an oracle of doom. For the rest, the substantial eighth-century figure of the prophet Hosea is directly or indirectly responsible. This is for the most part "the Word of Yahweh that came to Hosea the son of Beeri" (1:1) in the years shortly before the fall of Samaria and the extinction of the political entity of the Northern Kingdom of Israel.[6]

[6]See G. Fohrer's judicious discussion of Hosea in his *Introduction to the Old Testament,* trans. David E. Green, Nashville and New York, 1968, esp. pp. 422–25.

The Major Problems of Hosea

1–3

Two problems promise to remain problems and may well be ultimately insoluble. One is the relationship between chapters 1 and 3. The other, not unrelated, has to do with the interpretation of the personality of Hosea.

According to chapter 1, in which Hosea appears in the third person, the prophet is commanded by Yahweh to marry a prostitute and to accept offspring of this union whose paternal status must in fact remain in doubt. This Hosea does; and to the three children now born to Gomer he gives symbolic names, making them living oracles of indictment in the community:

Jezreel—for yet a little while, and I will punish the house of Jehu for the blood of Jezreel, and I will put an end to the kingdom of the house of Israel.

(1:4; cf. 2 Kings 9–10)

Lo'-Ruhamah ("Not Pitied")—for I will no more have pity on the house of Israel, to forgive them at all.

(1:6)

Lo'-'Ammi ("Not My People")—for you are not my people and I am not your God.

(1:9, with the Septuagint and the RSV)

Chapter 3 is a narrative in the first person: the prophet is himself the narrator. The Yahweh Word to the prophet is essentially the same: "Go again [a great deal hangs on this word: is it original or secondary?]; love a woman who is beloved of a paramour [anyone who loves or is loved illicitly] and is an adulteress—even as Yahweh loves the people of Israel, though they turn to other gods and love cakes of raisins [denoting idolatrous rites]."

The first problem, then, concerns the relationship between the two accounts. There are three possible answers:

1. Since chapter 1 is an account in the third person, and chapter 3 in the first person, the two accounts are parallel—descriptions in different terms of the same thing. The word "again" in 3:1 is an editorial insertion.
2. Chapter 3 preserves Hosea's own view of the matter *preceding* the actual marriage which is narrated in chapter 1.
3. Chapter 3 is a sequel to chapter 1. It is the same woman in both chapters. After the birth of the children in chapter 1, Gomer leaves Hosea, and he later buys her back; he redeems her from the life of prostitution to which she has returned.

The second problem arises out of the repeated statement that Hosea *knowingly* married a prostitute (1:2 and 3:1). For one whose moral constitution was as acutely sensitive as Hosea's, no undertaking could be more bitter. If in fact, then, Hosea married Gomer in the full knowledge of her previous professional standing either as an independent prostitute or as a sacred prostitute attached to one of the still-flourishing fertility cults (see, for example, Hos. 4:14), several interpretations are proposed:

1. Some, intrigued with the (dubious) game of fitting ancient figures into compartments of modern psychoanalysis, would see Hosea's act as symptomatic of a profound sickness. Hosea is a masochist: he takes upon himself the fullest possible measure of abuse in committing himself to sexual partnership with a confirmed whore.

   This is masochism in its original sense. The term has come into common use for that personality sickness in which one derives perverted pleasure from the endurance of pain. The term originally derives, however, from the title of an Austrian novel, *Masoch,* written in the nineteenth century by von Sacher, and describing in detail the case of one whose abnormal sexual appetite and passion find satisfaction in exquisite abuse by his partner.

   This view of a severely psychotic prophet has little to recommend it.

2. Others give a high religious interpretation to the reported fact of Hosea's foreknowledge of Gomer's unchaste status. This act—of all acts most repugnant to him—is one of supreme surrender to divine will. In this view, Hosea conforms to the not uncommon figure in the history of religions of the flagellant who, as an (perverted?) act of service to or contrition before the deity, heaps abuse upon himself. But this strictly "hair-shirt" explanation of Hosea is only a variant of, and no more satisfying than, the interpretation of masochism.

3. The simplest view—on the assumption still that Hosea did know the character of Gomer before their marriage—is that he loved her; that he believed this marriage to be according to the Word of Yahweh; and that he hoped, at least, that his love, like Yahweh's love for Israel, would ultimately bring a satisfying response and a fulfilled relationship.

It may be, of course, in spite of the statement of 1:2 ("Yahweh said to Hosea, 'Go, take to yourself a wife of harlotry'"), that Hosea did *not* in fact knowingly marry a prostitute. Someone has suggested that

the implication of "And the Lord said to Hosea" is simply that looking back on his life, Hosea realized that God had enabled him to turn his sorrow to the service of truth, and therefore he could feel that the good hand of God had been with him from the start, despite the personal tragedy for Gomer and for him.'

In any view of either problem, the central facts are unaltered. Whatever the relationship between chapters 1 and 3, and whatever the interpretation of Hosea's personality, the prophet was in marriage covenant with an unfaithful woman; and in his own anguish and love for his wife, he believed Yahweh had revealed the nature of the relationship between Yahweh and unfaithful Israel, the specific character of the divine compassion, and the precise quality of Israel's violation of covenant.

Hosea-Gomer: Yahweh-Israel

Is it possible that Hosea is *fictional* allegory? This suggestion has appeared with some persistence in modern interpretations of the book. It seems unlikely on a number of counts, and especially in view of the authentic appeal and the emotional intensity of the central analogy that as Gomer is to Hosea, so Israel is to Yahweh. In 2:2-7, for example, it is improbable, to say the least, that we are reading a theoretical, fictionalized allegory. In this brief section, and in others, the mingled fury, anguish, love, and hope tend to confirm the dual historical, existential reference—Israel *and Gomer.* In prophetic faith, this is revelation, this is Yahweh's self-disclosure, with double intensity. God is revealed in the most intimate and bitter relationship of Hosea's private life, in the prophet's personal history; and Hosea, recipient of the Word of Yahweh, is called to be the interpreter of that segment of history in which he is himself the center. His own agony is the key to the meaning of that history.

The intensity of the castigation in 2:2-5a (cf. 9:10-17) is derived from the same dual *historical* reference. So, too, is derived the pathos in the portrayal of a lack of knowledge in 2:5b and 8. From the same double reference comes the tender hope of a voluntary return in 2:7.

As Gomer is to Hosea, so Israel is to Yahweh. The wife is unfaithful. The husband's love is rejected. The marriage covenant is shattered. The most common Hebrew term for the sex act in mar-

'W. A. L. Elmslie, *How Came Our Faith,* New York, 1948, p. 269 n. For a superb and completely documented discussion of the Hosea-Gomer problem, see H. H. Rowley, "The Marriage of Hosea," *Bulletin of the John Rylands Library,* 39, no. 1, September 1956.

riage is the verb "to know." The phrase occurs again and again in the Old Testament: "and so-and-so *knew* his wife, and she conceived and bore. . ." The Book of Hosea repeatedly sets the appropriate Yahweh-Israel relationship in terms of "knowledge" or "knowing" and of course this conveys implicitly far more than the narrow analogue of contractual obligation. The knowledge of Yahweh embraces also the cognizance that in Israel and Israel's world there is no other; that in Israel's history and the broad history which it shares, Yahweh rules (see 13:4 f.). But in the context of Hosea we cannot escape the inference of the intimate and the particular. The lament that there is no knowledge of God in the land (4:1,6) and the plea for the restoration of that knowledge (6:6; cf. 2:20; 6:3; 8:2) imply so strong a relationship between Israel and Yahweh that the profound effect of its violation can be conveyed only by comparing it to the violation of the marital relationship when a wife wantonly offers a husband's sexual prerogatives to other men (10:11). Incidentally, in all of this Hosea merits a standing ovation for his unqualified assertion of a single standard in sex morality (4:14).

As Hosea is to Gomer, so Yahweh is to Israel, "How can I give you up, O Ephraim!" cries Yahweh (11:8), whose love and compassion are made known in one who has himself cried, night after lonely night, "How can I give you up, O Gomer!" Hosea knows that the unfaithfulness of the covenant partner invokes wrath, discipline, judgment; and that as Gomer must suffer, so also must Israel (see, for example, 2:10–14; 4:9–10; 7:11–13; 9:3,10–17; 11:5; 13:16). But Hosea also knows that unfaithfulness, even at its most lewd and shameless, does not stop the flow of love or assuage the anguish of woefully injured affection. His hopes and purposes for his life with Gomer, as Yahweh's with Israel, cannot be permanently frustrated. Compassion is of stronger, more enduring stuff than wrath. Discipline becomes only the necessity by which the relationship may be restored and redeemed.

These comments touch but lightly on this rich product of classical prophetism. Read Hosea again—and again. The theme of impending catastrophe is sounded no less forthrightly than in Amos. But the dominant theme is Yahweh's compassion for Israel and Yahweh's unimpedable purpose to produce out of Israel a people whose end it will be somehow to bless all the families of the earth.

In that day, says Yahweh. . . .
I will sow him [i.e., Jezreel: this is a play on the name] for
  myself in the land.
And I will have pity on Not pitied
And I will say to Not my people, "You are my people!"
And he shall say, "Thou art my God."

(2:21-23)

The Theological Ethic and History:
Isaiah 1-23, 28-33; Micah 1-7[8]

Yahweh alone will be exalted.

Isa. 2:17

Assyria, Israel, and Judah

Tiglath-pileser (745-727) first consolidated his eastern territories before turning west; but in 738 Rezin of Damascus and
Menahem of Israel render the tribute of vassals, and other small
western states capitulate. Pekah in Samaria and Rezin later con-
spire to throw off the Assyrian yoke, but needing the support of
Judah, and finding Ahaz (735-715?) unwilling to join, they lay
siege to Jerusalem in the hope of deposing Ahaz. In extreme
straits, Ahaz reverts to the crude rite, persistently condemned in
prophetic Yahwism, of child sacrifice, and offers up his own son
as a burnt offering (1 Kings 16:3). He also appeals to Tiglath-
pileser, against Isaiah's advice (2 Kings 16:7; Isaiah 7), which was
certainly prudentially given: since the Assyrian king would not in
any case tolerate for long such independent and insurrectionist action on the part of vassals, Ahaz obligated himself unnecessarily.

In 734, then, the Assyrians campaign in the west with bitter
vengeance. Damascus and Northern Israel are mercilessly
plundered and for the first time Assyria invokes in this area the
policy of deportation, the removal to other parts of the empire of
appreciable numbers of the population and particularly the real or
potential leaders around whom subsequent rebellion might form.
Judah is not molested at this time, but remains in diminished circumstances from the occupation of Rezin's and Pekah's armies.
And Ahaz the king is summoned peremptorily to Damascus

[8]Also read 2 Kings 15; 2 Chronicles 26; 2 Kings 16; 2 Chronicles 28-30; 2
Kings 17-21 (cf. 18-20 and Isaiah 36-39); cf. Psalm 46.

where, in partial token of his subservience to Assyria, he arranges for the erection of an altar in the temple in Jerusalem copied from an imported Assyrian altar in Damascus. This we suspect underlies the account of 2 Kings 16:10 ff. Ahaz hardly went to such pains and expense in the midst of his humiliation simply to satisfy his aesthetic delight in some Syrian altar he chanced to see in Damascus! Commonly in the ancient East, political dependence required formal recognition of the victor's gods, a fact explaining in part the common prophetic protest against any and all kinds of "alliances" with superior powers.

By 732 Tiglath-pileser had efficiently organized and consolidated his western territories north of Samaria into Assyrian provinces. It is important to remember that Hoshea of Samaria (732–724) owed his throne to Tiglath-pileser, a fact which made his subsequent rebellion all the more odious to Assyria. Early in the reign of Shalmaneser of Assyria (727–722) Hoshea begins a series of politically unfaithful flirtations with Egypt. Second Kings 17:4 puts it succinctly: "Assyria found conspiracy in Hoshea." The prophet Hosea speaks of the ultimate folly of this kind of action when he characterized the pro-Egypt party as silly doves without sense, calling to Egypt, going to Assyria (Hos. 7:11; cf. 8:9). King Hoshea in Samaria openly declares his intentions to divorce Assyria in 724 (2 Kings 17:4). Assyrian forces are able to imprison Hoshea; but probably to their surprise and dismay, Samaria does not surrender and Assyria is put to the effort of a three-year siege before the capital and kingdom of North Israel falls in 722–721, never again to be so reconstituted. Sargon II (722–705) may have succeeded Shalmaneser before the fall of Samaria. In Sargon's own annals, the conquest is claimed several times.[9] And again, Assyria follows its policy of shifting the best classes of populations, deporting thousands of Israelites eastward, and importing thousands from Aramaic-speaking countries, who in time lose their identity among the inhabitants of Palestine. The subsequent attitude of the Judean Jew toward the Samaritan (cf. John 4 in the New Testament) draws from the memory of this fusion of population elements. The immediate problems of the North are described in 2 Kings 17:29 ff.

[9]But according to C. Schedl, *Vetus Testamentum* 12, 1962, pp. 89 f., a newly discovered text supports 2 Kings 17:3 and 18:9–10 in maintaining that Shalmaneser was in reality the conqueror.

The history of surviving Judah is resumed in 2 Kings 18. Hezekiah (715–687?) had come to the throne in Jerusalem a few years after Samaria's fall (perhaps a few years before; his dates present particularly difficult problems). He defies Assyria in two ways: he institutes elaborate religious reforms, always in the ancient East a gesture of independence; and even more brazenly, he undertakes extensive defense measures. The outer fortifications of Jerusalem are strengthened, an act of military strategy against which the prophet Isaiah speaks a devastating theological word: it is right and good that this be done, he says in effect to the king, but you and your action are condemned in this kingdom of Yahweh unless it be done for Yahweh's sake, to God's honor and glory (see Isa. 22:8b–11). The same critical prophetic word appears in the same passage applied to Hezekiah's attention to the acute problem of the city's water supply in time of siege. The Gihon spring, outside the city wall—ancient Jerusalem's only unfailing source of water—is made inaccessible to attackers, and its waters channeled through a tunnel cut through the rock, into the city, for a distance of about 1700 feet. The spring, the tunnel, and a terminal pool are still in use today, although the original terminal was probably an underground cistern, not the present pool, Siloam.[10] In the tunnel's construction, workmen began at opposite ends. At the point of meeting, someone inscribed a brief account of this remarkable feat of ancient engineering in the limestone wall—soft when first exposed to air. It is one of our oldest and best Hebrew inscriptions, even though the first half is unfortunately missing:

[. . . when] (the tunnel) was driven through. And this was the way in which it was cut through:—While . . . (were) still . . . axe(s), each man toward his fellow, and while there were still three cubits to be cut through, [there was heard] the voice of a man calling to his fellow, for there was *an overlap* in the rock on the right [and on the left]. And when the tunnel was driven through, the quarrymen hewed (the rock), each man toward his fellow, axe against axe; and the water flowed from the spring toward the reservoir for 1200 cubits, and the height of the rock above the head(s) of the quarrymen was 100 cubits.[11]

[10]See Naseeb Shaheen, "The Siloam End of Hezekiah's Tunnel," *Palestine Exploration Quarterly* 109, 1977, pp. 107–12.
[11]Pritchard, op. cit., p. 321.

It is remarkable that Hezekiah got by for so long a time without a spanking from Assyria. In 711 he is party to a rebellious coalition of western states inspired by Egypt or Babylon, or both; yet he appears to escape the punishment which they receive. But in 701 Sennacherib (705–681) moves in to pour the wrath of Assyria on all the small western states, as well as Egypt. Jerusalem, besieged by Assyria, escapes destruction. Why and how? Why was the siege lifted?

Second Kings 18–19 lists three reasons:

1. Hezekiah's payment of tribute (18:14–16), a prodigious sum then—the equivalent of at least ten to fifteen million dollars. Assyrian records indicate a more critical tribute including some of Hezekiah's daughters, his "concubines, male and female musicians."[12]
2. Urgent military business elsewhere—rumor of trouble (19:7).
3. Plague (the angel of Yahweh, 19:35).

Some believe that three separate, conflicting accounts of the same episode are combined in the present Kings narrative—tribute, 18:14–16; rumor, 18:17–19:9a; and plague, 19:9b–35. Not uncommonly, this kind of explanation has been offered: "If *I* were Sennacherib [quite a stretch, even for the most elastic Old Testament scholar] the first two reasons would be enough—tribute paid and insurrection in the east. Since from my point of view the third is unnecessary, we will throw it out. Besides, we must remember the great Old Testament axiom that where two or three accounts of one episode are gathered together somebody lied." This kind of argument is dubiously climaxed with the assertion that Hezekiah's prayer in 19:14–19 is theologically incompatible with the eighth century (true enough of the prayer *in its present form*), and that therefore the *whole account* is obviously late and, of course, spurious.

Happily, this point of view even in the FBI itself—the Federated Biblical Investigators—is on the wane. It is clear that the payment of tribute alone was not enough. After receipt of it, and before joining battle with the Egyptians at Eltekeh in the Philistine plain region, Sennacherib expressed his continuing distrust of Hezekiah in a note of sharp warning which Hezekiah took as more than warning; he took it as a threat to return and demolish the city of Jerusalem. If such was, in fact, the Assyrian plan, as both Hezekiah and Isaiah believed, the deed of destruc-

[12]Ibid., p. 288.

tion could have been accomplished then as easily as at any time in the period of Assyrian ascendancy. Morale in Jerusalem was at a record low. On every hand, surrounding nation-states were prostrate. In Judah, forty-six cities had been destroyed. Sennacherib boasts, "As to Hezekiah, the Jew, he did not submit to my yoke; I laid siege to forty-six of his strong cities, walled forts, and to countless small villages in their vicinity, and conquered them. . . ."[13] No pride remained in Jerusalem. Hezekiah had stripped the temple, exhausted all wealth, and even surrendered members of his own family in tribute. The three practical explanations for Assyria's withdrawal seem probable, but we must examine the explanation in terms of Israel's history. For, as we have seen, the Old Testament sets down history as it has been interpreted by faith.

In accordance with the faith that Yahweh is effectively involved with Israel's history, Northern Israel does not perish accidentally by the impersonal exigencies of history. Destruction is *not* seen in the Old Testament as the inevitable culmination of a series of events. On the contrary, the catastrophe is explicitly the judgment of Yahweh. Now, the question arises: Is the *interpretation,* indigenous to the narrative and inextricable therefrom, right or wrong? The answer depends, does it not, upon each interpreter's response to the ultimate validity of the claims of faith. No one may determine another's answer. All readers of the Old Testament must answer for themselves the ultimate question of the validity of Israel's historical faith.

But on this all can agree. The Assyrian forces made a sudden, totally unexpected withdrawal, sparing Jerusalem from what had appeared to be certain doom. In the biblical perspective of faith it is a minor consideration indeed whether Assyrian forces were hastily moved for strategic reasons, or were driven back east by a devastating wave of virulent infection, or by severe food or water poisoning, or even by bubonic plague. It could well have been a withdrawal impelled by *both* the threat of serious trouble elsewhere in the empire *and* the ravages of epidemic illness or disease. In the faith of Israel and in the kingdom of Judah it was in either case, or both cases, another of Yahweh's redeeming acts. It was the power of his Word fulfilling itself in history. This kind of repeated application of the proposition that Yahweh's dominant

[13]Ibid.

sphere of self-disclosure is history rather than nature is responsible for the persistent biblical address to human history and the full range of human life and human existence.

Isaiah: Book, Person, and Prophet

Of the sixty-six chapters in the present Book of Isaiah, the final block, chapters 40–66, is demonstrably from the sixth century; and it is highly probable that chapters 34–35 date from the same century. Chapters 36–39, are narrative rather than oracular material, paralleled in 2 Kings 18–20. We look for the eighth-century prophet Isaiah, then, in chapters 1–33.

In this block, four units appear:

1–12 In large part authentically Isaianic; and mainly from the prophet's earlier ministry.

13–23 Oracles for the most part against foreign nations, some or many composed after Isaiah's time, perhaps by disciples of the eighth-century Isaiah; in that sense, therefore, the material may be termed Isaianic.

24–27 An apocalyptic section, probably later than anything in 40–66.

28–33 For the most part from Isaiah, and mainly from his later years.

To say that a text is Isaiah's does not mean necessarily that it comes unmediated, directly from the lips or "pen" of the prophet. Some material that is substantially his was no doubt committed to memory in the circle of his disciples (see, now, Isa. 8:16). The present book is the product of a number of "Isaiahs," but the first Isaiah is prominently, authentically represented, and as we shall see, strikingly influential in the utterances of subsequent prophets who are known by his name.

Of the person of the prophet, several details are clear. His orientation is that of an urbanite. He is a resident of Jerusalem to whom *the* covenant is the David-Zion covenant. His language, his politics, and even his theology are impressively shaped by his urban existence.

He is highly placed in Jerusalem either by virtue of professional status or possibly by royal birth or by both. King Ahaz listens to him, even if he does not heed him; and Hezekiah, by any standards one of Judah's most distinguished kings (see the deuteronomic estimate of him, 2 Kings 18:1–8, matched only by the

Josiah formula, 22:1-2), not only listens and heeds, but is strongly dependent on the prophet. Moreover, Isaiah moves and speaks, despite occasional public ridicule (28:9 f.), with the assurance of one who knows his position is fundamentally secure.

Isaiah is married and sufficiently content with the title "prophet" to refer to his wife simply as the "prophetess" (8:3).[14] To our knowledge they have two sons, both named, as were Hosea's children, symbolically: Shear-Jashub, "a remnant shall return" (7:3), obviously predicating the tragedy that will leave only a remnant but at the same time affirming the expectation of productive survival; and Maher-Shalal-Hash-Bax, "The spoil speeds, the prey hastes" (8:1-3), with initial reference to the imminent collapse of the Rezin-Pekah alliance against Jerusalem in 734, but perhaps later with reference to Judah itself as the soon-to-be spoil and prey of Assyria.

No prophet is "typical." But no prophet more forcefully, comprehensively, and eloquently represents classical Israelite prophetism than Isaiah. His power, comprehensiveness, and almost unmatched eloquence are, of course, factors in his great stature. But it is his own honest, unneurotic, thoroughly realistic appraisal of himself and his generation together with his historical and existential knowledge of the Word of Yahweh that create the essence of his distinction.

Now let me speak directly. Neither I, who write these present words, nor *anyone else* can convey to you in words *about* Isaiah what is so powerfully articulated in the oracles themselves. Indirectly, and occasionally directed, I have tried to say all along: Let no one else do your reading of the Old Testament for you! In another text I have presumed (admitting there the presumption) to discuss the content of Isaiah's prophetism under the seven headings of Covenant, Yahweh's Holiness, Judah's Pride, Judgment, Redemption, the Messianic Hope, the Quality of Faith.[15] It is presumption because neither Isaiah's prophetism nor that of

---

[14]And so comparable to "Duke-Duchess." But since the Hebrew word which he uses for her is the feminine form of the common noun for prophet, by which the women prophets Miriam (Exod. 15:20), Deborah (Judg. 4:4), and Huldah (2 Kings 22:14, and see below pp. 194 f.) are designated, one wonders whether the wife of Isaiah may have been herself a prophet. This, of course, would make the Isaiahs the biblical prototypes of the growing number of "couples in ministry" in our own time.

[15]B. D. Napier, *From Faith to Faith,* New York, 1955, chap 4.

any other prophet may be thus categorized. These are in no sense separable concepts. Any one is of an inextricable piece with all the others. Nevertheless, these categories point to the major emphases not only of Isaiah but of classical prophetism as a whole, and I will later attempt a somewhat similar summary view of all of prophetism (Chap. 10).

Let me now indicate briefly some of the lines, paragraphs, and chapters that for various reasons always stand out in my own perusal of Isaiah—and around these you may direct your own conversations with the prophet.

The account of his call, chapter 6, no doubt now colored by his postcall career, is unquestionably the most intimately revealing single chapter in Isaiah, embracing explicitly or implicitly all the persistently sounded notes of his prophetic voice.

Mark the moving, empathic indictment of chapter 1; the knowing ox and ass contrasted with unknowing Israel; the awful totality of the Yahweh-Israel alienation—all this with the key to Yahweh's controversy with Israel (v. 13), "I cannot endure iniquity *and* solemn assembly!" (cf. Amos 5:21b).

Observe the strange and stirring, but characteristic, alternation between oracles of wrath and compassion (seen also in Hosea and Amos), illustrated in the "floating oracle" (because it also appears in Micah 4) at the beginning of chapter 2, in which is envisaged the redemption that the very catastrophe of judgment makes possible.

The merciless castigation of human pride, repeatedly and brilliantly articulated and everywhere presupposed, even in the prophet himself in his own call, is characteristic of Isaiah:

They bow down to the work of their hands (2:8) . . . [they] carry out a plan, but *not mine* (30:1) . . . are wise in their own eyes, and shrewd in their own sight (5:21) . . . whose deeds are in the dark, and who say, "Who sees us? Who knows us?" [29:15; its Isaianic authenticity doubted by some] . . . who say to the seers, "See not"; and to the prophets, "Prophesy not to us what is right; speak to us smooth things, prophesy illusions" (30:10).

Now read that sweeping condemnation of human pride in 2:12–17 where,

on wings of furious prophetic indignation, Isaiah moves north to Lebanon, east across the Jordan to Bashan, on somewhere, anywhere to the mountains—and then to the symbols of human pride, the high towers, the fortified cities, and the proud, frail craft that sail the seas.

The pride that renders Judah sick unto dying is the more critical because it is shared—by all.[16]

The powerful prophetic Word to Assyria in chapter 10 is one of Isaiah's most notable passages.

The Song of the Vineyard, 5:1–7 (from whence the title of this book), with its devastating conclusion, is more intense for its play on words:

> [Yahweh] looked for justice [*mishpat*],
>   but behold, bloodshed [*mishpah*];
> for righteousness [*ṣᵉdaqah*],
>   but behold, a cry [*ṣᵉ'aqah*].

Isaiah offers prophetic encouragement under siege, both in 734 and 701 (see 7:7 and 37:29; 2 Kings 19:28), with the plea for a very different kind of response to Jerusalem's release from siege in 22:12–14 (here, as occasionally elsewhere, we cannot surely tell whether the reference is to 734 or 701).

Yet he persists in the prophetic conviction of cataclysmic judgment based on the proposition that "If you will not believe, surely you shall not be established" (7:9b):

> For thus said the Lord Yahweh, the Holy One of Israel,
>   "In returning and rest you shall be saved;
>   in quietness and in trust shall be your strength."
> And *you would not*, . . .
>
> (30:15)

> "Surely this iniquity will not be forgiven you till you die,"
>   says the Lord, Yahweh of hosts.
>
> (22:14)

Consider the unequivocal language of judgment earlier in chapter 30 (vv. 12–14); and these words, more bitter than anything else in Isaiah if intended (as may well be the case) as irony and not (as most translations) as a compassionate "evangelistic" invitation:

> Come now, let us reason together,
>   says Yahweh:
> though your sins are like scarlet,
>   shall they be as white as snow?!
> Though they are red like crimson,
>   shall they become like wool?!
>
> (1:18)

[16]Ibid., pp. 182 f.

"Egypt" again, certainly! But beyond?

> I will turn my hand against you
> and will smelt away your dross . . .
> and remove all your alloy.
>
> (1:25)

The fire will burn, but its ultimate function is to purify. A remnant, and the tragic conditions to produce it, will be—but that remnant *will return* (Shear-Jashub, 7:3). The fire from the altar of Yahweh by which Isaiah himself is cleansed for Yahweh's service (6:6 f.) symbolizes the nature and function of judgment and points beyond judgment to Yahweh's purposive redemption.

Finally, observe the two remarkable passages, 9:2–7 and 11:1–9 (which may be from Isaiah, despite considerable adverse critical judgment), looking forward to the ultimate fulfillment of the David-Zion covenant (for Isaiah, *the* covenant) in a Messiah, an "anointed one," in and through whose rule "the zeal of Yahweh of hosts" (9:7) will effect justice and righteousness not only in Israel but in all the earth (11:4–9).

This is Isaiah. He knows that he is a person of unclean lips, dwelling in the midst of a people of unclean lips. He knows this because he knows and "sees" the holiness of Yahweh, the quality without which Yahweh would not be Yahweh, that by which Yahweh *is* Yahweh, the justice and righteousness which *are* Yahweh, which may be appropriated as light is appropriated from the sun—and *must* be appropriated if covenant life is to continue at all, if covenant purpose is to be fulfilled.

All that is truly Isaianic derives fom this dialogue between human uncleanness which is pride and Yahweh's holiness which is the ultimate prophetic assertion of faith.

Micah—and Isaiah

Micah, youngest of the four great eighth-century prophets, is from the country. He is as much shaped by his orientation there as Isaiah is by the city of Jerusalem. His home is Moresheth, probably Moresheth-Gath, near the old Philistine city of Gath. We can imagine what his town and area suffered from every invading or even passing army in the last four decades of the eighth century; and we can better understand the intensity of his prophetic wrath, especially when the high fortress-city of Jerusalem is his target. Look at 3:2 f. Has any government seat, have any government personnel, ever been so bitterly castigated?

The present book and the relationship of its parts to the prophet himself may be thus briefly indicated:

1–3   With the possible exception of 2:12 ff., these chapters may with confidence be assigned to Micah.

4–5   Here 4:6–7 and 5:7–8 presuppose knowledge of the fall of Jerusalem and Judah. The rest would appear to be, if not from Micah, then from his time or from the reign of Manasseh (from *c.* 687) shortly after.

6:1–7:7   It is impossible to say whether this is or is not from Micah; but one can insist that in time and perspective it is removed from the prophet only a little, if at all.

7:8–20   This is certainly not from Micah. It reads like a cultic psalm and is patently postfall in origin. Its prophetic reaffirmation of the covenant, verse 20, is marred by a bitter, narrow nationalism.

Especially in the sections chapters 4–5 and 6–7, we sense an affinity with Isaiah and the circles of his disciples:

But you, O Bethlehem Ephrathah[17]
. . . . . .
from you shall come forth for me
   one who is to be ruler in Israel,
whose origin is from of old
. . . . . .
Therefore [Yahweh] shall give [Judah] up until the
time when she who is in travail has brought forth;
. . . . . .
And he shall stand and feed his flock in the strength of Yahweh
   in the majesty of the name of Yahweh his God.
(Mic. 5:2 ff.)[18]
But as for me [Micah? Or a prophet from the Isaiah circle?]
   I will look to Yahweh
   I will wait for the God of my salvation. . . .
(Mic. 7:7)[19]

We further note the strong anti-Assyrianism of 5:10 ff., reminiscent even in language of the Isaianic circle. If some of this material in chapters 4–7 is from Micah, or if it fairly represents what was in fact the prophetic mind of Micah, then it may be that we will have to predicate a relationship, if indirect, between Isaiah and Micah; and so see Micah, even as we see Isaiah, as holding in faith the prophetic expectation of redemption beyond judgment.

[17]Reference is the Davidic line; Bethlehem Ephrathah is the birthplace of David.
[18]Cf. Isa 9; 11; 40:11.
[19]Cf. Isa. 8:17.

The affinity between the Book of Micah and the Isaiah circle is further marked by the presence in both books of the floating oracle (Isa. 2:2–4 and Mic. 4:1–3). Whether it is the original utterance of one or neither of these eighth-century prophets, it is one of prophetism's finest and most lyrical expressions of the hope for covenant fulfillment. Micah 4:4 adds the verse:

> They shall all sit under their own vine and fig tree,
>   and none shall make them afraid;
> for the mouth of Yahweh of hosts has spoken.
>   (slightly emended)

The Book of Micah includes that matchless summary of the theological ethic ("man" may be translated as "humankind"):

> [Yahweh] has showed you, O man, what is good;[20]
> and what does Yahweh require of you
> but to do justice and to love kindness,[21]
> and to walk humbly with your God?
>   (Mic. 6:8)

The essence of prophetism is never the moral and the ethical. Micah 6:8 does *not*, as is sometimes loosely claimed, constitute a summary of classical prophetism. Prophetism is always theological-historical. The theological ethic is never an end in itself, but only the necessary condition for the *historical* fulfillment of the Yahweh-Israel covenant. This full prophetic faith is given climactic summary in the floating oracle; and even more eloquently, movingly, in this phenomenal utterance originating probably in circles of prophetism subsequent to Isaiah, but, perhaps not without some justification in view of his tremendous influence, attributed to him in Isaiah 19:23 f.

In that day there will be a highway from Egypt to Assyria, and the Assyrian will come into Egypt, and the Egyptians into Assyria, and the Egyptians will worship with the Assyrians.

In that day Israel will be the third with Egypt and Assyria, a blessing in the midst of the earth, whom Yahweh of hosts has blessed, saying, Blessed be Egypt my people, and Assyria the work of my hands, and Israel my heritage.

[20]Or, *Man* has showed you what is good, but what does *Yahweh* require of you.
    [21]*Hesed*, a covenant term denoting loyalty, faithfulness, and even something akin to the New Testament concept of grace, the giving of more than the relationship may properly demand.

8

Suspended Judgment:
The Seventh Century

Packaged Prophetism:
Deuteronomy[1]

> The word is very near you.
> *Deut. 30:14*

Manasseh succeeded Hezekiah about 687 (some competent chronologists would make it an earlier date). A fair impression of his reign, although only an impression, is returned in 2 Kings 21 and 2 Chronicles 33. He is bitterly condemned by DH. He was surely repudiated in prophetic-Yahwistic circles, and it may be that Yahwism during his reign was virtually forced to go underground. An extrabiblical tradition reports Isaiah's death under Manasseh's persecution.

His was a long reign, lasting until 642, when his son Amon succeeded to the throne. He appears as an Assyrian vassal in the annals of Esarhaddon (681–669) and Asshurbanapal (669–633?). The Chronicler reports an act of rebellion, or suspected rebellion; but if true, his relationship to Assyria as a subject king in good standing was quickly restored. As the Kings' account also reports of his grandfather Ahaz (in 2 Kings 16:3), Manasseh reverted to child sacrifice (2 Kings 21:6); and, also like Ahaz, he introduced, no doubt under the guise of what continued to pass for Yahweh worship and the Yahweh cult, extraneous practices denoting Judah's subservience to Assyria.

Amon's reign—indeed his life—was brief (642–640: he was killed at 24). DH formally condemns him, but it is interesting and perhaps significant that his assassination was avenged by "the people of the land," that is, the most influential citizens,[2] and his

---

[1]Essential readings for this chapter: 2 Kings 21; 2 Chronicles 33; 2 Kings 22–23; 2 Chronicles 35; Deuteronomy 1–8, 10; 12; 17; 22–25; 27–33.

[2]Cf. G. von Rad, *Studies in Deuteronomy*, in the series *Studies in Biblical Theology*, London, 1953, p. 63: "We may take it as certain that the term means the free, property-owning, full citizens of Judah."

son Josiah put on the throne at the age of eight to succeed him. During the years of Josiah's reign (640–609) Assyria was dying and Josiah was able to effect a drastic religious transformation because Judah gained again, and for the last time, a period of political independence.

The Kings Account

2 Kings
22–23

Unless these two chapters are a hoax, they are historically two of the most important in the Old Testament. Here is recorded the most extensive, thoroughgoing reform in the whole history of the Israelite kingdoms, a reform based upon a book of law found—or appearing, or now for the first time seriously heeded—in the eighteenth year of Josiah's reign (probably 621). Reform is already under way: Josiah has already set in motion the complete redecoration and restoration of the "house of Yahweh," the temple in Jerusalem. Manasseh had apparently permitted its shameful deterioration. The priest Hilkiah reports the finding of "the book of the law in the house of Yahweh" (2 Kings 22:8). Josiah's secretary, Shaphan, reads the book to the king, who is profoundly moved by the disparity between present practice and the book's admonition (22:11–13). The prophetess Huldah is consulted. She is apparently a professional prophet in her own right commanding vast respect in Judah, although we hear of her nowhere else. She returns the Yahweh Word validating the book, confirming Josiah's concern. She indicts and passes judgment upon Judah, but for Josiah she speaks gentle words of Yahweh's acceptance (22:14–20).

At once Josiah set about implementing the lawbook. He calls a popular assembly at the temple; gives the book a public reading; elicits the assembly's acceptance of "the words of the covenant" in the old covenant-making tradition (Joshua 24); and at once proceeds with appropriate reforms (see 23:4 ff.), including the excision from the whole temple cultus of objects and personnel alien, or deemed to be alien, to traditional Yahwism. Cult prostitution, scattered idolatrous sanctuaries, the practice of child sacrifice, and all objects and manifestations of astral worship (ancient Babylonian in origin, taken over by Assyria) are abolished. The Passover is reestablished, not afresh, but in a form deemed to adhere for the first time in centuries to ancient rite (23:21 f.;

observe that the Chronicler, 2 Chronicles 35, greatly expands and elaborates the account of this Passover celebration).

DH gives expression to unprecendented gratification in Josiah:

> Before him there was no king like him, who turned to Yahweh with all his heart and with all his soul and with all his might [cf. Deut. 6:5], according to all the law of Moses; nor did any like him arise after him.
> (2 Kings 23:25)

Josiah's death at the hands of the Egyptian Pharaoh Neco is recorded (2 Kings 23:28–30); but the details are decidedly unclear, and the Chronicler's account of the same tragic episode (2 Chron. 35:20 ff.) compounds the confusion. It is only clear that Josiah loses his life, still a relatively young man, at Megiddo. Egypt is allied in a hopeless cause with Assyria against the Medes and Babylonians. Perhaps the Kings and Chronicles accounts are both satisfied on the assumption that Josiah, forced into the battle by Egypt, loses his life in the fighting (Chronicles) and so, in a manner of speaking, at Neco's hand (Kings).

Josiah's Law-Book: Deuteronomy

For well over a century and a half this identification has been widely, and we think, rightly accepted. The basis of Josiah's reform, centering the cult practice of Yahwism exclusively in Jerusalem, purifying and simplifying Yahweh's worship, and rearticulating the "law of Moses," was the original unit of the present book of Deuteronomy, that is, chapters 12–26 (perhaps also including chapter 28), or even the larger block, chapters 5–26. This prevailing view has had its able opponents. A handful of scholars have argued that Deuteronomy was not in existence in Josiah's day and that Josiah's reform program was shaped by the J legislation in Exodus 12 and 32–34; or a brief collection of Jeremiah's oracles; or the Holiness Code of Leviticus 17–26 (conventionally dated in the sixth century, of course); or, if any part of Deuteronomy, the chapters 5–11 only.

Others have seen in Deuteronomy 12–26 (and 28) a very early North Israelite work—late tenth or early ninth century. Centralization of worship was out of the question at that time, and they rid Deuteronomy of any such program by ruling the passage 12:1–7 to be a later intrusion; and by reading 12:14 (RSV: "at the place which Yahweh will choose in one of your tribes, there you shall offer . . .") "in *any* place which Yahweh shall choose *in any one* of your tribes." The original and early Deuteronomy argued, they say, only for centralization by tribes and could not, therefore, have been the basis of Josiah's reform.

The case for identification nevertheless remains convincing. As many as twenty-six specific parallels between Deuteronomy and 2 Kings 22–23 have been cited; and it is difficult indeed to believe that the Kings account of Josiah's reform is an invention of DH. From a literary point of view, Deuteronomy shows dependence on JE, but no rapport with P. To narrow the span of years of Deuteronomy's possible origin, the eighth-century prophets betray no knowledge of it whatsoever, whereas late seventh- and sixth-century prophets (Jeremiah, Ezekiel, Second Isaiah, Haggai, and Zechariah) all show at least some indirect acquaintance with it. Style and vocabulary accord well with what we know of late eighth- and earlier seventh-century Hebrew.[3]

To many careful readers of Deuteronomy, the theological tone necessarily presupposes the preaching of the eighth-century prophets.[4] The strong theological ethic enunciated in Deuteronomy has a kind of post-Amos, post-Isaiah appeal. The central body, chapters 12–26, 28, gives in a considerably expanded and often significantly modified form virtually the full contents of the Covenant Code (E? Exod. 20:18–23:19; see above Chap. 3). There is, of course, new material in Deuteronomy, regulations specifically pertinent to the life of Judah in the years of Assyria's ascendancy around 725 to 625 B.C. Concern with the sociopolitical implications of war is marked both in the main body of Deuteronomy (20:1–20; 21:1–14; 23:10–14; 24:5; 25:17–19) and in the long introduction (see, for example, 7:16–26 and 9:1–6).[5] Some of this material no doubt originated centuries before, but in this century of Assyrian domination it is revived by Deuteronomy. A

[3]For an excellent summary of the major interpretations of Deuteronomy, see the symposium, "The Problem of Deuteronomy," *Journal of Biblical Literature,* 67, 1928, pp. 305 ff. For a briefer, able updating, see the article, N. Lohfink, "Deuteronomy," in *The Interpreter's Dictionary of the Bible, Supplementary Vol.,* Nashville, 1976, pp. 229–32.

[4]But see von Rad, op. cit., especially pp. 60 ff. "The prophetic in Deuteronomy is merely a form of expression, and a means of making the book's claim to be Mosaic real" (p. 69). For a view of Deuteronomy differing in some important respects from that taken here, see also his *Old Testament Theology,* New York, 1962, Vol. 1, pp. 219 ff.

[5]See von Rad, *Studies in Deuteronomy,* op. cit., pp. 50 ff. Cf. E. Voegelin, *Israel and Revelation,* Baton Rouge, 1956, pp. 375 f.

sense of crisis and urgency pervades the material. The tone of Deuteronomy is far less legal than hortatory: it is all cast now in the form of Moses' personal words to his own people in direct address, and the note of pleading (characterized in the phrase, "Hear, O Israel!" 5:1; 6:3 f.; 9:1; 20:3; cf. 12:28; 13:11 f.) is implicit throughout. It is Old Testament law, of course; but the content of the law provides as it were, the text for the sermon. This is Old Testament law not so much formally codified as preached, and preached with passion and conviction.[6]

Deuteronomy has been called a derailment of prophetism.

> Far from resulting in a new response of the people to the living word of Yahweh . . . the prophetic effort (Deuteronomy) derailed into a constitution for the Kingdom of Judah which pretended to emanate from the "historical" Moses. The past that was meant to be revitalized in a continuous present now became really a dead past; and the living word to which the heart was supposed to respond became the body of the law to which the conduct could conform.[7]

Deuteronomy was produced—like the Yahwist's work from a wide range of sources and including some very old materials—out of prophetic Yahwism in the century preceding Josiah.[8] Deuteronomy was probably already in process during the reign of Hezekiah (about 715–687) and influenced his reforms (2 Kings 18:3 ff.). The work which was ultimately to issue in the lawbook of Josiah's reform went underground during the reigns of Manasseh (*c.* 687–642) and Amon (642–640), and was "found" in the eighteenth year of Josiah's reign when a Yahwist king was ready to institute a Yahwistic reform and a Yahwistic program.

It *did* become a derailment of prophetism. Prophetism in a package cannot remain prophetic. And yet, the same commentator who so eloquently describes the derailment also declares:

> With all its dubious aspects admitted, Deuteronomy is still a remarkable recovery of Yahwist order, when held against the practice of Judah under Manasseh; and when held against the alternative of a complete destruction of Yahwist order through the Exile and the dispersion of the upper class, it has proved to be its salvation in the form of the Jewish postexilic community.[9]

[6]Cf. von Rad, *Studies in Deuteronomy,* op. cit., especially pp. 15 f.
[7]Voegelin, op. cit., p. 429.
[8]See also von Rad, *Studies in Deuteronomy,* op. cit., pp. 66 ff.
[9]Voegelin, op. cit., p. 377.

The Contents of the Package

Deuteronomy looks like this:

1-11   a. 1-4. A summary of the history recounted in Exodus and
          Numbers.
          b. 5-11 A forceful call to obedience, with repeated reference
          to the era of Israel's wilderness days.

12-26, 28 The main, and probably original, section: laws old and new,
          prophetically apprehended, compiled, and edited; suggesting
          a product not of altar or bench, but of the pulpit.

27, 29-31 A collection of heterogeneous character, relatively late.

32   The so-called "Song of Moses" (vv. 1-43), unmistakably a
          product of prophetic circles; a poetic, lyrical expression out
          of classical prophetism, interpreting the history of Israel in
          terms of the theology of Yahwism (cf. Psalms 78, 105, 106).

33   The so-called "Blessing of Moses," one of the Old Testa-
          ment's older long poems, probably premonarchic in origin,
          but showing signs of editing certainly in the tenth century and
          perhaps as late as the eighth century; preserving, in the form
          of individual blessings, characteristics of the tribes con-
          stituting the people Israel (and therefore to be compared
          closely with Genesis 49).

In three regards the law which Deuteronomy pleads (rather than strictly legislates) may be seen to express the prophetic temper which produced it. As compared with similar regulations of the Covenant Code, Deuteronomy (1) further tempers justice in behalf of the offender of any sort and any class; (2) takes a markedly more merciful, sympathetic view of the weak member of society by providing a sort of legal compensation for those who are victimized by social inequity or who suffer from the brutality and deprivation of the accidental in life; and (3) presupposes throughout a theological perspective indebted to classical Israelite prophetism and dependent upon its prior emergence.

In reading in Deuteronomy, one can have no better introduction than is contained in 4:31-39 and the moving *Shema Yisreal,* "Hear, O Israel," of 6:4-13 (a recitation in constant use in Judaism from Deuteronomy's day to the present). One will not miss the distinctive genius of the preaching: all that is urged is itself sustained by the sense of the merciful Yahweh who took a victimized nation from among the nations of the world and gave to it full life and enduring meaning. All that is urged is then caught up in the words, "You shall love Yahweh your God with all your heart!" It is all said, in a different way, in 9:6; and more fully in summary, in 10:12–22. With this done, and knowing the theme, read at random in the introduction (chaps. 1–11); read aloud, and you will be preaching in ancient Israel. But see that, like the prophets, you also stand as the recipient of the word that is spoken.

You will want to see for yourself the difference between Deuteronomy and the Covenant Code where both address the same problem. See, for example, Deut. 15:12–18 and then Exod. 21:2–11. The older law sets the Hebrew slave free after six years of servitude and legally determines related questions (Exod. 21:2 ff.); Deuteronomy restates the law but makes it subservient to the prophetic-theological ethic—when the slave goes free "you shall furnish him liberally . . . remember that you were a slave in the land of Egypt, and Yahweh your God redeemed you . . . it shall not seem hard to you, when you let him go free" (Deut. 15:14 ff.).

The peculiar character of Deuteronomy and his post-Amos-Isaiah status is equally revealed in regulations that are new, at least in the sense that they do not appear in the Covenant Code. By all means read

24:14 f. On the rights of hired servants.
23:15 f. On the sheltering of a runaway slave.
25:13–16 On weights and measures (cf. Amos 8:5!).
24:16   On the confinement of guilt to the guilty individual (and for an illustration of the application of the law, see 2 Kings 14:1–6).
22:6–7   On birds—"you shall not take the mother with the young. . . ."
25:4   On oxen—let him eat of the grain that he treads as he works!
22:8   On a railing round the roof.
23:12–14 And even on defecation; for the sake of cleanliness, of course, but—this is Deuteronomy—be clean because Yahweh walks in the midst of your camp!

An important element in the differences between the codes of Exodus and Deuteronomy is the emergence between them of classical prophetism; Leviticus 19, in the still later Holiness Code, reflects the further development of prophetism's theological ethic. One looks in vain in Deuteronomy for the statement of the equality of the stranger and the homeborn (Lev. 19:34). The nationalism mainly apparent in Deuteronomy's acute martial sensitivity speaks in discrimination against the stranger even in worship (alas, contemporary worship practices remain by and large in this sense deuteronomic), and toward the bastard child—then, as down to very recent times—there is harshness (23:3 ff. and 23:2, respectively). Inconsistencies of a theological-humanitarian kind are not uncommon: see, for example, 23:3 (Ammonites and Moabites forbidden Yahweh's presence) and 24:17 in implicit contradiction (the sojourner's justice is in no way to be perverted); or again, the contradiction between 12:29 f.; 20:16–18; and 7:3 on the one hand (all of which, in the category of Holy War, insist that there be *no* kind of intercourse between Israelite and non-Israelite), and 21:10–14 on the other hand (which not only permits intermarriage, but remarkably honors the rights of the non-Israelite wife). And sometimes, we suspect, what is represented as of nobler stuff is in reality hard, shrewd, brutal, and deeply selfish, as in 20:10–20.

Let the three underlying qualities long ago pointed up in Deuteronomy continue to testify to the fact that, package though it be, it *is* a prophetic package. First, Deuteronomy insists on the unity of God. Yahweh is *one*—and this is so emphatic (whether explicit or implicit) that it indirectly affirms that God *is alone.* Indeed, Deut. 6:4 can sustain four translations, all different but unified in meaning:[10]

> Yahweh our God is one Yahweh (RSV text)
> Yahweh our God, Yahweh is one ⎫
> Yahweh is our God, Yahweh is one ⎬ (RSV margin)
> Yahweh is our God, Yahweh alone ⎭

The second of these qualities, though perhaps narrow in itself, nevertheless grasps after what has been in Western religions a prominent and persistent hope—unity of sanctuary. In Deuteronomy it is conceived as a physical, geographical unity; but the symbol of such unity is still the yearning dream of the New Testament centuries later, a dream carried through from the old covenant to the new (see John 10:16 and 17:20). And in our own time modern Judaism with its exciting focus on the new Israel, Roman Catholicism, and world Protestantism with its increasing sense of unity—all know *now* in one form or another the worthy vision of a symbolic unity of sanctuary.

The third underlying principle or fundamental quality of Deuteronomy has been called "social morality and wholehearted worship." This is nothing other than what we have been calling

[10]On Exod. 20:3–6, see above, Chapter 3, and B. D. Napier, *Exodus,* Richmond, 1961.

the theological ethic. For all its limitations, Deuteronomy speaks for prophetic Yahwism when it pleads, as consistently it *means* to do, for righteousness and justice that issue from love of God involving all that one is—heart, soul, and might!

Faith and the Uncertain Present:
Nahum 1–3; Zephaniah 1–3; Habakkuk 1–3

> The righteous shall live by faith.
> *Hab. 2:4 (slightly modified)*

Ashurbanipal was the last strong Assyrian king. After his death in 633 or 632, Assyria's collapse was swift and sure. Babylon had its independence by 625. The Medes from the mountains of Iran pushed westward unhindered into Assyria's central domain. And out of the steppes of Russia marauding bands, probably Scythians, poured over the outlying reaches of the empire in the same decade of the 620s. The capital city of Ninevah fell in 612 to a coalition of forces involving all three of these peoples; and in 610 Assyria lost its last real battle. It was, then, no mere coincidence that Josiah expressed himself so freely in the year 621 with his Deuteronomic reform program: Assyria, liege lord of the vassal, Judah, was as good as dead!

Nahum

Nahum 1–3   With unrestrained gratification and unabashed glee, this resident of the town of Elkosh somewhere in southern Judah verbally celebrates Assyria's dying. He composes, apparently shortly before the fact in 612 B.C., a brilliant ode on the destruction of Nineveh.

> Nineveh is like a pool
>   whose waters run away.
> "Halt! Halt!" they cry;
>   . . . . . .
> And all who look on you will shrink from you and say,
> Wasted is Nineveh; who will bemoan her?
>   . . . . . .
> There is no assuaging your hurt,
>   your wound is grievous.
> All who hear the news of you
>   clap their hands over you.
> For upon whom has not come
>   your unceasing evil?
>
> (2:8; 3:7,19)

The physical text of Nahum has suffered as much abuse in transmission as any prophetic writing, as witness the excessive number of footnotes in the RSV translation. Chapter 1 may contain fragments of a prophetic oracle originally of a piece with chapters 2-3; but these Nahumesque lines, which appear only after verse 11 or 12, have been incorporated by an editor in what was intended to be an acrostic poem, a kind of alphabetical psalm. However, only fifteen lines remain of an original twenty-two, presumably one each for the twenty-two letters of the Hebrew alphabet.[11]

How is Nahum to be evaluated? What is his relationship to prophetism? Some interpret him as a cult prophet, a professional member of the temple staff, whereas others exclude him altogether from the company of the prophets. Admittedly, we have very little to go on; but tradition, never glibly to be set aside, ranks him with the prophets and his language is unmistakably prophetic:

Behold, I am against you, says Yahweh of hosts, and I will burn your chariots in smoke . . . and the voice of your messengers shall no more be heard.

Behold, I am against you,
    says Yahweh of hosts,
    and I will lift up your skirts over your face;
and I will let nations look on your nakedness
    and kingdoms on your shame.

(2:13; 3:5)

Furthermore, Nahum speaks not merely for Judah but for humanity: Assyria's death means longed-for peace and self-respect for all the small peoples of the world. How wrong he was in this; but how prophetically right in his participation in this event not merely as an Israelite, but as a member of the international community.

The central emphases of classical prophetism are lacking—the passionate address to the contemporary life of the covenant nation; the cry for justice and righteousness in the theological ethic; and the consuming concern for ultimate meaning in the events of history. But we could hardly expect to find them in such a narrowly focused subject.

[11]Cf. Duane L. Christensen, "The Acrostic of Nahum Reconsidered," *Zietschrift für die alttestamentliche Wissenschaft* 87, 1975, pp. 17-29.

For the rest, we affirm enthusiastically the judgment which ranks this brief utterance in its sheer power and skill of articulation with the best of the age of classical Hebrew—a piece toward the end of that epoch to be classed with David's Lament (2 Samuel 1) in the middle of it, and the Song of Deborah (Judges 5) from the years of its beginning.

Zephaniah

1-3   In the eruptive decade of the 620s—about ten years *before* Nahum—the prophet Zephaniah speaks out in accents strongly reminiscent of Amos and Isaiah. His place in the succession of classical prophets is unquestioned. In one or all of the several fierce new powers unleashed on dying Assyria he sees the day of Yahweh

> near and hastening fast;
> . . . . . .
> A day of wrath is that day,
>   a day of distress and anguish,
> a day of ruin and devastation,
>   a day of darkness and gloom,
> a day of clouds and thick darkness,
>   a day of trumpet blast and battle cry
>   (1:14 f.)[12]

The catastrophe of this day of Yahweh is of such magnitude as to engulf all humankind (1:18b, if original); but with the particularity characteristic of classical prophetism, the day is the day of Judah's judgment, fall, and destruction. In 1:7–9 a grim metaphor is used. On the day of Yahweh, it is none other than Yahweh who makes a sacrifice—*and Judah is the sacrificial victim!* Yahweh's guests, Israel's enemies, will consume the victim. Judah's official and ruling classes are especially singled out, a fact the more remarkable since Zephaniah is probably himself of royal descent. His genealogy (1:1) is the longest recorded of any prophet, reaching back four generations, apparently in order to name the great-great-grandfather, Hezekiah (king, *c.* 715–687).

At the end of chapter 1 (verse 18b, which *may* be secondary), Judah's fate is merged with the fate of the world. Chapter 2 opens with the prophetic plea that the covenant people of Judah-Israel turn back to Yahweh in righteousness and humility, so that

---

[12]Cf. Amos 5:18–20; Isa. 2:9 ff.; Ezek. 7:7,10,12; Lam. 1:21; and Ezek. 34:12.

"perhaps you may be hidden on the day of the wrath of Yahweh." And then, in order, Philistia (four of the five major Philistine cities are named), Moab and Ammon, and Ethiopia are all denounced in bitterest terms, capped with this eloquent description of desolate Nineveh:

> Herds shall lie down in the midst of her,
>   . . . . . .
> the vulture and the hedgehog
>   shall lodge in her capitals;
> the owl shall hoot in the window,
>   the raven croak on the threshold;
>   . . . . . .
> This is the exultant city
>   that dwelt secure!
> that said to herself,
>   "I am and there is none else!"
> What a desolation she has become,
>   a lair for wild beasts.
> All who pass by her
>   hiss and shake their fists.
>
> (2:14-15)

We are again confronted by the problem of originality and authenticity. We noted in the Book of Isaiah a miscellaneous collection of oracles against foreign nations in chapters 13-23. The books of Jeremiah (46-51) and Ezekiel (25-32) embrace similar collections. On a much smaller scale, Zephaniah 2 incorporates oracles of this same sort which must be later than the prophet himself. When Judah finally fell, its neighbors Ammon and Moab incurred the enduring hatred of all the surviving inhabitants by further humiliating the shattered people with acts of plunder and cries of derision. The oracle of 2:8-11 probably originates in those dark days, several decades after Zephaniah.

The more extreme critics have left nothing to the prophet in chapter 3; or, still with a large question mark, only verses 1-7. A more conservative judgment accepts the finely wrought indictment of Jerusalem (vv. 1-7; cf. Isa. 1:21-23); admits, at least in the present form of verses 14-20, evidence of firsthand knowledge of events in the next century; but holds the middle section, verses 8-13, so strongly in the tradition of Isaiah, to be very possibly or even probably the utterance of the seventh-century prophet.

If Isaiah 9:2-7 and/or 11:1-9 are oracles of Isaiah of Jerusalem in the eighth century, then it is Isaiah who first among the prophets speaks out in strong eschatological language. What do we mean by eschatology?

> Eschatology . . . while sometimes signifying (in the Old Testament) the abandonment of any hope for justice in this world, is essentially an expression of the sense of injustice in the world *as it is*, and the conviction that God is good and his justice must somewhere and somehow ultimately triumph.[13]

If we speak more narrowly of covenant eschatology, we mean the description of covenant fulfillment beyond the present or impending apparent frustration of covenant purpose and covenant ends. Quite apart from the specific question of the authenticity of Isaiah 9 and 11, Isaiah certainly envisaged destruction and, beyond destruction, productive, fulfilling survival: *"a remnant will return."* It is then certainly not impossible that Isaiah could have elaborated his own eschatology in one or both of these passages.

Isaiah speaks of his disciples (Hebrew, *limmudim*, 8:16). The so-called Second Isaiah (whose oracles appear mainly in chapters 40–55, but perhaps also in 34–35 and here or there in 56–66) almost two centuries later probably means to identify himself as among those disciples when he calls himself one of the *limmudim* (RSV, "those who are taught" Isa. 50:4, twice; and see below, Chap. 10). We have already suggested that Micah, if not in the circle of Isaiah's continuing discipleship, was apparently influenced by Isaianic prophetism. Zephaniah, who may borrow directly or indirectly from Amos, shows such strong affinity with Isaianic motifs as to raise the question of his possible connection with circles of Isaianic prophetism.

In any case, there is the strong possibility that the eschatological note is authentic. The skill, power, vigor of the prophetic utterance; the deftness in the use of metaphor; the brilliance of the whole prophetic production—all this is eminently worthy of the Isaianic tradition. More specifically, Isaianic influence asserts itself in the admonition to be silent, before Yahweh (1:7); the enumeration of the symbols of human pride like "the fortified cities" and "the lofty battlements" (1:16); the emphasis on humanity (2:3); the very language in which the prophet's anti-Assyrianism is couched (2:13–15; cf. Isaiah 10); the indictment of Jerusalem, as already noted; the eschatology implicit in Yahweh's

[13]M. Burrows. *An Outline of Biblical Theology*, Philadelphia, 1946, p. 286. (Italics mine.)

plea, "Wait for me!" (3:8; cf. Isa. 8:17; 30:15); and perhaps most compellingly,

On that day . . .
. . . . . .
. . . I will remove from your midst
  your proudly exultant ones,
and you shall no longer be haughty
  in my holy mountain.
For I will leave in the midst of you
  a people humble and lowly.
They shall seek refuge in the name of Yahweh,
. . . . . .
For they shall pasture and lie down,
  and none shall make them afraid.
                                        (3:11–13)

This is the distinguished seventh-century prophet Zephaniah, who pictured Yahweh as a kind of sinister Diogenes, holding aloft a lamp and searching out in Jerusalem all who, like coagulated wine, have "thickened on their lees," lost all their covenant sensibilities, and whose attitude toward Yahweh is the ultimate denial of prophetic Yahwism—"Yahweh will not do good, nor will Yahweh do ill" (1:12). Yahweh may *be*, but Yahweh does not *do*; the life of Yahweh is utterly unrelated to the living of our days; God is absent from our history.

This invokes the judgment, the "return to Egypt." Out of the second Egypt the purposes for which Yahweh chose Israel shall be fulfilled. In the traditional medieval representation of Zephaniah, the prophet himself holds the lamp and sheds the light; and so in fact he does.

Habakkuk

1–3

We have here only the scantiest direct information about the prophet himself. There is no authentic extrabiblical tradition about him; and the Old Testament gives us only the single line in the book which bears his name, "The oracle of God which Habakkuk the prophet saw" (1:1).

We cannot even fix his dates precisely. He speaks out in the face of Babylon's fresh aggression (Chaldeans, 1:6), probably in the decade of the 610s, perhaps closer to 600. Jerusalem was to suffer heavy deportation under neo-Babylonian conquest in 597 and, ten years later, destruction by the same armies. He raises the problem we have come to identify by the term theodicy (Greek: *theos*, God; plus *dikē*, right, justice). Theodicy presupposes the prophetic proposition that God rules *in history* and, of course, that God is just. What then of patent historical injustice? How injustice?

Specifically, Habakkuk proceeds as follows:

1:2–4   Forthright and bitter complaint over the wicked character of presiding power.

1:5–11   Yahweh's unapologetic response, not only not answering the prophet's lament but for the moment apparently confirming its validity. Chaldean power—magnificently described—*is* the power of "guilty ones whose own might is their God!"

1:12–17 The resumption of the prophet's complaint. He knows that Yahweh has "ordained them as a judgment," but what of Yahweh's judgment against *them*, when they go on "mercilessly slaying nations for ever!"?

2:1–3   The prophet now stations himself ("on the tower") to await "the vision," the divine answer to his anguished problem. The vision is delayed, but the Word of Yahweh assures its coming and demands that it be written "plain upon tablets," so that even a jogging runner may be able to read it. The vision—as we read Habakkuk—is recorded in the "prayer of Habakkuk" in chapter 3,[14] which, in the original arrangement of the text, may have immediately followed 2:1–3.

2:4–5   Any translation of the first two lines of verse 5 will represent some conjecture, since the Hebrew text is obscure. This little unit is in the form of a *mashal*, that is, a proverb or parable, designed to bridge the gap between the expectant prophet, waiting for his vision, and the five woes pronounced in the next section. Verse 4 nevertheless states the theme of Habakkuk and verse 5 is an appropriate prelude to the woes.

2:6–19   The five woes are invoked against Babylon, by the victimized nations. In this perspective, Babylon is, in the family of nations, (1) the despot, (2) the megalomaniac, (3) the perpetrator of violence, (4) a vicious tormentor, and (5) in Israel's book the worst offense, an idolater, worshiper of inanimate wood and stone! This last, but perhaps also all of these indictments, invokes the familiar lines,

> but Yahweh is in the holy temple;
> let all the earth keep silence in that presence.

And one is reminded again of the great Isaiah (cf. Isa. 2:17; 7:9b; 8:16; 30:15).

[14]See A. Weiser, *The Old Testament: Its Formation and Development*, trans. Dorothea M. Barton, New York, 1961, pp. 258 ff. I am indebted to Weiser's analysis of Habakkuk.

3:1-19   This is set now, like a psalm, with directions for its (cultic) performance. Conventional liberal criticism has deemed the
"prayer" of Habakkuk to be a later, and unauthentic, addition. We prefer the judgment of those who read here the report
of the promised vision, which, in its use of brilliant images,
reminds us of Judges 5 and Deuteronomy 33.

We hold to the substantial unity of the little book. Habakkuk
may well have been a cultic prophet, professionally attached to
the Jerusalem temple as a member of the temple staff. The forms
of prophetic utterance which he employs are disciplined forms, by
his time conventionalized in the institution of prophetism. We
sense in Habakkuk the meaning of the free-ranging prophetic
speech and the best of the long-disciplined liturgical expression in
temple cultus:

> O Yahweh, I heard the report of thee,
>   and thy work, O Yahweh, do I fear[15]
> In the midst of the years renew it;
>   in the midst of the years make it known;
>   in wrath remember mercy.
>
>   (3:2)

This is one of the great, timeless prayers of the Old Testament,
created out of a prophetic faith confronted by an uncertain present and an immediate *catastrophic* future.

The theme of Habakkuk is faith, and faith is not espoused as an
answer to the problem of theodicy. The prophet is content to live
with the problem in the conviction that faith can sustain any and
all seeming denials of the reign of God and the justice of God
(3:17-18). One thinks of Rainer Maria Rilke's words in his *Letters
to a Young Poet*:

Be patient towards all that is unsolved and try to love the questions
themselves. . . . Do not now seek the answers, which cannot be given
you because you would not be able to live them. And the point is to live
everything. Live the questions now. Perhaps you will then gradually,
without noticing it, live along some distant day into the answer.[16]

The stated proposition that "the righteous shall live by faith"
(2:4b) no doubt came to mean in subsequent Judaism that the
religious Jew is justified and fulfills covenant responsibility by
faithfulness—to the formal prescriptions of *torah*, the whole law
and instruction of "Moses." Yet even here, even in the circles of

---

[15]Fear in the sense of acknowledge, affirm, respect.
[16]Trans. M. D. Herter Norton, rev. ed., New York, p. 35.

much maligned (unjustly) postexilic legalistic Judaism (fifth and following centuries B.C.), if this kind of faithfulness in carrying out the (religious) law is what justifies and even defines "the righteous," it must be remembered that this was the best, and perhaps the only, way in which the prophetic Yahweh faith could now come to expression. And for the prophet Habakkuk, as always for prophetic Judaism and prophetic Christianity, the phrase carries the primary meaning—*the* biblical-theological theme—that the quality of righteousness is not first an item of performance but of faith; that the only righteous life is lived in faith, which alone is able to sustain life. The Yahwist knew this in the tenth century and affirmed it then (Gen. 15:6). It was Isaiah's fundamental affirmation (7:9). Indeed, the key word in both of these is "believe," from the same Hebrew root as Habakkuk's "faith." Paul, on behalf of the covenant community of the New Testament, is not wrong when he quotes and interprets Habakkuk as he does (Gal. 3:11 and Rom. 1:17; cf. Heb. 10:38); nor was Martin Luther guilty of any textual distortion when he took this declaration, originally out of classical prophetism, as the primary point of cohesion for the Protestant Reformation.

In ancient Israel's most dismal, hopeless hours, prophetism continued to speak with honesty, realistically acknowledging the anguish of Israel's existence and the fearful perplexities therein for the prophet; and yet at the same time it joyfully affirmed Yahweh's reign and the ultimate success of the Word. "The wicked surround the righteous and justice goes forth perverted!" (1:4). This *is*, says the prophet; I see it, I live with it, and I vigorously and even violently protest it. Nevertheless, and even though it continue and be intensified, "I will rejoice in Yahweh, I will joy in the God of my salvation!" (3:18).

This is the righteousness which lives only in faith.

Protesting Prophetism: Jeremiah 1–52[17]

> Before I formed you in the womb, I knew you.
>
> **Jer. 1:5**

The Time and the Book

The prophetic career of Jeremiah begins during the reign of Josiah (640–609), in the thirteenth year of that reign (1:2), and so

---

[17]In addition to the Book of Jeremiah, see 2 Kings 23:28–25:30.

in the turbulent decade of the 620s (or possibly, changing "thirteenth" to "twenty-three" in 1:2, in the decade of the 610s).[18] The bulk of material in the Book of Jeremiah relates to the years after the accession of Jehoiakim in 609; and we know that Jeremiah was still an active prophet long after Jerusalem's fall to Babylon in 587. His was, like Isaiah's, a long career.

Three kinds of material relating to Jeremiah and his times dominate the book: (1) prophetic oracles deemed in their freshness and vitality to be authentic, in the sense in which we have used this word before; (2) historical-biographical narratives, conservatively attributed (and rightly, we think) in first origin to Baruch, the prophet's personal scribe (36:4 ff.); (3) oracles related in essence to (1) but obviously edited by deuteronomists.

The contents of Jeremiah can be described as follows:

1   The prophet's introduction and call.

2–25   Oracles for the most part; and for the most part against Judah and Jerusalem. Here the reader confronts *the* problem of Jeremiah: the arrangement of the material is not consistently chronological and it is sometimes impossible to discover any sense or scheme behind the present arrangement. That the physical text of Jeremiah has suffered uncommon problems in transmission is apparent from a comparison of the Hebrew and Greek (Septuagint) forms of the text. Appreciable sections of the Hebrew are missing altogether in the Greek (about 12 percent, in bulk of words); and the block of oracles against foreign nations (chaps. 46–51) is placed in the Septuagint after 25:13, and in completely different order. On the other hand, this section does exhibit this much order: chapters 1–6 reflect Josiah's reign; 7–20 contain oracles for the most part from the reign of Jehoiakim (609–598); and 21–25 are largely later.

26–36   The dominant first-person, oracular, forms of the preceding section give way now to narration of episodes. Jeremiah's scribe, Baruch, is probably responsible for the basic structure of chapters 26–45. Chapters 7 and 26 offer instructive comparison. The first is preserved no doubt from Jeremiah's dictation, and reports what was spoken; the other, dealing with the same episode, is concerned much more with the *circumstances* of

<hr>

[18]J. P. Hyatt, "Jeremiah," *The Interpreter's Bible,* Nashville, 1956, vol. 5, has argued for the later date against the conventional date of 626 B.C. On this and other questions see the admirable study, William Holladay, *Jeremiah: Spokesman Out of Time,* Philadelphia, 1974.

Jeremiah's temple speech. The time sequence in 26–29 is chronological, moving from Jehoiakim's reign (26) to Zedekiah's (598–587); and chapter 29 is a letter to Babylonian exiles deported from Judah by Nebuchadnezzar in 597. Chapters 30–31 constitute the most important collection of prophetic promises of restoration; 32 contains Jeremiah's emphatic confirmation of this promise in his purchase of land; 33 reiterates, in different form, the essential message of ultimate hope; 34 dates from Jerusalem's final siege, which ended in the city's destruction in 587; 35 leaps back to the days of Jehoiakim and lauds the faithfulness of the Rechabites, a sect in Judah preserving the forms of wilderness existence; and 36 gives us the Old Testament's only description of the origin of a scroll, also in Jehoiakim's reign.

37–45   Here is recounted Jeremiah's experiences during Babylon's three-year siege of Jerusalem, which ended in the city's fall and destruction in 587. This takes, for the most part, the character of an intimately informed report from Baruch, who describes in detail the suffering and fate of his master through these days of catastrophe. Baruch remained to the end the faithful scribe and disciple; and this section appropriately concludes with a notice (chap. 45) reflecting Jeremiah's appreciation of Baruch.[19]

46–51   This is a collection of oracles against foreign nations (cf. Isaiah 13–23 and Ezekiel 25–32) almost certainly compiled after Jeremiah's day. Some of these oracles may originate in prophetic circles quite independent of Jeremiah; but others—for example, the oracle against Egypt (46:2–28) and those oracles directed against Moab, Ammon, Edom (48:1–49:27), and Elam (49:34–39)—may well be fashioned in present form from authentic oracles of Jeremiah.

52   An appended historical narrative, largely paralleled in 2 Kings 24:18–25:1–21,27–30.

The Prophetic Quality

The best introduction to Jeremiah is Jeremiah. The following selection of brief readings from the Book of Jeremiah represents some of the important forms, moods, and emphases, and the passionate self-involvement of the prophetism of Jeremiah. Read these, if possible aloud, without concern for critical questions of precise date and specific background. We know the broad character of Jeremiah's time; that is enough.

Yahweh to Jeremiah:

[19]Cf. Weiser, op. cit., pp. 214–15.

Run to and fro through the streets of Jerusalem,
look and take note!
Search her squares to see
if you can find a single
soul who does justice
and seeks truth,
that I may pardon her.

. . . . . .

Jeremiah:

Thou hast smitten them,
but they felt no anguish
thou hast consumed them,
but they refused to take correction.
They have made their faces harder than rock;
they have refused to repent.

Then I said, "These are only the poor,
they have no sense;
for they do not know the way of Yahweh,
the law of their God.
I will go to the great,
and will speak to them:
for they know the way of Yahweh,
the law of their God."
But they all alike had broken the yoke,
they had burst the bonds.

(5:1–5)

Yahweh:

For from the least to the greatest of them,
every one is greedy for unjust gain;
and from prophet to priest,
every one deals falsely.
They have healed the wound of my people lightly,
saying, "Peace, peace!"
when there is no peace!

(6:13–14)

Behold, you trust in lying [RSV, deceptive] words to no avail. Will you
steal, murder, commit adultery, swear falsely, burn incense to Baal, and
go after other gods that you have not known, and then come and stand
before me in this house, which is called by my name, and say, "We are
delivered!". . . Has this house, which is called by my name, become a
den of robbers in your eyes?

(7:8–11)

Therefore I still contend with you, . . .
and with your children's children I will contend.
. . . . . .
Has a nation changed its gods,
even though they are no gods?
But my people have changed their glory
for that which does not profit!
Be appalled, O heavens, at this,
be shocked, be utterly desolate, . . .
for my people have committed two evils:
they have forsaken me,
the fountain of living waters,
and hewed out cisterns for themselves
broken cisterns,
that can hold no water.

(2:9–13)

Have I been a wilderness to Israel,
or a land of thick darkness?
Why then do my people say, "We are free,
we will come no more to thee"?
Can a maiden forget her ornaments,
or a bride her attire?
Yet my people have forgotten me
days without number.

(2:31–32)

In anguish, now, Jeremiah cries out, seeing only destruction:

My grief is beyond healing,
my heart is sick within me.
Hark, the cry of the daughter of my people,
from the length and breadth of the land:
"Is Yahweh not in Zion?
Is her King not in her?
. . . . . .
The harvest is past, the summer is ended,
and we are not saved!"
For the wound of the daughter of my people is my heart
wounded,
I mourn, and dismay has taken hold on me.

Is there no balm in Gilead?
  Is there no physician there?
Why then has the health of the daughter of my people
  not been restored?
O that my head were waters,
  and my eyes a fountain of tears,
That I might weep day and night
  for the slain of the daughter of my people!

                                                    (8:18–9:1)

Finally, again the Yahweh Word looking beyond the catastrophe:

Return, O faithless children, says Yahweh;
  for I am your master;
I will take you, one from a city, and two from a family,
  and I will bring you to Zion.
And I will give you shepherds after my own heart,
  who will feed you with knowledge and understanding.
                                                    (3:14–15)

. . . I will make a new covenant with the house of Israel and the house of
Judah. . . . I will put my law within them, and I will write it upon their
hearts; and I will be their God, and they shall be my people. And no
longer shall each one teach one's neighbor . . . saying "Know Yahweh,"
for they shall all know me, from the least of them to the greatest; for I
will forgive their iniquity, and I will remember their sin no more.
                                                    (31:31–34)

A Prophet Among Prophets

Jeremiah's call took him to the capital city of Judah from his
native town of Anathoth, set in the rugged, barren hills a few
miles north of Jerusalem. He was the son of a priest in Anathoth
(1:1) who may well have found himself without employment when
Josiah's deuteronomic reform (in 621) centralized all of Judah's
worship in the Jerusalem temple.

Jeremiah, with Zephaniah, stands next in the succession of
great classical prophets after the giants of the preceding (ninth
and eighth) centuries. Some brief words of comparison may be instructive. Jeremiah was both like and unlike Elijah. He seems, like
Elijah, almost to have cherished his stark singularity, his
aloneness, his separateness. And yet, in one of a number of para-
doxical qualities in his personality, Jeremiah was more passionately gregarious than any prophet before him. It was one of the
major frustrations of his life that the city of Jerusalem, the largest
city by far in Judah, was never able to satisfy his love of people

and his intense desire to be warmly accepted, to be loved. To the end, Jeremiah resented bitterly his own alienation within the city. To the end he was baffled and outraged by the city's life and manner and disposition.

He was both like and unlike Amos. The strident prophetic note of denunciation and doom is familiar in both prophets. But while in Amos this note is struck with a force and persistence at best, for the most part, only implicitly relieved, it is sounded by Jeremiah consistently with compassion and personal anguish. For it is a part of the distinctive character of Jeremiah that he always sees himself in dual focus. He is the whip of God, called to wield the Yahweh Word which must first be a seemingly merciless lash. At the same time, the prophet sees himself standing under the abuse of the very weapon he wields, in full identification with those whom he is called to scourge with the Word of Yahweh. It is another paradox in Jeremiah that this prophet who defined (with his younger contemporary, Ezekiel) a new covenant between Yahweh and the individual (Jer. 31:31 ff.; cf. Ezek. 11:19–20; 37) bears in himself the strongest convictions of the solidarity of human life, the inescapable involvement of the life of the one in the life of the many, and the essentially corporate nature both of virtue and of sin. More closely than of any other person in the Old Testament—and quite without sacrilege—the words of the Servant Poem (in Isa. 53:4–5) may be applied to Jeremiah: "Surely he has borne our griefs and carried our sorrows . . . . he was wounded for our transgressions, he was bruised for our iniquities."

Jeremiah is also both like and unlike Isaiah. Each is called out of a quiet and relatively secure existence into the unpopular role of speaking, acting representative of an angry God, a Yahweh determined now to act in judgment. Both are initiated into uncommonly long prophetic careers by indescribably moving encounters with Yahweh, which both nevertheless attempt to describe. But while Isaiah enters this service as a kind of involuntary volunteer, Jeremiah sees himself from the beginning as a conscript, captive to a Word he would, if only he could, defy and ignore (see 20:7 ff.). And the glory and grandeur of Isaiah's vision (Isaiah 6) is in stark contrast to Jeremiah's consummate simplicity and his profound and bitterly protesting humility (see especially 1:4–10,17–19). But here, too, Israelite prophetism attains one of its highest peaks: for here there is no intermediary agency. In this one individual, Jeremiah, this lonely prophet, this exquisitely sensitive, turbulently loving person—here God and humanity meet! It is a meeting specifically direct and intensely personal—but at once involving all of human history, all of human existence. It is a relationship in which human and divine emotion are merged and in such a phenomenal union as ultimately to defy separation. In this person, classical prophetism comes as close to incarnation as it is to come.

Jeremiah in History

In Josiah's Reign (640–609)

Four events loom especially large in this epoch. (1) The call of Jeremiah sometime during the middle years of the decade of the 620s is coincident with the collapse of Assyrian power from assertive forces both within and without the empire. Jeremiah, through whom the Word of Judah's destruction has been spoken, sees one of these powers as the instrument of judgment (1:13 ff.). (2) A few years after his call, the prophet watches the process of Josiah's reforms. It is impossible now to recover his initial attitude. It is clear that he was later disillusioned. It is, on the other hand, not an unreasonable assumption that in its early enthusiastic introduction, he encouraged the reform. Long after Josiah's death, he held Josiah in high regard (22:15b,16); and if 11:1–8 refers to Josiah's reformation, there is no question about it: "Cursed be everyone who does not heed the words of this covenant. . . . Hear the words of this covenant and do them." Perhaps 8:8 is a considerably later reflection of the prophet on the same deuteronomic law; "How can you say, 'we are wise, and the law of Yahweh is with us'? But, behold, the false pen of the scribes has made it into a lie." Or are both of these references to other covenants, other laws? It is in any case clear that Jeremiah lived to see the collapse of Josiah's reformation. (3) There is no report of any response from Jeremiah to the fall of Nineveh in 612. (4) There is only the briefest passing word on Josiah's death (22:10).

In Jehoiakim's Reign (609–598)

Josiah is immediately succeeded by Jehoahaz, a *younger* son of Josiah, apparently the popular choice. He dares to defy Egypt and is deposed by Pharaoh Neco in favor of his older brother, Jekoaikim. Jeremiah apparently held Jehoahaz in respect and even affection, and laments his tragic fate of permanent exile (22:10–12; see also 2 Kings 23:30 ff.). One attempt on Jeremiah's life—there may have been several—occurs now at Anathoth (11:18–23), which gives rise to the same complaint in Jeremiah that is voiced about the same time by Habakkuk (12:1–6; cf. Hab. 1:2–4). Yahweh's answer to Jeremiah (12:5) is, in poetic effect, You haven't seen anything yet!

Some of the greatest prophetic utterances of Jeremiah originate in this period: the parable of the potter, chapter 18; the temple discourse, 7:1–8:3,26, with its expression of Jeremiah's characteristic tension between the Word of destruction and his own pleading word of mercy, 7:16 ff. (cf. 18:20 and 14:11); Jeremiah's profound grief, 8:4–9:1; his affinity with Hosea, 13:18–27 but in many other passages as well; the certainty of destruction, 14:10–18; the quality of the "confession" in 15:10–18 (as also elsewhere) that brings Jeremiah closer to us than any other figure in the Old Testament; the symbolic act again, chapter 19—only Ezekiel among the prophets performs more such acts than Jeremiah; the bitterest of his confessions, 20:7–18, matched in the Old Testament only in Job (cf. Job 3); his association with Baruch in the remarkable narrative of chapter 36, "in the fourth year of Jehoiakim"; and his devastating words on Jehoiakim, 22:13–19, bitter testimony to what was in Jeremiah's eyes the miserable rule of a miserable king.

In Zedekiah's Reign (598–587)

Jekoiakim dies (or is assassinated) while Jerusalem is under siege by Babylon in 598. His eighteen-year-old son, Jehoiachin, succeeds him and "reigns" for three months in the besieged city until he is forced to surrender. Jehoiachin gives himself up and the city is spared destruction for another decade; but the young king spends the next thirty-seven years in Babylonian prison until he is finally released in 561 (see Jer. 22:24–30; and 2 Kings 25:27–30). His weakling uncle, Zedekiah, presides over the last years of ancient Israelite Jerusalem. Jeremiah writes movingly to the company exiled with Jehoiachin to Babylon (chap. 29). It is still early in Zedekiah's reign when Jeremiah has his violent encounter with the prophet Hananiah (chap. 28). During the final three years of Zedekiah's reign, Jerusalem remains under Babylonian siege and Jeremiah remains the outspoken prophet of the impending tragedy as Yahweh's act of judgment. It is not strange that in a city straining every faculty toward the very faint hope of survival, such a line as Jeremiah's would be regarded not merely with distaste, but as defeatist if not downright seditious. Even when the siege is briefly lifted, while Babylonian forces frightened Egypt home again, Jeremiah declares once more Yahweh's totally negative Word—the Chaldeans will return, take this city, and burn it with fire (see 37:4–10). We cannot wonder, then, that Jeremiah is beaten and imprisoned (37:11–21). We wonder only that he survived at all—indirect tribute to the place of prophetism in ancient Israel, despite the individual unpopularity of most of the prophets. Earlier, in Jehoiakim's reign, Jeremiah's life was spared only, apparently, on the precedent of the prophet Micah, who had not been put to death by Hezekiah when he had, like Jeremiah, predicted the destruction of the city (chap. 26, the parallel and sequel to the temple discourse of chap. 7). Zedekiah remains eager to know the Yahweh Word from Jeremiah (37:17; 38:14), but he lacks the courage to support the prophet (38:4–5), swears Jeremiah to secrecy about their conversations (38:24), and ultimately rejects the counsel of submission to Babylon which Jeremiah gives him (38:17–20).

Jerusalem continues to resist until the wall is breached. Three years was a long siege and the long-frustrated, now victorious armies of Babylon take bitter vengeance (39:1–2,4–10 is an abbreviation of 52:4–16 and a repeat of 2 Kings 25:1–12). Jeremiah is set free under exceedingly liberal terms: in Babylon's eyes he had been, in effect, a collaborator (40:1–6). Those not taken captive—the poorest elements of Judah—set up a community at Mizpeh, a few miles north of the ruined Jerusalem, under the administration of Gedaliah, the appointive governor of Judah. Gedaliah is assassinated by a violently nationalist group under one Ishmael, whose bloody coup at Mizpeh is, however, quickly ended (chap. 41). The survivors at Mizpeh resolve to take up voluntary exile in Egypt and hope to have an affirmative word from Jeremiah, whose counsel they seek. Their piety is prodigious: "Whether it is good or evil, we will obey the voice of Yahweh. . . ." (42:6). The Word comes ("at the end of ten days"!): "Remain in this land" (42:10). But this is another instance when confirmation, not counsel, is sought. Jeremiah is again called a liar for representing the unpopular word as the Yahweh Word (43:2); and the whole Mizpeh community under

Johanan and "all the insolent men" go into Egypt, taking Jeremiah and Baruch with them (43:4-7).

And old Jeremiah? A tradition, unconfirmed and unconfirmable, reports that they stoned him to death there. It is certain that he found himself still proclaiming essentially the same word of violence and destruction which it had been his to speak from the beginning of his career, still no doubt to his own anguish. The last words we hear from him are like the first (see 43:8-11 and 44:26-30). The judgment, even on these survivors, is only suspended. "I am watching over them for evil and not for good; all the folk of Judah who are in the land of Egypt shall be consumed by the sword and by famine, until there is an end of them!" (44:27).

9

Applied Judgment:
The Sixth Century

Hope and Bitterness:
Jeremiah, Obadiah, Lamentations

> I am with you to save you [but] I will chasten you in just measure.
> *Jer. 30:11*[1]

Jeremiah: Prophet and Covenant

Since the days of Tiglath-pileser and Isaiah, Southern Israel, the little kingdom of Judah, had lived with and under prophetic Yahwism's persistent proclamation of death. Jerusalem surrendered to Babylon in 597, already a doomed state. In 587 the city was destroyed after a three-year siege by the forces of Nebuchadnezzar, Babylonian king. In both debacles, and indeed again in 582, Babylon, following Assyrian practice, forcibly deported large numbers of the surviving populations and particularly those deemed to be capable of leading any subsequent insurrection. A people whose faith attributed their very peoplehood to the gracious, purposive power of their God, Yahweh, now suffered, no doubt with bitter incredulity, the destruction of this wonderfully created people of Israel; and, according to the same Yahweh-faith, the end was effected as the beginning, by Yahweh and the power of Yahweh's Word. Out of Egypt into this land: out of chaos into meaning—but now back to Egypt, as it were, consigned again to the chaotic and the meaningless, to a state of oppression.

Prophetism *never* deemed this to be the end. Judgment is bitter, but its function is the restitution of productive order, its aim always positive (see below, chap. 10). We left Jeremiah in the preceding discussion breathing fire on the beaten survivors of 587. But we know the other side of this astonishing man's prophetism.

[1]Cf. Psalms 89, 137.

Exile would be long. It is twice stated in Jeremiah as seventy years (25:11 and 29:10). It was something less than this for the first returnees (c. 538), but approximately this length of time from 587 to the reconstruction of the temple in the years c. 520–515. Is "seventy" Jeremiah's round number, the maximum allotment of time to anyone, to encourage the exiles to unpack their bags and prepare to live and die in the "city where I have sent you into exile" (see again his letter to the exiles of 597, chap. 29)? Or is this number editorial, deeming "exile" to end with the reconstituted temple? For Jeremiah, in any case, exile would be long; but it would also be terminal and *all* Israel would participate in the restoration (see especially now chap. 31). We have already marked Jeremiah's concrete demonstration of the certainty of restoration: in the final year of the fatal siege,

I bought the field at Anathoth from Hanamel my cousin. . . . and I gave the deed of purchase to Baruch. . . . in the presence of all the Jews who were sitting in the court of the guard. And I charged Baruch in their presence, saying. . . . thus says Yahweh of hosts, the God of Israel; Houses and fields and vineyards shall again be bought in this land!

(32:9–15)

As has been most aptly remarked, Jeremiah's action here "smacks of the same paradox as if a contemporary should forecast nuclear warfare and then proceed to buy a choice piece of real estate on Manhattan";[2] yet even more—as if this were done when the sirens were already warning of the fatal attack!

All of the major emphases of classical prophetism are present in Jeremiah. But, as with every great prophet, there is that which is distinctive and even unique. In Jeremiah the impact of the *person* of the prophet is quite without parallel. Nowhere else do we encounter the depth and intimacy and force of Jeremiah's own self-disclosure; in no other Old Testament figure do we face so vividly, so realistically, this kind of personal anguish in unceasing tension with profoundly saintly faith. We are talking about *hope* in Jeremiah. One of the great paradoxes of the Judeo-Christian faith is for the first time made explicitly articulate in Jeremiah. It appears again in the Bible most notably in the New Testament in Jesus of Nazareth. In the "knowledge" of God's effective, mean-

---

[2]N. H. Gottwald, *A Light to the Nations*, New York, 1959, p. 370.

ingful involvement in the very substance of human history, Jeremiah and Jesus regard as indivisible, as faces of the same coin, God's love and wrath, God's grace and judgment. And they understand that redemption involves inseparably both peace and anguish. Jeremiah and Jesus affirm essentially the same paradox as regards prophet and people, whether of the old covenant or the new: if one would save one's life one must lose it. The finding lies always beyond, and only beyond, the losing. Peace is always beyond, and only beyond, anguish.

One will not want to miss the old prophetic emphasis, here renewed, confirmed, strengthened—the power and entity of the Word for Jeremiah (1:3,9,10,12,18,19; cf. again Isa. 55:10 f.); the remarkably forthright declaration on the subject of slaves and human liberty (34:12 ff.); the analysis, typical of Jeremiah, of the character of false prophetism (23:23–32; cf. Isa. 30:9–11); or this word on the nature of biblical faith:

Let not the wise glory in wisdom, let not the mighty glory in might, let not the rich glory in riches; but let all who glory, glory in this—that they understand and know me, that I am Yahweh who practices kindness [*hesed*], justice, and righteousness in the earth; for in these things I delight, says Yahweh.

(9:23 f., slightly emended)

But it must be finally the new covenant which stands as the last word. Again in the Judeo-Christian faith, this is the first expression of the indomitable hope which, in any ultimate analysis, is the saving source of the strength both of Judaism and Christianity:

Behold, the days are coming, says Yahweh, when I will make a new covenant with the house of Israel and the house of Judah, not like the covenant . . . which they broke. . . . I will put my law within them, and I will write it upon their hearts; and I will be their God, and they shall be my people. . . .

(see 31:31–34)

The Bitterness of Edom: Obadiah

Obad.
vv. 1–21

There is no bitterness like that between relatives. Ancestral tradition preserves the fact of the close relationship between Israel (Jacob) and Edom (Esau): Jacob and Esau are twins (Gen. 25:24–26). But in the day of Israel's final ignominy, in the collapse and destruction of Jerusalem in 587, Edom gave brotherly help—to the enemy! This littlest of prophetic "books" eloquently records the bitterness against Edom in surviving circles of prophetism.

> For the violence done to your brother Jacob,
>> shame shall cover you,
>> . . . . . .
> on the day that strangers carried off his [Jacob/Israel's] wealth and the foreigners entered his gates
>> and cast lots for Jerusalem,
>> you were like one of them.

(vv. 10–11)

The name Obadiah ("Servant of Yahweh") *may* be a later attachment to the oracles to honor the memory of Ahab's majordomo back in the ninth century (1 Kings 18:3 ff.); or it is possibly the real name of a sixth-century prophet on whose lips originated substantially what we have in verses 2–14. Verses 15–21 obviously reflect a different situation. Esau/Edom still figures, but now the fate of *all* Israel's enemies is contrasted with the ultimate glory of Israel. It has been common to attribute the second section to another source; but it may be that it should be assigned only to another mood and time in the life of the same prophet.

In the final arrangement of the canon, Obadiah follows Amos perhaps for two reasons. In Amos 9:12 the day is envisaged when Edom will be possessed by Israel. More important, we suspect, Obadiah takes up again (as Isaiah and Zephaniah had done earlier) Amos's theme of the day of Yahweh (v. 15).

It is interesting to note that one in the collection of oracles against the nations in Jeremiah is probably dependent upon Obadiah: there are a number of parallels between Jer. 49:7–22 and Obad. verses 1–9. One often has reason to suspect that the remarkable emotional vitality and equilibrium of Israelite Yahwism and subsequent Judaism is in part due to the verbal discharge of all widely suffered frustrations, antagonisms, and aggressions. Ancient Israel suffered intensely as a people, and, judged by any commonly employed criteria, it suffered its most exquisite abuse arbitrarily and unjustly (as did the Jews, the descendants of ancient Israel, particularly in the Holocaust, in World War II, Germany). But as a people, Israel never suffered mutely! And it was able to produce as a part of its phenomenal literature the skillfully wrought expression of the nature and the subjects of its wrath and ire, suffering and anguish. Both Obadiah and Lamentations (as well as numbers of psalms) are in liturgical form. See, for example, the refrain running through Obad. verses 12–14. With some persistent regularity this people was able thus to discharge the otherwise debilitating poison of profound feelings of injury and of impotence in the face of shameless abuse and aggression.

It would be wrong, we think, to dismiss Obadiah's sentiment as unqualified human hatred. Even this little piece comes appropriately into the canon of the prophets since "it is not fanatic nationalistic hate but rather the notion of an appropriately compensating divine justice that shapes the proclamation of Obadiah."[3]

Bitterness and Hope in Lamentations

1–5   The study of meter in Hebrew poetry had its beginnings in these five poems. The first four are acrostics (like Nahum 1, Psalm 119, Proverbs 31); that is, the twenty-two letters of the Hebrew alphabet are employed in succession, one at the beginning of each verse. The English versification in chapter 3 accords three verses to each letter. The fifth poem has twenty-two lines but does not follow the acrostic scheme.

The prevailing demands of this exacting form impose some restrictions on the free delivery of emotion. Nevertheless, taken together these dirges illuminate with brightness and a sense of reality the anguished reactions to 587 and its aftermath among Judah's survivors. All five poems are to be dated in the sixth century. Some expert readers have claimed to find internal evidence that chapters 2 and 4 stand closest to 587 (on the strength, chiefly, of an "eyewitness" quality allegedly not present in the others); that chapters 1 and 5 are a little later; and that chapter 3 is the latest of the five. Other equally expert readers admit of some unevenness from poem to poem, but cite comparable inconsistencies within the individual laments and a certain possibly calculated coordination in the present arrangement of the five poems. These readers conclude that while the issue of unity may remain in doubt, there is insufficient evidence to justify the firm assertion of a plurality of sources. In any case, the five poems represent the same epoch, the same experience, the same point of view.

[3]A. Weiser, *The Old Testament: Its Formation and Development*, New York, 1962, pp. 247–49.

The book of Lamentations was written, not simply to memorialize the tragic destruction of Jerusalem, but to interpret the meaning of God's rigorous treatment of his people, to the end that they would learn the lessons of the past and retain their faith in him in the face of overwhelming disaster. There is deep sorrow over the past and some complaint but there is also radiant hope for the future, particularly in ch. 3.[4]

This is an important observation. The tone of the dirge *is* seldom relieved; but here and there explicitly, and much more pervasively implicitly, Lamentations affirms Yahweh's continuous purpose in history and his reign over the world of nations. This is briefly illustrated in the fourth poem when Lamentations picks up the theme of Obadiah (the first line is surely ironic):

> Rejoice and be glad, O daughter of Edom,
> . . . . . .
> but to you also the cup shall pass;
> you shall become drunk and strip yourself bare.
> The punishment of your iniquity, O daughter of Zion,
> is accomplished, he will keep you in exile no longer;
> But your iniquity, O daughter of Edom, he will punish,
> he will uncover your sins.
>
> (4:21–22)

There is no substance whatsoever to the tradition attributing Lamentations to Jeremiah; but in such lines as this we understand why the identification was made and we strongly suspect dependence, conscious or unconscious, on Jeremiah's language:

> My eyes are spent with weeping;
> my soul is in tumult;
> my heart is poured out in grief
> because of the destruction of the daughter of my people.
>
> (2:11)[5]

And in the mood of Jeremiah's confessions, but with the "I" changed to "we":

> Thou hast wrapped thyself with anger and pursued us,
> slaying without pity;
> thou hast wrapped thyself with a cloud
> so that no prayer can pass through.

---

[4]T. J. Meek, "Lamentations Introduction," *The Interpreter's Bible*, Nashville, 1956, vol. 6, pp. 5 f. See also Delbert R. Hillers, *Lamentations* (*Anchor Bible*), Garden City, N.Y., 1972, especially the Introduction, pp. xv ff.

[5]Cf. 3:48–49 and Jer. 8:18 ff.

Thou hast made us offscouring and refuse
  among the peoples.
All our enemies
  rail against us;
panic and pitfalls have come upon us,
  devastation and destruction;

(3:43–47)[6]

To bring Jeremiah to mind is to bring hope to mind. In the passage—it stands solidly in the very center of Lamentations—where the note of hope is sounded most powerfully even Isaiah is recalled, if not to the author, then certainly to the reader:

"Yahweh is my portion," says my soul,
  "therefore I will hope in him."
Yahweh is good to those who wait for him,
  to the soul that seeks him.
It is good that one should wait quietly
  for the salvation of Yahweh.

(3:24–26)[7]

And at this climax, Lamentations embraces words that have continued to bring incalculable solace to persons in all branches of biblical faith in all time:

Yahweh will not
  cast off for ever,
but, though he cause grief, he will have compassion
  according to the abundance of his steadfast love [ḥesed];
for he does not willingly afflict
  or grieve [humankind].

(3:31–33)

The mood of the dirge returns. This *is* a bitter existence and the lament proudly rejects any stance of unrealistic piety. The concluding lines constitute as vigorous a protest against Yahweh's conduct of history as any in the Old Testament—but the power is the power of faith:

But thou, O Yahweh, dost reign for ever;
  thy throne endures to all generations.
Why dost thou forget us for ever,
  why dost thou so long forsake us?

[6]Cf. Jer. 20:7 ff.
[7]Cf. Isa. 8:17; 30:15.

Restore us to thyself, O Yahweh, that we may be restored!
Renew our days as of old!
Or hast thou utterly rejected us?
Art thou exceedingly angry with us?

(5:19–22)

Lamentations—and the Old Testament people's epoch of supreme despair—leave us here.

Insight and Resurrection:
Ezekiel[8]

> Son of man, stand upon your feet!
> *Ezek. 2:1*

What Manner of Man?

Like Jeremiah, Ezekiel is of a priestly family; but more, he is himself a priest (1:3), probably attached to the Jerusalem temple staff before the city's fall. He is among those deported in 597 (1:1; 33:21; 40:1), and he then lives at Tel-abib on the canal Chebar (3:15 and 1:1), which leaves the Euphrates north of Babylon and returns again near the mouth of the river. He occupies his own house (3:24; 8:1) with his wife who dies very suddenly in the course of his exile (24:15–18). Even apart from his prophetic role, he appears to have been a person of uncommon stature among the exiles (8:1; 14:1). "The thirtieth year" of 1:1 is a standing puzzle —the thirtieth year of what or whom? But the vision which inaugurated his career as a prophet is unambiguously dated in "the fifth year of the exile of King Jehoiachin," hence, in 593–592. Although he addresses himself repeatedly to Judah and Jerusalem,[9] his actual residence is exclusively Babylon where he remains the active prophet-priest for at least twenty years. His latest dated oracle ("the twenty-seventh year," in 29:17) is from the year 571 or 570.

Interpreters of Ezekiel have assessed him very differently. At least one book which purports to deal with the most significant aspects of the Old Testament omits altogether any discussion of

[8]See especially Ezekiel 1–4,8–9,16,18,22,27,33–39,47.
[9]A fact which has led a few interpreters of Ezekiel to conclude that the Babylonian setting is a later fiction, and that Ezekiel in fact fulfilled his career in Jerusalem.

Ezekiel except brief mention in a footnote or two.[10] Two summary statements by knowledgeable commentators illustrate the two extremes in the evaluation of Ezekiel:

Ezekiel is the first fanatic in the Bible. He is completely dominated by an uncompromising zeal for Jehovah's [Yahweh's] cause and the vindication of his name. He is filled with holy fury against Jerusalem's profanation of Jehovah's earthly abode and for its other insults on the deity. Although he is not devoid of human feelings—twice he cries out in anguish at the thought of the coming destruction, interceding for his people (9:1; 11–13)—he never yielded to them: he was a stern zealot with a forehead hard as a diamond (3:9). . . . Like most fanatics, Ezekiel was dogmatic. Unflinching zeal and doctrinal assurance, often inseparable, tend to produce what Edmund Burke called "a black and savage atrocity of mind," of which there are traces in our prophet, and utter intolerance, deaf to the voice of wisdom and common sense.[11]

It is hard to believe that the following paragraph addresses the same subject:

He is a man of rich and versatile mind, thoroughly alive to the problems and perplexities of the people he addresses, and well qualified, by discipline alike of head and heart, to bring to bear upon their situation words full of insight and consolation, of warning and of hope. . . . Further, he is sensitive to every current of life about him, he knows its every whisper. So far are his words from being abstract or theological discussions that they are frequently a direct reply to popular murmurs or challenges which he quotes. . . . No prophet ever took himself or his call more seriously. From the beginning to the end he devoted to his ministry all his powers of mind, heart and imagination.[12]

But it is significant that these same two commentators agree precisely in one particular. Writes the first: "Ezekiel wrote a book destined to exercise an incalculable influence on the history of his people and indirectly on Western nations." The second: "No influence was more potent than his in the shaping of that Judaism which has lived on unshaken through the centuries."[13]

[10]See W. A. L. Elmslie, *How Came Our Faith,* New York, 1949, pp. 37, 191 n., and passing reference to Ezekiel on p. 99.

[11]R. Pfeiffer, *Introduction to the Old Testament,* New York, 1958, p. 543.

[12]J. E. McFadyen, "Ezekiel," *Peake's Commentary on the Bible,* London, 1937, pp. 501, 503.

[13]Pfeiffer, op. cit., p. 565; ibid., p. 503. Perhaps the best study of Ezekiel is W. Zimmerli, *Erkenntnis Gottes nach dem Buche Ezekiel,* Zürich, 1954.

The Book

We would not now say so confidently that Ezekiel *wrote* the book, although most of its content is probably authentic—the accurate representation of at least the prophet's verbal record and report.

In gravest doubt are:

25–32 This is the block of oracles against foreign nations, the like of which we have already encountered in Isaiah (13–23) and Jeremiah (46–51). As also there, a few oracles originating with the prophet have provided the nucleus for the editorially expanded section.

40–48 The section deals in elaborate detail with all that has to do with Judah in the ideal age to come, the Messianic age; with its architecture, ritual, religious personnel, feasts and festivals, and finally even the physical features and properties of the land itself. There can be little doubt that this is, in its present form, the work of editors subsequent to the time of Ezekiel; but it is very possible that this is an editorial expansion and elaboration of an Ezekielian original, produced in the same priestly tradition responsible for the final form of the Tetrateuch.[14]

For the rest, we shall assume that we have to do with material substantially from the thoughts and visions and experiences of the prophet Ezekiel. This does not exclude some minor editorial work of later scribes. It is probable, for example, that the now enigmatic "Gog" of chapters 38–39 was originally Babylon, or some recognizable representation of that power, and that at a good many points the text of Ezekiel has suffered both accidental and well-intentioned alteration. Overall, the Hebrew text comes down to us in as poor condition as Samuel and Psalms. We are nevertheless confident that it is by and large the prophet himself who is returned to us in these sections:

1–24 This deals with or is related to the imminent destruction of Jerusalem. It comes out of the years between Ezekiel's call in 593 or 592, and the fateful year 587. The prophetic message, whether by word or vision or symbolic action, is of violence and destruction, doom, and Jerusalem's sure end.

33–35 This is not properly a major division in and of itself; but we list it

[14]Cf., for example, Weiser, op. cit., p. 223.

so because it marks rather clearly a historical transition, and bears affinity both with what precedes and what follows. In chapter 33, the prophet receives news of Jerusalem's fall. But the tone of the chapter continues harsh. In chapter 34 the shepherds of Israel receive a brilliant and finally moving indictment. Chapter 35, which purposes to make the turn to gentleness and hope, is an extended oracle against Edom (so also, as we have seen, Obadiah and Lam. 4:21-22).

36-39 In Chapter 36 hope is made articulate and restoration is assured:

> But you, O mountains of Israel, shall shoot forth your branches, and yield your fruit to my people Israel; for they will soon come home. For behold, I am for you, and I will turn to you, and you shall be tilled and sown; and I will multiply people upon you, the whole house of Israel, all of it; the cities shall be inhabited and the waste places rebuilt. . . . then you will know that I am Yahweh. (see 36:8-16)

Chapter 37 follows with the vision of the nation's resurrection and the restoration of life and vitality to Israel's vast valley of bones, long still and dry:

> Yahweh said to me, "Prophesy to these bones, and say to them, O dry bones, hear the Word of Yahweh. . . . Behold, I will cause breath to enter you, and you shall live. And I will lay sinews upon you, and will cause flesh to come upon you, and cover you with skin, and put breath in you, and you shall live; and you shall know that I am Yahweh!" (37:4-6)

And the prophet's sure hope of Israel's re-creation, of its restoration again to life and meaning, is climaxed in the stirring description of the overthrow of Gog—Babylon no doubt for Ezekiel, but certainly in subsequent centuries again and again the current oppressor, the most conspicuous contemporary source of injustice and brutality and anguish, whose overthrow must precede the reign of God in history, the establishment of Yahweh's just rule among humankind.

Ezekiel's Prophetism

There exists obviously a vast disparity between our ways and those of the ancient East, our thoughts and their thoughts, our disposition and psyche and theirs. Standards of judgment and norms of behavior are conspicuously and often radically removed from one another. If any biblical character were placed unchanged in our culture, he or she would likely appear to be a candidate for the psychiatrist's couch or perhaps, if the transportee were a Hosea or a Jeremiah or an Ezekiel, for the institutional straitjacket. In our own contemporary Western environment which, relatively speaking, rigorously inhibits virtually all the phenomena attendant upon the exercise of the prophetic role, not only an Ezekiel, but probably even an Amos or an Isaiah would appear to be mad. Certainly by our psychological standards Ezekiel's frequent symbolic actions, his strange visions, his trances, and his clairvoyance all consign him to one of our categories of emotional illness. But this is of course an illegitimate judgment. In an age which knew its own forms of severe emotional illness, the prophets were listened to, even though often mocked, were respected, if deplored, and were immortalized in subsequent generations. This judgment no doubt is also subjective, but it is on every count a more dependable judgment than one which exercises exclusively alien criteria.

The opening vision of Ezekiel, his call-vision, is a weird report (chap. 1), if only superficially regarded. But one clue is the recognition that the prophet attempts to describe what he himself knows to be indescribable. In the constant reiteration of such phrases as "the likeness of," "the appearance of," "as it were," and the variety of similes introduced by "like," the prophet is insisting that he knows full well that this is a vision only, that this kind of ultimate reality cannot be apprehended in substance, but only—and only in part—in meaning. The vision of the creatures with their wheels (1:15–21) verges on the grotesque. Yet what is conveyed to the prophet, and what he would in turn convey, is clear—the mobility and universality of the spirit of Yahweh. The four creatures move in every direction propelled by seeing wheels. This is, of course, not substance, not concrete form: this is only how it seemed, this is what it was "like," this was the "appearance" of the reality. And it is a reality about Yahweh of particular pertinence at that time: the temple of Yahweh lies in ruins and we are removed, we exiles, from Yahweh's land; but not from Yahweh!

Isaiah and Jeremiah, and now Ezekiel, all record their most revealing single "essays" in their call-accounts. Ezekiel's vision of Yahweh is the most sensitive and sophisticated of the three, and it is the more striking and moving for its humility. He does not claim to have laid eyes on Yahweh or even Yahweh's throne. The description of the vision is repeatedly punctuated with qualifying clauses (vv. 26–28a) and is climaxed with the vision of deity that is nevertheless four times removed:

Such
was the appearance of
the likeness of
the glory of
Yahweh.

He is overcome by what he sees. (It is utterly gratuitous to deduce from the words "I fell upon my face" and the prophet's occasional trances that Ezekiel was a cataleptic.) The call moves now to the prophet's charge, and the Word which first comes to him is emphatic and explicit: "Son of man, *stand upon your feet and I will speak with you!*" (2:1). And in what follows we hear in eloquent refrain the characteristic theme of classical prophetism: you shall speak to this people the Word of Yahweh "whether they hear or refuse to hear!" (see 2:5,7; 3:11,27).

We have seen the use of symbol in name and act in previous prophets; but more than any of these, Ezekiel is given to the dramatic *portrayal* of the Word's message. Before the actual destruction of Jerusalem, he shuts himself in to symbolize the siege (3:24–27) and plays in miniature scale the game of siege, as would a child (4:1–3,7), rationing out to himself publicly his own food and water supply (4:9–17).

Further graphic symbolisms are performed. Ezekiel cuts off his hair and divides it into equal thirds; one part he burns, another he assaults with a sword, and the third he scatters to the winds.

A third part of you [in Jerusalem] shall die of pestilence and be consumed with famine in the midst of you; a third part shall fall by the sword round about you; and a third part I will scatter to all the winds. . . .
(5:12)

Later (chap. 12), he carries his belongings out of his house through a hole in the wall, symbolizing the only possibility of escape from the doomed, besieged city. In the same chapter, driving home the same point, he eats and drinks publicly, quaking all the while. Like the prophetic understanding of the Word, the symbolic act is also deemed to be efficacious, involving the instrument of the message (the prophet) as a participant in the execution of the dramatized event. Ezekiel's seeming callousness is psychologically understandable. It is no less a reaction to anguish than

Jeremiah's tears and confessions—the anguish of participating in the "execution" of Israel-Judah (see further below, Chap. 10).

Another quality of Ezekiel's prophetism is illustrated in chapter 8. Here the prophet inveighs against pagan forms of worship practiced in Jerusalem—another characteristic expression of classical prophetism. But Ezekiel gives to his condemnation a new dimension of psychological depth which renders his prophecy at once more primitive and more modern than comparable words from his predecessors. To begin with, he sees the abominable forms of worship in a vision, 8:3b; and in verse 7, still in a vision, he is brought to the door of the temple.

Ezekiel often speaks from a position midway between fact and allegory, between actual visual perception and vision-imagination. He is psychologically able to move back and forth between the two easily and sometimes without distinction. It is apparent that the prophet's own mind makes a facile transition from sensory perception to psychic perception, that is, from what is seen and heard with eye and ear to what is, no less realistically for him, internally perceived and psychically apprehended. So, too, in his observation of others, he moves with equal facility from acute observation of the outward person to an even more acute and penetrating observation of the hidden realms of thought and imagination.

In verse 7a Ezekiel and Yahweh stand at the door of the outer court of the temple. The door was always open, the outer court of the temple always accessible to all. If Ezekiel goes through the open door into the court he will see what the patrons of the court expect him and all others to see—their pretensions, the façade of cleanness and decency, the guise of conformity and respectability. Ezekiel chooses another way, to enter not only the court of the temple but its very occupants:

When I looked, behold, there was a hole in the wall. Then Yahweh said to me, "Son of man, dig in the wall"; and when I dug in the wall, lo, there was a door. . . . "Go in, and see the vile abomination that they are committing here." So I went in and saw; and there, portrayed upon the wall round about, were all kinds of creeping things, and loathsome beasts, and all the idols of the house of Israel.

(8:7–10)

And who are the occupants of the temple court? None other than the seventy elders of Israel, in the outward act of utmost piety: "each had a censer in his hand, and the smoke of the cloud of incense went up" (v. 11). The prophet, we repeat, moves easily back and forth between the two realms of perception. But Yahweh now asks,

"Son of man, have you seen what the elders of the house of Israel are doing *in the dark,* every man in his chambers of imagery [RSV, room of pictures]? For [here] they say, 'Yahweh does not see us; Yahweh has forsaken the land.'"

(8:12)

This kind of sensitivity and insight is not matched anywhere else in prophetism.

The characteristic themes of classical prophetism are all here, but, as with every prophet in this succession, they are qualified by the particular strength and temper of the person of the prophet. Chapter 16 reminds us of Hosea, but the language is even stronger (probably offensive to the prudish) and the allegory has its own originality. Chapter 22 takes up the now familiar theological ethic. But this is the prophet Ezekiel who is even more prophet-priest than Jeremiah. The old cultus of the temple and the whole external institution of Yahwism which earlier prophets condemned because popular observance was unaccompanied by the doing of justice—all of that is now for the exiles beyond reach, and in Jerusalem itself is about to be extinguished. In the full reconstitution of Yahwism, Ezekiel wants the formal ritual performance inseparably linked to the covenant justice-righteousness which appears with such signal force in earlier prophets (who, we think, would have concurred *now*, in Ezekiel's time). See how Ezekiel brings ritual and righteousness together, especially in 22:6–12.

Ezekiel's Faith

All of this discussion is simply to cite some of the qualities of Ezekiel's prophetism in the pre-587 epoch of his career. We have already noted that the prophet's dominant note of doom changes dramatically to one of hope and resurrection with word of the disaster. However, the strongest and most persistent single criticism of Ezekiel from modern commentators is precisely here in the charge that the proclamation of redemption betrays no more of human compassion and gentleness than his treatment of the theme of destruction.

Thus says Yahweh God: It is not for your sake, O house of Israel, that I am about to act [in redemption], but for the sake of my holy name. . . . I

will vindicate the holiness of my great name. . . . which you have pro-
faned. . . . that the nations may know that I am Yahweh.

(see 36:22 ff.)

Now certainly the quality of compassion does not dominate the
personality of Ezekiel as it does Jeremiah. But it would be instructive to ask why Ezekiel (with the Second Isaiah; cf. Isa. 48:1–11)
stresses the point of Yahweh's acting "for the sake of my holy
name." He does so because he fears with good reason that with
the promise of restoration, the narrow, short-sighted, vicious
pride of covenant Israel will return in full measure. He does so
because he knows all too well the popular tendency to make
Yahweh the *junior* party to the covenant, dependent for glory and
perhaps even for *being* upon Israel. Ezekiel knows that Israel was
created for Yahweh's purposes and is now brought under sentence
of death to make possible the reconstitution and re-creation of a
new Israel made fit by the very judgment for Yahweh's original
purpose—to bless the families of the earth and to bring to the nations the knowledge of Yahweh.

And the alleged hard-heartedness of the word even of resurrection is denied by what Ezekiel says:

A new heart I will give you, and a new spirit I will put within you. . . .
I will put *my* spirit with you. . . . You shall dwell in the land which I gave
to your ancestors and you shall be my people, and I will be your God.

(see 36:26 ff.)

Although Ezekiel stresses Yahweh's self-sufficiency, he is not a
prototype of modern proponents of a theology in which the
human role in redemption is reduced to a cipher. Humankind,
persons, have a position of critical significance in the fulfillment
of Yahweh's historical purpose. Nowhere is this brought out more
emphatically than in the vision of the valley of dry bones (chap.
37). Yahweh's purposes require a redeemed community which
knows itself to be constituted by the resurrecting spirit of God.
Here is Yahweh's Word to an Israel dead and buried:

Behold, I will open your graves, and raise you from your graves, O my
people; and I will bring you home into the land of Israel. And you shall
know that I am Yahweh when I open your graves, and raise you from
your graves, O my people. And I will put my Spirit within you, and you
shall live, and I will place you in your own land; then you shall know
that I, Yahweh, have spoken, and I have done it!

(37:11–14)

Judah and Israel, South and North, are reunited in this vision of resurrection (as also in Jeremiah 31):

My servant David shall be king over them; and they shall have all one shepherd. . . . I will make a covenant of peace with them; it shall be an everlasting covenant. . . . then the nations will know that I Yahweh sanctify Israel, when my sanctuary is in the midst of them for evermore.
(see 37:24 ff.)

We encounter in Ezekiel two very important items of prophetism already met in Jeremiah. The new covenant (Jer. 31:31–34), while not thus specifically indicated, is a repeated explicit and implicit theme in Ezekiel. It is envisaged in what we have just quoted from chapter 37; and, in terms especially reminiscent of Jeremiah, the substance of the new covenant is stated in 11:19–20. And we find in Ezekiel, as in Jeremiah, what has been called perhaps inadvisedly a "doctrine of individualism." The two prophets quote, in order to refute it, the same proverb: "The fathers have eaten sour grapes, and the children's teeth are set on edge" (Jer. 31:29; Ezek. 18:2). In these critical years before Jerusalem's final destruction, the proverb is much in vogue: *we* are not responsible for this debacle, people are saying, but the generations that preceded us. We are suffering for the sins and stupidities of those who went before us. And the inference in all of this is, of course, that *we* are innocent and God is unjust! Now it is important to insist that neither Jeremiah nor Ezekiel means in refuting the proverb to propound a "doctrine of individualism" which would deny communal responsibility and the inescapable corporateness of human existence. Nothing that either prophet says can be legitimately interpreted as advocating religious individualism, and certainly not the kinds of pious privatism so prevalent in Western religious practice. These two prophets are the most community-conscious, Israel-conscious, corporate-conscious of the prophets: it is inceivable that either would deny the covenant solidarity of Israel. But they are faced with a rampant conceit, a self-righteousness which absolutely blocks any reconciliation with Yahweh; and both prophets are sufficient realists to know that *no* generation may with impunity declare itself guiltless. The popular proverb—which is in certain lights profoundly true—is *in this crisis and in its present interpretation* refuted. The teeth set on edge are specifically those of the eater of sour grapes (see Jer. 31:30). "Behold, all souls are mine [says Yahweh]; the soul of the [parents] as well as the soul of the [children; soul here in the sense of entity or being —the total person]: the soul that sins shall die" (Ezek. 18:4).

There can be no mistake about the prophetic *intent*: the popular proverb is denied in its pointed use as a declaration of the innocence and the consequent unjust suffering of the prophets' own generation (see also Ezek. 12:6 and 14:12–23).

Finally, do not overlook in Ezekiel the superb description of the city of Tyre as a majestic ship (chap. 27, especially vv. 1–11, 26–32); or what is surely one of the Old Testament's most sensitive creations, the oracle against the shepherds in chapter 34; or in chapter 47, the moving description of the stream flowing from the temple, increasing in breadth and volume and majesty as it flows, bringing life, healing, and fruitfulness all along its redemptive course.

And do observe in Ezekiel that (1) Yahweh's ways, if sometimes unfathomable, are deemed to be just and right; (2) history, even in its anguish, is interpreted in terms of Yahweh's concerned, purposeful participation in it; (3) Yahweh's ultimate purpose is confidently assumed to be redemptive—to recreate by resurrection a people who will be God's people and (certainly implicitly) will even yet fulfill the purposes of their creation as a people; and (4) the bold faith that despite any appearances to the contrary, the Word of Yahweh *is* accomplishing itself and cannot be thwarted in any future.

IV
EXISTENCE:
THE MEANING OF YAHWISM

10

The Culmination, Summary, and Projection of Prophetic Faith

Comfort and Light: Second Isaiah[1]

> You are my servant.
> *Isa. 49:3*

From Nebuchadnezzar to Cyrus

Two kings span the major part of the seventy years of neo-Babylonian ascendancy (in round numbers, 610–540 B.C.). Nebuchadnezzar (605[4]–562) was one of history's strongest rulers. He *was* Babylon; and as long as he lived, Babylon's power was unassailable. He administered Jerusalem's surrender and the first deportation in 597; the city's three-year siege, its fall and destruction, and the second deportation of 587; and a third act of aggression and deportation in 582. The number of these involuntary exiles was not large—about forty-six hundred according to Jer. 52:28–30; but since this is probably the number of adult males, we would not be far wrong in assuming a grand total of, say, fifteen to seventy thousand. It is clear that their lot, as exiles, was uncommonly good. This last fact, together with the dismal physical state of Judah, no doubt attracted some voluntary Jewish exiles to Babylonian settlements. Other Judeans certainly moved, out of preference, to Egypt (Jeremiah 42–43).

Babylon's collapse began in the years immediately following Nebuchadnezzar's death (562). The Babylonian demise was presided over by Nabonidus (556–539), who seized the throne after its occupancy by several other ill-fated rulers. It is possible that Nabonidus would have looked better in some other historical epoch: it was his personal misfortune to share his years with Cyrus the Great, who literally took Babylon and its empire away from him.

[1] Essential reading for this chapter: Isaiah 34–35, 40–55.

Like Nebuchadnezzar, Cyrus stands as one of history's most powerful personalities. But he is also one of history's wisest emperors. Of Persian origin, he appears as early as 559 as an administrator of promise in Ansham, an Elamite province belonging to Media. From Ansham he gained control of the empire of the Medes, which by treaty had been able to maintain nominal independence even through the years of Babylon's strength. Having won all the Median territory, Cyrus moved west and north and with remarkable ease annexed the Lydian empire (Asia Minor). Astutely, he did not hurry to conquer Babylon. Time, Babylon's internal confusion, and his own growing prestige all worked for him; and when at last in October 539, he moved in battle array against the city, the populace threw open the gates and poured out of the city to welcome him.

So it was that Cyrus, this combination of Mede and Persian, became the ruler of the ancient world, the first non-Semitic occupant of the emperor's throne in the ancient Middle East. He ruled as had none of his predecessors. It is a fundamental fact of his administration that he respected the dignity and the integrity—short of political independence, of course—of all subject peoples; and in consequence he not only permitted, but apparently on occasion encouraged and supported, the reestablishment of broken peoples and their traditional ways and institutions. It was in the first year of his assumption of Babylonian rule that he set in motion the machinery for Judah's renewal with a favorable edict permitting and supporting the return of exiles and the rebuilding of the temple. We say "exiles"—they were by that time for the most part second and even third generation "Babylonians":

The restoration project was placed in charge of Shesh-bazzar, prince of Judah. Presumably he set out for Jerusalem as soon as practicable, accompanied by such Jews (Ezra 1:5) as had been fired by their spiritual leaders with a desire to have a part in the new day. How large a company this was we cannot say. The list of Ezra, ch. 2, which reappears in Neh., ch. 7, belongs later. . . . But it is unlikely that any major return of exiles took place at this time. After all, Palestine was a faraway land which only the oldest could remember; and the journey thither difficult and dangerous: the future of the venture was at best uncertain. Moreover, many Jews were by this time well established in Babylonia. . . . It is probable that only a few of the boldest and most dedicated spirits were willing to accompany Shesh-bazzar.[2]

Others came back to the old "land of promise" in the years to

[2]John Bright, *A History of Israel*, 2nd ed., Philadelphia, 1972, p. 363.

The Culmination, Summary, and Projection of Prophetic Faith / 242

follow, probably never in large numbers. But there *is* a sense in which "Israel" was gathered again. Houses and fields and vineyards were again bought and sold in the land even as Jeremiah had boldly predicted (Jer. 32:15). The temple and its cultus were reconstituted, the walls of Jerusalem finally rebuilt, and covenant life in covenant community was resumed—not, to be sure, in demonstrable terms of Jeremiah's and Ezekiel's new covenant, but at least so as to provide substance for the preservation of that hope and expectation.

From Isaiah to Second Isaiah

The prophet of this epoch is nameless. We call him the Second Isaiah because the substance of his prophetism—such as we have —is preserved in the *Book* of Isaiah. Probably chapters 34–35 are his; certainly chapters 40–55; and perhaps some of the oracles in chapters 56–66. This is the extent of Second Isaiah, either as directly recorded or as "remembered" in the same prophetic circles to which he himself had belonged.

It was no accident that brought together the prophetic utterances of these two Isaiahs. Their prophetism (as well as that of "Third" Isaiah in 56–66 and "Fourth" Isaiah in 24–27) is of the same essential character. It is prophetism out of a common, enduring Yahwistic tradition; but even more, it is out of a distinctively cultivated and maintained Yahwistic prophetism. The oracles of the Isaiah were preserved, if not all originally created, in circles of prophetism which knew a common and sustained theological discipline. This theory predicates a peculiarly "Isaianic" prophetic tradition the major record of which, created over a number of centuries, is the Book of Isaiah.

The explicit and implicit theme throughout is the holiness of Yahweh which is the "godness" of Yahweh—characteristics of greatness, unqualified adequacy, absolute sufficiency. And yet at the same time holiness means

. . . above all else that Yahweh keeps close to Israel. . . . The holy one dwells in the high places, yet comes down to the contrite and humble (Isa. 57:15), for although holiness is that which qualifies God as god it is also that in God which is most human. The holy one of Israel gives the Word (Isa. 5:24; 30:12,15); is always near to help (Isa. 31:1; 37:23), with blessings so evident that the peoples will exclaim: "Yahweh is only found in thee" (Isa. 45:14).[3]

[3]E. Jacob, *Theology of the Old Testament*, New York, 1958, p. 90.

The holiness of Yahweh is at once distinct and radiant.[4] This quality, which removes Yahweh from the human scene as the heavens are removed from the earth, conveys *at the same time* Yahweh's immediate impingement, "historicity," self-disclosure in human life and human community, Yahweh's "in-the-midst-ness" (notice the repeated phrase throughout the Book of Isaiah, "the holy one *of Israel*"). This holiness of Yahweh is the explicit theme of Second Isaiah, as it is also of Isaiah of Jerusalem some two centuries earlier. There is, however, a significant difference. For the eighth-century Isaiah, the understanding of Yahweh as holy devolves *from* history. It is history which informs the prophet of this essential quality of Yahweh. In Second Isaiah's prophetism, demonstrably nurtured in a solidly Isaianic tradition, the holiness of Yahweh takes priority over history, that is, it is history now which devolves from Yahweh's holiness. It is *from* the holiness of Yahweh that *all history* is informed. Yahweh's holy nature is the prior fact which conditions history. It is in this sense and for this reason that Second Isaiah has been called "the originator of a theology of world-history."[5]

The common theme of Yahweh's holiness in both Isaiahs and their common use of closely related subthemes could hardly account for the anonymity of the Second Isaiah. By any criteria—literary, poetic, theological—he can be ranked second to none of the classical prophets. The movement of classical prophetism attains its ultimate expression in him. The finest qualities of his predecessors are his, some of those qualities more intense, or more subtle, or still further refined; and to an extent unmatched in any other prophet, the prophetism of Second Isaiah gives coherent unity to virtually the whole range of prophetic Yahwism, embracing at once all the centuries from the two previous "beginnings" in Moses and the Yahwist's days to this new beginning in his own and Cyrus's day. How right that one should say, "In many ways he stands closest to the writer of Israel's most glorious epic, the Yahwist, and he grasps the distances and guises of the epic with . . . fidelity and certitude."[6]

Now it is simply unthinkable that the *name* of this most power-

<hr>

[4]Cf. Martin Buber, *The Prophetic Faith*, New York, 1949, pp. 128 f.
[5]Ibid., p. 208.
[6]J. Muilenberg, "Introduction, Isaiah 40-66," *The Interpreter's Bible*, Nashville, 1956, vol. 5, p. 397. See the whole of his superb essay, pp. 381–414. And see the more recent concise review of Isaiah 40-66, by J. M. Ward, in *The Interpreter's Dictionary of the Bible, Supplementary Vol.*, pp. 459 f.

ful prophet should have fallen into obscurity—unless the prophet himself had regarded his work as an extension of Isaiah's prophetism and had insisted that this name be also his own identification. Such would appear to be the case. We have already observed the apparent fact that Isaiah of Jerusalem, at some point in his career, deemed inappropriate further proclamation of the Word of renewal beyond the coming catastrophe.

Bind up the testimony, seal the teaching among my disciples. I will wait for Yahweh, who is hiding his face from the house of Jacob, and I will hope in him.

(Isa. 8:16–17)

The word for disciples is *limmudim*. This is the first occurrence of this form from its root *lmd* and the first instance in the Old Testament of a word which is properly rendered "disciples." The same form of the word does not occur again until Second Isaiah, and it is subsequently found nowhere else. The original Isaiah proposed in effect that it was not yet time for the full-scale prophetic Word of redemption. Let the Word be *sealed* among his disciples until the hour of its fulfillment, lest its premature preaching lend itself to the increase of popular complacency, pride, and injustice.

And so, a year or two before the fall of Babylon, with Cyrus long in the public eye and his administrative policies long known and admired, this prophet from among Isaiah's continuing circle of disciple-prophets breaks the living seal. The message of redemption from this second Egypt of a second exodus and a second entrance into the land of promise, is brought forth from its place of living seclusion in the hearts of Isaiah's disciples.

> The Lord Yahweh has given me
>> the tongue of *limmudim* [disciples: RSV, "those who are taught"]
> that I may know how to sustain with a word
>> (the) weary.
> Morning by morning [Yahweh] wakens . . .
>> my ear to hear as *limmundim*.

(Isa. 50:4)

The term is used once more by Second Isaiah, this time to express the expectation in faith that as the prophet is among Isaiah's *limmudim*, so Israel shall be *limmudim* of Yahweh: All your *people* "shall be *limmudim* of Yahweh!" (54:13).[7]

---

[7]Cf. Buber, op. cit., pp. 201–5.

From Cyrus to Servant

The main body of Second Isaiah's oracles, chapters 40–55, is perhaps intentionally divided into two sections. In chapters 40–48 the subject is almost exclusively the deliverance of the captive people—their physical, political release from "captivity" in the very near future. Chapters 49–55 differ from this first section in two more or less subtle regards. The sense of immediate deliverance is heightened: one wonders if these oracles may not have been created in the very year of the first return, although still before the actual fact. And the *quality* of deliverance takes on a more pronounced spiritualization: much more prominently now, the expectation of Jacob/Israel's reconstitution is charged with meaning and consequences more theological than political although that quality is not wanting in the first section. The hope, rapturously articulated throughout, is in the second section much more conspicuously a sweeping, profound *interpretation* of the sharply anticipated event. It is an interpretation that gathers up in essence and projects in essence the substance of Israelite Yahwism, daringly embracing again the whole world, and, with the consummate audacity of bold faith, bringing into single focus all generations in all time. What does this event of redemption mean, together with all that was Israel before? Altogether it means nothing less than light to the nations of the world and salvation "to the end of the earth" (see 49:6). Now certainly this is an expectation—a projection of faith—never literally realized; and it may well be that it remains ultimately beyond historical realization. And yet, in the last analysis, it is this essential interpretation which nurtures and motivates the faith of Judaism and Christianity. Second Isaiah's phenomenal articulation of faith, hope, and love has known *this* kind of reality through a long past, and will surely continue to know it into an indefinite future in the biblical religions.

This movement from 40–48 to 49–55 is most sharply pointed up in the shift of emphasis from the political figure of Cyrus to the theological figure of the Servant. On the eve of Cyrus's elevation to the pinnacle of world power, this prophet of the Isaiah name speaks of Cyrus in terms that sound in the Old Testament almost —but certainly not—sacrilegious. From chapter 40 to chapter 45, the word is one of comfort and high expectation. The creator of these soaring lines lyrically enunciates the single dominant theme: It's over! The anguish and the sorrow, the bitterness and the loneliness are behind us now. Israel will be Israel again. Our chaos is about to be transformed into joyful order, our previous bleak, unloved existence into loving security. Yahweh is about to

> . . . feed his flock like a shepherd;
>   he will gather the lambs in his arms,
> he will carry them in his bosom,
>   and gently lead those that are with young.
>   (40:11)

The creation faith is articulated and emphasized as it has not been since the Yahwist's day, but *in no sense* as abstract support for a proposition of "theoretical monotheism." Second Isaiah remains a prophet, not a philosopher or even a theologian. This faith in creation is *nowhere* abstracted; it is *nowhere* propositional. It is always enunciated specifically for "existential" reasons—to support, undergird, substantiate the prophetic Word of impending release. This message seems incredible—but it is Yahweh who will do this! And who is Yahweh?

> Have you not known? Have you not heard?
>   Has it not been told you from the beginning?
>   Have you not understood from the foundations of the earth?
> It is [the one] who sits above the circle of the earth,
>   . . . . . .
> who stretches out the heavens like a curtain.
>   (40:21 f.)

The power of the Creator in the first exodus is recalled, not now for itself, but in support of the prophetic Word of the imminent second exodus from the second Egypt, as a historical witness to the creation faith:

> I am Yahweh, your Holy One,
>   the Creator of Israel, your King.
>   . . . . . .
> Who makes a way in the sea,
> A path in the mighty waters,
>   . . . . . .
> Behold, I am doing a new thing;
>   now it springs forth, do you not perceive it?
> I will make a way in the wilderness
>   and rivers in the desert
>   . . . . . .
> to give drink to my chosen people,
>   the people whom I formed for myself
> that they might declare my praise.
>   (see 43:15–21)

And the instrument by which this event of Isreal's re-creation will be effected?

> Thus says Yahweh, your Redeemer, who formed you from
>   the womb,
>   . . . who made all things
>   . . . who confirms the world of his servant
>   . . . who says of Jerusalem, 'She shall be inhabited'
>   . . . who says of the deep, 'Be dry'
>   . . . who says *of Cyrus, 'He* is my shepherd. . . .'

> Thus says Yahweh to his anointed [*m^eshiah* = messiah], to
>   Cyrus, whose right hand I have grasped,
>   . . . . . .
> "I will go before you and level mountains,
>   . . . . . .
> For the sake of my servant Jacob,
>   and Israel my chosen,
> I call you by your name. . . ."

(see 44:24–45:4)

> Thus says Yahweh,
>   the Holy One of Israel.
>   . . . . . .
> I made the earth,
>   and created humankind upon it;
> It was my hands that stretched out the heavens,
>   and I commanded all their host.
> I have aroused him [Cyrus] in righteousness,
>   and I will make straight all his ways;
> he shall build my city
>   and set my exiles free.

(see 45:11–13)

Cyrus does not appear again. The figure which takes his place is the figure of the Servant. It is not impossible (we do not and cannot *know*) that the prophet has Cyrus in mind in the first of the four Servant Songs (42:1–4). Compared to his predecessors on the thrones of the Middle East, this Cyrus was indeed gentle and just and faithful. His own words on the Cyrus Cylinder (inscribed on a clay barrel) support this characterization:

(Marduk, God of Babylon) scanned and looked through all the countries, searching for a righteous ruler. . . . He beheld with pleasure Cyrus' good deeds and his upright heart (and therefore) ordered him to march against his city Babylon. . . . going at his side like a real friend. His widespread troops—their number, like that of the water of a river, could not be established—strolled along, their weapons packed away. Without any battle, he made him enter his town Babylon, sparing

The Culmination, Summary, and Projection of Prophetic Faith / 248

Babylon and calamity. . . . Happily [the inhabitants] greeted him as a master through whose help they had come (again) to life from death (and) had all been spared damage and disaster, and they worshipped his (very) name.[8]

But in three subsequent poems dealing with the person of the Servant, his function and mission, all in the second division of chapters (49:1–6; 50:4–9; and 52:13–53:12), the Servant clearly cannot be Cyrus, and the Servant's mission has gone quite beyond any historical accomplishment of Cyrus.

Can the Servant in the four songs be Israel? In a number of other contexts, all but one in the first division, Israel is collectively identified as servant:

But you, Israel, my servant, Jacob whom I have chosen (41:8)
You are my witnesses. . . . and my servant (43:10)
But now hear, O Jacob my servant, Israel whom I have chosen (44:1)
Remember these things, O Jacob, and Israel, for you are my servant; I
    formed you, you are my servant (44:21)
For the sake of my servant Jacob, and Israel my chosen (45:4)
Declare this with a shout of joy. . . . "Yahweh has redeemed his servant
    Jacob!" (48:20)

Yet the specific identification of Servant and Israel appears only once (49:3) in the four songs, and in a line suspected of having been tampered with (but suspected chiefly because it alone of the Servant Songs expressly equates Servant and Israel).

The identity of the Servant will remain indefinitely a matter of debate. *You* draw your own conclusions on the strength of a fresh, contemplative reading of the four songs in immediate sequence. There can be absolutely no doubt that collective Israel— judged, smitten by Yahweh, disfigured, uprooted—has at least *influenced* the understanding of the meaning and mission of the Servant. Even *if* the Servant figure is consistently or only at times conceived as an individual (on the pattern of a second Moses, a Jeremiah, perhaps the prophet himself, a contemporary, or someone yet to appear), the very individualization is obviously shaped in the prophet's mind, consciously or unconsciously, by his people's corporate experience in the days from Nebuchadnezzar to Cyrus. The rule holds: the great affirmations of the Old Testament people are all historically conditioned; and it is again the

[8]For the full text of the cylinder, see James B. Pritchard, ed., *Ancient Near Eastern Texts*, 2nd ed., Princeton, N.J., 1955, pp. 315 f.

major events of Exodus, David-Zion, destruction, and now reconstitution which most radically determine the structure of their faith. To be sure Second Isaiah is able to begin with the holiness of Yahweh; and he does indeed see all history devolving in meaning therefrom. But the precise form of this "theology" is as powerfully influenced by the events of his own century as the prophetism of Isaiah by events of the eighth, or Jeremiah by those of the seventh and sixth centuries.

Prophetic Understanding

> I am God and not man.
> *Hos. 11:9*

If we essay a single broad look at classical prophetism as a whole, a number of concepts emerge as most crucial and characteristic. The essence of prophetism is embraced in the prophets' understanding of (1) Word and symbol, (2) election and covenant, (3) rebellion and judgment, (4) compassion and redemption, and (5) consummation.

Thus Says Yahweh: Word and Symbol

As we have seen, the Word was regarded as an entity containing and releasing divine power to accomplish itself, that is, to perform or bring to pass its content. In relationship to the prophet and the prophet's call, we witness the phenomenon of the psychology of captivity—a self-consciousness in vocation characterized by feelings of having been overpowered by the Word of Yahweh. This is evident in the three remarkable call-narratives of Isaiah 6, Jeremiah 1, and Ezekiel 1; pointedly in Amos 3:8, 7:15; and in Jer. 20:8b f.

We have seen that this sense of the entity and power of the Word explains in great part the concentrated emotional character of the prophets and their deep anguish in proclaiming the negative message. To announce catastrophe under the formula "Thus says Yahweh" is in the prophetic psychology to take a direct hand in the destructive event. The very proclamation of doom releases the power to produce the debacle.

What is true of the Word is also true of the prophets' symbolic acts. The devices of symbolism (such as the use of the names,

Hosea 1 and Isaiah 7 and 8, and the singular, sometimes weird dramatizations of Jeremiah and Ezekiel) are simply graphic extensions of the Word which possess for both prophet and people a quality of realism ultimately unfathomable to the Western mind. The dramatized Word, like the uttered Word, is deemed by the prophet to be charged with the power of performance.

Now, if we recall another psychological phenomenon in ancient Israel, the normative sense of corporate personality, the identity of the one in the many and the many in the one, we are able to understand that in their application of Word and symbol the prophets became not only executioners of Israel, but at once also their own executioners. In the destructive Word and symbol directed at the people they are themselves destroyed in profoundly realistic psychological meaning.

All of this may be (and probably is) a survival from primitive, mimetic magic. But the transformation is striking. Magic coerces the unseen powers. But the prophet is overwhelmed by the sense of Yahweh's coerciveness. Rather than aiming at control of the deity, the prophetic symbol is inspired, performed, and interpreted at the behest of the Word of Yahweh, to bring to pass the judgment and will of Yahweh in Israel and the world.[9]

Election and Covenant

> Out of Egypt I called my son[s and daughters].
> *Hos. 11:1*

The sense of election, of having been specially chosen for a special function, is not limited to the prophets; and the actual Hebrew term for covenant appears rarely if at all in the classical, preexilic prophets. But in prophetism election takes on a prophetically refined meaning; and covenant is a concept everywhere assumed, despite the striking absence of the term itself. The prophets may have deliberately avoided using the term because of the widespread popular misunderstanding which made the idea of covenant the food for a narrow, prideful, exclusive nationalism.

Covenant is the working extension of election, the implementation of election. In the Old Testament, covenant is the working

[9]For a fuller discussion of this idea, see B. D. Napier, "Prophets, Prophetism," *Interpreter's Dictionary of the Bible*, Nashville, 1962, and *Prophets in Perspective*, Nashville, 1963.

contract between unequal parties, initiated by the senior party in the act of election.[10] And in prophetism, the concept of election/covenant is basic to the interpretation of Israel's existence. If the prophets speak on behalf of social and economic justice, they do not preach a general abstract morality, but pointedly and specifically proclaim an election/covenant ethic, the sense of which is something like this: You shall refrain from this practice, or you shall do thus-and-so, because I am Yahweh who brought you up out of Egypt (election) and you are a people voluntarily committed in return to the performance of my righteous will (covenant). The motivation of the prophetic ethic is election. The nature of that ethic is determined by the covenant. And so it is that we speak of the theological ethic of the prophets.

Rebellion and Judgment

They went from me. . . . they shall return to the land of Egypt.
Hos. 11:2,5

The prophetic indictment is not merely of Israel (see Isa. 10:5 ff.; Amos 1–2; and the blocks of oracles against the nations in Isaiah 13–23; Jeremiah 46–51; and Ezekiel 25–32). It is the rebelliousness of *humanity* against God that is ultimately indicted. But for the prophet, Israel nevertheless stands at the very hub of existence as the nucleus of the vast area of God's concern. Israel is peculiarly electee and covenanter. In its relationship to Yahweh there is a special intensity and intimacy, a more specific and immediate purpose and mission. Therefore, the judgment of Israel's rebelliousness is unique.

Israel's alienation from Yahweh is willfull and complete, the shocking exhibition of pride and arrogance, which appear all the more reprehensible against the background of such relationships as parent-child (Isa. 1:2 ff., for example), or owner-vineyard (Isaiah 5), or even husband-wife (Jer. 2:2–7; Ezek. 16:8–15; and of course Hosea). Israel's rebelliousness is infidelity; its infidelity, pride. Prophetism is persuaded that this is the sickness-unto-death not only of Israel but all people. It is the condition which brings Israel, and ultimately the world, under judgment.

The Hebrew root "to judge" conveys an act by which wrong is righted by punishment of the aggressor, restitution to the victim,

[10]Cf. G. E. Mendenhall, *Law and Covenant in Israel*, Pittsburgh, 1955.

or both. Offenders of all sorts are to be judged, but so are the victims of abuse and misfortune (for example, Isa. 1:17). Thus, judgment is the realization of justice.

We have already marked classical prophetism's orientation in catastrophe, the fall of either North or South Israel. This is divine judgment, the establishment of justice, the rebalancing of the scales between Yahweh and Israel. It means political death for Israel, a figurative return to Egypt. But at the same time it rights the wrong and, more than this, it provides—it is intended by Yahweh to provide—the context for the resumption of a productive, meaningful relationship between Yahweh and Israel, one in which justice and righteousness in all interpersonal, social, and economic relationships will prevail.[11]

We have seen the staggering power and stunning language of the proclamation of judgment characteristically elicited by the ruthless exploitation of the poor and dispossessed by the more secure, the more comfortable, and the more powerful. If the prophets entertain personal hopes that judgment may be averted (as they surely do) or that it will work for good in an Israel that loves God (as emphatically they do), the character of the proclamation remains nevertheless uncompromised. The force of the judgment is appropriate to Israel's rejection of Yahweh manifested in the social corruption of its ways.

> Thou hast smitten them,
>> but they felt no anguish;
> thou hast consumed them,
>> but they refused to take correction.
> They have made their faces harder than rock;
>> they have refused to repent. . . .
>
> They have spoken falsely of Yahweh,
>> and have said, [lit., "Yahweh is not"]
>>> . . . . . .
> Therefore thus says Yahweh, the God of hosts:
> "Because they have spoken this word,
> behold I am making my words in your mouth a fire,
>> and this people wood, and the fire shall devour them."
>> (Jer. 5:3, 12,14; but see also vv. 1–17)

[11]On the singular, consistent, passionate, prophetic emphasis on justice to the poor, see Julio de Santa Ana, *Good News to the Poor*, Maryknoll, N.Y., 1979, esp. pp. 1–11; and José Porfirio Miranda, *Marx and the Bible*, Maryknoll, N.Y., 1974, perhaps esp. pp. 44–53, although this quality of the prophetic is sounded throughout the work.

At the same time, prophetism always intends and wants to proclaim judgment in the *full* sense of justice—the setting right of the woefully wrong, the reordering of that which is tragically awry—so that the very objects of judgment are restored. It does this in part by setting the issue between Yahweh and Israel in terms of current judicial practice (cf., for example, Amos 3:1; Hos. 4:1; Isa. 1:2,18 ff.; 3:13; Mic. 6:1 ff.). It is the just and righteous Yahweh who accuses. Yahweh renders the verdict. And it is Yahweh who is responsible for the execution of the judgment.

The positive quality of judgment becomes clearer in the brief discussions that follow.

Compassion and Redemption

> How can I give you up, O Ephraim! . . . I will return them to
> their homes.
> *Hos. 11:8,11*

As a whole, the prophets give passionate testimony to their faith that, in the context of Israel's life under election/covenant, its rebellion and judgment call forth at once Yahweh's compassion and redemption.

The term *hesed* best conveys the unique quality of Yahweh's compassion. It is variously rendered mercy, kindness (or lovingkindness), devotion, faithfulness, or even grace. In the RSV it is most commonly "steadfast love." The root sense in Hebrew conveys the quality of sustaining strength. *Ḥesed* is often an attribute of covenant, either the Yahweh-Israel covenant or a family covenantal relationship such as husband-wife or parent-child. But as the prophets use the term (notably Hosea, Jeremiah, and 2 Isaiah), *ḥesed* is no longer dependent upon covenant or one of a number of covenant's attributes; but covenant becomes subordinate to *ḥesed*. Covenant is subject to control and transformation by compassion that is *ḥesed* (see, for example, Hos. 2:16 ff.; 11:8 ff.; Jer. 3:12; Isa. 54:7 f.). If *ḥesed* begins in the structure of covenant, it ends with covenant as its own renewed creation.

> For the mountains may depart
> and the hills be removed,
> But my *ḥesed* shall not depart from you
> and my covenant of peace shall not be removed,
> says Yahweh, who has compassion on you.
> (Isa. 54:10)

Compassion of the *ḥesed* quality is compounded of grace and is, of course, rooted and sustained in the love of God:

> I have loved you with an everlasting love;
> > this is why I have maintained my *ḥesed* toward you.
> > > (Jer. 31:3)

Out of Egypt into this land, back to Egypt again. But "I am God and not *'adam*" (Hos. 11:9). Prophetism, in the knowledge of Yahweh's compassion, sees a second act of Yahweh's redemption of Israel from chaos—a redemption to be effected by Israel's return to the land, redemption by the reconstitution of Israel. And this insight, this faith, this expectation was already a part of prophetism in the eighth century. If the first Isaiah was convinced of Israel's doom, he was also persuaded of Yahweh's compassionate purpose in judgment-justice; he was persuaded of a judgment-justice never primarily punitive in intention but redemptive in Yahweh's conception. If judgment is wrath at all, it is purposive wrath, not vindictive wrath. Yahweh's judgment is not an end in itself, but the necessary measure to make redemption possible:

> I will turn my hand against you
> > and will *smelt away your dross.* . . .
> > and *remove all your alloy.*
> > > (Isa. 1:25)

The use of the term remnant (surviving the catastrophe: Isa. 7:1 ff.) is in the same way at once negative but also predominantly positive in its import.

Hosea warmly expounds the same theme (2:14-23; 5:15; 7:13,15; 11:11). It is pervasive, if sometimes implicit in Jeremiah, as witness, for example, the familiar lines on the new covenant (Jer. 31:33 f.). In Ezekiel this conviction that Yahweh's judgment is ultimately positive is given singularly moving expression in the prophet's vision of the valley of death, that vast, open grave exposing the skeletons of all the house of Israel (Ezekiel 37).

So, deep in the sixth century, on the very eve of the second exodus, the voice of prophetism, summoning into a single moment of time the act of creation and the first Exodus, proclaims the now old prophetic faith in the redemptive purpose of Yahweh's judgment:

Awake, awake, put on strength,
  O arm of Yahweh;
awake, as in the days of old,
  the generations of long ago.
Was it not thou that didst cut Rahab in pieces,
  that didst pierce the dragon? [a reference to the destruction
    of chaos at creation]
Was it not thou that didst dry up the sea,
  the waters of the great deep;
that didst make the depths of the sea a way
  for the redeemed to pass over? [the Exodus from Egypt, of
    course]

(Isa. 51:9–10)

And now, having brought into the same moment of time the creation of the world and the creation of Israel, the prophet proclaims a third comparable event which is about to be, the end and purpose of judgment—a new creation, a new people, a new world!

And the ransomed of Yahweh shall return,
  and come with singing to Zion;
Everlasting joy shall be upon their heads;
  they shall obtain joy and gladness,
  and sorrow and sighing shall flee away.

(Isa. 51:11)

Faith in such measure, proclaimed with such rapture, cannot be and is not contained in any concept of one people's redemption, of Israel's redemption alone.

A Light to the Nations: Consummation

In its ultimate projection, prophetic faith points, if not beyond history, at least to a history radically transformed. In the face of an existence which appeared to be as hard and as compassionless as a rock, this faith, grounded in the conviction that existence is nevertheless Yahweh-given and Yahweh-ruled, came to insist finally that such an existence would have only limited duration. The totality of existence is Yahweh's, who is neither hard nor without compassion:

[Yahweh] is gracious and merciful,
  slow to anger,
and abounding in ḥesed.

(Joel 2:13)[12]

[12]Cf. Jon. 4:2.

Moreover, Yahweh has spoken the Word that in Abraham/Israel all the nations of the earth shall be blessed (Gen. 12:3), and the Yahweh Word cannot but accomplish that purpose which calls it forth (Isa. 55:11).

The notion of the historical redemption of Israel alone was never able to contain the prophetic faith or answer prophetism's pressing questions about the meaning of Israel's existence. Even, sometimes, where the *terms* are of Israel's redemption, the prophetic intensity of feeling and pressure of conviction mark the intent to be universal. This is true of Isaiah 51:9-11 which we have just quoted above. It is also true of such passages as Hos. 2:18-23, Jer. 23:5 f., and especially Isa. 9:2-7. In all these the prophetic disposition and intention embraces all humanity in all the earth.

It is appropriate in any summary such as this that prophetism speak its own concluding lines to express its faith in consummation; and it is perhaps inevitable that these lines should most naturally be drawn from the tradition of the Isaiahs. Whatever the identity of the Servant, one thinks at once of Yahweh's Word in address to the Servant of Yahweh:

> It is too light a thing that you should be my servant
>   to raise up the tribes of Jacob
>   and to restore the preserved of Israel;
> I will give you as a light to the nations,
>   that my salvation may reach to the end of the earth.
>   (Isa. 49:6)

Whatever the identity of Servant and speaker in the next lines, the sense of the redemption of corporate human life is unambiguous:

> Surely he [the Servant] has borne our griefs
>   and carried our sorrows;
> yet we esteemed him stricken,
>   smitten of God, and afflicted.
> But he was wounded for our transgressions,
>   he was bruised for our iniquities;
> upon him was the chastisement that made us whole,
>   and with his stripes we are healed.
>   (Isa. 53:4-5)

From the line of David, out of the stuff and substance of history, "a shoot from the stump of Jesse" (David's father) will be endowed with the spirit of Yahweh:

He shall not judge by what his eyes see,
    or decide by what his ears hear;
but with righteousness he shall judge the poor,
    and decide with equity for the meek of the earth.[13]

                    (Isa. 11:3 f.)

The vision moves now tenderly to the lower orders of creation to make the consummation complete and concludes with reference to all things under creation:

They shall not hurt or destroy
    in all my holy mountain;
for the earth shall be full of the knowledge of Yahweh
    as the waters cover the sea.

                    (Isa. 11:9)

[13]*The Jerusalem Bible,* Garden City, N.Y., 1966, aptly translates:
He does not judge by appearances,
he gives no verdict on hearsay,
but judges the wretched with integrity,
and with equity gives a verdict for the poor
of the land.

11

Yahwism into Judaism

Reconstitution in Temple and Cultus:
Isaiah, Haggai, Zechariah, Malachi[1]

> Has not one God created us? Why then are we faithless
> to one another, profaning the covenant. . . .
>
> *Mal. 2:10*

"Third" Isaiah

The question of authorship and date of the various poems brought together at the close of the Book of Isaiah, in chapters 56–66, involves us in uncertainty. As a *collection*, this block cannot be earlier than the last ten or fifteen years of the century. Some sections seem to presuppose a firmly reinstituted temple cultus, which was not realized until after the rebuilding of the temple in the years from 520–515 (see especially chaps. 56 and 58). Although the literary quality of the whole is worthy of its position in the Book of Isaiah, at points there is a conspicuous unevenness in verbal texture and theological point of view, precluding, we think, the possibility of unity of authorship.

On the other hand, we read here several poems hardly distinguishable from the work of Second Isaiah; and we must conclude, therefore, that Isaiah 56–66 must have come out of continuing Isaianic circles of prophetism surviving the sixth-century debacle, and having as its nucleus a small collection of Second Isaiah's oracles not incorporated in 40–55 and perhaps of somewhat later origin (see especially the three chapters 60–62 and the Servant Song in 61:1–4).

Some of classical prophetism's persistent themes are sounded again, reinterpreted out of the broadening experiences of the sixth century. Of "foreigners who join themselves" to this religious community of Jews, this is the Yahweh Word:

---

[1]Essential reading for this chapter: Isaiah 55–66; Ezra 1, 3–6; Haggai 1–2; Zechariah 1–8; Malachi 1–4.

> these I will bring to my holy mountain,
>> and make them joyful in my house of prayer;
>> . . . . . .
> for my house shall be called a house of prayer
>> for all peoples.
>
> (56:7)

The bitter prophetic word of "peace, peace, when there is no peace" (Jer 8:11) of the preceding century is answered out of the same essential prophetic faith addressing now a new time:

> Thus says the high and lofty One
>> who inhabits eternity, whose name is Holy:
> I dwell in the high and holy place,
>> but also [those] of a contrite and humble spirit,
>> . . . . . .
> I will lead [my people] and requite [them] with comfort,
>> . . . . . .
> Peace, peace, to the far and to the near, says Yahweh.
>
> (see 57:15–19)

If Sabbath observance and other external features of the revived cultus are enjoined (56:2–5; 58:13–14), the classical prophetic note, the theological-social ethic, is still resoundingly here:

> Behold, in the day of your fast you seek your own pleasure.
> . . . . . .
> Is such the fast that I choose,
>> a day for one to humble oneself?
> Is it to bow down one's head like a rush,
>> and to spread sackcloth and ashes . . .?
>> . . . . . .
> Is not this [rather] the fast that I choose:
>> . . . . . .
> to let the oppressed go free,
>> and to break every yoke!
> Is it not to share your bread with the hungry,
>> . . . . . .
> when you see the naked, to cover him,
>> . . . . . .
> Then shall your light break forth like the dawn.
>
> (see 58:1–12)

Israel's mission is nothing less than the world's redemption: "Nations shall come to your light, and kings to the brightness of your rising" (see 60:1–3).

The Servant is here the anointed one, the *Messiah* (a resurrected, personified Israel, or one out of Israel nevertheless embodying all Israel?)—the Servant, prophetism's boldest and most profound conception, the assertion of the fulfillment of the cove-

Yahwism into Judaism / 260

nant, and implicitly the assurance that Yahweh's promissory Word to bless the families of the earth is now accomplished (61:1–4, cf. Luke 4:16–21).

The Return

These are relatively dark years. Throughout the two centuries of Persian dominance (in round numbers, 540–330) it is always difficult and sometimes impossible to know the nature and sequence of events in Jerusalem and Judah. What we know of the first century of the Persian period *in Palestine* comes (in addition to what we can glean from Isaiah 56–66) from five Old Testament writings. Two of these purport to be historical books: Ezra and Nehemiah. Three are in the prophetic canon: Haggai, Zechariah, and Malachi.

When we moved into the *fourth* century, it is clear that we have to do with a theocratic community, a state ruled by priests. The temple and walls of Jerusalem have been restored. But exactly how and in what sequence all of this occurred in the sixth and fifth centuries we can only conjecture.

The books Ezra and Nehemiah are unmistakably the editorial work of the Chronicler. First and Second Chronicles, Ezra, and Nehemiah, were originally a single book, dating probably from 300 B.C. or later. The Chronicler employed a wide range of sources, with which he apparently exercised great freedom. He is not a historian in any sense of the word, but an apologist: he conceives his task as that of glorifying the kingdom of David, its history, its people, its city, its temple, and its theocratic life. To this end, he happily preserves for us some of the Old Testament's most valuable *historical* material, including the memoirs of Ezra (Ezra 7:27–28; 8:1–34; 9:1–15) and Nehemiah (but more extensively edited, in Nehemiah 1–7).

The verbal accuracy of Cyrus's decree as "remembered" by the Chronicler in Ezra 1:2–4 has been doubted; but the fact of a favorable edict and the first return, substantially as described, is certain. Formalized worship of some sort was no doubt reinstituted early; but if the Chronicler exaggerates the returnees' ardor in this regard (he has them beginning intensive work on the temple almost immediately, Ezra 3:8 ff.), his date for the completion of the work (the sixth year of the reign of Darius I, 521–485, that is; 516[15]) is supported, although not confirmed, by Haggai and Zechariah. The number of persons (and animals) participating in the first return is grossly excessive:

The whole assembly together was forty-two thousand three hundred and sixty, besides their menservants and maidservants, of whom there were seven thousand three hundred and thirty-seven; and they had two hundred male and female singers. Their horses were seven hundred and thirty-six, their mules were two hundred and forty-five, their camels were four hundred and thirty-five and their asses were six thousand seven hundred and twenty.

(Ezra 2:64–66)

The first-century Jewish historian Josephus makes us appreciate the relative modesty of this inflation of numbers: Josephus makes it 4,628,000!

Haggai and Zechariah

The first rapture fades quickly. It is, of course, a trying, frustrating existence in this land of physical destruction and utterly deflated morale. The Jerusalem community finds itself hungry and ill clothed. They cannot build the temple when the fundamental necessities are in woefully short supply. Haggai succeeds in getting the task of building under way (see Hag. 1:1–15). But a few weeks later the work has flagged and he is hard put to get the task resumed (2:3–5,9). At the close of the little book of Haggai, this stalwart leader and prophet interprets the current trouble suffered by Darius I within his empire (around 520 B.C.) as a sign of the new era in which, under Jerusalem's own Zerubbabel as the messiah, the nation will be reborn into a glorious future (2:20–23).

Haggai and Zechariah agree in dating the beginning of the temple's reconstruction in the second year of Darius, that is, 520 (Hag. 1:1; 2:1; Zech. 1:1,7). Neither specifically dates its completion, but, as we have already noted, the Chronicler's date (516[15]) accords very well with the words of Haggai and Zechariah.

Zechariah worked, with Haggai, at the task of encouraging the rebuilding of the temple (Zech. 1:16). He is of a priestly family (see Neh. 12:16; Ezra 5:1; 6:14). Of the fourteen chapters in the Book of Zechariah, chapters 9–14 chiefly comprise a series of five apocalypses pointing to a date several centuries after the time of Zechariah (see below, Chap. 12). For the rest, substantially a unit from the priest-prophet Zechariah, the first six chapters contain eight symbolic visions and one symbolic action, whereas chapters 7 and 8 comprise historical narrative.

Zechariah is not one of the greatest of the prophets. He exhibits little originality. At points he appears unable to make up his own mind. On the other hand, one appreciates that Zechariah apparently knows this about himself. We observe that he stands in the very dim twilight of the dying day of classical prophetism, the successor in a tradition of giants from Amos to Second Isaiah. Being of priestly affiliation and standing at the beginning of a strongly priestly era, he nevertheless courageously repeats some of the best of the earlier age. At his best in symbolic vision and act he is in close affinity with Ezekiel. He reiterates the old prophetic theological ethic. His primary aim, frustrated at times to his own discontent, is to stand in the Isaianic tradition, as a disciple of the Isaiahs.

Look at the first vision (1:7-17, signifying liberation and restoration). Zechariah was always in tension between his own peaceful, universalistic leanings and the powerful, popular, militant nationalism of his own time. It was a nationalism fed by Persia's internal confusion following the death of Cyrus's successor, Cambyses (529-522). Darius I (521-485) was several years in bringing order and Haggai, as we saw, voiced at this same time the hope of national independence for Jerusalem and Judah under Zerubbabel. But Zechariah refuses to espouse this position. In 1:11 he is in effect counseling quietness. Accept the present order—"All the earth remains at rest." Underlying this counsel is, of course, the prophetic conviction that Yahweh alone is the sufficient strength of the nation; and in this counsel one wonders whether Zechariah may not be ultimately and perhaps consciously dependent upon Isaiah of Jerusalem (cf. again Isa. 7:9; 8:17; 30:15). The tender lines that follow, 1:12-17, are strongly reminiscent of Second Isaiah.

Again in the third vision (2:1-13) Zechariah rejects nationalistic hopes pinned upon physical defense. To be sure, he appears sometimes to lack the courage and strength of conviction to stand unequivocally against popular hopes. He joins in the expectation of the overthrow of all national enemies and in the identification of Zerubbabel as the messiah. But in one significant respect these concessions to popular nationalism are sharply qualified: whatever is done in the realization of national aims is done not by people, or by might, or by ruler, but specifically by Yahweh, for Yahweh's ultimate purpose.

This is the Word of Yahweh to Zerubbabel: Not by might, nor by power, but by my Spirit, says Yahweh of hosts!

(4:6)[2]

[2] Cf. Jer. 9:23-24.

Malachi

This is an anonymous writing. Malachi is not a proper name, but means simply "my messenger" (see 3:1). The simplest statement of the content of the writing is, after the introductory verses 1:1–5, a twofold division: (1) 1:6–2:9, the prophet's words to the priests, and (2) 2:10–4:3, his address in the main to the people. The closing verses 4:4–6 are commonly regarded as an editorial conclusion to the book, or perhaps and even probably, to the whole volume of the Twelve Prophets (Hosea-Malachi).

Malachi dates from the first half of the fifth century. The temple is rebuilt but the excitement is gone. Cultic observance is stale, joyless, and uninspired. Not only is the ritual carelessly observed (1:12), but there is widespread, brazen denial of any deviation on the part of priests responsible for this cultic demoralization (2:7–10a). Haggai, a few decades earlier, had assured the nation that its economic plight would somehow be resolved with the rebuilding of the temple. He and Zechariah breathed the confidence that when this was done, Yahweh would bless the community with peace and plenty. But now the temple stands completed, its ritual long since resumed—and the same wretchedness and economic frustration prevail. Understandably, the temple itself suffers from the reaction of disillusionment. Malachi's message in this time and situation is summarized in these words:

> Bring the *full* tithes into the storehouse. . . .and thereby put me to the test, says Yahweh of hosts, if I will not open the windows of heaven for you and pour down for you an overflowing blessing.
>
> (3:10)

This is the central issue. It is essentially the question of theodicy that we met first explicitly in Habakkuk and Jeremiah, which appears repeatedly in the wisdom writings and most pointedly in Job. The orthodox proposition holds that Yahweh, being just and righteous, tangibly rewards the faithful performance, the fulfillment of divine command. Now Malachi, no more than the people, is disposed to dispute this proposition; but the prophet simply insists that they have *not* in fact acted in faithfulness. They have, he insists, failed to earn the mercies of Yahweh not only by their carelessness, boredom, and abuse of the cultus, but also in their contamination of the purity of the community by intermarriage (2:10–16).

The one distinguishing literary feature of Malachi is the frequent and very effective use of the question. The message of Malachi can be summarized by citing instances of this kind of dialectic discourse:

I have loved you, says Yahweh. But you say, "How has thou loved us?" (1:2)

A son honors his father, and a servant his master. If then I am a father, where is my honor? and if I am a master, where is my fear? (1:6)

Have we not all one father? Has not God created us? Why then are we faithless to one another, profaning the covenant of our fathers? (2:10)

Has not one God made and sustained for us the spirit of life? And what does he desire? (2:15)

You have wearied Yahweh with your words. Yet you say, "How have we wearied him?" By saying, "Everyone who does evil is good in the sight of Yahweh, and he delights in them." Or by asking, "Where is the God of justice?" (2:17)

Return to me, and I will return to you, says Yahweh of hosts. But you say, "How shall we return?" Will one rob God? Yet you are robbing me. But you say, "How are we robbing thee?" In your tithes and offerings. (3:7b,8)

Your words have been stout against me, says Yahweh. Yet you say, "How have we spoken against thee?" You have said, "It is vain to serve God. What is the good of our keeping his charge or of walking as in mourning before Yahweh of hosts? Henceforth we deem the arrogant blessed; evil-doers not only prosper but when they put God to the test they escape." (3:13–15)

The Book of Malachi is a more eloquent and revealing link than Zechariah or any other writing between the earlier Old Testament world of prophetism and the emerging form of Judaism. It throws light on the crucial and otherwise dark half-century in which the transformation was in most active process, and it gives strong support to the contention that prophetic Yahwism and priestly Judaism were in closer and more conscious continuity than is sometimes alleged. Malachi tends to confirm three common, binding characteristics. (1) In Judaism as in Yahwism, history is devoutly interpreted: the meaning of existence is derived from Yahweh's concerned and purposive involvement in history. (2) Far from any intention of invalidating the prophetic tradition, it was assumed from the beginning that prophetic faith was gathered up and translated into the structure of Judaism. This is explicitly reflected in Malachi 3:5 and implicitly in the dialectic discourse, the statement-question-answer form of proclamation from which we have just quoted. (3) The clearest single motive behind the earlier Yahwism of the prophets is the creation and continued realization of devoted community. The real aim of

Judaism, from its earliest beginnings as expressed in Zechariah and Malachi, is to render tangible, and to fix inescapably in practice, both the law of Moses and the Word of the prophet:

Has not one God created us? Why then are we faithless to one another, profaning the covenant...?

(Mal. 2:10)

Judaism emerges in a different time, with a different program, a different disposition, and even a different mind—but no less concerned than prophetism with the realization *in fact* of the devoted and consecrated community.

City, Law, and Prayer Book:
Nehemiah, Ezra, the Psalter[3]

> Out of Zion shall go forth the law.
> *Isa. 2:3 (Mic. 4:2)*

Nehemiah

The trustworthiness of the Nehemiah Memoirs has rarely been questioned. This includes Nehemiah 1–7, 13, and perhaps also 11:1–2 and 12:27–43. Evidence of editorial work appears here and there and especially in chapter 3, but this

autobiography of Nehemiah. . . .is admittedly genuine beyond the shadow of a doubt. . . .Written by Nehemiah himself after 432 (5:14) and recounting his activities during the twelve preceding years, these Memoirs report frankly and vividly, as one would do in a personal diary not intended for publication, the actual events and the emotions which they aroused in the writer. . . .[The Memoirs] are not only one of the most accurate historical sources in the Old Testament, but they pierce for a moment the darkness enveloping the political history of the Jews during the Persian period.[4]

---

[3]Nehemiah 1–2, 4–7, 13; Ezra 7–10; Psalms 1, 6, 8, 14, 18 (= 2 Samuel 22), 19, 22–24, 27, 29, 42–43, 46, 48, 51, 65, 67, 72, 74, 84, 89–91, 93, 95–100, 103–106, 110, 114, 121, 122, 130, 132, 136–139, 150.

[4]R. Pfeiffer, *Introduction to the Old Testament,* New York, 1958, p. 829. Cf. the word of G. Fohrer, op. cit., p. 246 (under the heading "Historical Reliability"): "There can also be no doubt concerning the importance of the Memoirs of Ezra and Nehemiah, especially because they contain not only unintentional portraits of the two figures but also important information about the post-exilic period, which is for the most part historically obscure."

We assume, on the basis of considerable evidence, that it is to the years and reign of Artaxerxes I (465–424) that Nehemiah refers, not Artaxerxes II (404–358). The Memoirs open (1:1) "in the twentieth year [hence, 445 (4)], as I was in Susa the capital" (of Persia). Nehemiah holds a highly trusted position vis-à-vis the king: he is Artaxerxes's cup-bearer and personal steward. Not only that; his relationship to the Persian monarch is uncommonly intimate. Having heard earlier (1:3) of the continuing plight of Jerusalem with its walls still in ruins and its gates gutted by fire, he enters the king's presence in a mood of deep melancholy.

Now I had not been [previously] sad in his presence. And the king said to me, "Why is your face sad, seeing you are not sick? This is nothing else but sadness of the heart."

(see 2:1–2)

Nehemiah asks and is granted permission to return and rebuild the city's defenses. This work was completed in the phenomenally short space of fifty-two days (6:15), and that despite the best efforts of malicious obstructionists to defeat the task (2:19 and 4:7). In view of his nearly incredible feat of persistence, leadership, and skilled administration, it is no wonder that he was made governor of the province of Judah for a twelve-year term (444—432; see 5:14) and that at the end of this term he apparently embarked upon a second. In any case, he takes up work anew in Jerusalem (13:6–7). And here our knowledge of Nehemiah ends. We know from the Elephantine Papyri[5] that in 408 one Bagoas, a native Persian, was serving as governor. Did he, sometime earlier, succeed the aging Nehemiah? Or was Nehemiah recalled to Persia or removed from office in 424 at the death of his patron, Artaxerxes I?

Chapter 13, and probably also chapter 5, reflect Nehemiah not as wall-builder, but as governor. In both roles he exhibits vast resources of strength and leadership. He has the prophet's concern for justice and something of the old Yahweh faith (see, for example, 6:15–16). But he is primarily a man of action who obviously believes that Yahweh helps those who help themselves. He trusts in God but keeps his powder dry. He tells us that he consults *with himself* (5:7). In the face of social inequities he rests his reform program primarily on his own example (5:10–19). When his constitu-

[5]These are documents on papyrus of the fifth-century B.C. Jewish community at Elephantine, an island in the Nile facing Assuan (Aswan).

ents are in any disorder he personally sees to the immediate restoration of order!

Chapter 13 admirably illustrates the kinds of problems Nehemiah faced throughout his administration. All four of these issues are characteristic of the emergent theocratic state. They are, broadly speaking, priestly concerns.

1. The sanctity of the temple is desecrated by one Tobiah's residence in one of the rooms.

I was very angry, and I threw all the household furniture of Tobiah out of the chamber. . . .and I brought back thither the vessels of the house of God.

(13:8 f.)

2. The temple personnel, the Levites and singers, are in hardship because the people are not paying the tithe that is due the temple (13:10–14). Malachi's reforms obviously haven't held. Nehemiah acts with his usual force and efficiency and adds the characteristic note:

Remember me, O my God, concerning this, and wipe not out my good deeds that I have done for the house of my God and for his service.

(13:14, but also vv. 22,29,30)

3. Nehemiah institutes Sabbath reform (13:15–22).

Merchants and sellers of all kinds of wares lodged outside Jerusalem [on the Sabbath]. But I warned them and said to them, "Why do you lodge before the wall? If you do so again I will lay hands on you." From that time on they did not come on the sabbath.

(13:20f.)

Amen. This is Nehemiah.

4. The problem of marriages, first vocalized in Malachi, appears again (13:23–31). Nehemiah moves in frontally and personally against parents responsible for arranging such marriages outside Judah:

And I contended with them and cursed them and beat some of them and pulled out their hair; and I made them take oath in the name of God, saying, "You shall not give your daughters to their sons, or take their daughters for your sons or for yourselves. . . ."

(13:25)

Note now that Nehemiah says nothing of divorce, of severing such marriages already established. We can well believe that as long as Nehemiah was around, the business of marriage in Judah involved exclusively home-grown participants.

This is Nehemiah. No more personally forceful administrator appears in the Old Testament, but on the other hand, none acted with greater integrity and persistence, nor followed any more consistently than he the dictates of the best that he knew.

Ezra

The Ezra Memoirs, Ezra 7:27-28; 8:1-34; and probably 9:1-15, have not enjoyed so secure a reputation as the Nehemiah Memoirs. It is certain that the Chronicler draws the picture of an Ezra somewhat more massive and significant than in fact he was; and it is probable that the Cronicler errs in making Ezra an older contemporary of Nehemiah. The Ezra Memoirs—in any case the most reliable information we have about Ezra— are also dated according to the years of the reign of Artaxerxes. But there is some support for the view that Ezra's monarch is Artaxerxes II (404-358), and that Ezra began his work in Jerusalem about 397—"the seventh year of Artaxerxes" (7:7). If it were Artaxerxes I, the year would be 458(7), more than a decade before Nehemiah returned to build the walls. The powerful priest Ezra would have shared responsibility for Nehemiah's Jerusalem in the years 444-432. But they do not mention one another in the respective memoirs. Ezra occupies a restored Jerusalem (9:9), restored *earlier,* one might conclude, during the reign of Artaxerxes I, by Nehemiah. The Ezra Memoirs generally reflect a more densely populated and more thoroughly settled community than Nehemiah knew. Nehemiah's high priest was Eliashib (Neh. 3:1,30 f.; 13:4,7) but Ezra's Eliashib's son,[6] Jehohanan (Ezra 10:6), who was serving in the capacity as early as 408, as we know, again, from the Elephantine Papyri. Nehemiah never appeals to the law which Ezra brought with him, which Ezra promulgated and had ratified, precisely because neither Ezra nor that law had yet appeared in Jerusalem. The problem of mixed marriages is in Ezra's time and perspective far more acute than in Nehemiah's, so much so, in fact, that Ezra insists now upon divorce in existing mixed marriages (9:12; 10:2-4).

---

[6]Or possibly uncle (Neh. 12:10-11, 22). Perhaps both names were used by the same person. G. Fohrer, op. cit. p. 247, is in accord with the position taken here: "Nehemiah worked at Jerusalem in the period of Artaxerxes I, but Ezra under Artaxerxes II, from 398 on. When all the arguments are weighed, this view appears most probable."

Ezra is much more probably the first Jew of the fourth century than a contemporary of Nehemiah in the fifth. He may not have been the giant the Chronicler makes him out to be—a new Moses, the founder of the new nation, and a new Josiah, revealing afresh the law of Moses (see Neh. 8:2–3,13–18). On the other hand, accepting the tradition that Ezra was among the Babylonian priests, it is in every way credible that he did introduce *torah* (instruction) in the form of legislation formulated and codified during the two preceding centuries of exile. We cannot now determine the limits or otherwise identify the law of Ezra. What he promulgated is no doubt now incorporated in the Pentateuch as we have it, but scholars' guesses through the years still remain only guesses.

In further support of the reality of the person and work of Ezra, the character of the Judaism which emerges more fully into the light in the Greek period (in the late fourth and third centuries especially) is best explained and understood on the assumption of the substantial historicity of the role of Ezra. The prayer put on Ezra's lips in Neh. 9:6 ff. (Nehemiah 8 and 9 belong to Ezra's work, not Nehemiah's) may represent that notable priest himself. It is a moving penitential psalm reminiscent of other great confessional recitations on the theme of the history of God and people.[7] It is right that this prayer-psalm has been called "the birth-hour of Judaism,"[8] and that Ezra is commonly called the father of Judaism.

The Psalter

A few decades ago it was common to regard the Psalms as a collection of varied devotional pieces for the most part composed and first employed by individuals in postexilic times. In contradiction to this older view, two points of interpretation are now widely held. A great number of the psalms are preexilic; and the vast majority came into existence and were regularly employed in the formal, rhythmic celebration of the cultic year in Israel, the round of Yahwism's ritual expression.

There are one hundred fifty psalms in both the Hebrew and Greek Old Testaments, but the identification of specific psalms by number differs in the two. One suspects elements of the arbitrary and the haphazard in the division of the Psalter both by individual

[7]One thinks especially of the short cultic credos of Deut. 6:20 ff. and 26:5 ff. and the longer recitations of Joshua 24 and Psalms 104–106.

[8]Cf. H. W. Robinson, *Inspiration and Revelation in the Old Testament,* Oxford, 1946, p. 23.

psalms and by "books." For example, 9–10 and 42–43 are each original units; and the five "books." (note the repeated benediction closing the first four at the end of Psalms 41, 72, 89, and 106) are in conformity to the "five books of Moses," the Pentateuch. The superscriptions, attributing large blocks of psalms to David (3–41, 51–71, 108–110, 138–145, and a number of individual psalms), two to Solomon (72 and 127), and one even to Moses (90) are hardly consistently reliable, although they do indicate how, in later postexilic Judaism, the psalms were read and interpreted.

Many psalms have already been listed for reading in conjunction with preceding sections where the psalm is itself a commentary on the biblical text under discussion. A selection of psalms is included with the list of readings for this section (see note 3). Our understanding of the Psalter as a whole is probably most enhanced by the recognition and consideration of the major types of psalm and the corresponding occasions in the cultic life of Israel-Judah on which they were employed.

The Lament

The lament type is conspicuous in the Psalter and is, of course, represented elsewhere in the Old Testament (for example, Jeremiah, Lamentations, and Job). A few psalms in this category (such as 74 and 106) are demonstrably laments of all Israel, while many more *appear* to be individual laments (to mention only a few from our own selection, 6; 22; 27:7–14; 42–43; 51; 130). But as we have had occasion to remark before, the line between the individual and the community among the Old Testament people is often very lightly drawn. If the individual lament survived, it did so because it successfully articulated *for the many* a sense of impending or consummated calamity and the appropriate response in the Yahweh faith. The lament was recited in the temple, probably in the presence of a priest and it may well be that the present exultant conclusion to some of the psalms of lament is in response to the priestly oracle of reassurance (not, of course, a part of the psalm). This priestly oracle may well account for the sudden change of mood characteristic of many of the psalms of lament (see, for example, Ps. 6:8–10).[9]

---

[9]One of the milestones of the form critical method is the article of J. Begrich, "Das priesterliche Heilsorakel," *Zeitschrift fur die alttestamentliche Wissenschaft*, 2, 1934, pp. 81–92, in which he proposes and supports this explanation for the characteristic change of mood in the psalm of lament.

The Thanksgiving

This type of psalm, in its pure representation, appears in the Psalter relatively infrequently. From our selection of psalms, 18 (also a Royal Psalm), 46, 67, and 138 are psalms of thanksgiving. Two excellent examples appear outside of the Psalter, in psalms attributed to King Hezekiah (Isa. 38:10–20) and Jonah (Jon. 2:2–9). The thanksgiving psalm no doubt had its regular cultic use as a part of the sacrifice of thanksgiving. Its very close relationship to the lament is obvious, since its "description of the distress (the removal of which is the subject of the Thanksgiving) is often so elaborate and dominating that it can be difficult to determine if the psalm in question is a psalm of thanksgiving . . . or a psalm of lamentation with anticipation of the thanksgiving."[10]

The Hymn

Dominant in the Psalter, it appears in wide variation (examples from our list: 8, 19, 29, 65, 98, 100, 103–105, 114, 136, 150) but typically opens on the note of praise (often "Hallelujah!" meaning "Praise Yahweh!"); elaborates in the body of the psalm on the object and cause of praise which is Yahweh's power in Word and deed; and concludes either as it began, or on a note of dedication, intercession, or benediction (see, for example, 29:11; 104:35; and 19:14). Outside the Psalter, the hymn form appears in the Song of Miriam-Moses (Exod. 15:1–18), and the psalm attributed to Hannah (1 Sam. 2:1–10).[11]

Other Types

By a flexible definition of these three main types, the vast majority of psalms are included. Hermann Gunkel (who died in 1932) and Sigmund Mowinckel (1884–1965), the two pioneering giants in modern study of the Psalter,[12] properly distinguished several other types, but all have some affinity with these three major categories. Gunkel's Songs of Zion (46, 48, 76, 87) and Songs in Celebration of Yahweh's Enthronement as King over All

---

[10]A Bentzen, *Introduction to the Old Testament,* 2nd ed., Copenhagen, 1952, vol. 1. p. 154.

[11]In the New Testament, the Magnificat (Luke 1:46–55) and the Benedictus (Luke 1:68–69) perpetuates the hymn form.

[12]H. Gunkel, *The Psalms: A Form-critical Introduction,* trans. Thomas M. Horner, Philadelphia 1967; S. Mowinckel, *The Psalms in Israel's Worship,* 2 vols., trans. D. R. Ap-Thomas, New York, 1962. Unfortunately, some works of both these giants remain untranslated into English.

(47, 93, 97, 99) are variations of the hymn. Mowinckel's very large category of psalms assigned by him to the occasion of the celebration of the New Year Festival is also drawn largely from the hymn type.[13] It may be that we should retain as a major category Gunkel's Royal Psalms (including, from our selection, 18, 72, 110, 132), which have to do with the life and function of the king of ancient Israel—his enthronement (2, 101, and from our selection, 110), the occasion of his marriage (45), or some other auspicious or particularly significant occasion in his reign (see, for example, 18, 20, 21, 72). Some few psalms are unmistakably in the category of liturgy. Thus, Psalm 50 would appear to have had its liturgical cultic setting in the repeated ceremony of covenant renewal; and Psalm 24 has long been recognized as a liturgy recited at the temple doors antiphonally between the temple personnel within and the procession of newly arrived pilgrims without. And this brings to mind the two psalms which Gunkel classified as Songs of Pilgrimage (84 and 122) which "point to the existence of a type of psalm which was composed for use of pilgrims to one or another of the annual festivals, and, as such, might be sung by them on their way to the holy city, for example while they were assembling for the road or when they had reached their journey's end."[14]

Some psalms, assigned to other types, contain instructional or oracular lines; thus, the office of both priest and prophet is reflected in the Psalter (for example, 4, 15, 24, and some of the Royal Psalms cited above). Finally, a few psalms are of the wisdom type (see below, Chap. 12), a typical example being Psalm 1 (cf. 37, 49, 73, 112, 128).

The present Psalter is Judaism's work in the centuries following ancient Israel's destruction and exile. The voice of Yahwism's successor, Judaism, is heard repeatedly in the Psalms. But we know now that the life of the days of the kingdoms and the kings and the sanctuaries and the first temple is also mirrored here, and that in the Psalms we witness afresh the faith and devotion of the Old Testament people over the vast span of perhaps a thousand years.

[13]For a knowledgeable summary of Mowinckel's position in this regard, see Aubrey Johnson, "The Psalms," in H. H. Rowley, ed., *The Old Testament and Modern Study,* Oxford, 1951.
[14]Ibid., p. 176.

12

Tensions of Mind and Faith

Time and Apocalypse:
Fourth Isaiah, Joel, Second Zechariah[1]

> On that day. . . .Yahweh will become king over all the earth.
>
> *Zech. 14:8 f.*

"Fourth" Isaiah

These four chapters, Isaiah 24–27, cannot be the creation of one of the earlier Isaiahs (First, Second, or "Third"), although marked affinities exist. What we loosely call "Fourth" Isaiah is certainly in the broad sense Isaianic: it comes, we suspect, out of the still continuing Isaianic circles. But the last critical Old Testament scholar of any great stature to defend the eighth-century Isaiah's authorship of 24–27 was the remarkable Franz Delitzsch (1813–1890); and almost reluctantly, he himself came finally to abandon the identification.

Three sections in Isaiah 24–27 are more strongly apocalyptic than anything else we have yet read in the Old Testament (24:18c–23; 25:6–9; 26:20–27:1). A now classic definition of this term *apocalyptic* (literally, "uncovered") properly sees the transition from prophetic to apocalypic literature as

really scarcely traceable. But it may be asserted in general terms that whereas prophecy foretells a definite future which has its foundation in the present, apocalyptic directs its anticipation solely and simply to the future—to a new world-period which stands sharply contrasted with the present. The classical model of all apocalyptic may be found in Daniel 7 [see below]. . . .it is only after a great war of destruction, a "Day of Yahweh" or day of the Great Judgment, that the dominion of God will begin.[2]

Isaiah 24–27 is not entirely apocalyptic: now and again readers

---

[1]Essential reading for this chapter: Isaiah 24–27; Joel 1–3; Zechariah 9–14.

[2]From an article by W. Bousset, "Jewish Apocalyptic," in J. Herzog, ed., *Realencyclopadie*, quoted in O. C. Whitehouse, *Isaiah*, in the *Century Bible Series*, Edinburgh, 1905, vol. 1, p. 267.

come to feel that they have their eye on history. But as the sensitive Delitzsch expressed it long ago, "if we try to follow out and grasp these [historical] relations, they escape us like will o' the wisps; because . . . they are . . . made emblems of the last things in the distant future."[3] Delitzsch is arguing with discernment that where we think we have hold of a projection of history—that is, where we think we have moved in unbroken continuity from history past and present to distant history—we discover that it is in fact no projection at all, that while the passage started us off in history, it leaves us at the end in seeming discontinuity with history and the historical process.[4]

The dating of the section with any measure of certainty is impossible. Seeming historical allusions have been variously identified with events in the history of the Middle East from the beginning of the Persian period down through the Maccabean Wars of the second century B.C. Happily, since the major thrust of Isaiah 24–27 is apocalyptic, the matter of date is not crucial. By universal consent it is postexilic; and we should guess that it is best assigned to the fourth century. Arguments for and against the unity of the four chapters are equally inconclusive but again not of great importance. Most frequently suspect as breaking the unity are the three songs (25:1-5, 9-12; 26:1-19; and 27:2-6). If these are not of a piece with the rest, but are themselves a unity, they should probably be dated later than the long apocalyptic poem into which, in that case, they have been inserted.

In chapter 24 the reader will not fail to note a point of emphasis strongly reminiscent of the First Isaiah—the subjugation and humiliation of the proud (see especially vv. 4b and 21). Apocalyptic's characteristic discontinuity with history is expressed in verses 19, 20, and 23:

> The earth is utterly broken,
>   the earth is rent asunder,
>   the earth is violently shaken.
> The earth staggers like a drunken man
>   it sways like a hut;
>   . . . . . .
> Then the moon will be confounded,
>   and the sun ashamed;

[3]B. Duhm, *Biblical Commentary on the Prophecies of Isaiah,* 3rd ed., trans. J. Denney, New York, n.d., vol. 1
[4]The question remains in my own mind whether the canonical Old Testament ever sees a future in total discontinuity with the present.

Sun and moon will have no function any longer: Yahweh is the Light.

The voice of classical prophetism with its theological ethic is revived in the first of the songs:

> For thou [Yahweh] hast been a stronghold to the poor
> a stronghold to the needy in [their] distress,
> a shelter from the storm and a shade from the heat.
>
> (25:4)

The universalism of Second Isaiah is reflected in the prose lines of 25:6:

On this mountain [Jerusalem's Mount Zion; see 24:23] Yahweh of hosts will make *for all peoples* a feast of fat things, a feast of wines on the lees, of fat things full of marrow, of wine on the lees well refined.

This universalism is not as consistently maintained as it is in Second Isaiah, as witness the bitter words against Moab in the same passage, 25:10–12.

Discontinuity in history again voiced in 25:8:

[Yahweh] will swallow up death forever, and will wipe away tears from all faces. . .for Yahweh has spoken.

This is not a reference to life after death, but to a radically transformed age in which, simply, there will be no death.

In several ways 26:3–5 is suggestive of First Isaiah:

> Thou dost keep him in perfect peace,
> whose mind is stayed on thee,
> because he trusts in thee.

Compare, for example, Isa. 7:9 and 28:16. One could almost say that the apocalyptic hope is the inevitable and ultimate extension of Isaiah's so-called quietism, his insistence that the fulfillment of existence is only in faith. And now Isaiah's eloquent castigation of pride (see especially Isa. 2:12–17) is resounded:

> For [Yahweh] has brought low
> the inhabitants of the height,
> the lofty city.
> [Yahweh] lays it low, lays it low to the ground,
> casts it to the dust.
>
> (26:5)

There are probably only two passages in the Old Testament that state explicitly—beyond possibility of doubt—the belief in full life after death. One is Dan. 2:12; and the other is before us now in Isa. 26:19:

> Thy dead shall live, their bodies shall rise.
> O dwellers in the dust, awake and sing for joy!

One nevertheless recalls other lines which push hard *in the direction* of resurrection—Ezekiel's vision in the valley of death (Ezekiel 37); some of Job's penetrating questions (Job 14:14 f.; 16:18 f.; 19:23; 27); Psalms 16, 73, and 139; and at least for this reader, the Servant in the fourth of Second Isaiah's Servant Songs, Isa. 52:13–53:12.[5]

Finally, we cite the appropriateness of "Fourth" Isaiah's place among the Isaiahs as that place is supported by the affinity between the earliest and latest Isaianic Songs of the Vineyard in Isaiah 5 and 27. For the First Isaiah, Yahweh's vineyard (Israel) was the object of Yahweh's offended concern, his indignation, his wrath and judgment (5:1–7). Now, after the long passage of time and in the perspective of apocalyptic, the same vineyard is

> A pleasant vineyard, sing of it!
> I, Yahweh, am its keeper.
> (27:2)

It is the same Song of the Vineyard, but a song transformed. It sings now of a vineyard brought out of judgment, through judgment, into fulfillment and redemption.

Joel

The three chapters of Joel (four in Hebrew) fall into two major divisions. The first is 1:1–2:27. Two overwhelming natural disasters (accompanied by lesser calamities) are described—a plague of locusts and a severe famine. These appear to have no direct connection with one another (although 2:3a may reflect an effort to relate them), since the famine is caused not by locusts but by drought (see 1:18–20). This first division of Joel closes with the community's confession and petition to Yahweh with the consequent deliverance from the disasters.

The second division is 2:28–3:21. This is an apocalypse in which

---

[5]Cf. S. Mowinckel, *He That Cometh,* trans. G. W. Anderson, New York-Nashville, 1954, p. 205.

Yahweh visits in exterminating wrath all of Judah's enemies, and establishes the utopian age in Jerusalem, to be enjoyed forever by Yahweh's chosen people.

Specifically, all we know of the author is his name and the name of his father. Beyond this, it is a good guess that he was a priest, and if so, a priest possessed of the articulate gift of the classical prophet—almost. Joel speaks with a style and power which come very near meeting that very high standard. And in part for this reason a preexilic date for Joel was long maintained (one of the last scholars to abandon it was, again, Franz Delitzsch). In recent decades Joel has commonly been assigned to the fourth century, or even the early third century. A recent survey of all evidence for the date of Joel sets the time between 323 and 285 (that is, between the death of Alexander the Great and of Ptolemy I), "when the northern tribes had disappeared, the Jews were scattered . . . the temple was functioning, Mt. Zion was the only Holy Mountain, the wall was standing, the priests ruled Jerusalem, the Jews had no armies, Egypt oppressed Judea, and the Greeks bought Jewish slaves."[6]

The locust plague is one of a series of natural disasters which, for Joel, are sure signs of the day of Yahweh. The plague is so graphically described after the analogy of an invading army that interpreters have occasionally (but probably wrongly) supposed that Joel envisages *in fact* the catastrophe of military invasion (2:25 seems clearly to refute this possibility).

Mark now the tender lines of 2:12–13:

> "Yet even now," says Yahweh,
> "return to me with all your heart,
>
> . . . . . .
> And rend your hearts and not your garments."
> Return to Yahweh your God. . .
> . . . gracious and merciful,
> Slow to anger and abounding in steadfast love.

If something of prophetism's verbal gift and theological insight still live in Joel, the universalism of prophetism at its highest is missing—according to the usual interpretation of Joel. "All flesh" of 2:28 is commonly taken in context as a reference only to

[6]Marco Trevis, "The Date of Joel," *Vetus Testamentum*, 7, no. 2, April 1957, p. 155.

all Judah. But is it clearly so limited? This is the beginning of the apocalypse of Joel:

> And it shall come to pass afterward
> [after the calamitous day of Yahweh]
> that I will pour out my spirit on all flesh;
> your sons and your daughters shall prophecy,
> your old men shall dream dreams,
> and your young men shall see visions.
>
> (2:28)

And what shall we say of the breadth of faith and expectation in 2:32:

And it shall come to pass that *all* [?] who call upon the name of Yahweh shall be delivered [from Yahweh's wrath in the day of Yahweh] . . . .

But in what follows, Joel sees the survival and restoration of Judah and Jerusalem and Zion, and Yahweh's devastating judgment upon the nations that have participated in the abuse of Yahweh's people. This is not necessarily a denial of Yahweh's ultimate purposive concern for "all flesh." The old covenant faith, with possible universalistic overtones, is still brilliantly sounded:

> Multitudes, multitudes,
> in the valley of decision!
> For the day of Yahweh is near
> in the valley of decision.
> The sun and the moon are darkened,
> and the stars withdraw their shining.
>
> And Yahweh roars from Zion. . .
> and the heavens and the earth shake.
> But Yahweh is a refuge. . .,
> a stronghold to the people of Israel.
>
> (3:14–16)

It was in any case this faith, accommodating itself in one form or another to almost every conceivable circumstance of existence, which was responsible for the survival of Judaism's essential integrity, its unique entity—and, historically assessed, for the subsequent creation of the Christian faith.

Second Zechariah

It may be that three prophetic supplements have been appended to Zechariah 1–8: (1) Zechariah 9–11 (13:7–9 is clearly out of place, and no doubt originally concluded Zechariah 9–11); (2) Zechariah 12–14; and (3) Malachi.

Second Zechariah (9–14) is in general character apocalyptic. As such, it is distinguished for the variety in which it presents the apocalyptic form. Five distinct apocalypses are recorded, which have no relationship to each other except the typical apocalyptic style, and, probably, a chronological arrangement and reference.

In the first of the apocalypses, 9:1–10, Yahweh's wrath is visited on Judah's immediate neighbors, Syria, Phoenicia, and Philistia. The instrument of divine wrath envisaged by the writer is probably the brilliant son and successor of Philip II of Macedon, Alexander the Great (336–323), who brought the Persian empire to its end and who in the name of Greece conquered the world. The apocalypse closes with the advent of the Messiah and the establishment of universal and everlasting peace in verses 9–10.[7]

In the second apocalypse, 9:11–17, Greece is destroyed. All Israel, in the land of Judah and everywhere in dispersion, knows peace and security.

Upon the death of Alexander, the Greek empire was divided and the fortunes of Palestine were for a time determined by the Ptolemies of Egypt and the Seleucids of Syria (Ptolemy I and Seleucus I were both generals under Alexander). For more than a century after Alexander's death, Egypt maintained dominant political control of Palestine although until the turn of the century (301 B.C. at the battle of Ipsus in Phrygia) that control was sharply contested by the Seleucid rule. This third apocalypse, 10:3–11:3, describes ostensibly the overthrow of Assyria and Egypt; but there can be no doubt that these two divisions of Alexander's empire are meant to be designated. It is the overthrow of the Ptolemies and the Seleucids, the empires of Egypt and Syria, that is envisaged, with particular emphasis on Syria (11:1–3).

In 12:1–13:6 Judah and Jerusalem are vindicated against the nations and made victorious by Yahweh's intervention; the city repents and mourns for someone martyred in a just cause (the

[7]Matthew 21:5 quotes these verses together with Isa. 62:11. The evangelist's staggering affirmation is possible only out of the remarkable claims of earlier Jewish apocalyptic. The heavy use of Old Testament apocalyptic in the New Testament underlines the conviction of the early church that the advent of Christ was God's great redemptive act fulfilling the ultimate apocalyptic hope.

historical allusion is unknown); and Yahweh now removes all idolatry and prophecy (degenerate prophecy, prophecy of a mercenary and corrupt form), and effects Jerusalem's spiritual cleansing in a divine fountain. If the order of the apocalypses continues chronologically, we can only assume that this is a little later in the Greek period (which is the general designation of the epoch from Alexander's conquest to the time of Rome's annexation of Palestine in 67 B.C.).

Like the fourth, the fifth apocalypse, chapter 14, is also obscure; but its stress upon Egypt suggests a time still a little later in the Greek period. If one may so speak, it is the most apocalyptic of all, that is, it is on a vaster scale and presents by far the most radical break with history. The catastrophe is again (as in the fourth apocalypse) an attack upon Jerusalem by all nations—but this time the city falls and half the city is taken captive. *Now* Yahweh intervenes. The topography of Palestine is transformed. The living waters (cf. Ezekiel 47; and Joel 3:18) flow again. All the mountains are leveled except the Jerusalem hill which is raised to a still higher elevation. The nations fighting against Judah are punished; but the survivors go up to Jerusalem to worship Yahweh. *Our* tastes would call for the close of the apocalypse at the end of verse 16, perhaps, but the following verses do not annul its universalism; and the concluding note of priestly piety (14:20–21) intends to say simply and essentially that the community is completely devoted to Yahweh.

This brief survey of five apocalypses covers all of Zechariah 9–14 except 11:4–17 and 13:7–9. Like Jer. 23:1–4 and Ezek. 34 and 37:16–28, these two passages are in the form of an allegory of the shepherd; but unlike the shepherd allegories of Jeremiah and Ezekiel, the apparent detailed historical reference here remains utterly enigmatic, totally mystifying.

Time and apocalypse. When faith was able to see no possibility of the fulfillment of Yahweh's historical purposes *in the historical process,* it was history, not faith, that was broken. Apocalyptic preserved the faith and made it still articulate in the vision of time and history interrupted and transformed by the decisive invasion of Yahweh.

Yahweh will become king over all the earth. On that day Yahweh will be one and [Yahweh's] name one!

(Zech. 14:9)

Pride and Justification: Job

> . . .then will I also acknowledge to you that your own right hand
> can save you!
> *Job 40:14*

Introduction and Outline

The book of Job belongs among the most significant works in world literature. Not only its aesthetic value, which is apparent in the power of its expression, in the depth of its sensitivity, and in its monumental structure; but also its content—the bold and colossal struggle with the ancient, and at the same time always new, human problem of the meaning of suffering—all this puts the work, in its universal significance, in a class with Dante's *Divine Comedy* and Goethe's *Faust*.[8]

Throughout the centuries, Job has received extravagant praise from literary artists and critics. Thomas Carlyle, for example, is reported to have said, "There is nothing written, I think, in the Bible or out of it, of equal literary merit."[9] The name of Job has become a commonplace in our language in the phrase "the patience of Job." This work is, of course, beyond dispute a literary masterpiece. But the hero appears as a person of distinguished patience only in the relatively brief prologue of the work; and the sensitive reader of Job may well wonder whether the primary concern of the writing is the problem of suffering or that one vast, central problem of life under God, the life of faith.

Job is an anonymous writing. We are able to form an image of the creator of the literary Job only from the book. Job is not biography in any conventional sense of that word. It may well be that there once lived an actual historical Job; but from the once-upon-a-time beginning of the work and the overwhelming evidence throughout of a purpose quite transcending the merely biographical-historical, it is clear that only a known historical *name* has been employed. It was a name which traditionally conveyed an example of ultimate human righteousness, as is evident

---

[8] A. Weiser, *Einleitung in das Alte Testament,* 2nd ed., Gottingen, 1949, p. 186 (my translation). Cf. the English translation of Weiser, *The Old Testament: Its Formation and Development,* trans. Dorothea M. Barton, New York, 1961, p. 288.

[9] See S. Terrien's superb tribute to the "style" of Job in "Job Introduction," *The Interpreter's Bible,* Nashville, 1956, vol. 3, pp. 892 f.

from Ezek. 14:14 (cf. 14:20) where the name of Job is coupled with the names of Noah and Daniel.

The Book of Job presents this clear outline:

1–2	Prologue.
3–31	Dialogue: a debate in three cycles between Job and his three friends, Eliphaz, Bildad, and Zophar. Chapter 28, in praise of wisdom, has no intrinsic relationship to the dialogues but may nevertheless appear here in accordance with appropriate editorial design.[10]
32–37	The speeches of Elihu, a younger bystander.
38:1–42:6	The Yahweh speeches.
42:7–17	Epilogue.

The composition of the present Book of Job cannot be dated. The prologue and epilogue may derive from a preexilic Job story, perhaps an ancient and certainly widely known tale. The Elihu speeches[11] and segments of the Yahweh speeches (notably on the ostrich, 39:13–18, and Leviathan, 41:1–34) may be added after the creative unification of the rest of the literary Job; but the work as a whole unmistakably reflects Israel's own corporate catastrophic experience of the bitter sixth century. The "biography" of Job is like the "biography" of the Servant of Second Isaiah: both are created and conditioned out of Israel's anguished existence through destruction and exile. The purpose of Job is essentially that of Second Isaiah: to restore a lost faith and lost meaning in existence.

The Literary Problem

The prose prologue and epilogue and the body of poetry in between betray many differences other than merely form. There are striking differences in vocabulary. In the poetry of Job, the deity is rather consistently designated by terms other than Yahweh (127 times it is *'el, 'eloah,* or *shadai*). But not one of these terms appears in the prose prologue or epilogue where, in contrast, the specific Israelite name, Yahweh, is used. In the poetry, the name

[10]H. Lamparter has written one of the most acute interpretations of Job ever produced. He holds that chapter 28 belongs to the whole, is appropriate to the whole, and speaks eloquently to the whole *where it is.* See his *Das Buch der Anfechtung,* in the series *Die Botschaft des Alten Testaments,* Stuttgart, 1951. pp. 162–71 (unfortunately not in English translation).

[11]For an able defense of the integrity of the Elihu discourse, see again Lamparter's discussion, ibid., pp. 192 ff.

Yahweh occurs once only in speech (12:9, but this is commonly regarded as a later editorial addition). In the speeches of Yahweh, 38:1–42:6, the name is never used in actual monologue or dialogue, but only in simple identification of the speaker, as "Job answered Yahweh" (40:3) or "Yahweh answered Job" (40:6).

The point of view and tone differ markedly in prose and poetry. The folk quality of prologue and epilogue is pronounced. Here one is confronted by that kind of brilliant, disarming naïveté which, while appearing naive, is nevertheless informed by the accumulated understanding of the centuries.[12] One observes the highly stylized form with its effective use of repetition, a device characteristic of Israel's oldest folkloristic traditions. One delights in the deftly humorous use of hyperbole—surely this is the intention, for example, of 1:13–19.[13] But these qualities do not appear in the dialogues. The poetry of Job is certainly also stylized, but it is stylization of a totally different character: the style of wisdom, familiar all over the ancient Middle East and quite at home in Israel from the time of Solomon.

The Yahweh of prologue and epilogue is much more intimately and charmingly envisaged than the relatively sophisticated deity of the speeches. And the character of Job himself appears to be of different stuff. The prologue justifies the popular image of Job as a man of unparalleled (indeed incredible and inhuman) patience; but in all the poetry that follows there is nothing to confirm this quality in Job, not even in the Job who accepts at last the rebuke of Yahweh (40:4–5 and 42:2–6).

In view of these and other decisive differences between the prose and poetry of Job[14] we must assume that the poet, the creator of this unique work, employed an already existent prose narrative as the occasion and setting for his own brilliant literary creation. At the same time we recall emphatically that literary-theological creativity in Israel was never exclusively a product of single authorship. From the time of the Yahwist, through the Deuteronomists and the complex of the Isaiahs and into the

---

[12]S. Terrien speaks of Job's "profound psychology under the cover of naïveté," op. cit., p. 878.

[13]See further N. M. Sarna, "Epic Substratum in the Prose of Job," *Journal of Biblical Literature,* 74, March 1957, pp. 13 ff.

[14]For more detailed discussion, see Terrien, op. cit., pp. 885 ff; and M. H. Pope, *Job (Anchor Bible),* Garden City, N.Y., 3rd ed., 1973, pp. xxiii–xxx.

postexilic days of the priests, creativity was conspicuously a more corporate achievement wrought by the judicious, inspired use of existent material as well as by the artistic creation of the new.

The physical text of Job presents its own peculiar problems. The Hebrew of Job is notoriously difficult. Every page of the RSV translation betrays in footnotes the varied problems of the translator. Occasionally the structure of the underlying Hebrew is unintelligible or ambiguous and the translator must resort to the reading in the Greek or the Syriac text or even to conjecture.

In one notable case the text has suffered major disarrangement. As we move into chapter 25 we have had two speeches by each of the three friends, with Job's reply to each; and in addition Eliphaz has delivered his third speech (chap. 22) and Job has given his response (23–24). We now naturally expect the completion of the cycle of three, with a third speech from Bildad and Zophar and corresponding responsive speeches from Job. *As the text now stands* Bildad speaks (it is the briefest of all the speeches) in 25:1–6. All that follows, chapters 26–27, is represented as the words of Job, together with the wisdom poem of chapter 28, and the extended final Job speech of 29–31. Not only is Zophar not heard from in the third cycle, not only is Bildad cut short, but parts of the speeches of Job in chapters 24–27 would come much more appropriately from the lips of the friends than from Job (see 24:13–25 and 27:7–23).[15] These peculiar problems of the text are answered by the following reconstruction:

Job's answer to the third speech of Eliphas	23:1–24:12
Bildad's third speech	25:1–6; 24:13–25
Job's answer to Bildad	26:1–27:6
Zophar's third speech	27:7–23

This reconstruction[16] gives the fullest possible endorsement to the text as it stands, and achieves the logically anticipated sequence of speeches with minimal rearrangement. Job's answer to Zophar's

[15]Reconstructions vary, of course. See, for example, R. Pfeiffer, *Introduction to the Old Testament,* New York, 1958, pp. 671 f., and for differing proposals, Terrien, op. cit., p. 888b, and R. Laurin, "The Theological Structure of Job," *Zeitschrift für die alttestamentliche Wissenschaft,* 84, 1972, pp. 86–90.

[16]After Lamparter, op. cit. pp. 143 ff. See also M. K. Reddy, "The Book of Job—A Reconstruction," 84, 1972, pp. 86–90; *Zietschrift für die alttestamentliche Wissenschaft* 90, 1978, pp 59–94.

third speech has not been lost: in chapter 28 the author employs (it is unimportant whether he wrote it or not) this exquisite poem on wisdom as his own answer, not only to the friends, but to Job as well. In advance of Job's self-indicting rebuttal (29-31), it provides the clue, reiterated in the Yahweh speeches (38-42), to the problem of Job.

The Interpretation

The real problem of Job is not his suffering, but his status in existence. It is not affliction and anguish that he cannot accept, but his own fundamental impotence to control the terms of his total environment. Job is all of us; he is everyone.

The old problem of theodicy—the problem of vindicating the justice of God in the face of its seeming denial—is raised again. We have met the same problem earlier in Habakkuk and Jeremiah. The increasingly vigorous and sometimes almost violent running dialogue between Job and the three friends seems to center on the tension between the proposition of a just and righteous God and the fact of innocent suffering. But what is always more deeply at issue is the question of existential sovereignty: who is in control in time and history and in human life, who set the terms of existence, who commands in life. In the last analysis Job protests, not his suffering, but an *order* of existence in which he is unable by his own devices to maintain his life in security and to achieve its fulfillment.[17] It is his *role* against which he rebels. And this is the same age-old theological problem which the Yahwist so brilliantly presented to Israel in the primeval stories of Genesis 2-11. It is the essential problem which prophetic Yahwism always addressed. It has been and is and will remain the primary issue in the life of faith.

Here again it is Job/Israel—as it was Jacob/Israel, king/Israel, Servant/Israel. Biblical theology is a product of history. It is the historical experience of a people that predominantly shapes the faith of the Old Testament.

[17]In the play *JB*, Archibald MacLeish has written a sensitive, moving drama which purports to render Job in modern guise. But it is precisely at this point that it misses altogether the theological sense of the biblical Job. *JB* affirms human lordship and Job, the lordship of God: Boston and Cambridge (Sentry ed.), 1958; see especially on this point the concluding (and climactic) lines of the play, pp. 149-53.

Job/Israel was indeed unique, the only one who knows Yahweh.

There is none like him on the earth, a blameless and upright man, who fears God and turns away from evil.

(1:8)

Job/Israel looked back from post-tragedy to pretragedy and saw a relatively idyllic existence (1:3–5, 10). Job/Israel suffered an incredible sequence of disasters resulting in the loss of everything (1:13–19). And Job/Israel bore the suffering and survived it (2:10). But the conditions of survival were unrelentingly oppressive, and Job/Israel was inevitably proffered the "friendly" counsel of neighbors (2:11–13). This is the sense of the prologue as it is used by the author of Job.

The dialogue opens (chap. 3) with Job's consummately articulate elaboration of the death wish, reminiscent in the Old Testament only of Jeremiah (20:14–18). In Moses (Num. 11:15), in Elijah (1 Kings 19:4), in Jonah (4:3), as also in Jeremiah and Job, the wish or request for death is seen in the Yahweh faith as an act of defiance of deity, an unwarranted gesture of independence, a bitter—perhaps the bitterest—protest of disrespect of Yahweh. Job/Israel has come to this. This is the measure of bitterness.

The "friends" deliver the timeless note of religious piety and orthodoxy, known in and out of ancient Israel, known long before, and alas, still longer after. It is as thin as this: as one appears, so *is* one. One's status and condition are the sure measure of one's intrinsic worth and worthiness. Job/Israel has descended to the most miserable level of existence and therefore must be correspondingly evil.

This piece of stupidity is picked up, dusted off, examined from all sides, and powerfully shattered in Job's several brilliant responses on this theme. But while Job devastates the friends as well as their arguments (see, for example 6:15 ff.; 12:1 ff.; 13:45; 16:1 ff.; 19:1 ff.; 26:1 ff.), his hardest words and increasingly his attacks are directed at God, in the strongest and certainly the most sustained language of its kind in the Old Testament (see for example, 7:11–21, with a vitriolic parody of Psalm 8 in vv. 17–19; 9:7–12,30–35; 10:1–9,18–22; 13:3,14–15,20–28; 14:1–2,7–12,14–15,18–22).

The second cycle of speeches begins with Eliphaz's second

discourse in chapter 15, and the third cycle at chapter 22. The passage most difficult to interpret and perhaps most disputed in Job falls in the course of the second cycle, in Job's response to the second Bildad speech:

> Oh that my words were written!
>   Oh that they were inscribed in a book!
> Oh that with an iron pen and lead
>   they were graven in the rock for ever!
> For I know that my Redeemer lives,
>   and at last he will stand upon the earth;
> and after my skin has been thus destroyed,
>   then without my flesh I shall see God,
> whom I shall see on my side,
>   and my eyes shall behold, and not another
>   [or, not as a stranger?].
>
> (19:23–27)

So the RSV renders the passage, but the notes indicate the ambiguity or uncertainty of the Hebrew text. The question under debate is whether the character of Job is here intentionally represented as affirming faith that he will achieve his justification with God in life beyond death, or whether the redeemer is in the orginal sense of the word (in Hebrew, *go'el*), a person of close kin who, in this case, succeeds in ultimately exonerating Job. In the second of these alternatives, the crucial verses yield to this interpretation:

But I know that my defender lives! He will survive my unjust death, and over the dust of my grave [cf. the use of the word "dust" (*'aphar*) in 7:21, 7:16, 20:11, 21:26; also 10:9; 34:15; Ps. 104:29] he will stand at the last instant. Through his intermediation, by his activity, he will summon God and me together, and bring me before the face of God![18]

If, on the other hand, Job affirms that God will indeed redeem him in death, it is a position only very fleetingly held, since Job has consistently defied God up to this point and continues to do so in following speeches. But this by no means rules out this interpretation. It is not at all beyond the author's superb gifts of imagination and subtlety to effect precisely this kind of summit in the center of the dialogues.

[18]Terrien, op. cit., p. 1052. See also Pope, op. cit., for his translation of 19:23–27, p. 139, and his commentary on it, especially p. 146 f.

But now Job/Israel is brought to the ultimate declaration of worthiness and righteousness which is self-indicting in its very vehemence. The prophetic code of morality has already been extensively stressed in chapter 22 where Eliphaz, in his third speech, accuses Job of its wholesale violation. Job, in his long speech of final rebuttal in chapters 29–31, makes Israel's prophetic code his theme and in effect claims its absolutely flawless performance. In having him speak so, it may well be that the author means to present us with the prototype of that perennial breed of the self-righteous who justify themselves by their overt performance of a set of relatively agreeable prescriptions, and in that performance take an inordinate and insufferable pride. The days before tragedy are recalled:

> Oh, that I were in the months of old,
>   as in the days when God watched over me
>
> . . . . . .
> When the ear heard, it called me blessed
>   and when the eye saw, it approved;
> because I delivered the poor who cried,
>   and the fatherless who had none to help them.
> The blessing of these who were about to perish came upon me,
>   and I caused the widow's heart to sing for joy
> I put on righteousness, and it clothed me;
>   my justice was like a robe and a turban.
> I was eyes to the blind,
>   and feet to the lame.
> I was a father to the poor,
>   and I searched out the cause of those whom I did not know.
> I broke the fangs of the unrighteous,
>   and made them drop their prey from their teeth.
> Then I thought, 'I shall die in my nest,
>   and I shall multiply my days as the sand
> My roots spread out to the waters,
>   with the dew all night on my branches,
> My glory fresh with me,
>   and my bow ever new in my hand.'
> People listened to me, and waited,
>   and kept silence for my counsel.
> After I spoke they did not speak again,
>   and my word dropped upon them.[19]

[19]This concept of "word" is otherwise employed in the Old Testament only of the Word of Yahweh. Job here utters several Yahwehlike assertions. In this extended quotation, I have deviated from the RSV only in rendering in the inclusive plural certain corporate but male singulars and in substituting "people" for "men" in v. 21.

They waited for me as for the rain;
  and they opened their mouths as for the spring rain.
I smiled on them when they had no confidence;
  and the light of my countenance they did not cast down.
I chose their way, and sat as chief,
  and I dwelt like a king among his troops,
  like one who comforts mourners.

(29:2,11–25)

In view of earlier prophetic castigations of pride, this sweeping, exhaustive claim of prophetic virtue becomes its own denial; and in the next line the code which the speaker thought to uphold is brutally shattered in one of the most arrogant statements in the Old Testament:

But now they make sport of me,
  men who are younger than I,
whose fathers I would have disdained
  to set with the dogs of my flock!

(30:1)

The vacuous piety of the orthodox friends is rebuked, but so is the colossal pride of Job/Israel. Perhaps the most significant lines in the often soaring rhapsodic Yahweh speeches are these categorical words—strongly in the Isaianic tradition—calling Job/Israel away from pride to the life of faith again. It is Yahweh's turn to speak with defiance and sarcasm:

Gird up your loins like a man;
  I will question *you*, and *you* declare to *me*.
Will you even put me in the wrong?
  Will you condemn me that you may be justified?
  . . . .
Deck yourself with majesty and dignity:
  clothe yourself with glory and splendor.
Pour forth the overflowings of your anger—
  and look on every one that is proud, and abase him.
Look on every one that is proud, and bring him low;
  and tread down the wicked where they stand.
Hide them all in the dust together;
  bind their faces in the world below.
Then will I also acknowledge to you,
  that your own right hand can give you victory.

(40:7–8,10–14)

The deftest touch of the whole composition of Job is the use of the epilogue from the old Job story. It is affirmed in the charming, naïve language of the folktale that Job's and Israel's true fulfillment (indeed, everyone's fulfillment) is in abandonment of pride, in acceptance of the status of servant, and in cheerful acquiescence in the given condition and existent role.

And that note of universalism, present in the Old Testament faith from earliest times, is subtly sounded yet again in words taken over unchanged from the old tale. The same sense of covenant destiny affirmed in the call of Abraham (Gen. 12:3) is reiterated:

Yahweh said to Eliphaz the Temanite: "My wrath is kindled against you and against your two friends; for you have not spoken of me what is right, as my servant Job has. Now therefore take seven bulls and seven rams, and go to my servant Job, and offer up for yourselves a burnt offering; and *my servant Job* shall pray for you, for I will accept his prayer not to deal with you according to your folly. . . .So Eliphaz the Temanite and Bildad the Shuhite and Zophar the Naamathite went and did what Yahweh had told them; and Yahweh accepted Job's prayer.

And Yahweh restored the fortunes of Job, *when he had prayed for his friends.* . . .

(42:7-10)

Faith and the World's Wisdom:
Proverbs, Ecclesiastes, Song of Solomon[20]

> Behold, the fear of Yahweh, that is wisdom.
> *Job 28:28*

The Wisdom Type

From relatively early preexilic times, Israel's religious leadership was of three major types, set forth explicitly in the words of Jer. 18:18:

. . . the law shall not perish from the priest, nor counsel from the wise, nor the word from the prophet.

Wisdom literature represents, then, the utterance not of priest nor of prophet, but of the "wise." In the Hebrew canon Proverbs, Ecclesiastes, and a number of psalms (conspicuously those

[20]Proverbs 1, 8, 10, 25, 30–31; Ecclesiates 1–12; Song of. Solomon 1–8; Psalms 1, 37, 49, 73, 112, 128.

listed in note 20) belong to this type. Job is sometimes assigned to this category, but it is certainly not typical and in our judgment it is on the whole inappropriately classified with the wisdom writings even though it employs the wisdom style. Among the apocryphal writings (rejected by the Hebrew canon, but present from the beginning in the Greek) 1 Esdras, Tobit, and Baruch may be classified as wisdom writings, and Ecclesiasticus and the Wisdom of Solomon are consistent and classical models of the wisdom type. In addition, a number of such writings have been preserved outside both the Hebrew and Greek canons.[21]

What are the characteristics of the wisdom writing? It tends to be nonnationalistic, although in its later development in the dispersion of Jews over the Greek world the apologetic note grows stronger and the specifically Jewish is more and more stressed. It tends to its own kind of orthodoxy, but an orthodoxy freer and more flexible than most. The wisdom writing characteristically gives advice in some form, and it proffers this advice generously and with confidence. The words of wisdom are prevailingly words of counsel uttered on rational grounds, but the appeal to common or uncommon good sense is never (not even in Ecclesiastes) a denial of or in opposition to the mode of inspiration and revelation. The sage is, for the most part, in accord with both priest and prophet. The prophetic ethic is prominent, although the sense of the immediacy of its theological justification is largely lost. The demands of the priest are honored.

The wisdom school flourished in Yahwism and Judaism for more than a thousand years. There are marked affinities with precisely the same type of expression among Babylonians and Egyptians and there can be no doubt that Yahwism-Judaism is often the borrower. The contents of Prov. 22:17–23:10 appear substantially (and certainly originally) in an Egyptian writing called the Teaching of Amen-em-ope, variously dated in the early centuries of the first millennium B.C. But this is not to say that the product of wisdom in the biblical tradition is merely a copy of Egyptian or Babylonian wisdom writings. Canonical wisdom is for the most part distinctly and creditably its own. Like everything that the Old

[21]Notably, the Letter to Aristeas, 4 Maccabees, the Sayings of the Fathers. In the New Testament, James is most clearly influenced by the wisdom school, as is also the Didache, a noncanonical Christian manual of the second century A.D.

Testament borrowed, it is substantially altered, if not in form then in essence, by the distinctive *faith* of Yahwism-Judaism.

Wisdom was early domiciled in Israel. There is no reason to doubt that Solomon was a generous and even enthusiastic patron of the school. In the broad development of the biblical wisdom tradition, the pattern of wisdom, thus early made indigenous, continued by and large to shape and control its continuing expression.

And finally, what is wisdom?

Wisdom was the first product of God's creative activity, for it is the condition and instrument for the creation of all things. Before there were deeps and their fountains, before the mountains were sunk into their places, before the earth and its fields existed, Wisdom was present to assist in fixing the heavens and in tracing the great circle of the farthest horizon. . . . Wisdom was to Yahweh an intimate friend, as well as agent and overseer in all this work, finding delight in the creation of all things. . . .

The precise origin of the figure of Wisdom in Hebrew usage is obscure and disputable. . . . Its unifying function in regard to Nature is obvious. The world becomes a revelation of the divine wisdom, and Nature is a unity in the sense that it exhibits the wisdom of its divine Creator and Upholder. Whilst the mystery of Nature. . . .tended to separate God from man, this revelation of the divine Wisdom constitutes a bond of union between them, capable of further development in the Logos background of the Incarnation, to which Wisdom was an important tributary.[22]

Several descriptions of wisdom merit special mention. Job 28 lyrically probes the question, where is wisdom to be found and what, in fact, is it:

> God understands the way to it,
>   and he knows its place.
>
>   . . . . . .
>
> When he gave to the wind its weight,
>   and meted out the waters by measure;
> when he made a decree for the rain,
>   and a way for the lightning of thunder;
> then he saw it and declared it;
>   he established it and searched it out.

[22]H. W. Robinson, *Inspiration and Revelation in the Old Testament,* Oxford, 1946, p. 11. Cf. Prov. 8:22 ff. Pursue the study of Wisdom in G. von Rad, *Wisdom in Israel,* trans. James D. Martin, Nashville, 1973; and R. B. Y. Scott, *The Way of Wisdom in the Old Testament,* New York, 1971.

And he said to 'adam (humankind),
"Behold, the fear of Yahweh, that is Wisdom;
and to depart from evil is understanding."
(Job 28:23,25–28)

In Proverbs 8 wisdom is hypostatized, that is, wisdom assumes
the reality of a distinct being:

I, wisdom, dwell in prudence. (v. 12)
I love those who love me, and those who seek me diligently find me.
  (v. 17)
I walk in the way of righteousness, in the paths of justice. (v. 20)
And now, my [children], listen to me; happy are those who keep my
  ways. (v. 32)
For whoever finds me finds life. (v. 35)

In the Apocrypha, two remarkable chapters, the Wisdom of
Solomon 7 and Ecclesiasticus 24, also make this same kind of
hypostasis. The composers of these three essays hardly intended a
literal hypostasis. Wisdom is personified but not personalized.[23]
Wisdom is not seen as incarnate in a distinct being. This occurs in
the New Testament in the identification of Jesus and Wisdom, a
fact which speaks again of the incalculable influence of the Old
Testament on the New. The priests' cultus, the prophets' Word,
and the sages' wisdom are all three essentially a part of the immediate background of the New Testament faith in the person of
Jesus.[24]

The hypostasis of wisdom in these passages and others
represents the wisdom school at its best and most refined
theological attainment. When we turn now to Proverbs, it is

[23]Cf. G. F. Moore, *Judaism,* Cambridge, 1927, vol. 1 pp. 415 ff., on the
distinction between personification and personalization and also on Philo's use
of *Logos* as related to wisdom. It may be noted here that Judaism's hypostasis of
wisdom suggests in the third century B.C. the influence of the Egyptian Isis cult,
and in the second, the influence of the comparable Syrian orbit. See further, W.
L. Knox, *St. Paul and the Church of the Gentiles,* Cambridge, 1939, pp. 58 ff.
Ultimately, having claimed for wisdom the central attributes of Isis and Astarte,
Judaism identified wisdom and the *Torah* of Moses: "All these things [i.e., these
attributes of wisdom] *are* the book of the covenant of the most high God, the law
which Moses commanded for a heritage to the congregation of Jacob" (Ecclus.
24:23).

[24]Paul's Christology was influenced by the wisdom concept and in Hebrews,
Colossians, and the Fourth Gospel the attributes of personified wisdom are
unmistakably applied to Jesus Christ. See further, John Knox, *On the Meaning
of Christ,* New York, 1947, p. 55; and H. Conzelmann's article "Wisdom in the
New Testament," in *Interpreter's Dictionary of the Bible, Supplementary Vol.,*
Nashville, 1976, pp. 956 ff.

apparent that wisdom's more common theme is one of practical, often pithy, and sometimes quasi-philosophical, or better, folk-philosophical counsel.

Proverbs

Although traditionally ascribed to Solomon, the writing itself does not make that claim for the full contents. Indeed, there can be no question that the book, like the Psalter, attained in present form in an extended process involving several collections of proverbs.

By general consent, the oldest collection is contained in 10:1–22:16, parts of which may possibly come down from Solomon himself and the time of Solomon. Other preexilic collections include, probably, 22:17–24:34 (the first part closely paralleling the Egyptian Amen-em-ope) and chapters 25–29, a section ascribed (see 25:1) to the time of Hezekiah (about 700).

Chapters 1–9 represent, on the other hand, a relatively late collection, probably from the Greek period. It appears that this section was added to the older collections by an editor of the whole book. He also appended chapters 30–31, which include proverbs attributed to Agur (30) and King Lemuel (31:2–9), and a final acrostic poem on the ideal woman, wife, and mother. We certainly do not intend to disparage womanhood, marriage, and the home when we say that this proverbial creature is about as realistically depicted in her remarkable relationships and enterprises as Snow White and the Seven Dwarfs.

A few representative chapters from Proverbs have been suggested in note 20, page 292. Here is a representative selection of individual proverbs.

> Trust in Yahweh with all your heart,
>   and do not rely on your own insight.
> In all your ways acknowledge him,
>   and he will make straight your paths.
>
> (3:5–6)
>
> Keep your heart with all vigilance;
>   for from it flow the springs of life.
>
> (4:23)
>
> For the lips of a loose woman drip honey,
>   and her speech is smoother than oil;
> but in the end she is bitter as wormwood,
>   sharp as a two-edged sword.
>
> (5:3–4)

Go to the ant, O sluggard;
   consider her ways, and be wise.
Without having any chief,
   officer or ruler,
she prepares her food in summer,
   and gathers her sustenance in harvest.
How long will you lie there, O sluggard?
   When will you arise from your sleep?
A little sleep, a little slumber,
   a little folding of the hands to rest,
And poverty will come upon you like a vagabond,
   and want like an armed man.

                   (6:6–11)

Like a gold ring in a swine's snout
   is a beautiful woman without discretion.

                   (11:22)

The way of a fool is right in his own eyes,
   but a wise man listens to advice.

                   (12:15)

Anxiety in one's heart weighs one down,
   but a good word makes one glad.

                   (12:25)

Hope deferred makes the heart sick,
   but a desire fulfilled is a tree of life.

                   (13:12)

Righteousness exalts a nation,
   but sin is a reproach to any people.

                   (14:34)

A hot-tempered man stirs up strife,
   but one who is slow to anger quiets contention.

                   (15:18)

Better is a little with righteousness
   than great revenues with injustice.

                   (16:8)

Pride goes before destruction,
and a haughty spirit before a fall.

                   (16:18)

Even a fool who keeps silent is considered wise;
   when one closes one's lips, one is deemed intelligent.

                   (17:28)

The words of a whisperer are like delicious morsels;
   they go down into the inner parts of the body.

                   (18:8)

Love not sleep, lest you come to poverty;
   open your eyes, and you will have plenty of bread.

"It is bad, it is bad," says the buyer;
but when he goes away, then he boasts.

(20:13–14)

Train up children in the way they should go,
and when they are old they will not depart from it.

(22:6)

Who has woe? Who has sorrow?
Who has strife? Who has complaining?
Who has wounds without cause?
Who has redness of eyes?
Those who tarry long over the wine,
those who go to try mixed wine.
Do not look at wine when it is red,
when it sparkles in the cup,
and goes down smoothly.
At the last it bites like a serpent,
and stings like an adder.
Your eyes will see strange things,
and your mind utter perverse things.
You will be like one who lies down in the midst of the sea,
like one who lies on the top of a mast.
"They struck me," you will say, "but I was not hurt;
they beat me, but I did not feel it.
When shall I awake?
I will seek another drink."

(23:29–35)

I passed by the field of the sluggard,
by the vineyard of one without sense;
and lo, it was all overgrown with thorns;
the ground was covered with nettles,
and its stone wall was broken down.
Then I saw and considered it;
I looked and received instruction.
"A little sleep, a little slumber,
a little folding of the hands to rest,"
And poverty will come upon you like a robber,
and want like an armed man.

(24:30–34)

A word fitly spoken
is like apples of gold in a setting of silver.

(25:11)

Like clouds and wind without rain
is one who boasts of a gift one does not give.

(25:14)

Let your foot be seldom in your neighbor's house
lest [your neighbor] become weary of you and hate you.
(25:17)

If your enemies are hungry, give bread to eat;
and if thirsty, give water to drink;
for you will heap coals of fire on their heads,
and Yahweh will reward you.
(25:21-22)[25]

One who meddles in a quarrel not one's own
is like one who takes a passing dog by the ears.
Like a [lunatic] who throws firebrands,
arrows and death
is one who deceives one's neighbor
and says, "I am only joking!"
For lack of wood the fire goes out;
and where there is no whisperer, quarreling ceases.
(25:17-21)

Faithful are the wounds of a friend;
profuse are the kisses of an enemy.
(27:6)

Three things are too wonderful for me;
four I do not understand;
the way of an eagle in the sky,
the way of a serpent on a rock,
the way of a ship in the high seas,
and the way of a man with a maiden.
(30:18-19)

Wisdom must not be sold short; and a sense of wonder is not the least of the gifts of theological insight.

Ecclesiastes

This is represented to be "the words of the Preacher [Hebrew, *Qoheleth*], the son of David, king in Jerusalem" (1:1; cf. 1:12). The intention to impersonate Solomon is unmistakable. But the Preacher is not Solomon and what appears as his work in Ecclesiastes is hardly, in its entirety, the words of a single author. The proverbs which are interspersed throughout may be extraneous; and some of the more pious statements of conventional orthodoxy must certainly be regarded as editorial, especially chapter 12. The finished work of Ecclesiastes can with virtual certainty be dated in the third century B.C. The broad mind of the Greek world is a part of its background, a fact which requires its

[25]Cf. Rom. 12:20

being dated after the era of Alexander (he died in 323 B.C.). At the lower extreme of possible date, nothing of the tight, defiant mood of the Maccabean recovery of Jewish independence (from 167 B.C.) appears; and from the additional fact that fragments from two manuscripts of Ecclesiastes were found among the Dead Sea Scrolls, one of them older than the other and hardly later than the early second century, a date later than about 200 B.C. is improbable.[26]

Ecclesiastes has a special place in the canon of Judaism with four other writings. It is one of the five *megilloth,* "scrolls," read on the occasion of special religious festivals during the cultic year:

Ecclesiastes	Feast of Tabernacles
Ruth	Pentecost
Lamentations	9th of Ab (the fall of Jerusalem)
Esther	Purim
Song of Solomon	Passover

Of the Preacher himself, by which we mean the dominant author, one can assert only that he is well along in years; that he would heartily concur with the words originally attributed to G. B. Shaw that youth is a wonderful thing but wasted on the young; and that he possessed both the means and position to have the best of this world's goods. His skepticism has been overemphasized. He does challenge sharply some of the major orthodox tenets of his day. But at the same time he repeatedly affirms the greatness and power of God; the fact, in faith, that human life stems from God and is the gift of God; and that all that has been, is, or ever shall be is ordained of God. As in the dialogues of Job, the name Yahweh is avoided: the argument is intended to have a setting broader then Yahwism-Judaism. The insight of this sage, the Preacher, centers on the human predicament, the plight of humankind. The conventional orthodox answers are not ultimate answers. These are God's alone. The folk of earth can only ask the ultimate *questions*—and the Preacher does this brilliantly and with zest.

The substance of the Preacher's thought is, of course, best conveyed in his own original words. The selection of verses and paragraphs that follows is designed to suggest some of his major

[26]Cf. M. Burrows, *More Light on the Dead Sea Scrolls,* New York, 1958, pp. 143 f. The interested reader is further referred to Charles T. Fritsch, *The Qumran Community: Its History and Scrolls,* New York, 1972.

themes and to illustrate the power and appeal of his mind and language. The key word is "vanity," occurring more frequently in this one writing than in all other Old Testament writings combined. All aspects of existence are in the last analysis vanity—*from human perspective*. Undergirding the Preacher's words is the faith that vanity, the absence of meaning, the "striving after wind" (1:14,17, and repeatedly), and all frustration and vexation (2:23) are resolved in the life and purpose (one might almost but not quite say "the love") of God. The sense of the proverb, whether original or inserted, is authentic (4:6), "Better is a handful of quietness [this is the Isaianic quietness of faith, Isa. 30:15] than two hands full of toil and a striving after wind."

I have seen the business that God has given to humankind to be busy with. [God] has made everything beautiful in its time, and has even put eternity into the human mind yet so that *one cannot find out what God has done* from the beginning to the end. I know that there is nothing better for them than to be happy and enjoy themselves as long as they live; also that it is God's gift . . . that everyone should eat and drink and take pleasure in all one's toil. I know that whatever God does endures forever. . . .

(3:10–14)

In a mood which does not necessarily deny this, the Preacher states with candor his basic empirical observation:

I saw that under the sun the race is not to the swift, nor the battle to the strong, nor bread to the wise, nor riches to the intelligent, nor favor to those of skill; but time and chance happen to them all!

(9:11)

One suspects that the Preacher enjoyed his role as burster of the balloons of the pious (as one of his twentieth-century counterparts, H. L. Mencken, certainly did).

I commend enjoyment, for men [and women] have no good thing under the sun but to eat and drink and enjoy themselves, for this will go with them in their toil through the days of life which God gives them under the sun. When I applied my mind to know wisdom, and to see the business that is done on earth . . . then I saw all the work of God, that one cannot find out the work that is done under the sun. . . .

(8:15–17)

But all this I laid to heart, examining it all, how the righteous and the wise and their deeds are in the hand of God; whether it is love or hate *one does not know*. Everything before *them* is vanity, since one fate comes to all. . . .

(9:1–2)

It has variously and sometimes ludicrously been asserted that the Preacher is a disciple, a "school" spokesman. One commentator sees him under the influence of the Stoics. Another makes him an Epicurean. Some would take Aristotle to be his master. Still others have alleged that he shows Buddhist leanings. The Preacher must be contemplating with delight all this idle speculation in the immortal life which he accepted, I am sure, with genuine, but controlled astonishment. In the tradition that produced the likes of a Moses, an Elijah, an Amos, and a Nehemiah, this Preacher is his own soul—a child of Yahwism-Judaism, gifted with uncommon insight and uncommon candor, whose work was wisely admitted into a canon properly and magnificently representing the full range of life and thought of the Old Testament people.

Song of Solomon

We rejoice that this writing also made the canon. In no technical sense is it in the category of wisdom, but it falls appropriately under the heading "faith and the world's wisdom," since, like wisdom, it is peculiarly in rapport with the world at large.

Debate over the interpretation of this little writing has exceeded that of any other Old Testament writing, and while this is perhaps an understandable fact, it is also lamentable, and a rather pitiful commentary on the history and problems of biblical interpretation.

Suppose we see what some of these interpretive opinions are and have been.

1. The modern, uninitiated reader, running through the poems for the first time, is likely to react with some surprise and the exclamation, "Now how did that get in the Bible?" The Song of Solomon made the canon on the merits of the oldest orthodox view: these poems (which are in reality songs of erotic love) are allegorical of the love of God for the congregation of Judaism. Christian orthodoxy accepted them on the corresponding analogy of the love of Christ for the church.

2. In the light of documents from Ugarit-Ras Shamra in Syria, dating from a time before Moses, the song is interpreted as liturgical material in common use in the Jerusalem temple until Josiah's reform in 621 B.C. This position takes for granted the virtually complete triumph of Canaanite fertility cultism in the very temple itself.

3. A comparable view sees the song as an ancient Tammuz liturgy from the Adonis cult, originating in and borrowed from an early Canaanite fertility cult.[27]

4. In another interpretation, the song is read as poems originally employed regularly in connection with wedding festivities.

5. The prevailing view, and perhaps still the simplest and best, regards the Song of Solomon as a collection of frank, uncomplicated poems of erotic love. As such they may be, as some insist, substantially folk poetry. If so, they display at points a rather high degree of sophistication. Or, it may be that this is poetic drama, although proponents of the view have been unable to agree on the intended plot of the alleged drama.

We would continue to read the Song of Solomon as simply a collection of love poems, from different poets and from different times. But there is something of truth in all the interpretations, even the first. If the theological perspective has any depth at all, then erotic love will always have its sacramental overtone: this love is born of God's love, is a reflection of that love, and may be in a real sense participation in that love. The play of erotic love falls always into a plot; it is always something of a drama. The various cultic interpretations of the poems remind us that such poetry as this is never created new, but rather always draws from the articulate lover of last spring and the spring before that, and so on back not merely over the years, but over the centuries and even the millennia. The theories of folk, liturgical, or ceremonial dependence all underscore not only the full measure in which the world loves and creates the lover, but also the singular beauty and insight and sensitivity of the ancient Israelite tradition in treating the love of a man and a woman.

So, nowhere in the Old Testament does the question of date seem less important. In any case, the only clues are internal. *In its present form* it is of course postexilic, but whether late fourth century, or early, or middle third—who knows, and who loses sleep

[27]The finest and most exhaustive modern commentary is by M. H. Pope, *Song of Songs (Anchor Bible)*, Garden City, N.Y., 1977. He writes: "No composition of comparable size in *world literature* has inspired such a volume and variety of comment and interpretation as the biblical Song of Songs." And then he comments: "Modern research has tended to relate the origins and background of the Songs to the sacral sexual rites of ancient Near Eastern fertility cults wherein the issues of life and death were the crucial concern . . . the impression has grown (in me) to conviction that the cultic interpretation . . . is best able to account for the erotic imagery" (p. 17).

over it. Perhaps only those who must have their biblical love from the lips of Solomon.

It has on occasion been carelessly said that the song has no religious-theological value. I must take emphatic personal exception. If it informs and nourishes and enriches the category of joyful, rapturous, sexual love, and if it has power to restore something of tenderness and freshness to the marriage relationship, then surely in the sense to which we have consistently held in these pages the Song of Solomon has even theological justification. As one who continues to delight in the poems, I cheer the ingenuity and inspiration of the allegorical interpretation which preserved the Song of Solomon. The song properly belongs in a canon of sacred literature from a people who were able to look at *all* the gifts of a rich creation with gratitude to the Giver and joy in the gift.

Judaism and the World: Daniel, Esther, Jonah

> . . . and also much cattle.
> *Jon. 4:11*[28]

The Last Chapter

Recall, now, the major events out of which the latest writings in the Hebrew canon were produced. Alexander the Great died in 323 and Palestine fell to Ptolemy, his governor in Egypt, in whose hands and the hands of his successors it remained throughout the next century. It was all the while coveted by the Seleucids who ruled to the north in Syria; but they were unable to take it from Egypt until Antiochus III (223–187) brought the Seleucid state to the peak of its power, and finally crushed Ptolemy V and acquired Palestine in 198.

Our knowledge of Jerusalem and Judaism in the second century is at best sketchy. But we know that the faith of Yahwism-Judaism was maintained in essence and in practice not only in Palestine but in other areas of the Greek Hellenistic world and especially in the ptolemaic capital city of Alexandria. Here the

[28]Cf. Psalms 73, 84.

thriving community of Judaism was sufficiently vigorous to attract proselytes; and in this century the Greek-speaking community of Judaism began the translation of its sacred writings from Hebrew (by some forgotten and by others never known)[29] The details are obscure, but the central fact is not in question. What was to become in time the Septuagint, the Greek version of the Hebrew canon, was begun at this time with the translation of the Pentateuch.[30]

At about the same time, Samaritan Judaism cut itself off from the Jerusalem center and established its own exclusive cultus on Mount Gerizim adjacent to ancient Shechem. It was a schism long a-brewing; indeed, it was centuries in the making. Antipathy between North and South Israel existed before the monarchy in the tenth century and was in evidence, sometimes violently, through all the succeeding centuries. Understandably, Jerusalem never "recognized" the Gerizim cultus.

In the end, however, the Samaritans shared the fate of all those who, though appealing perhaps to age-old traditions, rebel against a situation that has evolved over a long period of time, and try to base their life on historical conditions which have long since disappeared. They gradually degenerated and became almost completely uncreative. Today there is a tiny remnant of Samaritans in the city of *nāblus* (Shechem); they celebrate their Passover on the Gerizim but have otherwise become a mere historical curiosity.[31]

Judaism's welcome to the Seleucids at the beginning of the second century was quickly turned to bitterness. After the reign of Antiochus III, his son Seleucus IV (Philipator, 187–175) ascended to the throne, and, among other insults to Judaism, attempted to confiscate the temple treasury in Jerusalem. Upon his violent death at the hands of one of his ministers, Antiochus IV, known

[29]Hebrew survived the death of the old Israelite state in the sixth century. Aramaic, a related Semitic dialect, slowly took its place among Palestinian Jews who by Jesus' time, were speaking Aramaic. Hebrew continued to exist as a literary language to be revived as a living spoken language among Jews of Palestine in the nineteenth and twentieth centuries, to become the national language of the modern state of Israel.

[30]The name "Septuagint" and its common symbol LXX derive from the story or legend that the translation was undertaken by *seventy-two* scholars. See further, E. Wurthwein, *The Text of the Old Testament*, trans. P. R. Ackroyd, Oxford, 1957.

[31]M. Noth, *The History of Israel*, 2nd ed., rev. trans., London, 1960, p. 356.

as Epiphanes ("revealer" of God; but known by his enemies as Epimanes, "madman"), presided over events which led ultimately to Jewish independence in the Maccabean Revolt.

Greek culture and language, the cultivation of the body, sex and family mores at odds with the traditions of Yahwism-Judaism, fascination with the visual arts—all of this Hellenistic world pressed in upon Judaism and Jerusalem and even infiltrated in the persons of regularly visiting Jews from communities outside Palestine. In the early decades of the second century, the Jerusalem community was itself divided and in painful conflict over the issue of Hellenism, from the priesthood on down. The priesthood by and large accepted it, and large numbers of Jews saw no wrong in it. Antiochus Epiphanes, a most ardent patron of Hellenistic culture, precipitated an explosion during the course of a three-way contest within Judaism for the office of high priest. He was appealed to, and indeed, bribed, by the contesting parties with the result that the office of high priest became Antiochus's appointment. When in 169 one of the contestants, Menelaus, was returned to the office, Antiochus, who had already incurred the bitter resentment of faithful Jews by his interference, sought to correct his financial plight by entering the temple himself and stripping it of its considerable movable wealth.[32] Antiochus became at once the object of Judaism's bitterest hatred; and no doubt in part in retaliation but also as an expression of this ardent Hellenist's frustration with a people slow to change, he effected an otherwise quite unprovoked attack on Jerusalem in 168. And as if this were not enough, he took steps to exterminate the practice of Judaism, prohibiting all major festivals, sacrifice, Sabbath observance, circumcision. Attendance upon cults to Zeus both in Jerusalem and on Gerizim was made compulsory and in December 167, this pagan sacrifice was instituted in the Jerusalem temple.

Judaism faced the alternative of eclipse or armed resistance. When a priest named Mattathias, from the little town of Modein about twenty miles northwest of Jerusalem, killed a cooperating Jew as well as the official enforcing the pagan sacrifice, he and his sons became the nucleus of a resistance movement which was able

[32]See in the Apocrypha, 1 Macc. 1:17 ff. and 2 Macc. 5:15 ff. These two writings are our best sources for this period. First Macc., the more reliable of the two, covers the years 175 to 143 and 2 Macc., the shorter period 175 to 161.

to achieve the purification and restoration of the temple by December 164. This remarkable family, descendants of one Hasmon and therefore called Hasmoneans, is more popularly known by the name Maccabee, originally a nickname, probably meaning "hammerer," for the oldest son, Judas. The Maccabean Revolt, under the leadership of Mattathias's sons, led ultimately even to an uneasy political independence which was not brought to a conclusive end until Rome annexed Palestine in 63 B.C.

Daniel

The latest writings in the Hebrew canon are Daniel and Esther.[33] In its present form, Daniel can be positively dated after Antiochus's desecration of the temple in 168 and before its restoration in 164. Esther cannot be so narrowly dated. There is every possibility that it comes from the Maccabean period; and from the fact that of all the canonical Old Testament writings, only Esther yields no trace among the Qumran Dead Sea Scrolls (which date from the second century B.C. and later), we may be justified in taking Esther as the latest canonical book.

Daniel 1-6 purportedly describes real historical events in the lives of Daniel and his three friends Hananiah, Mishael, and Azariah, or, by their Babylonian names, Shadrach, Meshach, and Abednego (1:7), in the years between 606(5) and 536(5) (1:1 and 10:1). The theme is simple and single: they stoutly refuse to make any theological or cultic compromise in the face of the king's dire threats (it is Nebuchadnezzar by name, but obviously Antiochus Epiphanes in intent), and through every trial they emerge unscathed. Two of these remarkable episodes are almost universally known, being fodder in every Sunday School as well as Skeptics' Club, to say nothing of folk song and spiritual—the three friends in the fiery furnace and Daniel in the lions' den (chaps. 3 and 6).

Chapters 7-12 consist of a series of Daniel's visions which refer in varying symbol to the four empires of the Babylonians, the Medes, the Persians, and the Greeks. The point of focus for the

---

[33]Daniel is written in Hebrew except for one Aramaic section, 2:4b-7:28. It is surprising that so little Aramaic appears in the Old Testament (although aramaisms are not uncommon). In addition to the Daniel section, Ezra 4:5-6:18 and 7:12-26 are also in Aramaic. Jeremiah 10:11 and a single phrase in Gen. 31:47 ("the heap of witness") are the only other instances of Aramaic in the Old Testament.

whole structure of visions is the reign of Antiochus Epiphanes. That this is "prediction" after the event is confirmed as follows:

1. History is viewed with increasing accuracy down to the time of Antiochus.
2. The purported gift of vision collapses when it attempts to see beyond 165.
3. The example of Daniel and company is irrelevant to Israel's life in the days of neo-Babylonian ascendancy; but their heroic adherence to the faith and practice of Judaism is sharply coherent in that one bitter biblical epoch when Judaism was forced to fight for its very existence.

The readers of Daniel will especially appreciate the dream sequence, 2:1-5,36-44. They will observe the apocalyptic note through both sections and especially in 2:44, 7:13-14, and 12:1-4. Knowing now something of the history, reader's will read with understanding the brilliantly partisan description of Antiochus in 11:21-45. They will not fret over the question of literary unity, whether 1-6 and 7-12 stem originally from different sources. But they will take with pleasure and gratification a tale which so intimately reveals one of the most anguished crises in the life of the Old Testament people.

Esther

Esther is a good story. The title role is that of a beautiful Jewish girl, an orphan, who wins, against the best competition available, the crown of Miss Persia, or Miss Universe, 478 B.C. Not only is Esther superlatively beautiful. She is also a person of unparalleled courage, for virtually singlehandedly she turns upon the nasty heathen a diabolical plot to decimate the Jews. Instead, gloriously, the Jews dispatch 75,510 non-Jews in a single day—and that without the loss of a single Jew.

Esther is a good story. One wants to say yarn. This gentle and beautiful child is reared by a remarkably gentle and noble cousin, Mordecai by name, who is even more remarkable for the weight of years he apparently carries with such grace. He "had been carried away from Jerusalem among the captives carried away with Jeconiah (= Jehoiachin) . . ." (2:5). Assuming that he was an infant at the time, 597 B.C., this makes him about 120 years old when Esther becomes queen.

Esther is a good story. It boast a female villain, Queen Vashti, who is "justly" deposed because, silly girl, she refuses to appear, presumably *sans* apparel, before the drunken king and his drunken lords. This is for them no lost weekend, but a lost week:

it has been for these worthies a seven-day bout. The spinner of the tale himself appears to be ready to recognize the sensibilities of a modest woman; but unfortunately Vashti's refusal to obey the order of the king constitutes an irreparable blow to male prestige throughout the realm:

> Memucan [one of the Persian king's sages] said in the presence of the king and the princes, "Not only to the king has Queen Vashti done wrong, but also to all the princes and all the peoples ("male" peoples, of course) who are in all the provinces of King Ahasuerus. For this deed of the queen will be made known to all women, causing them to look with contempt upon their husbands. . . . This very day the ladies of Persia and Media who have heard of the queen's behavior will be telling it to all the king's princes, and there will be contempt and wrath in plenty. . . . let the king give her royal position to another. . . ."
>
> (1:16–19)

And where will one find a better stock villain than Haman, whose enormous conceit, malice, and cruelty are appropriately recompensed with death on the very gallows which he had especially constructed for the noble Mordecai. The whole tale is finally rounded out with the character of the king (Ahasuerus = Xerxes I of Persia, 486–465), who aids the plot considerably by being unable to remember his own decrees, and who is made the pale instrument through which the brilliant victory of Mordecai, Esther, and the Jews is won.

It is a good story; but it isn't history, and it certainly isn't theology. Like Daniel, it is a strongly nationalistic writing. Unlike Daniel, it has no religious reference whatsoever. God is not mentioned under any name[34] in the Hebrew text of Esther. The story gives vent to a narrow patriotism (understandable enough in view of the age which produced it), a kind of patriotism transcended centuries before in Yahwism and, happily, never normative in Judaism. An occasional interpreter has produced a few insipid moral bromides from 4:13–16, and the sermons preached on the text "Who knows whether you have not come to the kingdom for such a time as this?" (Mordecai to Esther, 4:14) if laid end to end would be laid end to end.

On the other hand, it must be reiterated that the Old Testament

---

[34]The Septuagint text of Esther is nearly twice as long as the Hebrew (270 verses against 163). It piously remedies the conspicuous absence of reference to the deity and adds other notes of a prayerful and worshipful nature.

canon reflects the full range of the life of that people; that the spirit of Esther was *provoked* in their history, again and again; that Jews have known in their long history one Haman after another (the most recent conspicuous Haman being Adolph Hitler); and that if Esther isn't history or theology in any direct sense, it nevertheless informs us more richly of the whole of human life and points up one of the universal deterrents to the exercise of the love of God. In this perspective, and in view of all subsequent Jewish history, it is not difficult to understand why Esther was accorded a place of increasing prestige in Judaism until it came to be known not simply as one of the *megilloth* (plural, "scrolls") but the *megillah* (singular), at the head of the other four *megilloth* (Song of Solomon, Ruth, Lamentations, Ecclesiastes).

In the continuing life of Judaism, Esther has aways been intimately associated with the Feast of Purim, "the day of lot, in which Israel relives its deliverance from the hands of Haman and takes renewed faith in its ability to outlive the Hamans of other times."[35] It appears probable, indeed, that the story of Esther actually created the feast. No reference to either story or feast appears until the mention of Mordecai's Day in 2 Macc. 15:36 (a writing, in its present form, not earlier than the first century B.C.). It is significant that in an exhaustive list of heroes in Ecclesiasticus 44–49 (in the Apocrypha) neither Esther nor Mordecai is named. Ecclesiasticus dates from *c.* 180–170. It is very probable, then, that Esther was written, and the Feast of Purim instituted, sometime in the latter half of the second century. And since, as we have already noted, no fragment of Esther appears at Qumran, it would appear probable that Esther is the latest writing in the Hebrew canon.

Jonah

He [Jeroboam II, *c.* 786–746] restored the border of Israel from the entrance of Hamath as far as the Sea of the Arabah, according to the word of Yahweh, the God of Israel, which he spoke by his servant Jonah the son of Amittai, the prophet, who was from Gath-hepher.

(2 Kings 14:25)

Now the word of Yahweh came to Jonah the son of Amittai, saying, "Arise, go to Nineveh, that great city, and cry against it. . . ."

(Jon. 1:1 f.)

[35]M. Steinberg, *Basic Judaism,* New York, 1947, p. 131.

The author of Jonah means to write his fabulous, moving, tongue-in-cheek tale around an obscure but historical prophet. But he hardly meant for his story to be taken as history. It is obviously a storyteller's story with one of the Old Testament's most powerful prophetic messages.[36] By general consent, the only considerable addition to the text of Jonah is the prayer of chapter 2. Jonah is in the canon of the minor prophets which was completed probably before 200 B.C. It can hardly be later. At the upper extreme, it is clearly dependent upon Joel (cf. Joel 1:13 f. and Jon. 3:5; Joel 2:14 and Jon. 3:9; and especially Joel 2:13 and Jon. 4:2) and cannot therefore be earlier than the fourth century. Jonah is commonly dated in the third.

The most winsome, imaginative, compelling biblical rebuke of all provincial pride, all arrogance born of parochialism, is the story of Jonah. Here is the slyest, deftest, most charming and humorous, most timelessly pertinent repudiation of exclusivism—religious, theological, ethnic, political, national—anywhere to be found. The story is a story, and let it be repeated, the author never meant it to be taken any other way. He rebukes with charm and humor a claim made among his own people in Jerusalem (and by some among every people in any time)—the claim of exclusivism and superiority. In the case of the story of Jonah, it is a claim with special theological overtones: we have God in our camp, on our team, packaged, as it were, in our church; our concerns are God's concerns, and God's concerns are ours; and we have a formula, a ritual, a cultus, a program of worship which guarantees God's exclusively favorable relationship to us. If one wishes to inquire after God, let one come here to Jerusalem where God dwells among this people, in this house, and is made accessible by this formula.

The story of Jonah cheerfully, brilliantly, and unrelentingly proclaims the central Word of all Yahwism-Judaism; and it does so by means of an inspired series of incongruities. To the pious protest of orthodox institutionalism that God is architechturally contained, Jonah's author simply laughs. "Don't be ridiculous," he says in effect, "here God is now, receiving praise in the most incongruous of all places, the belly of a great fish swimming in the

---

[36]The best that I know, unfortunately never translated, is the fine monograph by E. Haller, *Die Erzahlung von dem Propheten Jona,* In the series *Theologische Existenz Heute,* Munich, 1958.

bowels of the vast uncharted sea!" Aldous Huxley admirably appropriates the mood of Jonah's author:

> Seated upon the convex mound
> Of one vast kidney, Jonah prays,
> And sings his canticles and hymns,
> Making the hollow vault resound
> God's goodness and mysterious ways,
> Till the great fish spouts music as he swims[37]

To all claims of God's exclusive love and concern for one people (or one class or one color or one sex or one race) this preaching storyteller replies in effect, "Don't be ridiculous; for here God is now loving the most incongruous, the most improbable, of all people, the Assyrians—murderers, from your point of view, plunderers, godless, amoral!"

You pity the plant, for which you did not labor. . . . should not I pity Nineveh, that great city, in which there are more than a hundred and twenty thousand persons who do not know their right hand from their left—and also much cattle?

(Jonah 4:10 f.)

Now, to compound the incongruous, the great, pagan capital city of Assyria hears Jonah's reluctant revivalism and repents, not merely to the last person but down to the very beasts (3:8). The threat of destruction, the core of Jonah's preaching is removed; and Jonah, who knows but refuses to accept the breadth of God's love, flings himself sulkily away and asks peevishly for death since God has played God as God sees God, not as Jonah sees God. Impertinently and with profound disapproval, Jonah reminds God of what he, Jonah, had insisted was the untenable case from the beginning:

I knew that thou art a gracious God and merciful, slow to anger and abounding in steadfast love [*hesed*]. . . . Therefore, now, O Yahweh, take my life from me for it is better for me to die than to live.

The problem for Jonah (and certainly as understood in the biblical faith, the problem for everyone) is the abandonment of the cherished hatreds, the nurtured antipathies, the cultivated distastes, the snide comparisons by which persons and groups and

[37]Aldous Huxley, "Jonah," in *Leda*, London, Chatto and Windus, 1920, p. 25.

classes and nations maintain their own flattering images, their own sense of superiority and exclusiveness.

"Do you do well to be angry?" (4:4; 4:9). This is the summation of the old, unquenchable theological ethic. Here prophet, priest, and sage again raise in chorus their strongest and most persistent common note. Here Word, law, and wisdom all concur. Know the world from Yahweh's perspective, who ordained it, created it, and in love sustains it. It is your world because it is God's world. *All* its people are your people because they are Yahweh's, who loves when you cannot. Let this at least temper the quality of your unlove.

This is the age-old, liberating Old Testament and biblical faith—that against all indications to the contrary, in all of time, God remains the presider over history—a gracious God and merciful, slow to anger, and abounding in steadfast love. Jonah is called, as Israel is called, as God's people are always called, to the proclamation of such a God, and the meaning of such a God in time and history and in all of human existence.

The Bookshelf

Additional reading is recommended from the following list.

Albright, W. F., *From Stone Age to Christianity,* Garden City, N.Y.: Doubleday, 1957.

Alt, A., "The God of the Fathers" and "The Origins of Israelite Law," in *Essays on Old Testament History and Religion,* Garden City, N.Y.: Doubleday, 1966.

Anderson, B. W., *Understanding the Old Testament,* 3rd ed., Englewood Cliffs, N.J.: Prentice-Hall, 1975.

Bentzen, A., *Introduction to the Old Testament,* Copenhagen: Jesaja, 1952.

Bright, J., *A History of Israel,* Philadelphia: Westminister Press, 1972.

Buber, M., *Moses,* New York: Harper & Row, 1968.

Buber, M., *The Prophetic Faith,* New York: Harper & Row, 1977.

Childs, B., *The Book of Exodus,* Philadelphia: Westminster Press, 1974.

Childs, B., *Introduction to the Old Testament as Scripture,* Philadelphia: Fortress Press, 1979.

Childs, B., *Memory and Tradition in Israel,* London: SCM Press, 1962.

Childs, B., *Myth and Reality in the Old Testament,* London: SCM Press, 1960.

DeVaux, R., *Ancient Israel: Its Life and Institutions,* New York: McGraw-Hill, 1961.

DeVaux, R., *The Early History of Israel,* Philadelphia: Westminster Press, 1978.

Ehrlich, E. L., *A Concise History of Israel,* New York: Harper & Row, 1965.

Eichrodt, W., *Theology of the Old Testament,* Philadelphia: Westminister Press, vols. 1 and 2, 1961 & 1967.

Eissfeldt, O., *The Old Testament: An Introduction,* New York: Harper & Row, 1965.

Fohrer, G., *Introduction to the Old Testament,* Nashville: Abingdon Press, 1968.

Gottwald, N. K., *A Light to the Nations,* New York: Harper & Row, 1959.

Gottwald, N. K., *All the Kingdoms of the Earth,* New York: Harper & Row, 1964.

Gottwald, N. K., *The Tribes of Yahweh,* Maryknoll, N.Y.: Orbis Books, 1979.

Habel, N., *Literary Criticism of the Old Testament,* Philadelphia: Fortress Press, 1971.

Hahn, H., *The Old Testament in Modern Research,* Philadelphia: Fortress Press, 1966.

Harrelson, W., *Interpreting the Old Testament,* New York: Holt, 1964.

Hayes, J. H., *An Introduction to Old Testament Study,* Nashville: Abingdon Press, 1979.

Hayes, J. H. and Miller, J. M., *Israelite and Judean History,* Philadelphia: Westminster Press, 1977.

Herrmann, S., *A History of Israel in Old Testament Times,* Philadelphia: Fortress Press, 1975.

Heschel, A. J., *The Prophets,* New York: Harper & Row, 1962.

Hillers, D. R., *Covenant: The History of a Biblical Idea,* Baltimore: Johns Hopkins University Press, 1969.

Holladay, W., *Isaiah: Scroll of Prophetic Heritage,* Grand Rapids: Eerdmans, 1978.

Holladay, W., *Jeremiah: Spokesman Out of Time,* Philadelphia: Pilgrim Press, 1974.

The Interpreter's Bible, Nashville: Abingdon Press, vols. 1–6, 1952–1957.

The Interpreter's Dictionary of the Bible, Nashville: Abingdon Press, vols. 1–4, 1962; Supp., 1976.

Jacob, E., *The Theology of the Old Testament,* New York: Harper & Row, 1958.

Koch, K., *The Growth of the Biblical Tradition,* New York: Scribners, 1969.

Kuntz, J. K., *The People of Ancient Israel,* New York: Harper & Row, 1974.

Lindblom, J., *Prophecy in Ancient Israel,* Philadelphia: Fortress Press, 1962.

McKenzie, J., *A Theology of the Old Testament,* Garden City, N.Y.: Doubleday, 1974.

Miller, J. M., *The Old Testament and the Historian,* Philadelphia: Fortress Press, 1976.

Miranda, J. P., *Marx and the Bible,* Maryknoll, N.Y.: Orbis Books, 1974.

Mowinckel, S., *He That Cometh,* Nashville: Abingdon Press, 1954.

Napier, B. D., *Come Sweet Death: A Quintet from Genesis,* Philadelphia: Pilgrim Press, 1967.

Napier, B. D., *Exodus,* Richmond, Va.: John Knox Press, 1963.

Napier, B. D., *From Faith to Faith,* New York: Harper & Row, 1955.

Napier, B. D., *Prophets in Perspective,* Nashville: Abingdon Press, 1963.

Napier, B. D., *Word of God, Word of Earth,* Philadelphia: Pilgrim Press, 1976.

Noth, M., *The Laws in the Pentateuch and Other Essays,* Philadelphia: Fortress Press, 1967.

Noth, M., *Numbers: A Commentary,* Philadelphia: Westminster Press, 1968.

Peake's Commentary on the Bible, rev. ed., New York: Thomas Nelson, 1962.

Pedersen, J., *Israel: Its Life and Culture,* Oxford: Oxford University Press, 1926.

Pritchard, J. B., ed., *Ancient Near Eastern Texts Relating to the Old Testament,* 3rd ed., Princeton, N.J.: Princeton University Press, 1969.

Ringgren, H., *Israelite Religion,* Philadelphia: Fortress Press, 1966.

Robert, A., and Feuillet, A., *Introduction to the Old Testament,* Garden City, N.Y.: Doubleday, 1968.

Rowley, H. H., *Worship in Ancient Israel,* Philadelphia: Fortress Press, 1967.

Scott, R. B. Y., *The Relevance of the Prophets,* rev. ed., New York: Macmillan, 1969.

Snaith, N. H., *The Distinctive Ideas of the Old Testament,* Naperville: Allenson, 1944.

Tucker, G. M., *Form Criticism of the Old Testament,* Philadelphia: Fortress Press, 1971.

Voegelin, E., *Israel and Revelation,* Baton Rouge: Louisiana State University Press, 1969.

von Rad, G., *Deuteronomy: A Commentary,* Philadelphia: Westminster Press, 1966.

von Rad, G., *Genesis: A Commentary,* rev. ed., Philadelphia: Westminster Press, 1973.

von Rad, G., *The Message of the Prophets,* New York: Harper & Row, 1972.

von Rad, G., *Old Testament Theology,* New York: Harper & Row, vols. 1 and 2, 1962 and 1965.

Vriezen, T. C., *An Outline of Old Testament Theology,* Newton Centre: Charles T. Branford Company, 1969.

Ward, J. M., *Amos and Isaiah: Propets of the Word of God,* Nashville: Abingdon Press, 1969.

Weiser, A., *The Old Testament: Its Formation and Development,* New York: Association Press, 1961.

West, J. K., *Introduction to the Old Testament,* New York: Macmillan, 1971.

Wilson, R. R., *Prophecy and Society in Ancient Israel,* Philadelphia: Fortress Press, 1980.

Wolff, H. W., *Joel and Amos,* Philadelphia: Fortress Press, 1977.

Wright, G. E., *Biblical Archaeology,* Philadelphia: Westminster Press, 1957; 1961.

Zimmerli, W., *Ezekiel 1,* Philadelphia: Fortress Press, 1979.

Zimmerli, W., *Old Testament Theology in Outline,* Atlanta: John Knox Press, 1978.

Index of Names & Subjects

Baal, 39, 115, 161, 172
Babylon, 5; archaeological evidences in, 53–54; captivity in, 169; code of law in, 72–73; collapse of, 242; creation myth in, 41, 41n., 53; Cyrus and, 242; Daniel on, 307; deportation as policy of, 206, 211, 221, 241; Egypt and, 169, 194–195, 218; exile in, 85; Ezekiel and, 228; fall of, 245, Habakkuk on, 207; Jeremiah and, 218; Jerusalem and, 210–211, 217–218, 221, 241; wisdom writings of, 293
Balaam, 97–98
Balak, 97–98
Barth, K., 86
Barton, D. M., 207n., 283n.
Baruch, 210–211, 217, 219, 293
Bashan, 97
Bathsheba, 68, 131 ff., 136
Begrich, J., 271n.
Benaiah, 137
Benjamin, 119; in Canaan, 110–111; Joshua and, 106; Philistines and, 120
Bentzen, A., 272n.
Bethel, 55, 58; Ai and, 105; Amos in, 172; bull image at, 80
Bethlehem Ephrathah, 191n.
Bethshemesh, 123
Bildad, 284, 286, 289, 292
Black, M., 45n.
Blessing, 93–94; of Moses, 198; universality of, 257, 260, 277, 313
Bousset, W., 275n.
Breasted, J. H., 53
Bribery, 74
Bright, J., 54n., 106n., 242n.
Buber, M., 35n., 244n., 245n.
Burke, E., 229
Burning bush, 26, 79
Burrows, M., 205n., 300n.

Cain, Abel and, story of, 48–49, 55, 67, 86, 129
Caleb, 95
Calebites, 107
Calfhill, J., 117
Cambyses, 263
Canaan, 4, 22–23; Bedouins in, 115; conquest of, 99, 104, 105 ff.; Egypt and, 104–105; entry into, 30, 75, 82, 92, 95–96; ethical practice in, 70, 72–73; fertility cults of, 39, 302; Jerusalem and, 107; Joseph in, 111; Judges and, 103; monarchy in, 63; prophecy in, 150–153, 154–157
Canon, Hebrew, 113n., 114
Carlyle, T., 283

Carmel assembly, 162
Carruth, W. H., 21n., 54n.
Chaldeans, 168, 218
Childs, B. S., 21n., 113n.
Christ, see Jesus
Christensen, D. L., 202n.
Christianity, Decalogue and, 63; Sabbath of, 66n.
Chronicler, the, 261–262
Chronicles of the Kings of Israel, Books of the, 145
Circumcision, 25; Antiochus IV and, 306; as ritual, 55–56, 76, 105
Clapham, H., 117–118
Classical prophetism, see Prophetism, classical
Coats, G. W., 59n.
Code, in Covenant, 70–76, 83, 88–89; Deuteronomy and, 198–199
Collingwood, R. G., 157n.
Colossians, 295n.
Communion, sacrifice as, 117
Conduct, in Covenant, 72–75
Confession, defined, 3, 27; faith through tribal, 108
Conzelmann, H., 295n.
Covenant, the age of code of, 88; Code in, 70–76, 83, 88–89, 198–201; consummation of, 256–257; of David, 147; Deuteronomy and code of, 198–200; election and, 251–252; ethics in, 85–92; God and, 61–100, 124, 254–255; golden calf as denial of, 78–80; Jeremiah and, 221–223; Moses and renewal of, 80–82; patriarchal, 19, 79; occupation as fulfillment of promise, 99–100; redefined, 82–84; renewal of, 80, 84–85, 237, 243; Ritual Decalogue and code of, 61, 82; sealing of, 75–76; theo-ethical summary of, 90–91; universalism and, 292; in wilderness and occupation, 92–93; see also Word, the; Yahweh speech in, 91–92
Covenant Code, 70–76, 83, 88, 98–99
Covenant of the Patriarchs, 19, 75
Covetousness, 69
Creation, 37–43; Fifth Commandment and, 66–67; order and, 76, 124; Sabbath and, 66; stories of, 40–41; wisdom and, 294
Credo, consummation of, 7–8; cultus and, 169; Egyptian captivity and, 169; Exodus and, 3, 100
Crenshaw, J. L., 59n., 118n.
Crim, K. R., 135n.
Cross, F., 33n.
Cultus: apodictic law and, 74–75; Canaan, 39; creation and, 39; credo

and, 169; ethic and, 85–92; etiology and, 55; faith and, 70; formula, 103; institutions, 77; language, 6, 17; priesthood in, 85, 96; prophetism and, 208; prostitution and, 39, 88; purification under Josiah, 194–195, 216; ritual and, 270, 273, 302–303; Ritual Decalogue and, 61–62, 82–83; of Samaritan Judaism, 305; scrolls in, 300; Solomon's temple and, 4, 144; Song of Miriam and, 33; theology and, 17, 27, 30, 100; time and, 29; traditions in, 77

Cyrus, 242, 245, 248, 261, 263

Dagon, 123
Dallas, A. K., 21n.
Damascus, 138, 158, 175, 181–182
Dan, 80, 119
Daniel, 307–310
Darius I, 261–263
Dathan, 96
Dating, see Sources
David, 4, 5; Absalom and, 133–134; Bathsheba and, 68, 131–133; birthplace of, 191n.; Cain, Abel and, story of, 129; dotage of, 136; full accession of, 126–127; Isaiah on, 257; Jeroboam and, 146; lament of, 203; as monarch, 128–134; monarchy establishment by, 4, 12, 75; psalms of, 271; relation of, to God, 125, 127, 129, 140; Ruth and, 114–115; Saul and, 125–126, 150–151; Solomon and, 135–140
Day, 44; of Yahweh, 65–66
Day, Seventh, see Sabbath
Dead Sea scrolls, 300
Death: motif, 14; etiology, 46; sentence, 73
Deborah, 109–112, 152–153, 187n.
Decalogue, 60–70; age of, 83; as covenant, 76; ethics and, 82, 89; as history, 61; Leviticus and, 90; Moses and, 78–82, 84; ritual, 82–83
Delitzsch, F., 275–276, 279
Deluge, see Flood
Denney, J., 276n.
Deuteronomic Code, 71, 88, 91, 100
Deuteronomy, 193–201; Book of Kings and, 143–145; classical prophecy in, 193–199; code in, 71, 88, 91; editors, 75; Jeremiah and, 210; Joshua and, 99; Judges and history in, 108; Ruth and, 114; Sabbath and, 66
Didache, 293n.
Dietary laws, 75, 83
Dinah, 58

Dispersion, geographical, 46
Documentary hypothesis, see Sources
Driver, S. R., 20
Duhm, B., 276n.

Ebla, 54
Ecclesiastes, 292, 299–301, 310
Ecclesiasticus, 293, 295, 310
Eden, see Garden of Eden
Edom, 18, 58, 138, 223–224; Ezekiel on, 231; Jeremiah on, 211
Egypt, 11–19, 26, 48, 61; 'Apiru in, 14, 18; Babylon and, 169, 195, 218; Canaan and, 104–105; Eighteenth Dynasty in, 13; flight from, 31–33; Hezekiah and, 184; history of, 29, 31; Hoshea and, 182; invasions from, 146; Isis cult in, 295n.; Israel in, 11–12; Israel out of, 26–35, 103; Jehoahaz and, 216; Josiah and, 195; Judea and, 279; Moses and, 22–25, 27, 56, 84; Nineteenth Dynasty in, 13; Philistines and, 122; plagues of, 28–30; prophets and, 167; Ptolemies of, 281; as symbol, 7, 12–13, 169, 192, 206, 245; tribes in, 12–13; voluntary exiles to, 241; wisdom writings of, 293
Ehud, 109
Eighth century, anticipated judgment in, 167–192
Eissfeldt, O., 20, 113n.
Ekron, 122
Elam, 211
Eldad, 95
Elephantine Papyri, 267, 267n., 269
Elhanan, 122
Eli, 122–123
Eliashib, 269
Elihu, 284
Elijah, 145, 160–163; Ahab and, 160n., 171; Amos and, 162; death wish in, 288; Elisha and, 158–159; Jeremiah and, 214; Moses and, 81; as prophet, 157, 169, 173; Word and, 161–162
Eliphaz, 284, 286, 288–289, 292
Elisha, 145; Elijah and, 158–159; Jehu and, 160; as prophet, 157–159, 172
Elmslie, W. A., 118n., 179n., 229n.
'Elohim, 19, 21, 27, 41–42, 73
Emerton, J. A., 59n.
Emma Elish, 40
Ephod, 116
Ephraim, 4n., 106, 110–111, 117
Esarhaddon, 168, 193
Esau, 44, 54, 223–224
Eschatology, defined, 205
Esdraelon, 110

Esdras, 293
Esther, 307–310
Etham, 31
Ethics, in covenant, 85–92; theology and, 174, 199–200
Ethnic groups, see Races; Tribes
Ethnology, 54
Etymology, of Hormah, 97; as interpretation of meaning, 54, 65; of nabi', 150; in Ruth, 114
Exodus, 11–15, 70–85, 92; Book of Numbers and, 94–95; creation and, 4, 42; credo and, 3, 100; date of, 18; Deuteronomy and, 198–199; God disclosed in, 14, 19–20; Israel before, 11–12; Kadesh tradition in, 61; humankind's alienation and, 47; Moses as figure in, 15–16; Passover and, 74; sources of, 20–21, 26–28, 32–33, 37–38, 62, 77, 83
Ezekiel, 99, 228–238; as book, 230–231; Deuteronomy and, 196; faith in, 235–238; Jeremiah and, 215; on judgment, 255; prophetism in, 231–235; prophetism, classical and, 148; on resurrection, 278; Word in, 251; Zechariah and, 263, 282
Ezion-geber, 139n.
Ezra, 242, 261, 269–270

Faith: confession of, 24; covenant and, 92; cultus and, 70, 265; event and, 11; history and, 282; holiness and, 190; Israel's, 38, 57; judgment and, 280; manifestations of, 56–57, 58, 235–238; order and, 112, 155; prophecy and, 147, 156; prophetic, culmination of, 241–257; righteousness and, 208–209, 223; tribal confederation through, 108; wisdom writings and, 294
Falsehood, 68–69, 90, 212
Fathers, Sayings of the, 293n.
Feast: ingathering, 30, 75; harvest, 74–75; tabernacles, 75, 300; unleavened bread, see Passover
Fertile Crescent, 53
Fertility rites, 39
Firstborn, 25, 30; killing of, 15; see also Passover
Flood story, 43, 45–46, 48–49, 56, 86
Fohrer, G., 176n., 266n., 269n.
Form criticism, 20
Freedman, D. N., 24n., 35n.
Freedom in Covenant, 71
Fritsch, C. T., 300n.

Garden of Eden, 48, 55, 86, 98, 129
Gath, 122, 190
Gaza, 104, 122
Gedaliah, 218
Genealogy: Edomite, 58; Genesis, 43–44; Levite, 27
Genesis, 37–60, 129
Gibeah, 119
Gibeon, 104
Gideon, 109, 115–116
Gilead, 117
Gilgal, 105
Gilgamesh Epic, 46
Globe, A., 111n.
Glory of God, see God, glory of
God: alienation from, 48–51; commitment of, to covenant, 61, 75–76, 78, 91, 124, 236; compassion of, 254–256; as creator, 25, 41–43, 60, 66; disclosure on Sinai, 11; in Exodus, 11, 19–20; Ezekiel's relation to, 232; glory of, 60, 61–63, 81; history's relation to, 1–2, 11, 38, 141, 149, 152–153, 158, 171, 174, 184–185, 227, 238, 287; holiness of, 88, 243–244; identity of, 63–64; Jeremiah and, 215; Moses' relation to, 26, 81–82, 84–85, 94; names of, 20–21, 65, 284–285, see also 'Elohim, Yahweh; nature of, 27–28, 64, 76, 82, 190, 312–313; prophecy and, 149–151, 155–156; in secular law, 73–74; Word of, see Word, the
Gods, Egyptian, 14
Golden Calf, 78–80, 82
Goliath, 122
Gomer, 176–180
Goodman, S., 106n., 126n., 160n., 168n.
Goshen, 104
Gospel Forth, 295n.
Gottwald, N. H., 41n., 113n., 222n.
Grace, concept of, 192n.; in Davidic covenant, 6; in Genesis, 50
Graf, K. H., 20
Greece, 157; Daniel on, 307; Judah and, 279, 281–282, 304–306
Green, D. E., 176n.
Greenberg, M., 14n.
Gunkel, H., 21n., 54n., 272n.
Gunn, D. M., 141n.

Habakkuk, 206–209; Jeremiah and, 217; Job and, 287; theodicy in, 264
Hadad, 138
Haggai: Deuteronomy and, 196; history in, 262–263; on the temple, 261, 264

Murder, 67; David and, 68, 131–132
Myth, creation in, 2, 40, 42, 43; history and, 141; Samson and, 118; theology and, 104

Naaman, 159
Nabonidus, 241
Nahum, 201–203
Naioth, 151
Names, meaning of, 54
Naphtali, 110
Napier, B. D., 46n., 54n., 58n.; on David, 133n.; on election, 251n.; on Exodus, 31n., 66n., 200n.; on God, 60n.; on Isaiah, 187n.; on Jacob, 58n.; on Joseph, 60n.; on prophecy, 155n., 251n.; on Sabbath, 66n.
Nathan, as prophet, 157, 158; role of, 132, 133; Solomon and, 136
Nationalism, 263, 309
Nature, fertility of, 30
Nazirite Law, 93, 118
Nebuchadnezzar, 211, 221, 241–242, 307
Neco, 195, 216
Negeb, 22, 104
Nehemiah, 266–269; Ezra and, 261, 270; history in, 261
New Testament, apocalyptic in, 281n.; wisdom and, 295
New Year Festival, 273
Niebuhr, R., 86
Nineveh, 54, 201, 204, 216, 312
Noah, 44–46
Nomads, Semitic, 53
Noth, M., 4n., 21n., 38n., 54n., 63n., 67n., 68n., 83n., 139n., 160n., 305n.; on Assyria, 168n.; on David, 126n.; on prophecy, 152n.; on tribe of Benjamin, 106n.
Numbers, 16, 92–99; Deuteronomy and, 198; history and, 93
Numerology, 93
Nuzi, 54

Obadiah, 160, 172, 223–225
Offerings, 85; sin, 87
Omri, 144–145, 147–148, 158
Oracles: in Amos, 170; in Book of Numbers, 98–99; cultic, 271; of Ezekiel, 204, 230–231, 238; in Hosea, 176; in Isaiah, 188, 204, 243, 246, 259; of Jeremiah, 204, 210–211; in Micah, 192; of Obadiah, 224; of Second Isaiah, 246, 259; of Zephaniah, 204
Oral history, see history, oral
Ordeal of Jealousy, 93

Order: creation and, 47, 76, 124; faith and, 112, 155–156; God and, 39, 43; prophecy and, 168
Othnielites, 107, 109

Paran, Wilderness of, 22
Parents, dignity of, 66, 67, 72
Passover, 17n., 29–30, 74–75, 83, 105, 300; Josiah and, 195; Ritual Decalogue and, 83; Samaritan, 305
Patriarchs, 53–60
Paul, St., 86, 209, 295n.
Peake, A. S., 45
Pederson, J., 17n.
Pekah, 176, 181, 187
Pekahiah, 176
Peniel, 58
Pentateuch, 44, 99, 305
Pentecost, 74
Persia, 261, 267, 269, 281, 307
Person, Decalogue on, 66–68
Peterson, D. L., 46n.
Pfeiffer, R., 20, 229n., 266n.; on Job, 286n.
Pharaoh, 12–14, 18, 25, 27, 29; Eighteenth Dynasty, 13; Nineteenth Dynasty, 13; Seventeenth Dynasty, 31; Word and, 26–27
Philistia, 281
Philistines: cities of, 204; invasions of, 146; monarchy and, 119, 121, 122, 130; origin of, 122
Philo, 295n.
Phoenicia, 137–138, 281
Phrygia, 281
Pilgrimage, 273
Pithom, 13
Plagues: in Assyria, 184–185; of Egypt, 28–30; of locusts, 278–279; of Philistines, 123
Pope, M. H., 285n., 289n., 303n.
Pride and alienation, 252; Isaiah on, 188; of Job, 290–292; Jonah on, 311; Zephaniah on, 206
Priesthood, 79, 85, 96, 268
Pritchard, J. B., 16n., 40n., 145n., 175n., 183n., 184n., 249n.
Promised land, 80
Property, Decalogue on, 68
Prophetism, 148–155; degenerate, 282; eighth century, 167–192; in Ezekiel, 231–235; faith and, 7, 147; God and, 149, 151–152, 154, 156; as a group phenomenon, 151–152, 160; history and, 192; of Jeremiah, 214–216; of Nahum, 202; preclassical, 155–163; premonarchic, 152–155; professional, 171; tradition of,

Shalmaneser V, 168, 176
Shalom, 93
Shechem, 105–106, 115, 146, 305
Shem, 44
Shesh-bazzar, 242
Shiloh, 122
Shishak I, 146
Sholomon ben Isaac, Rabbi, 87
Shur, Wilderness of, 33
Simeon, 103, 107
Sin: as alienation from God, 48, 50, 58, 86, 129, 188; apostasy as, 140; in Cain and Abel story, 86; in Flood story, 49, 86; original, 86
Sin, Wilderness of, 33
Sinai, 19–20, 92; Decalogue and, 61; Moses on, 23–27, 77–80; Mount Ebal and, 105; site of, 18, 22, 33, 60
Sirbonis, Lake, 31
Sisera, 110, 111
Slavery, 12–13, 18–19, 31, 71–72, 79, 104, 199, 279
Solomon, 4, 75; architecture under, 137, 139; art under, 137, 139; Book of Acts of Solomon, 140, 145; Ecclesiastes and, 299; kingdom of David and, 135–141; legend of, 137–138; monarchy and, 132, 135–141; proverbs and, 296; psalms of, 271; Rehoboam and, 146; Song of Solomon, 131, 302–304; wisdom writings and, 295; *see also* Solomon's temple
Solomon's temple, 77, 138, 140–141; Ahaz and, 181–182; Book of Kings and, 144; cultus and, 259; Josiah and, 194; reconstruction, 222; records, 145
Song: of Deborah, 203; of Hannah, 123; of Moses, 198; of Moses or Miriam, 33; of Solomon, 131, 302–304; of the Well, 97
Sorcery, 73
Sources: Amos, 170; of Balaam story, 97; Book of Judges, 108–109, 112; Book of Kings, 137–138, 140, 143–145, 159–160, 185; Book of Numbers, 93, 97–98; Book of Proverbs, 296; Daniel, 308; Decalogue, 83; Deuteronomy, 100, 103, 195, 197; Ecclesiastes, 299; Esther, 307; Exodus, 21, 26–28, 32, 61, 77, 153–154; Ezekiel, 230; Ezra, 269, 270; Ezra and Nehemiah, 261; Genesis, 21–22, 41, 43–45, 47, 55, 59; Habakkuk, 206–208; Hexateuch, 96; Hosea, 175–176; Isaiah, 186, 275–277; Job, 283–286; Joel, 278; Jonah, 310–311; Lamenta-

tions, 226; Leviticus, 88; Malachi, 264; Micah, 190–191; Nahum, 201–202; Nehemiah, 266–267; of the Psalter, 270–271, 295–296; Samson, 117–118; Samuel, 121–122, 123, 125, 128, 230–231; Song of Solomon, 302–303; Tetrateuch, 100; Third Isaiah, 259; Zechariah, 262, 280–281; Zephaniah, 204
Speiser, E. A., 40n.
Stalker, D. M. G., 15n., 40n.
State, theocratic, 55
Status, Decalogue on, 69
Steinberg, M., 86n., 310n.
Suez Canal, 31
Sunday, 66
Symbolism, of atonement, 86–87; in Book of Numbers, 97; of Egypt, 7, 12, 13, 14–15, 19, 170, 192, 206; in Exodus, 14, 15, 24, 62; in Ezekiel, 232, 235, 238; in Genesis, 55, 56; in Hosea, 179–180; in Isaiah, 189–190; in Job, 287; in the Servant Song, 248–249; Word and, 250–251; in Zechariah, 262, 263
Syria, 159, 161n., 281, 302–304
Syrians, 109, 138, 146, 147

Tabernacle, 77, 80–81, 87
Tabernacles, Feast of, *see* Feast of Tabernacles
Taboo, 62, 74
Tamar, 53, 59, 133
Tammuz, 303
Tanis, 13
Temple, Antiochus and, 305–307; reconstruction of, 243, 279
Ten Commandments, *see* Decalogue
Tent of Meeting, *see* Tabernacle
Terah, 44
Terrien, S., 283n., 285n., 286n., 289n.
Tetrateuch, 37–38; Deuteronomy and, 62; as literature, 99–100; sources of, 230
Thanksgiving, 272
Theft, 68
Theocracy, *see* State, theocratic
Theodicy: defined, 206–207; God's relation to history, 1–3, 11, 140, 149, 152, 157, 171, 174, 185, 186, 207, 227, 237–238, 287; of Job, 287; in Malachi, 264–265
Theology; cultus and, 17, 27, 28–29; of Deuteronomy, 196; in Esther, 309–310; ethics and, 174, 200, 251–252; Hexateuch as, 99–100; history and, 129, 144, 287; myth and, 40, 43, 104; and political changes of

Israel, 55–58; prophetism as, 192; Song of Solomon and, 303
Tiamat, 40
Tiglath-pileser, 168, 181; annals of, 145n., 175; as prophet, 221; reign of, 182
Tigris-Euphrates valley, 46
Timsah, Lake, 31
Tithes, 85
Tobiah, 268
Tobit, 293
Torah: apodictic law in, 74, 85, 88; Decalogue and, 63, 69; Leviticus and, 85–92
Tower of Babel story, sin in, 43, 48, 56, 86; Solomon and, 129, 140; as symbol, 56
Trevis, M., 279n.
Tribes: confederation of, 4, 93, 107, 110, 111, 119, 122, 127; division of, 143–147, 155, 156; during period of Judges, 107; in Egypt, 12; interrelations of, 54
Tutmose, 17

Ugarit, 53–54
Ugarit-Ras Shamra, 302
Umman-manda, 168
Unleavened Bread, *see* Passover
Uriah, 132, 135
Utnapishtim, and Noah, 46

Vanity, 301
Vashti, 308–309
Vaux, R. de, 139n.
Violence, control of, in covenant, 71–72
Voegelin, E., 155n., 157n., 196n., 197n.
von Rad, G., 4n., 15n., 21n., 40n., 46n., 50n., 76n., 88n., 135n., 154n., 157n., 170n., 193n., 197n., 294n.; on Deuteronomy, 196n., 197n.; on Moses, 154n.; on salvation, 50n.
Vulgate, 85

War, cessation of, 7
Ward, J. M., 244n.
Weeks, Festival of, *see* Feast, of Weeks

Weiser, A., 207n., 211n., 225n., 230n., 283n.
Wellhausen, J., 20
Westermann, C., 51n.
Whitehouse, O. C., 275n.
Wilderness, covenant in, 92–94; Israel in, 33–35
Wilson, R. A., 14n., 73n.
Wisdom Literature, 292–302; *see also* specific writings, e.g., Ecclesiastes
Word, the, in Amos, 173; as covenant, 23–24, 26–27, 30, 35, 56, 59, 69–70, 99; as creator, 39–40, 41, 76; in Elijah, 162; Elisha and, 159; as history, 162–163, 171, 185; in Hosea, 179; idolatry, 78–80; in Isaiah, 215, in Jeremiah, 215, 218, 223; in Job, 290n.; nature of, 250–251; as prophecy, 149, 156, 158; Yahweh speech in, 91–92
Wright, G. E., 106n., 139n.
Wurthwein, E., 305n.

Xanthus, 98
Xerxes I, 309

Yahweh: nature of, 27–28, 64, 76, 82, 190, 312–313; prophecy and, 149–151, 155–156; in secular law, 73–74
Yahwism, into Judaism, 259–273; meaning of, 241–258
Yom, 44–45
Yom Kippur, 86–87

Zadok, 136
Zebulum, 110
Zechariah, 175, 262–263, 280–282; Deuteronomy and, 196, Ezekiel and, 263, 282, Haggai and, 262–263; Malachi and, 266, 280–281; as prophet, 262–263; Second Zechariah, 280–282
Zedekiah, reign of, 211, 217–219
Zephaniah, 203–206; as prophet, 214
Zerubbabel, 262, 263
Zimmerli, W., 229n.
Zimri, 145
Zion, 4–5, 7, 280
Zok, 87
Zophar, 284, 286, 292

Index of Biblical References

108–110 — 271
110 — 155n., 266n.,
273
112 — 273, 292n.
114 — 92n., 266n., 272
119 — 225
121, 122 — 266n., 273
127 — 271
128 — 273, 292n.
130 — 266, 271
132 — 5n., 266n., 273
135 — 92n.
136–139 — 266n.
136 — 272
137 — 221n.
138–145 — 271
138 — 272
139 — 278
150 — 266n., 272

Proverbs
1–31 — 292n., 296–299
8:22 ff. — 294n., 295
22:17–23:10 — 293
31 — 225

Ecclesiastes
1–12 — 292n., 299–302

Song of Solomon
1–8 — 292n., 302–304
2:10–13 — 131

Isaiah
1–33 — 186
1–23 — 181–192
1:2 ff. — 252, 254
1:17 — 253
1:21–23 — 204
1:25 — 6n., 255
2:3 — 266
2:2–4 — 7n., 192
2:9 — 203n.
2:12–17 — 277
2:17 — 277
3:13 — 254
5 — 252, 278
5:1–7 — xv, xvi
5:24 — 243
6 — 88, 215, 250
7–8 — 251
7 — 181
7:1 ff. — 255
7:9 — 207, 209, 263,
277
7:17 — 155
7:18 — 75
8:16 — 186, 205,
207, 245

8:17 — 191n., 206,
277n., 245, 263
9 — 191n., 205
9:2–7 — 204, 257
9:7 — 7
10 — 205
10:5 — 252
11 — 191n., 205
11:1–9 — 204
11:3 f. — 258
11:6–9 — 7
11:9 — 258
13–23 — 204, 211, 230,
252
19:23 f. — 192
19:25 — 119
22:8–11 — 183
19:24 f. — 7
19:25 — 119
23 — 138
24–27 — 243, 275–278
27 — 278
27:1–5, 7 — xvi
28–33 — 189
28:16 — 277
30:9–11 — 223
30:12–14 — 5
30:12 — 243
30:15 — 88, 206, 207,
227n., 243, 263, 301
31:1 — 243
34–35 — 186, 205,
241n., 243
36–39 — 181n., 186
37:23 — 243
37:29 — 189
38:10–20 — 272
40 ff. — 6
40–55 — 241n., 243,
246–249, 259
40–66 — 39, 186, 205,
244n.
40:11 — 191n.
45:14 — 243
49:3 — 241
49:6 — 60, 257
50:4 — 205, 245
51:1 f. — 19
51:9–11 — 256, 257
52:13–53:12 — 278
53:4–5 — 215, 257
54:7 f., 10 — 254
54:13 — 245
55:10–11 — 7, 161, 223
55:11 — 155, 257
56–66 — 205, 243,
259–260
57:15 — 243
62:11 — 281n.

Jeremiah
1–52 — 209–219,
221–223
1 — 250
2:2–7 — 252
3:12 — 254
5:1–17 — 253
7:18 — 73
8:11 — 260
8:18 ff. — 226n.
9:23–24 — 263n.
10:11 — 307n.
18:18 — 292
20:7 ff. — 227n.
20:8 — 250
20:14–18 — 288
23:1–4 — 282
23:5 f. — 257
30:11 — 221
31:3 — 255
31:29 — 237
31:31 ff. — 7, 237
31:33 f. — 255
32:15 — 243
42–43 — 241
44:15 — 73
46–51 — 204, 230, 252
49:7–22 — 224
52:28–30 — 241

Lamentations
1–5 — 225–228
1:21 — 203
4:21–22 — 231

Ezekiel
1–48 — 228–238
1–2 — 149
1 — 250
7:7, 10, 12 — 203
11:19–20 — 215
12:6 — 238
14:12–23 — 238
14:14, 20 — 284
16:8–15 — 252
18:2 — 237
18:4 — 238
25–32 — 204, 211, 252
27 — 138, 238
34 — 238, 282
34:12 — 203
34:23 f. — 5n.
37 — 215, 255, 278
37:16–28 — 282
41 — 139n.
43:13–17 — 70
47 — 238, 282